ROBERT BURNS

*From the painting by Alexander Nasmyth in the Scottish National
Portrait Gallery, Edinburgh.*

The Poems of
ROBERT BURNS
1759-1796

*Containing 'Homes and Haunts of
Robert Burns' by James MacKenna,
the Poems and Songs, Index to
first lines and Glossary, and
Pictorial Section*

COLLINS
LONDON AND GLASGOW

CONTENTS

Printed in Great Britain

HOMES AND HAUNTS OF
ROBERT BURNS

SINCE Robert Burns set out on a borrowed nag from Mossgiel to Edinburgh, methods of locomotion have been revolutionised, and to-day the automobile has made it possible for the tourist to cover great distances in a short space of time. The poet spent twenty-two days in traversing the highways enclosed in the square Stirling, Inverness, Aberdeen, Edinburgh, and the same area can be covered in a leisurely fashion now in three days.

The Burns country may be said to be embraced in a triangle with the out-points at Ayr, Edinburgh, and Dumfries, and the tourist may compass this in two or three days' time. An attempt is made in this little work to retell the story of the poet's life, giving the salient facts only, and avoiding anything in the nature of criticism. The aim is to provide a guide to the homes and haunts of the poet and to indicate everything of historical interest, be it a building, a household relic, or a MSS., that has survived the passage of time.

The scheme is literally to follow the poet " from the cradle to the grave," providing in concise form a complete guide to the Burns country and Burnsiana for the tens of thousands who seek annually to pay homage to the memory of the greatest lyric poet of all time.

THE POET'S PARENTAGE

In 1748, Robert and William Burness, sons of
Robert Burness, tenant of Clochnahill, Kincardine-
shire, left their home to seek their fortunes in the
south. Robert, the elder of the two, went to
England, and William, after a short stay in Edinburgh and Fairlie, secured in 1752 a situation as
gardener to Mr. Crawford of Doonside, near the
town of Ayr. In 1756, William Burness leased $7\frac{1}{2}$
acres of land at Alloway from Dr. Campbell of
Ayr. He laid out this ground as a market-garden,
and in a corner of it he built the clay cottage consisting of a " but and ben," with byre and barn all
under one thatched roof, which is known to-day as
Burns's Cottage. To this humble home on 15th
December, 1757, William Burness brought his
bride, Agnes Brown, the merry-hearted daughter
of a Kirkoswald farmer, whom he had met at
Maybole Fair.

ALLOWAY, 1759-1766

The poet was born on 25th January, 1759, and
lived in the cottage until his eighth year. From his
sixth year he attended school at Alloway Mill under
Campbell, on whose retiral the school was closed
when the poet's father and four of his neighbours
started a school (1765) and selected John Murdoch
as tutor. Murdoch was possessed of " linguistic and
literary talent " and has put it on record that the
future poet as a tiny pupil of six " was grounded a
little in English grammar." The poet's first school
books were the Bible and Masson's *English Grammar*
and *Collection of Prose and Verse* (c. 1755). In 1766

the poet's father moved to Mount Oliphant, but the distance proved too great for Robert and his brother Gilbert and the father was compelled to continue the education of his boys at home. Robert went to Dalrymple School for a period and had further tuition from Murdoch in Ayr in English and French and from Robinson of Ayr Grammar School in Latin. His general reading expanded with his years. In the end Burns, the youth of fourteen, with a summer three years later at Kirkoswald school under Hugh Rodger, a master mind on mathematics, entered the years of manhood well grounded in religious doctrine and with a fair education and an awakening ambition.

BURNS'S COTTAGE

The cottage, with the land surrounding it, was sold by William Burness in 1781 to the Incorporation of Shoemakers in Ayr, for the sum of £160. It was converted into an alehouse sometime before 1800 by the tenants. After 100 years' ownership by the Incorporation, it was purchased in 1881 for the sum of £4000 by the Alloway Burns Monument Trustees, who set about transforming it into a memorial worthy of the poet. The sale of liquor was discontinued, and a restoration as near as possible to the original condition was commenced. The " but " and the " ben " with the byre and the barn communicating as we now see it, is actually the building as planned and erected by the poet's father.

On the word of the Hon. Secretary to the Trustees, Mr. Dunlop, we may take it for granted that except for the fixtures of strong, sound workmanship, none of the original furniture exists. Old furniture of the period has been installed, giving a sense of authenticity to the home. Even the bed where in all probability the poet was born has a genuine eighteenth century appearance. The humble cottage has a sweet savour of homely reality.

The description in *The Cottar's Saturday Night*, inscribed by the poet to Robert Aiken, writer in Ayr, may be visualised without effort :

" His wee-bit ingle, blinkan bonilie,
His clean hearth-stane, his thriftie wifie's smile,
The lisping infant, prattling on his knee,
Does a' his weary kiaugh and care beguile,
An' makes him quite forget his labour and his toil."

RELICS IN THE COTTAGE AND MUSEUM

These number over 400 exclusive of the Bennett and Henderson libraries, but only the more valuable and noteworthy are recorded here. A complete catalogue with historical notes may be purchased at the cottage.

The cottage catalogue number of each item is given to assist identification by the tourist.

IN THE COTTAGE (KITCHEN)

Bed in which the poet was born (2).

Dresser and plate rack probably made for William Burness (3).

Stool for washing tub which belonged to Mrs. Burns (7).

Milking stool from Mossgiel (12).

Chair which belonged to William Burness (12A).

IN THE COTTAGE (ROOM)

Two chairs said to have been used by Tam o' Shanter and Souter Johnnie (15-16).

Table which belonged to Burns when at Dumfries (17).

Sign board fixed outside the cottage when it became an inn (25).

Grate from Ellisland Farm (32).

Trunk which belonged to Betty Burns, daughter of the poet (34).

Copestone of the auld Brig of Ayr (34A).

IN THE MUSEUM
(in safe, centre of East Room)

Holy Bible. Edinburgh, printed by John Reid, 1766, folio (66).

The poet's family Bible, with the following entries :—
In the handwriting of the poet :

" Robt. Burns was born at Aloway in the Parish of Ayr—Janry. 25th, 1759."

" Jean Armour, his wife, was born at Mauchline—Febry. 27th, 1767."

" Septr. 3d, 1786, were born to them twins, Robert, their eldest Son, at a quarter past Noon : & Jean, since dead at fourteen months old :—March 3d, 1788, were born to them twins again, two daughters, who died within a few days after their birth.—August 18th, 1789, was born to them Francis Wallace, so named after Mrs. Dunlop of Dunlop ; he was born a quarter before seven, forenoon.—April 9th, 1791, between three & four in the morning was born to them William Nicol, so named after Willm. Nicol of the High School, Edinr.—November 21st, 1792, at a quarter past Noon, was born to them Elizabeth Riddel, so named after Mrs. Robt. Riddel of Glenriddel."
In the handwriting of James Glencairn Burns :

" James Glencairn, born 12th Augt., 1794, named after the late Earl of Glencairn."
In the handwriting of William Nicol Burns :

"Maxwell. Born 26th July, 1796, the day of his father's Funeral. So named after Dr. Maxwell, the Physician who attended the Poet in his last illness.

"*Inserted by W. N. Burns, 9th April, 1867.*"

The Bible, which cost the poet £2, was bequeathed by Jean Armour Burns to her eldest son, Robert.

As the property of Mrs. Burns Hutchison, niece of the poet, the Bible was offered at auction in 1904, and was purchased for £1560 by Mr. Bernard Quaritch, bookseller in London. Eventually it was acquired by the trustees for £1700.

Robert Burns : copy of the bust by Sir John Steell, R.S.A., for the poets' corner in Westminster Abbey (51).

Eight-day clock which belonged to Isabella Burns Begg, youngest sister of the poet (53).

Three panes of glass from the Globe Inn, Dumfries, 18 lines of poetry, written with a diamond by the poet (56).

Shelved press and cupboard, used as a bookcase by the poet (59).

Mahogany writing desk belonging to Burns, purchased for £600 (60).

Chair on which the poet's mother nursed her children (62).

Chair which belonged to the poet (63).

Oak chair made from the printing press on which the first Kilmarnock Edition of Burns's poems was printed, 1786 (64).

CASE A

Alloway : The Burness Family.

Contract of feu betwixt Alexander Campbell, physician in Ayr, and William Burness, gardener for present at Doonside-Miln, 22nd June, 1756, concerning the land on which " the auld clay biggin " was erected by the poet's father and to which he brought his bride, Agnes Brown, in 1757 (67).

Silver watch which belonged to William Burness and afterwards to his son, the poet (69).

Holy Bible. Edinburgh: printed by Alexander Kincaid, 1762, 4to. The family Bible of William Burness, father of the poet, containing the register of his family. The date of birth of himself, and of his wife, of their marriage, and of the births of their seven sons and daughters, are entered in the hand of William Burness; the date when his father " departed this life " at Lochlea, is entered by the poet; and that of Agnes Brown's death at Grant's Braes, by James Burns, second son of Gilbert.

The Bible is doubly interesting on account of the poet's reference to it as " the big ha'-Bible, ance his father's pride " in *The Cottar's Saturday Night*. Purchased by the Trustees for £450 (72).

Tack between William Fergusson of Doonholm and William Burness, of lands of Mount Oliphant: dated 11th Dec., 1765 (73).

Collection of documents (seven in all) relating to William Burness (74).

A manual of religious belief composed by William Burness for the instruction of his children. MSS. 11 pp., printed 1875 (76).

CASE B

Holograph letter from Robert Burns to his brother Mr. William Burns, Saddler, Middle Street, Newcastle-on-Tyne, 1790 (83).

Jean Armour—Hair bracelet with lock of Mrs. Burns's hair (85).

Gold brooch belonging to Jean Armour, with lock of her hair (86).

Eighteen silver spoons and two sauce ladles presented to the poet's wife by her son James Glencairn Burns, 1824 (87).

Psalms of David in metre, 1796, with Mrs. Burns's name inscribed (90).

Seal which belonged to the poet (98).

Six buttons which belonged to the poet (100).

Cast in plaster of the skull of the poet, taken on 31st Mar., 1834 (101).

One guinea note of Bank of Scotland, 1st Mar., 1780, with 12 lines of poetry by Burns on reverse side (102).

CASE C

Many holograph letters from Burns, including one to the Bailies of the Canongate, Edinburgh, asking permission " to lay a simple stone over the revered ashes " of Robert Fergusson, the poet (110).

Burns's second commonplace book, in manuscript, 1787-90 (111).

Burns's Journal of his tour in the Highlands, 1787 (116).

CASES D AND E

A collection of Holograph Letters from Burns to correspondents, numbering 38 in all, including 5 to Mrs. Dunlop and 5 to Mrs. McLehose (Clarinda) (123-157).

CASE F

The Cunningham Collection of Holograph Letters (158).

Punch-bowl of Inverary marble presented to the poet by James Armour, his father-in-law (copy) (159).

CASES G AND H

The Graham of Fintry Collection of holograph letters and poems of Burns, 22 in all (161).

ON PEDESTAL BESIDE CASE K

Poems, chiefly in the Scottish dialect, by Robert Burns, Kilmarnock : printed by John Wilson, 1786, 8vo. (162).

The first edition of the *Poems* published on 31st July, 1786, price three shillings. Only a very few copies in uncut condition and with the original blue-paper wrapper are known to be in existence. This is one of those few copies—probably the finest of all—and was acquired in 1908 from Mr. George Seton Veitch of Paisley for £1000.

CASE K

Proposals for publishing by subscription Scotch poems by Robert Burns. The work to be elegantly printed in One Volume Octavo. Price stitched Three Shillings (163).

The only known copy of the prospectus of the world-famous Kilmarnock Edition.

Poems, chiefly in the Scottish dialect. By Robert Burns. The second edition considerably enlarged. Edinburgh, 1793, 2 vols., 12mo. (164).

The Stair Manuscripts. Poems and songs (eight in number) sent to Mrs. Stewart of Stair, 1786 (166).

The Afton Manuscripts (fourteen in number) with inscriptions by the poet (168).

A collection of books from Burns's library, including Shakespeare, 20 vols., 12mo, Moliere's works, 8 vols., Life of Wallace, Sterne's works, English Songs, 3 vols. (170-177).

Stirrup-cup or caup from the Tam o' Shanter Inn, Ayr (178).

CASE L

A collection of over 50 holograph verses and songs by the poet and a selection of Excise documents and books relating to the poet's service as an Excise Officer (179-219).

CASE M

Agreement between William Creech, publisher, Edinburgh, and Mr. Burns, respecting the property of Mr. Burns's poems, 17th April, 1787 (220).

Promissory notes for 100 guineas granted by William Creech to Robert Burns, 23rd Oct., 1787 (221).

Various editions of the poet's works including :
2nd Edinburgh Edition, 1787 (222).
3rd London Edition, 1787 (225).
Belfast, 1787 (226).
Dublin, 1787 (227).

Philadelphia, 1788 (228).

New York, 1788 (229).

The Jolly Beggars—a cantata, by Robert Burns, first published Glasgow, 1799 (235).

Letters addressed to Clarinda, etc., by the poet, published surreptitiously and interdicted by Court of Session, 1802 (237).

Holograph letter from Thomas Carlyle to Mrs. Isabella Burns Begg, sister of the poet, intimating that the Prime Minister, Sir Robert Peel, had agreed to bestow on her a small pension of twenty pounds a year (242).

EAST AND WEST ROOMS

On the walls of both rooms are displayed over 100 paintings and etchings of the poet, his relatives, friends, patrons and correspondents.

No. 301 is a copy in oils made from the original pencil sketch of the poet by Alexander Naysmith in 1787. On the walls are 20 portraits reproduced by many processes, based on the Naysmith.

Among the famous reproductions are :

The meeting of Burns and Scott in Sciennes Hill House, Edinburgh, the residence of Professor Adam Ferguson in 1787. Engraving by Chas. Martin Hardie, R.S.A. (392).

Inauguration of Robert Burns as poet laureate of Lodge Canongate Kilwinning, Edinburgh, 1787 (393).

Burns in Edinburgh—1787, reading his poem of the " Winter Night " before a literary gathering at the Duchess of Gordon's. Gravure after C. M. Hardie, R.S.A. (394).

Collection of editions of the poetical and prose writings of Robert Burns, and of books relating to his life and work. The library contains over 1300 volumes and of these Col. Robert James Bennett bequeathed in 1916, 523 volumes. A handsome collection of books and portraits were acquired in 1935 from Mr. Henderson, Dumfries, for £450 (408).

The most notable Burns manuscripts, letters and relics acquired within recent years are here recorded together with the prices paid by the trustees. The latter are evidence of the enhanced value of the poet's work and property:

1933

" The Vision," a very fine autographed MSS. of 7 verses, price paid, £450.

Volume of English Songs which belonged to the poet, price paid, £150.

Letter to James Hamilton, dated from Ellisland, 27th April, 1789, price paid, £210.

1934

First edition (Edinburgh) *Shakespeare*, 18 vols. and other relics, property of Burns—price paid, £150.

A letter to Mr. R. Cleghorn, Saughton Mills, dated 29-8-1790, price paid, £245.

Manuscript of Heron Election Ballad No. 1, price paid, £385.

1935

Collection of editions of Burns, works and books about his life, and portraits, price paid, £450.

Holograph letter from Burns to Richard Brown, price paid, £170 10s.

1937

Poetical epistle from Burns to Robert Graham (1791), price paid, £380.

1939

Letter from Burns to Capt. Johnston with poem, price paid, £130.

1941

Manuscript of Burns a Birthday Ode, price paid, £105.

ALLOWAY KIRK

A pre-Reformation sanctuary, now scheduled as
an Ancient Monument, it stands to the south of the
cottage, roofless and ivy grown, its belfry still
crowning the eastern gable. Even in Burns's day
the church was a ruin, and interments took place
within its walls. Here is interred William Burness,
the father of the poet, and on the back of the
memorial stone may be read the epitaph composed
by the poet and read with reverence by the countless thousands who visit the kirkyard :

" Here lie the loving husband's dear remains,
    The tender father, and the gen'rous friend.

The friend of man, to vice alone a foe,
    For even " his failings leaned to virtue's side."

Burns, when later he met Captain Grose, who was
at work on his *Antiquities of Scotland*, urged him to
include Alloway Kirk, and this led to the produc-
tion of that masterpiece *Tam o' Shanter*, with which
Alloway Kirk is associated in a vivid scene of
weirdest revelry. First there is the prophecy of his
" ain wife Kate," that Tam, forgetful of " time
or tide,"

" ——wad be found, deep drowned in Doon,
    Or catch'd wi' warlocks in the mirk,
    By Alloway's auld haunted kirk."

Then the tale proceeds to tell of Tam rising from
his carousal with the Souter and setting forth,
" well-mounted on his grey mare, Meg " on his
adventurous ride into Carrick :

" Kirk-Alloway was drawing nigh
    Where ghaists and houlets nightly cry."

Then, after passing the ford, and " thro' the whins"
and " by the cairn," Tam beholds a wondrous
sight :

" When glimmering thro' the groaning trees
    Kirk-Alloway seem'd in a bleeze
    Thro' ilka bore the beams were glancing,
    And loud resounded mirth and dancing."

Everyone has read of that " unco sight " at which
Tam o' Shanter " glowr'd amaz'd, and curious "
and of how, chased by Nannie and the hellish
legions, Tam's grey mare Meg did her " speedy
utmost " and won " the Keystane o' the brig."

BURNS MONUMENT

On the 17th March, 1814, on the initiative of
Sir Alexander Boswell of Auchinleck, a meeting
was called in the town of Ayr " to commence a
subscription " for the erection of a monument to
Robert Burns within his native county. After vary-
ing fortune, the sum of £800 having been raised by
subscription, and a design by Thomas Hamilton,
architect, approved by the committee, it was
decided that " the sum of £1200 shall be expended
in erecting and finishing the proposed monument."

The choice of a site was a matter of grave concern
to the committee, but eventually it was agreed that
on the banks of the Doon, between the Auld Brig
and Alloway's Auld Haunted Kirk was the most
appropriate position, and posterity has pronounced
favourably on the choice of site.

The total number of subscribers was 700, and the
sum raised was £2611, which included a donation

of fifty guineas from the Prince Regent, afterwards George IV.

The next step was to raise money " for enclosing the monument in a handsome manner and ornamenting the grounds round the building." The total cost of the monument, including the buying and enclosing of the extra acre of ground, was £3247.

On the top of the triangular building each of the sides of which faces approximately the three divisions of Ayrshire—Carrick, Kyle and Cunningham—is the circular base of the monument from which gracefully rise nine fluted Corinthian columns thirty feet high, with elaborate capitals. Surmounting the columns is the dome carrying a sculptured vase and tripod, the whole from base to tripod measuring 70 feet in height. A circular staircase within gives access to the base of the temple, and from this platform a delightful prospect is unfolded to the view.

As showing the universal interest in all things pertaining to the National Poet, it is worthy of note that the yearly number of visitors from all parts of the world to the monument and cottage exceeds 130,000. Within the monument may be seen a wonderful collection of very precious relics of the poet and his friends. The following are worthy of attention :

BIBLES which belonged to Highland Mary. These Bibles were presented by the poet to Mary Campbell on the eve of her setting out to visit her relatives. After her death they were taken out to Canada, and in 1840 were purchased by admirers of the poet and handed over to the Trustees of Burns Monument (2).

Lock of Highland Mary's hair, which was preserved in the Bibles (4).

Case containing Bonnie Jean's Wedding Ring ; Ring containing portion of Burns's hair ; and Ring containing lock of Burns's wife's hair (5).

The poet's seal, which was designed by Robert Burns, purchased in 1907 for £210 (7).

Cairngorm brooch, presented to Robert Burns by the Dumfries Volunteers (8).

Snuff-box which belonged to the poet (9).

Pair of glasses given by Burns to Clarinda (10).

Nanse Tinnock's quaich (12).

Kilmarnock Edition of Burns, 1786 (13).

First Edinburgh Edition, 1787 (17).

Copies of Edinburgh *Evening Courant* of 23rd, and 28th July, 1796, giving first public account of the poet's death and funeral, also the response made to the appeal on behalf of the poet's wife and family (26).

Bust of Burns by Patrick Park (32).

IN THE STATUE HOUSE

While in the garden may be seen the slightly defaced statue of Nanse Tinnock, by the sculptor Thom, attention will at once be directed to the masterpieces of the self-taught artist in stone, as seen in the Statue House.

TAM O' SHANTER and SOUTER JOHNNIE, the two drouthy cronies of Burns's great poem, have celebrated their centenary, having been fashioned in rough grained sandstone in the year 1828 by James Thom, a native of Tarbolton parish. Startlingly lifelike and represented in the garb of the period, the pose of the figures is so natural and true to type that it requires little imagination to conjure up a vision of the scene described by the poet in the lines :

> " . . . Ae market night
> Tam had got planted unco right,
> Fast by an ingle, bleezing finely
> Wi' reaming swats, that drank divinely ;
> And at his elbow, Souter Johnnie,
> His ancient, trusty, drouthy crony."

It is an interesting fact that these realistic figures were exhibited throughout the British Isles, and the admission fees amounted to £3600 before the statues were returned to Ayr.

AULD BRIG O' DOON

Four centuries have passed since this fine single arched bridge, steep and narrow, was built. It was the only bridge across the Doon linking Kyle with Carrick and its causeway has rung with the clatter of mail-clad warriors and plundering raiders as well as staid travellers and benighted roysterers. In 1813, when the new bridge was built, the auld brig was doomed to destruction. Burns's admirers protested, and for a time it was saved, but through neglect its disappearance was only a matter of time. To Hamilton Paul, preacher, poet, and editor, its final salvation is due for his petition to the Trustees of the Roads in the county of Ayr stirred up an enthusiasm which ensured its preservation for all time. The appeal began as follows :

" Must I, like modern fabrics of a day
　Decline unwept, the victim of decay.
　Shall my bold arch that proudly stretches o'er
　Doon's classic stream, from Kyle to Carrick's
　　shore,
　Be suffered in oblivion's gulf to fall,
　And hurl to wreck my venerable wall ?
　Forbid it every tutelary power
　That guards my *Keystane* at the midnight hour."

The Auld Brig stands as it did in Burns's day, but strengthened, and it is now scheduled as an Ancient Monument. It is visited by thousands who with knife and chisel incise their name or initials on the unprotesting parapets. Standing on the crown of the bridge, and gazing on the beautiful gardens to the west, it is difficult to realise that here is the veritable scene of that weird chase when Nannie and her fiendish followers sallied forth determined on the capture of Tam, the disturber of their revels :

" Now do thy speedy utmost, Meg,
      And win the keystane o' the brig ;
There at them thou thy tail may toss
A running stream they daurna cross,
But ere the keystane she could make
The fient a tail she had to shake
            .   .   .
Ae spring brought off her master hale
But left behind her ain grey tail ;
The carlin caught her by the rump,
And left poor Maggie scarce a stump."

AYR

As boy and man Burns must have been familiar with every nook and corner of the county town. Baptized in the Auld Kirk by Dr. William Dalrymple of " *The Kirk's Alarm*," Burns attended worship there with his parents while they resided at Alloway. In 1773, as Murdoch his teacher relates, " Robert Burns came to board and lodge with me (Ayr) for the purpose of revising English Grammar." From Mount Oliphant, Lochlea, and Mossgiel, he visited Ayr for pleasure or for business at the Mealmarket, and he reports : " My vicinity to Ayr was a great advantage to me."

Of the friendships formed in Ayr much might be written, but for all time he has endowed the natives with the greatest of the virtues, according to Carlyle :

" Auld Ayr, wham ne'er a town surpasses
For honest men and bonie lassies."

Of honest men there was Robert Aiken, his patron,
whom he addressed as " My lov'd, my honour'd,
much respected friend ; " Provost Ballantine, to
whom was inscribed " The Brigs o' Ayr " ; Major
Logan of Parkhouse, " the thairm-inspiring rattling
Willie," and lawyer Willie Chalmers, an adviser
and correspondent of the poet. Then there was his
minister, Dr. Dalrymple, for whom the poet's
father also had a deep regard :

" D'rymple mild ! D'rymple mild !
Though your heart's like a child,
And your life like the new-driven snaw."

Dr. McGill, the minister of the second charge,
denounced as a heretic and referred to in *The Kirk's
Alarm* as Doctor Mac, and Dr. Peebles of Newton-
on-Ayr, " frae the water fit " church, whose
criticism of Doctor Mac induced Burns to place
him in the pillory in two satires, were both a source
of inspiration to the poet.

THE AULD KIRK is situated between High
Street and the river. Although reconstructed
internally it is much in the same condition as in
Burns's day. The Rev. Dr. Dalrymple, "D'rymple
mild " of *The Kirk's Alarm*, Robert Aiken, to whom
The Cotters Saturday Night was dedicated, and
Provost Ballantyne, of Ayr, all friends of the poet's,
are interred in the churchyard.

TAM O' SHANTER INN.—In the High Street. This
old thatched inn with its pictorial signboard is the
same hostelry from which Tam, " weel mounted
on his grey mare, Meg," set off by way of the
Carrick Vennel on his famous ride. Several Burns

relics may be seen within. The Town Council of
Ayr purchased the Tam o' Shanter Inn for the sum
of £4000 in September, 1943.

THE BRIGS O' AYR.—By a strange coincidence
the three rivers round which Burns has cast his
lyric spell, the Doon, the Nith, and the Ayr, are
spanned by old and new bridges. The Auld Brig
of Ayr, dating from the middle of the fifteenth
century, was erected by two sisters named Lowe,
and is now as it was in Burns's day, but renovated
and strengthened. The bridge was closed for
traffic from 1907-10 while undergoing restoration
under the superintendence of James A. Morris,
R.S.A., distinguished architect and Burns en-
thusiast. It is now scheduled as an Ancient
Monument :

" Auld Brig appear'd of ancient Pictish race,
   The very wrinkles Gothic in his face."

The new bridge referred to by the poet in the lines :

" ' New Brig ' was busket in a braw new coat
   That he at Lon'on frae ane Adams got " ;

met the fate predicted by the Auld Brig, in 1877.

" Then down ye'll hurl (deil nor ye never rise)
   And dash the gumlie jaups up to the pouring
   skies."

The Auld Brig is surveyed periodically, and this
venerable relic of medieval times should with-
stand flood and tide for many years to come.

SIMPSON'S INN, mentioned by the poet, stood at
the Brig End, and near the Fishmarket.

DUNGEON-CLOCK.—This was one of the two
steeples in Ayr and was situated in the Sandgate.

" The drowsy Dungeon clock had numbered two."

WALLACE TOWER.—The present tower was built on the site of the original tower, in 1834, the clock and bells having been transferred :

" And Wallace Tower had sworn the fact was true."

The exploits of Wallace in and around Ayr were the inspiring source of the " patriotic " tide which coursed in the veins of the poet. The Burning of the Barns (Barns Street is suggested as the scene of the gruesome incident), and Wallace's retreat in ·Leglen Wood, Auchincruive, historically examined by the late Marquis of Bute, were both familiar scenes to the poet. A memorial was erected at Leglen recently by the Rev. J. C. Higgins of Tarbolton, to commemorate the association of the two great Scotsmen.

BURNS STATUE. Beautifully located in Station Square, this fine piece of sculpture is the work of John Lawson. The handsome decorative railings were the gift of the late Sir William Arrol of Forth Bridge fame.

MOUNT OLIPHANT, 1766-77

(4 miles from Ayr)

" But now the plains of Mount Oliphant began to whiten and Robert was summoned to signalise himself in the fields of Ceres."—So runs Murdoch's narrative. William Burness, the poet's father, was ambitious, and sought larger scope for his energy. The other motive was worthy of his good heart, the provision of means to retain his growing family around him until they were fitted to take their place in the world.

In 1766 he obtained a lease of Mount Oliphant, a farm of about 70 acres, at an annual rent of £40, and there the poet's boyhood years were spent. "The farm proved a ruinous bargain," as according to Gilbert's narrative, "Mount Oliphant is almost the very poorest soil I know of in a state of cultivation. To the buffetings of misfortune we could only oppose hard labour and the most rigid economy. My brother (the poet) at the age of thirteen, assisted in threshing the crop of corn, and at fifteen was the principal labourer on the farm, for we had no hired servant. I doubt not but that the hard labour and sorrow of this period of his life was in a great measure the cause of that depression of spirits with which Robert was so often afflicted through his whole life afterwards."

Burns's first songs were composed from 1773 onwards at Mount Oliphant—among them *Handsome Nell*, beginning : "O once I loved a bonie lass," and *The Ruined Farmer*, recounting in song his father's brave struggle with the barren soil, and a "factor's snash." The bitter memories of hardships endured by Burns and his parents at Mount Oliphant are set forth in *The Twa Dogs*.

KIRKOSWALD, 1775

(12 miles south of Ayr)

Before leaving Mount Oliphant William Burness desired to advance the education of his son Robert, and sent him to a noted school—at Kirkoswald in Carrick—there to benefit by Dominie Rodgers's tuition in mensuration, surveying, dialling, etc. In the neighbourhood at Craigenton his mother's kinsfolk resided, and for three summer months Burns shared an attic with his friend, John Niven of Maybole, in the farmhouse of Ballochniel. The schoolroom in which Rodger taught was at first in a portion of the church, vacated since 1777, but it was transferred to a dwelling-house opposite the churchyard, now marked by a commemorative tablet. These were eventful days for the young poet. Besides his study of the dry sciences, he cultivated an intimate knowledge of good prose and poetry, and became crazed with love for " Peggy Thomson," the charming *fillette* who lived next door to the school. From this episode sprung that tender early " song composed in August," beginning :

" Now westlin' winds and slaught'ring guns
    Bring Autumn's pleasant weather."

Ten years after, when Peggy Thomson was quietly settled as Mrs. Neilson, at Minnybae Farm, Kirk-oswald, Burns presented her with a copy of his poems inscribed on the fly leaf :

" Once fondly lov'd, and still remembered dear
.   .   .   .   .
    Accept this mark of friendship, warm, sincere."

Two of Burns's best known poems are definitely associated with Kirkoswald, *Tam o' Shanter*, completed during the Ellisland period, and *Hallowe'en*, written during the Mossgiel tenancy.

TAM O' SHANTER. Founded on incidents of his Kirkoswald days, the poem was completed in 1791 and regarded by Burns as his *chef d'œuvre*. It has been suggested that the early drafts of the poem were made at Ballochniel when he resided with his uncle in 1775. At anyrate the characters have all been identified, and their resting places in Kirk-oswald churchyard are now clearly marked for the guidance of visitors.

Douglas Graham, tenant of Shanter Farm (now demolished) was the original Tam o' Shanter, possessed of a rustic ready wit and reputedly convivial in his habits. Kate, his wife, was Helen McTaggart, "queer and abnormally superstitious."

John Davidson, the Souter Johnnie of the poem was a shoemaker of skill, with a ready wit and famous for his "jests and smart sayings." When Burns first knew him in 1775, he dwelt at Glenfoot in the neighbourhood of Shanter Farm. Farmer and Souter were cronies and periodic visits to Ayr on business were occasions for celebration.

Davidson built himself a house in Kirkoswald which he occupied in 1785 and therein lived his descendants until the year 1893. The Rev. Mr. Muir of Kirkoswald set out to acquire the property and to him and his committee is due all credit for the restoration and preservation of this house of historic interest.

Kirkton Jean (Kennedy) and her sister kept the hostelry next to the church. It was known as The Leddies' House. The traditional site is occupied by the Smithy.

The Miller, Hugh Brown, and The Smith, John Niven, companions of Tam o' Shanter, came from Ardlochan, which stands near Maidens village by the seaside.

The Witch, "lang after kenn'd on Carrick shore," is said to have been Julia Robinson, a receiver of contraband stores.

The Souter's House is open to the public and contains an important collection of relics of which the following is representative :

The Souter's Bible—printed by Alexander Kincaid, Edinburgh, 1762, with family register on leaf preceding the Apocrypha. The leather cover was tanned by the Souter.

Hugh Rodger's Family Bible (Burns's schoolmaster at Kirkoswald).

A small jug which belonged to the poet's wife.

Missive of Lease : The Earl of Cassillis to John Davidson (Souter), 1786.

A " Manual of Religious Belief " compiled by William Burness, the poet's father, for the use of his children.

The old tongue of the bell in Alloway Kirk.

Latter Will and Testament of Samuel Brown, Ballochniel, Burns's maternal uncle, 1811.

Souter's set of china.

Two Vol. Bible (1743) gifted by Hugh Rodger to his wife on 21st July, 1757, the date of their marriage in Ardmillan Castle, near Girvan.

Souter Johnnie's Will—6th April, 1806.

A framed pane of glass from the Globe Inn, Dumfries, which bears upon it four lines of poetry inscribed with a diamond by Burns.

Armchair stated by grandsons William and Matthew Davidson to have " belonged to their grandfather," the Souter.

Souter Johnnie's chest.

Among other holograph papers are two very interesting letters :

(1) Letter from William Burness to Thomas Orr at park, Kirkoswald, of date 8th September, 1780, requesting Orr to go to Lochlie to help in shearing corn.

(2) Letter from Robert Burns to Thomas Orr, at Park, dated Lochlie, 17th November, 1782, in which the poet indulges in a homily on life.

OUTSIDE THE HOUSE may be seen Four life-size Stone Figures representing, "Tam o' Shanter," "Souter Johnnie," the Innkeeper of the Tam o' Shanter Inn, Ayr, and his wife. These were sculptured by James Thom of Tarbolton and after being exhibited in many cities in England and

Scotland found an appropriate resting place in Kirkoswald. Two other items should be noted—Souter Johnnie's Sundial, and an ancient Louping-on-Stone.

HALLOWE'EN

This descriptive poem was the product of the Mossgiel period, but is definitely associated through the characters with Kirkoswald. Cassillis Downans, the fairy haunt, is fast by Cassillis Castle, two miles from Maybole. " Or for Colean the rout is taen " refers to the seat of the Marquis of Ailsa. The allusion to Bruce proclaims the proximity of Turnberry Castle, the patriot's birthplace :

" Where Bruce ance ruled the martial ranks,
    An' shook his Carrick spear."

There are many references in Burns's and Scott's poems to Bruce and the Men of Carrick, who are reputed to have formed his bodyguard. The remains of this great stronghold are to be seen at Turnberry Point, now surmounted by a lighthouse and overlooked by a sumptuous hotel.

The persons mentioned in *Hallowe'en* have been identified as neighbours and friends of the poet during his Kirkoswald residence. His visits to the district continued, and Craigenton, his mother's birthplace, and Ballochniel, his uncle's home, were not forgotten after he had left the district. No doubt the quaint rustic games and the invocation by charm and spell so prevalent amongst the peasantry of Scotland in the eighteenth century were much practised in Kirkoswald district and Burns, the growing man, some years later, when his genius had flowered, endowed those scenes with a permanence that he alone could give them.

CHURCHYARD AT KIRKOSWALD. Here lie buried
the Browns, Burns's maternal relations, Hugh
Rodger, Burns's teacher at Kirkoswald ; Douglas
Graham, " Tam o' Shanter " ; Helen McTaggart,
" Kate " of the poem ; John Davidson, " Souter
Johnnie " ; and many of the persons named in the
poem *Hallowe'en.* Each memorial stone is clearly
marked by a metal tablet.

LOCHLEA, 1777-84
(10 miles from Mt. Oliphant, 2½ miles from Tarbolton)

The farm of Lochlea, extending to 130 acres, in
Tarbolton parish, was, with the exception of a
short interval at Irvine, Burns's home for seven
years. An interesting period in the poet's life was
now opening up. His muse became more active,
and experience of social life on a wider scale
ripened his genius. In 1780 he helped to found the
Bachelor's Club at Tarbolton. In 1781 Burns was
entered as an apprentice of Lodge St. David's at
Tarbolton, and in 1784, he was appointed Depute-
Master of Lodge St. James. He is regarded as the
Bard of Freemasonry.

Sickness and differences with his landlord result-
ing in litigation in which he was worsted, under-
mined the health of the poet's father, and in
February, 1784, he passed away, a worthy and
much respected parent. Many songs and poems
were composed by the poet during his residence at
Lochlea, and among others the following are
popular to this day :

O Tibbie I hae see the day.	The Lass of Cessnock
The Tarbolton Lasses.	Banks.
Mary Morrison.	The Rigs o' Barley.
Montgomerie's Peggy.	My Nanie O.

TARBOLTON

The site of the house where John Wilson, "Doctor Hornbook," lived may be seen in Cunningham Street :

"That's just a swatch o' Hornbook's way
    Thus goes he on from day to day,
    Thus does he poison kill and slay,
        An's weel paid for 't."

THE BACHELOR'S CLUB. Founded by Burns and his brother, was in the Sandgate, and the house where he was made a mason, situated in Burns Street, may still be seen. The old minute book records " Robert Burns in Lochly was passed and raised." This minute book may be seen in the Burns Tavern.

NEW MASONIC TEMPLE. Rebuilt on the site of the old Lodge St. James Tarbolton Kilwinning, there are housed within the following interesting Burns relics, which are shown to visitors on request :

Chair and footstool used by the poet when Depute-Master.
The mallet used by the poet.
The poet's apron.
The jewels which the poet wore.
The Bible presented by the poet.
The old minute book in which his name is inscribed many times.

WILLIE'S MILL.—This famous place lies between Tarbolton and Mauchline. Tradition affirms that here at honest William Muir's house the poet used to meet " Montgomery's Peggy." Of more human

interest is the fact that here Jean Armour in her
distress found shelter and kindness. On the miller
the poet penned a beautiful epitaph, beginning :

> " An honest man here lies at rest,
>   As e'er God with his image blest."

The stone on which Death and the poet rested
while they held their weird conversation is pointed
out on the road to the village of Tarbolton :

> " We'll ease our shanks and tak a seat—
>   Come, gie's your news."

IRVINE, 1781-2

Burns, in his autobiography, has written, " My
twenty-third year was to me an important era.
Partly through whim, and partly that I wished to
set about doing something in life, I joined a flax-
dresser in a neighbouring town, to learn his trade."
Burns came to Irvine in the autumn of 1781, and
remained until the spring of 1782. He set himself
to learn the business of flax-dressing or heckling
with one Peacock, a distant relative and a "rogue,"
but the venture came to an untimely end, for, in
his own words, " the shop took fire, and burnt to
ashes, and I was left like a true poet, not worth a
sixpence."

A friendship formed in Irvine with Richard
Brown, a sailor, who rose to be shipmaster,
although it may not have had beneficial moral
results, at the very least gave a stimulus to the
poet's ambition. Burns refers in a letter to a
Sunday they spent together in Eglinton Woods, and
credits Brown with having " encouraged me to
endeavour at the character of a poet." Another

source of inspiration for the poet was found in the perusal of Fergusson's poems, to which he was led by Provost Hamilton, and Burns confesses the effect on him was such " I strung anew my wildly-sounding lyre with emulating vigour." Fergusson emphasised to Burns the beauty and virility of the vernacular, and as Henley has expressed it, " when he used the language which he had babbled in babyhood, and spoken as boy and youth and man, he at once revealed himself for its greatest master since Dunbar."

PARISH CHURCH. The original church, founded in the tenth century, was rebuilt in 1774. The minister during Burns's residence in Irvine was Dr. Richmond, and the poet was admitted to membership in 1781. The pew where the poet sat is still pointed out. In the churchyard are two memorial stones of interest. One indicates the resting place of David Sillar, born near Tarbolton, and for a time in business in Irvine as a grocer. Two very fine " epistles " to Davie, a brother poet, were addressed to this great friend by Burns, the second of which ends as follows :

" Haud to the muse, my dainty Davie :
  The Warl' may play you monie a shavie :
  But for the muse, she'll never leave ye
    Tho' e'er sae puir,
  Na, even tho' limpin' wi' the spavie
    Frae door to door."

The other tribute stone is to the memory of the wife of Dr. Mackenzie, who was the Miss Miller of the *Belles of Mauchline.*

KING ARMS HOTEL, High Street.—For many years the landlord was Samuel Dunlop of Tarbolton, whose wife was one of *The Ronalds of the*

Bennals. This song was one of the poet's early productions, and has associations with the Bachelor's Club in Tarbolton :

> " In Tarbolton, ye ken, there are proper young
>   men
>   And proper young lasses and a', man,
>   But ken ye the Ronalds that live in the Bennals?—
>   They carry the gree frae them a', man."

It is noteworthy that the Irvine Burns Club has met here for over one hundred years, and the present landlord has many interesting relics on view.

TEMPLETON'S BOOKSHOP (High Street).—Regularly frequented by Burns, where in 1781-82 he conned old ballads and chap books, and extended his knowledge of the English novel.

WHEAT SHEAF HALL (High Street), where Burns attended Masonic meetings.

DAVID SILLAR'S SCHOOL.—Unsuccessful as a grocer, " Dainty Davie " took to teaching, and the old school (now a dwelling-house) still stands in East Road.

PORT HEAD INN (High Street).—In Burns's day this house was occupied by Provost Hamilton, who was a nephew of Hamilton of Gilbertfield, a poet greatly admired by Burns.

> " My senses wad be in a creel
>   Should I but dare a hope to speal
>   Wi' Allan, or wi' Gilbertfield,
>   The braes o' fame."

Burns was a frequent visitor, and the provost's son, Dr. Hamilton, was one of those who stood surety for the publication of the Kilmarnock Edition of 1786.

HECKLING SHOP AND LODGINGS.—Both were situated in the Glasgow Vennel and have been marked by a commemoration tablet.

BURNS STATUE.—Erected on the banks of the River Irvine on the town moor, this handsome statue of the poet was the gift of Mr. John Spiers of Glasgow. The work of Dr. Pittendreigh McGillvray, the memorial was unveiled by the Poet Laureate Alfred Austin in 1896.

EGLINTON WOODS.—The friendship between Burns and Richard Brown produced at least seven letters, still extant, from the poet. In one of these he refers to "A Sunday we spent together in Eglinton Woods." A memorial tablet on the Drukken Steps (St. Bride's Well) on the edge of the woods commemorates this meeting.

BURNS CLUB AND RELICS.—The club is one of the oldest, having been founded in 1826, and it holds an unbroken record. The Dr. McKenzie mentioned before was the first president, and David Sillars, the poet's friend, the first vice-president.

The club possesses some of the most interesting and valuable Burns MSS. Chief of these is the printer's copy for the first edition published in Kilmarnock in 1786 containing the following poems :

> The Cottar's Saturday Night.
> The Twa Dogs.
> The Holy Fair.
> The Author's Earnest Cry and Prayer.
> Address to the Deil.
> Scotch Drink.

Originally in the possession of Gavin Hamilton of Mauchline, to whom the poet dedicated his first volume of poems, the MSS. have been carefully

treasured for over one hundred years. They may
be seen on application to the Hon. Secretary of
the club.

MOSSGIEL, 1784-8

(1 mile north of Mauchline)

Three months before the death of William
Burness, Robert and his brother Gilbert leased the
farm of Mossgiel, extending to 118 acres, at a rental
of £90. It was a joint concern, and every member
of the family was allowed ordinary wages for their
labours. The brothers' allowance was £7 each per
annum. " I entered on this farm," says the poet,
" with a full resolution, come, go to, I will be wise !
I read farming books—I calculated crops—I
attended markets—and, in short, in spite of ' the
devil, and the world and the flesh,' I believe I
should have been a wise man ; but the first year
from unfortunately buying bad seed, and the
second, from a late harvest, we lost half our crops.
This overset all my wisdom."

The four years during which Burns resided on
the cold and unfruitful farm of Mossgiel were the
most important of his life. It was there his genius
developed its highest energies, and as Henley has
said, " at Mossgiel he did nearly all his best and
strongest work." Local fame, he reports, was
already his, for " I now began to be known in the
neighbourhood as a maker of rhymes." Songs,
epistles, satires and homely descriptive poems came
from the poet's pen, and when his first volume, the
priceless Kilmarnock Edition of 1786 was published, it contained no fewer than forty-five poems,
the product of his early years. Although many of
the poems in that volume, such as *The Twa Dogs*,

The Holy Fair, The Cottar's Saturday Night, Hallowe'en,
and the *Vision* may be regarded in a sense as autobiographical, it may be said of all Burns's poetry
that it is intensely realistic in that he finds his
theme and his inspiration in nature, and the folk
among whom he lived.

Mossgiel, and the little town of Mauchline, a
mile or so to the south, are linked closely in Burns's
career for a period of four years. The poet
frequented church, hostel, and Masonic lodge in
Mauchline, and found in his everyday life the
subjects for many of his brilliant satires, songs, and
poems. *The Jolly Beggars, Holy Willie's Prayer,* and
The Holy Fair are vivid word pictures of Mauchline
life at the end of the eighteenth century. One of the
far-reaching episodes in the poet's life was his wooing of Jean Armour, the master mason's daughter,
and one of the Belles of Mauchline of whom he
sang :

" There's beauty and fortune to get wi' Miss
     Morton,
  But Armour's the jewel for me o' them a'."

Burns's pledge to Jean Armour, her father's
persecution, his public appearance for reproof at
the hands of " Daddy Auld " in Mauchline Church
are facts known to every reader of Burns's life.

The poet's adoration of the Highland maid,
Mary Campbell, object and inspirer of many
beautiful songs, is an incident of the Mossgiel
period that has appealed to the sentiment of the
nation. Crushed by the stern attitude of mason
Armour, forsaken by his Jean, Burns formed an
ardent attachment with Mary Campbell, and, on
his own avowal, marriage was arranged between
them. They met on a Sunday in May, 1786, on the

banks of the Fail, and pledged their troth, when Burns presented Mary Campbell with a Bible. Thereafter she embarked for her home in the West Highlands, and on her return voyage died of a malignant fever at Greenock. That this *affaire de cœur* made a lasting impression on the poet's mind is evidenced by the number of beautiful songs such as *Flow Gently, Sweet Afton*, of which she was the inspiration. Many years after at Ellisland on the anniversary of her death, he composed the beautiful poem, *To Mary in Heaven*.

Mention has been made of the chief poems of the Mossgiel period, but the songs were many in number and of great variety and all of them lyrical gems. *Corn Rigs*, *Green Grow the Rashes*, *The Braes of Ballochmyle*, *Will ye go to the Indies*, *Mary*, *Farewell the bonie banks o' Ayr*, are all worthy of first place in the long line of Scots minstrelsy.

MAUCHLINE

MAUCHLINE CROSS.—The epistle to John Kennedy, factor to the last Earl of Dumfries, and an early friend of the poet, begins :

> " Now Kennedy, if foot or horse
> E'er bring you in by Mauchline Cross."

In HIGH STREET, nearby, resided John Richmond, the writer, with whom Burns stopped on his first visit to Edinburgh. Close at hand is the New Road, where stood the shop of James Smith, " the sleest pawky thief," a great friend of the poet, and whose sister was one of the Mauchline belles of which Burns sang : " Miss Smith she has wit, and Miss Betty is braw . . ."

NANSE TINNOCK'S HOUSE, fast by the cross, is identified as the change-house of *The Holy Fair*.

> " Now butt an' ben the change-house fills
> Wi' yill-caup commentators."

JEAN ARMOUR BURNS HOUSES.—Situated in Castle Street and marked by a marble tablet, is the house where Burns and Jean Armour began their married life in 1788. In the adjoining property lived Dr. McKenzie, friend and brother mason of the poet, and these houses and Nanse Tinnocks change-house were purchased, repaired and gifted by Charles R. Cowie of Glasgow to the Glasgow and District Burns Association, 1915. Burns's first home has been furnished in period fashion, and a museum of Burns relics incorporated in the building. But what must give great joy to all lovers of Burns is the knowledge that the greater part of the three properties is occupied by elderly ladies, who not only sit rent free but are in receipt of annual grants of money from the Association and the Little Bequest. In the Museum may be seen the Armour Family Bible and several Burns Manuscripts.

THE CHURCHYARD.—The scene of *The Holy Fair*, written by Burns in 1786 and appearing in the first or Kilmarnock Edition of his poems, is a place of deep interest to the visitor. Here lie Burns's contemporaries, some of them his dearest friends, many of them endowed with that immortality the pen of a genius alone can give.

The more noteworthy places of sepulture are : the burial place of the Armour family, Rev. William Auld, the " Daddy Auld " of *The Kirk's Alarm*, John Richmond, the poet's friend and host, the Alexanders of Ballochmyle, Auld Nanse Tinnock, George Gibson and his spouse Agnes Ronald, and their daughter, " Racer Jess," all of the Poosie Nansie hostelry, the Fisher family, of whom " Holy Willie " is the most notable member, and Gavin Hamilton, the bosom friend of Burns (no tombstone marks this grave).

MAUCHLINE CASTLE.—Adjacent to this ancient building stands the house where Gavin Hamilton, the poet's patron and friend, resided. Here the poet spent many of his happiest evenings, and amongst others he met there Miss Kennedy whose ill-fated love affair prompted the composition of the world-famous lyric, *Ye Banks and Braes o' Bonie Doon.*

POOSIE NANSIE'S HOSTELRY. — Opposite the churchyard gate was in Burns's day a common lodging house kept by George Gibson, his wife, and their daughter " Racer Jess." The howf of " The Jolly Beggars " is changed little since that night when Burns saw the motley gathering and transmuted their song revelry through the alchemy of his genius.

> " Ae night at e'en, a merry core
> O' randie, gangrel bodies,
> In Poosie Nansie's held the splore
> To drink their orra duddies."

BURNS NATIONAL MEMORIAL AND COTTAGE HOMES.—Situated at the junction of the Kilmarnock and Tarbolton roads, this practical memorial of the poet of humanity for which the Glasgow Mauchline Society is to be credited, was opened in May, 1898, and commemorates the centenary of the poet's death. The sum originally collected by the Society for their noble scheme was £8751. A square baronial tower, 67 feet in height, wherein is a museum containing many interesting Burns relics, it is flanked by twenty substantial and artistic cottage homes, where many deserving old folk find a quiet anchorage for life. Each occupant of these pleasant little homes sits rent free and receives annually a monetary grant from the Trustees. Here is a fulfilment of the poet's social programme, " A brother to relieve, how exquisite the bliss."

MAUCHLINE HILL TOP.—The ascent of this slight hill brings into view many places associated in the poet's life. The groves of Barskimming, the River Lugar, Montgomery Woods and Castle, Ochiltree where dwelt his brother bard, " winsome Willie " Simpson, and Catrine House, the home of Professor Dugald Stewart, are in the vicinity. It was at Prof. Stewart's house that the poet met Sir John Whitefoord and Lord Daer (both of Edinburgh) :

> " Ne're-to-be-forgotten day,
> Sae far I sprachled up the brae
> I dinner'd wi' a Lord."

Ballochmyle, the home of the Miss Alexander whom the poet saw, admired, and celebrated in the song, *The Lass o' Ballochmyle*, and Failford, the scene of Burns's parting with " Highland Mary," now marked by a commemorative stone, may be observed from the hill. Glenconner, the home of the Tennant family, much respected by the poet, and the subject of an epistle beginning, " Auld comrade dear, and brother sinner," is also in the vicinity.

KILMARNOCK, 1786

While resident at Mossgiel, the poet, disappointed in the farm, and under the ban of the Armour family and the church, resolved to

emigrate to Jamaica. His first act was to give up
his share in the farm to his brother Gilbert, and
his next, to decide on the publication of his poems.
To Kilmarnock, some seven miles north of Mossgiel, his eyes were bent, and encouraged by Gavin
Hamilton, his landlord, and R. Aiken, " my lov'd,
my honor'd, much respected friend," he entered
into negotiations with John Wilson, printer, for an
edition of 600 copies. Published at three shillings
per copy, the thin octavo volume in blue boards,
when offered for sale in these days, realises many
thousands of pounds.

It is of interest to know that some of the poems
were written while the printing was in progress, and
The Twa Dogs, with which the Kilmarnock Edition
opens, was one of them.

The profits of the edition, twenty pounds, in his
pocket, and having failed to affect a reconciliation
with the Armours, the poet, " skulking from covert
to covert, under all the terrors of a jail," secured a
passage in a ship that was to sail from the Clyde
to Jamaica. " I had taken the last farewell of my
few friends ; my chest was on the way to Greenock;
I had composed the last song, I should ever measure
in Caledonia, *The gloomy night is gathering fast,* when
a letter from Dr. Blacklock to a friend of mine over-
threw all my schemes, by opening new prospects to
my poetic ambition."

So writes Burns in his autobiography, but there
were interesting events worthy of record ere the
fateful letter arrived. The slender volume brought
him the friendship of many good neighbours of
high social standing. Professor Dugald Stewart of
Edinburgh, then residing in Catrine, Dr. Hugh
Blair, a leading literary light, Mrs. Dunlop of
Dunlop, an unfailing friend, and the beautiful Mrs.

Stewart of Stair, celebrated in several songs, all paid tribute to his genius and extended to the poet a warm and friendly welcome. To Dr. Lawrie of Loudon House, a wise counsellor, is to be credited the change in the plan which a desperate situation had thrust on the poet. Forwarding a copy of the poems with a sketch of the poet's life, to Dr. Blacklock of Edinburgh, and a request that he should invite the interest of the prominent literary men in that city, a reply was received by Dr. Lawrie, urging the poet to visit the capital with a view to preparing a second edition of his poems. This was an invitation which could not be resisted, and having failed to persuade " Wee Johnnie " Wilson of Kilmarnock to print a second edition unless he advanced the cost of the paper, Burns set out at the close of November, 1786, for " fair Edina " on a pony borrowed from his patron, Dalrymple of Orangefield.

THE MONUMENT AND STATUE, situated in Kay Park, are of comparatively recent date. The erection of a statue in Glasgow by shilling subscriptions gave an impetus to similar schemes throughout Scotland. Gothic in design, the memorial building, consisting of two storeys and a tower, rises to a height of 75 feet, and is the conception of a local architect, Mr. R. S. Ingram. The statue of the poet, sculptured in Sicilian marble, and modelled on the Nasmyth portrait, is the work of Mr. W. G. Stevenson, Edinburgh. Altogether the memorial cost £2000, and it was declared open to the public on 9th August, 1879, by Col. Alexander of Ballochmyle, before a vast assembly of people.

THE MUSEUM, within the monument, is the richest in the world in respect of Burns MSS., and besides possesses the wonderful collection of Burns's

Works made by the late James McKie, publisher, Kilmarnock. The catalogue of the McKie Burnsiana Library, prepared by Mr. David Sneddon, runs to 160 pages, and contains over 1300 items, consisting of holograph MSS. by Burns, editions of the poet's works, foreign editions, Clarinda letters, chapbooks, pamphlets, relics, paintings and etchings.

The following is a list of the Burns Holograph Manuscripts in the museum:

BURNS'S HOLOGRAPH MANUSCRIPTS

1. *The Holy Fair*—composed in Autumn, 1785.
2. *Hallowe'en.*
3. *Address to the Deil.*
4. *The Auld Farmer's New Year Morning Salutation* to his auld meere, on givin' her the accustom'd ripp o' corn to hansel in the New Year.
5. *John Barleycorn*—a ballad.
6. *Scotch Drink.*
7. *Man was made to Mourn*—a ballad.
8. *The Twa Dogs*—a tale.
9. *The Cottar's Saturday E'en.*
10. *The Author's Earnest Cry and Prayer* to the Rt. Honble. The Scotch Representatives in the House of Commons.
11. *Address to J. Smith.*
12. *Winter*—a dirge.
13. *An Epistle to Davy*, a brother poet.
14. *The Death an' Dyin' Words o' Poor Mailie*—my ain pet yowe. An unco mournfu' tale.
15. *Poor Mailie's Elegy.*
16. A Letter from Burns to Mr. Wm. Stewart, Closeburn, dated Glencairn Kirk, Thursday Even.
17. A Letter from Burns to David Staig, Esq., Dumfries, dated Friday noon.
18. *Lassie wi' the lint white locks.*

19. A ballad—*Last May a braw wooer cam down the Lang Glen.*
20. *Tam o' Shanter*—a tale.
21. *Lament of Mary Queen of Scots.*
22. Letter to Robert Muir, Merchant, Kilmarnock, dated Mossgiel, Friday Morn, 1786.
23. *Holy Willie's Prayer.*
24. Letter to Robert Ainslie, dated Ellisland, 30th June, 1788.
25. *Occasional Address,* spoken by Miss Fontonelle on her benefit night, December 4th, 1793, at Dumfries Theatre.
26. *Epistle to a Young Friend,* dated Mossgiel, 15th May, 1786.
27. Letter to Gavin Hamilton, dated Mauchline, August 18th, 1783.
28. Letter to Gavin Hamilton, Writer, Mauchline, dated Stirling, 28th Augt., 1787.

EDITIONS OF THE POET'S WORKS

There are over 400 editions in the McKie Collection, and these include the Kilmarnock or First Edition.

1786. *Poems,* chiefly in the Scottish dialect, by Robert Burns. Kilmarnock, printed by John Wilson. (Presented by Dr. A. C. MacLaren, London).

The First Edinburgh Edition—

1787. *Poems,* chiefly in the Scottish Dialect, by Robert Burns. Edinburgh, printed for the author and sold by William Creech.
1787. The Second Edinburgh Edition (Creech).
1787. The Third Edition. London, printed for A. Strahan ; T. Cadell in the Strand, and W. Creech, Edinburgh.
1787. The Dublin Edition (Gilbert).
1788. The American Edition (Stewart and Hyde).

RELICS

Among the most interesting relics of the poet to be seen in the Museum are the following :

Draught-board, used by Robert and Gilbert Burns at Lochlea.

Tam Samson's gun and dram glass.

> " That woefu' morn be ever mourned,
>   Saw him in shootin' graith adorned."

The Earl of Glencairn's sword.

Old Piano (Mrs. Gregory's) of date 1786. Burns greatly enjoyed Mrs. Gregory's playing on this piano.

Frying pan which belonged to Burns, at Ellisland.

Chair and dram glass which belonged to Burns.

Plate and silver teaspoons which belonged to Mrs. Burns.

Two cups and saucers and three jugs which belonged to the poet's mother.

TAM SAMSON'S HOUSE.—One of Burns's great friends, Thomas Samson, the subject of an elegy, a flattering epitaph, and a glorious resurgence, lived in Rosebank, Braehead, and the house still stands little altered from the poet's time, opposite the entrance to Kay Park. The elegy begins thus :

> " Has Auld Kilmarnock seen the Deil
>   Or great McKinlay thrawn his heel ?
>   Or Robinson again grown weel
>   To preach an' read ?
>   Na, waur than a' ! cries ilka chiel,
>   ' Tam Samson's dead.' "

Tam Samson, a fine old sportsman, lies in the Laigh Church burying ground, close beside the two reverend preachers mentioned in the first stanza of the elegy. The words of the epitaph are inscribed on Mr. Samson's headstone.

BEGBIE'S INN (now the Angel Hotel) still stands in Market Lane. The place is mentioned in the poet's daring satire, *The Ordination*:

> " Swith ! to the Laigh Kirk, ane an' a',
>   An' there tak up your stations ;
>   Then aff to Begbie's in a raw,
>   An' pour divine libations,
>   For joy this day."

JOHN WILSON'S SHOP.—" John Wilson," the printer and publisher of the world-famous Kilmarnock Edition of the poet's works, had his shop at the corner of King Street and Waterloo Street, now occupied by D. Brown & Co., Publishers. The printing office was on the third flat of a tenement in Waterloo Street. The printer is interred in the burial ground of the High Church, where John Russell, the " Rumble John " of the satire, " his piercin' words like Highlan' swords," preached strong Calvinistic doctrine.

THE LAIGH KIRK.—Apart from its Burns associations, the Laigh Kirk situated in Bank Street near the Cross, marks the site of the ancient shrine of St. Marnock. The many references made by the poet in *The Ordination* and other satires, have made the old church and burying ground places of abiding interest to all students of the poet's life.

Burns had many friends in Kilmarnock, whose homes have disappeared with the rebuilding of the town. John Goldie, " Goudie, terror o' the whigs," Robert Muir, who subscribed for seventy-two copies of the First Edition, Bailie Gregory, at whose home Burns heard the piano now in the museum played by Mrs. Gregory, are worthy of mention.

EDINBURGH, 1786

Burns, hospitably entertained by farmers *en route*, on arrival at the capital took up quarters on 28th November, 1786, in Baxter's Close in the Lawnmarket with John Richmond, a clerk of his acquaintance hailing from Ayrshire. It was the Edinburgh of Sir Walter Scott's day, gay, squalid, venerable, literary, with its " season " when every family of quality in Scotland was in residence. The brilliant society of the capital welcomed the rustic poet, introduced as he was by noblemen and learned professors, and Henry MacKenzie, in the *Lounger*, wrote so glowingly of his poetic genius that the doors of Edinburgh were flung open to him. Dalrymple of Orangefield introduced him to the Earl of Glencairn, and as friends and patrons Burns reckoned the Duke and Duchess of Gordon, Lord Eglinton, Lord Daer, Lord Monboddo, Henry Erskine, Dr. Blacklock, and Professor Dugald Stewart. The first few weeks in Edinburgh seemed to the poet a realisation of the prophecy contained in the quaint lines of an old ballad he hummed to himself many times :

> " As I cam o'er by Glenap
>   I met an aged woman
>   Who bade me keep up my heart,
>   For the best of my days were coming."

" The attention he received," says Professor Dugald Stewart, " from all ranks and description of persons, were such as would have turned any head but his own." Burns was too big to be spoiled, and his independent spirit and strong intellect carried him safely through the Edinburgh period.

Yet, as Henley has said, " Edinburgh was a triumph for Burns ; but it was also a misfortune. It was a centre of conviviality and a dangerous place for a peasant to be at large in, especially a peasant of the conditions and stamp of Burns." Freemasons welcomed him, the Caledonian Hunt assumed him, and the Crochallan Fencibles enrolled him, but withal he did not forget the purpose of his visit to the capital.

The second edition of Burns's poems advertised on the 14th December was published on 21st April, 1787, by Creech. It was dedicated to the Noblemen and Gentlemen of the Caledonian Hunt, and there were 1500 subscribers, who called for 2800 copies.

No. 447 LAWNMARKET, Baxter's Close, (now demolished), was the residence of Burns on his first visit in November, 1786. Here dwelt his friend John Richmond of Mauchline.

THE NEW COUNTY BUILDINGS mark the line of Liberton's Wynd where stood JOHNNIE DOWIE'S TAVERN, patronised by Fergusson the poet, and a resort of Burns where he met frequently Willie Nicol and Allan Masterton and other convivial friends.

GENERAL'S ENTRY (called after General Monk), in the Potterow, was the residence of Mrs. MacLehose (Clarinda). The house stood on the site of Marshall Street School. Better known as Clarinda's home is 14 Calton Hill (with tablet) where she lived for 25 years and died on October 22, 1841.

ANCHOR CLOSE (243 High Street), contained Dawny Douglas's Tavern, the meeting place of the famous Crochallan Club. In this close was William Smellie's printing office, where Burns read the proofs of his poems.

BELL'S WYND (146 High Street), where James

Johnson, engraver, produced the *Scot's Musical Museum*, to which Burns contributed nearly 200 songs without fee or reward.

STEVENLAWS CLOSE (No. 132 High Street), where Allan Masterton, of the High School, one of the heroes of *O Willie Brewed a Peck o' Maut*, dwelt.

AULD GREYFRIARS. In this ancient and famous God's acre lies " Patrick Miller, Esq., of Dalswinton," laird of Ellisland, a friend in need and indeed to the poet, as he was also to Alexander Nasmyth, the painter of the Bard.

CANONGATE CHURCHYARD. In the graveyard may be seen the simple monument Burns erected to the memory of Fergusson, the poet. Here also are interred " Clarinda " and Professor Dugald Stewart, associates of the poet.

ST. JOHN STREET (N. 182 Canongate). The Canongate Kilwinning Lodge of Freemasons, of which Burns was Poet-Laureate, met in the turreted building on the right through the arch.

ST. JAMES SQUARE (off Princes Street), where Burns lived for several months in 1787.

SCIENNES HILL HOUSE (Braid Place, Causewayside), was the residence of Professor Adam Ferguson, and here the historic meeting of the two great Scotsmen, Burns and Scott, took place. It was early in 1787 and the incident of Scott receiving his literary baptism at the hands of the Ayrshire poet has been permanently portrayed on canvas by Hardie the artist. The picture is now in the Chambers's Institute, Peebles.

OLD CALTON BURYING-GROUND. This interesting God's acre contains the unmarked grave of Willie Nicol, companion and fellow-lodger of the poet, and also that of the mother of Dr. Candlish, one of the five " Belles of Mauchline."

CALTON HILL. One of the view points of the city has many monuments of national interest. Professor Dugald Stewart, Burns's warm friend, is commemorated in stone and on a lower spur of the hill stands one of Edinburgh's memorials to the poet she honoured in his day. Burns's monument, imposing yet graceful, is Grecian in character and consists of twelve Corinthian pillars on a circular foundation supporting a cupola surmounted by griffins. It was erected in 1831 from the designs of Thomas Hamilton.

GEORGE SQUARE. This famous residential quarter has at least two dwellings associated with the poet. In No. 55 Henry MacKenzie, editor of the *Lounger*, whose bold recognition of the Poet's genius paved the way for Burns's welcome by literary circles in Edinburgh, lived and entertained for many years. In No. 23 Lord Craig, a distinguished judge and relative of Burns's "Clarinda" had his home.

BURNS STATUE. The last work of Flaxman, the sculptor, who did not live to finish it. This statue of white marble representing the poet contemplating the daisy's fate, may be seen in the Scottish National Portrait Gallery.

BURNS STATUE (Leith). Not to be outdone by its great neighbour, Leith has a very fine statue of the poet, the work of D. W. Stevenson.

GLASGOW

The poet's association with the city of the West has been the source of much speculation. Recent research has revealed that only on five occasions did Burns visit Glasgow. In his day the population did not exceed 45,000 whereas Edinburgh, with almost double the population, was not only the

Capital, but, the literary centre of Scotland. It
does not appear that the poet made contacts with
the nobility, professors, or literary circles and his
correspondence, with natives mainly, consisted of
letters to a few business friends.   And yet two
Glasgow people very closely identified with the
poet in his later years were productive of much
letter writing.   The " Clarinda " of the world
famous correspondence with " Sylvander " was a
daughter of Surgeon Wm. Craig of Glasgow, whom
Burns first met in Edinburgh, and one of the poet's
most notable friends, also of Glasgow, was Dr. John
Moore, author of *Zelucca* and other works, who was
the recipient of that most valuable autobiographical
letter written to him by the poet from Mossgiel in
August, 1787.

Burns's visits to Glasgow were as follows :

In June, 1787, shortly after the issue of the
Edinburgh edition of his poems, he wrote from
Glasgow to Creech, his publisher, asking him to
" send fifty copies to Mr. Smith, Bookseller, here."
In August he was again in the city for he reported
to Dr. John Moore that the " history of myself was
unluckily forgot among other papers at Glasgow."
On 18th February, 1788, Burns arranged to meet
his friend, Richard Brown, and his own brother
William at Durie's Black Bull Inn, Argyle Street,
north side of the street (now marked with a tablet),
and three weeks later in a letter to Robert Muir,
the poet intimated he was going to Glasgow via
Galston and Newmilns to collect "small sums
owing to me for my first Edition." And finally having
settled his affairs with Creech, his publisher, Burns
travelled via Glasgow to Dumfries and may have

spent a day or two in the city. Burns has nowhere in his poems or letters commented on the city of St. Mungo and its inhabitants but it is fact and not tradition that he found one very good friend in John Smith, bookseller, for he thanked him personally for disposing of so large a number of his poems on such a low commission as five per cent. In no city in the world has there been such appraisal of Burns's genius. To-day the city has 25 Burns Clubs with a membership exceeding 4,000

THE BURNS HOUSE CLUB. A central meeting place for members of Burns Societies was inaugurated in the city in 1920. The Burns Club House Chambers at 27 India Street, are available for ordinary and committee meetings and social and literary functions. The quarterly meetings of the Burns Federation are held there.

MITCHELL LIBRARY. In the Mitchell Library, North Street, is to be found the largest collection of Burns literature in the world, consisting of 3000 volumes including 700 editions gathered over a period of 62 years. A unique feature of the Library is that it contains two copies of the priceless first Kilmarnock edition of 1786 and of the second or Edinburgh edition of 1787 and the third or London edition of 1787. The " Burnsiana " has been subdivided into 26 sections and full indexes provide easy references for students.

BURNS EXHIBITION. One outstanding tribute to Scotland's greatest poet was " The Burns Exhibition " held in Glasgow to commemorate the centenary of the death of the poet. The Exhibition was opened on 15th July, 1896, by Lord Rosebery who delivered an eulogy on the occasion that has passed into the literature of the nation. The number of items exhibited was 2994.

Burns Statue. Glasgow's statue of Burns, sculptor C. E. Ewing, stands in George Square and is noteworthy for the four fine panels in bronze also designed by Ewing. It was unveiled by Lord Houghton on 25th January, 1877. An interesting fact is that the funds required were raised by a shilling subscription—an example followed by other cities and towns.

BURNS'S TOURS, 1787

The Edinburgh edition published, Burns set out on a tour of the border counties with his friend Robert Ainslie. After visiting Ainslie's home at Berrywell in Berwickshire, they passed through the romantic Scott country (as it is now known), to Newcastle, returning by Carlisle and Dumfries to Dalswinton, when the poet looked over Mr. Miller's property which he was soon to lease and make a home for Jean Armour. It was a triumphal tour for his fame had preceded him, and entertainment and honours were thrust on him wherever he halted.

Arriving at Mauchline on the 8th of June, he set out shortly for a solitary journey to the West Highlands by way of Greenock to Inveraray, returning by Loch Lomond to Glasgow and Mauchline.

After a period at Mossgiel he again visited Edinburgh, residing with his friend Nicol in Buccleuch Street.

On 25th August, 1787, Burns set off with his friend William Nicol in a chaise for the Highlands travelling as far north as Inverness. The route taken was through Linlithgow, Bannockburn and Stirling, by Strathallan and Killiecrankie, to Blair

Atholl. Culloden Moor was visited as well as Falls of Foyers, Nairn, Forres, Elgin, and many other places, and the return journey was made along the coast by way of Aberdeen and Montrose, in which town he made the acquaintance of his paternal kindred. This journey was an interesting one for the poet, for besides stimulating his muse to sing of the natural beauty and romance of the country, he was entertained royally by the Duke of Athole, the Duke of Gordon, Sir William Murray of Ochtertyre, and many others. Of more importance to Burns was his meeting with Mr. Graham of Fintry, a friend to him on many occasions, and Neil Gow, who played old Scots music to him and no doubt stirred within him a thrill of patriotic fervour. His visit to the battlefields of Bannockburn, Killiecrankie and Culloden Moor were fruitful, and later he embedded in imperishable songs the surging sentiment aroused on the occasion.

A further excursion in the company of Dr. Adair was made a month later. Starting from Edinburgh, Burns and his friend went to Stirling, thence up the River Devon to Harviestoun where they found friends, proceeding by Clackmannan and Kinross to Dunfermline, where the poet visited the grave of the Bruce. Some beautiful lyrics were composed by Burns during this tour.

After a period at Mossgiel, interrupted with a visit to Ellisland, Burns returned to Edinburgh, presumably to complete his business with his publisher, and to discuss with Johnson the Museum of Scottish Songs, to which he had become an enthusiastic contributor. To this period also belongs the acquaintance and correspondence with " Clarinda."

Burns, confined to his room as the result of an accident, took counsel with himself, and as a provision for the future, applied for an Excise appointment. Through the influence of his good friend, Mr. Graham of Fintry, his name was placed on the roll. Eventually he secured a settlement with his publisher, Creech, and found himself the possessor of £500 capital, with which sum he turned his back on Edinburgh and retraced his steps to Mossgiel. There he disbursed £200 to his brother Gilbert to help him to retrieve the position at the farm, and sought to fulfil his own ideal " to make a happy fireside clime for weans and wife," by taking Jean Armour to wife in August, 1788, in the chambers of his friend Gavin Hamilton.

ELLISLAND, 1788-1791

(6 miles from Dumfries)

Burns entered on possession of the farm of Ellisland with its hundred acres, six miles north of the town of Dumfries, at Whitsuntide, 1788. A generous landlord, Mr. Miller of Dalswinton, made the terms easy for the poet farmer, and granted £300 for the erection of suitable buildings. As Mrs. Burns could not join her husband until the house was habitable, he journeyed many times between Dumfries and Mauchline. The farmhouse was not ready for occupation until August, 1789, and in the interval the Burns family resided at a placed called " The Isle," half a mile to the south.

Installed in their home, which consisted of one storey of four apartments, with garrets for the servants, Burns and his " Bonnie Jean " settled down to the busy domestic life of a farmhouse. It may be remarked here that although alterations have been made, the plan of the house remains very much as it was in the poet's day. Very early it dawned on Burns that happy as was his life at the farm, his success as a farmer was doubtful. In July, 1789, he applied to his patron, Graham of Fintry, urging that he be appointed Excise officer for the district. His application was successful and for two years he combined the duties of farmer at Ellisland and Exciseman for ten parishes at a salary of fifty pounds.

The reason given in rhyme to Dr. Blacklock for taking this step was an eminently practical one :

> " I hae a wife and twa wee laddies
>   They maun hae brose and brats o' duddies ;
>   Ye ken yoursels my heart right proud is,
>   I need na vaunt,
>   But I'll sned besoms, thraw sauch woodies
>   Before they want."

The poet's survey covered a tract full fifty miles each way, and his excise duties necessitated two hundred miles journeying each week. The farm was wrought by his wife and the servants in the poet's absence, but bad crops and unfavourable seasons augured disaster. Meanwhile the poet sang, sometimes on a note of great uplift, not seldom in a burdened and sorrowing strain. When his Jean was at Mauchline and he was lonely at Ellisland, he penned to her the beautiful song, *Of a' the airts the wind can blaw*. A few months later, in a mood of deepest despondency and unrest, casting the eye backward to one of the sacred memories of his life, he wrote that beautiful lyric :

> " Thou ling'ring star, with less'ning ray
>   That lov'st to greet the early morn,

> Again thou usher'st in the day
> My Mary from my soul was torn."

Burns carried through his duties as Exciseman
with faithfulness and humanity, and in his wanderings made many friends. It is said that he knew
the River Nith better than his Ayrshire rivers, and
he certainly found inspiration in the beautiful
country surrounding Ellisland. Friars Carse and
Dalswinton, Maxwelton and Glenriddel, Craigdarroch and Woodley Park, were visited by the
poet, who was entertained hospitably, and his muse
cast its mantle generously alike over scenes of
tender and humorous experience. Northward,
where flows " Sweet Afton Water," the poet found
friends and cronies from New Cumnock, through
Sanquhar, where he encountered the funeral of
Mrs. Oswald, on a stormy night to his discomfiture,
to Thornhill, Drumlanrig, Wanlockhead, Dalgarnock and Closeburn. Even as far as Moffat the
poet wandered to spend a night with his old friend
Nicol and celebrate the event in his famous
bacchanalian song :

> " O Willie brewed a peck o' maut
> And Rob and Allan cam to pree."

This song was followed by another effusion of
the same character, when three lairds, neighbours
of Burns, met at Friars Carse to contend for the
prize of an ancient whistle, which was won by a
former laird of Maxwelton from a Dane who came
to Scotland in the train of Anne of Denmark :

> " Three joyous good fellows, with hearts clear of
>   flaw ;
> Craigdarroch, so famous for wit, worth, and law ;

And trusty Glenriddel, so skill'd in old coins ;
And gallant Sir Robert, deep-read in old wines.''

At Friars Carse the poet made the acquaintance of Mrs. Riddel of Woodley Park, a good friend to the poet in Dumfries, Miss Davies, immortalised in that tenderest of love songs, *Bonnie wee thing, cannie wee thing*, and most noteworthy of all Captain Francis Grose, author of the *Antiquities of Scotland*, for whom Burns composed that masterpiece, *Tam o' Shanter*. It is recorded and not doubted that the poet composed this matchless poem in one day in the autumn of 1790 as he paced by the side of the River Nith. To this period belong such songs as *Auld Lang Syne*, *John Anderson my Jo*, *The Silver Tassie*, *The Banks o' Doon* and the beautiful lament over the death of the poet's first friend and patron, the Earl of Glencairn :

" The bridegroom may forget the bride
   Was made his wedded wife yestreen ;
The monarch may forget the crown
   That on his head an hour has been ;
The mother may forget the child
   That smiles sae sweetly on her knee ;
But I'll remember thee, Glencairn,
   And a' that thou has done for me.''

But Ellisland as a farm was a failure, and Burns decided to throw up his lease. Mr. Miller, his laird, agreed, and in August, 1791, the auctioneer appeared, and the crop and stock was disposed of. Mrs. Burns and family had gone to Ayrshire for a few weeks, and Burns passed from the pleasant holms of Ellisland to a house in the Wee Vennel of Dumfries.

The final disposal of Ellisland and its lands is of

interest to all Burns lovers. In 1921 they were offered for sale but failed to find a purchaser. George Williamson of West Quarter, Lanarkshire, had vowed once that if it ever came into the market he would purchase it. This admirer of the poet negotiated and secured it and in due course through his brother it was bequeathed to the nation for all time.

DUMFRIES, 1791-1796

Burns removed from Ellisland to Dumfries in December, 1791, and settled down in his modest home of three apartments in the Wee Vennel, now Bank Street. Prior to this the poet, hearing that " Clarinda " was about to sail for the West Indies, paid a visit to Edinburgh and renewed the platonic friendship of an earlier date. Of the many songs he wrote at this time one may be singled out as a beautiful example of his lyrical genius. One of the stanzas of the *Parting Song to Clarinda* was declared by both Scott and Byron to contain " the essence of a thousand love-tales " :

" Had we never lov'd sae kindly,
    Had we never lov'd sae blindly ;
    Never met—or never parted,
    We had ne'er been broken-hearted."

Much foolishness has been perpetrated by biographers when dealing with the closing years of the poet's life in Dumfries. A closer study of the social habits of the worthy townspeople of this and other county towns in Scotland at the close of the eighteenth century would have resulted in a juster appraisement of Burns as a citizen and husband. In the prime of life Burns carried through his duties as exciseman, distasteful though they were, with faithfulness and zeal. He worked hard for promotion, and was on the list for a Supervisor, notwithstanding his unfortunate entrance into politics, when he purchased four carronades and sent them with his compliments to the French convention.

The French Revolution exercised a sinister influence on his mind and estranged him from many friends, yet when his country was involved in conflict with Napoleon he joined the volunteer corps and hurled defiance in songs that flew throughout the land. This was the period that gave birth also to two songs widely different in sentiment, but produced in the white heat of tempestuous feeling. *A man's a man for a' that* and Robert Bruce's march *Scots wha hae* are among the best known songs of the poet.

During the Ellisland-Dumfries period Burns contributed gratuitously almost two hundred songs, original or amended, to James Johnson's *Museum*. Following on this he engaged to lend his lyrical genius to the collecting of Scottish melodies and words for George Thomson of Edinburgh, and in regard to remuneration for this work it is interesting to quote the poet's own words :

" In the honest enthusiasm with which I embark in your undertaking, to talk of money wages, fee or hire, would be downright prostitution of soul."

In this spirit he worked almost to his dying day, singing with gay abandon or with a native tinge of gloom, and the letters with critical notes which he sent to Thomson with wondrous regularity exhibited a judgment and knowledge of minstrelsy rarely if ever surpassed. His contributions to Thomson exceeded sixty songs.

Besides the songs, Burns threw off political

ballads, epistles, toasts and epigrams in great numbers, and the Dumfries period was prolific of much fine if minor work. He maintained a great correspondence with George Thomson, almost ninety letters being extant, and with Mrs. Dunlop, William Nicol, Robert Ainslie, Francis Grose, and A. Cunningham.

With the exception of a short tour in Galloway with his friend John Syme, the poet seldom left Dumfries except when on duty or to visit his friend Mrs. Ridley of Woodley Park. He walked much in the early evening, when the urge of composition flowed in his veins, and a favourite resort was by the Nith towards the ruined abbey of Lincluden.

Towards the close of 1794 Burns was an acting Supervisor of Excise and there was a possibility of his being moved to another centre, but his health was poor and by the end of 1795 serious illness had attacked him. The death of an only daughter in the autumn filled the cup of affliction. His days were numbered, and full well the poet knew it. A brief stay at Brow, on the Solway Firth, brought no relief. On the 7th July, 1796, he is writing his friend Cunningham, " I fear the voice of the bard will be heard among you no more." About the same date he is writing his wife, addressing her as " My dearest love," and to his brother Gilbert he writes, " I am dangerously ill and not likely to get better. God keep my wife and children."

Home to Dumfries to die ! Nursed tenderly by Jessie Lewars, to whom the poet addressed the beautiful song, *O wert thou in the cauld blast*, the waiting was not long. On the 21st July, 1796, Burns died. His kinsman Carlyle, in a glowing panegyric, has written :

" And thus he passed, not softly, yet speedily,

into that still country, where the hail storms and fire-showers do not reach, and the heaviest-laden wayfarer at length lays down his load."

Four days later the remains of the poet were interred with military honours in St. Michael's Churchyard.

BURNS'S FIRST HOME IN DUMFRIES. At the foot of Bank Street (originally called the Wee Vennel), left-hand side, will be found a house bearing a tablet which reads :

" Robert Burns, the national poet, lived in this house with his family on coming to Dumfries from Ellisland, 1791."

BURNS'S HOUSE, in Burns Street, off St. Michael Street, the home of the poet for three years, is now under the care of Dumfries Burns Club. In a niche may be seen a bust of the bard gifted by the late William Smart, M.P. There is little change since the poet occupied it, and the apartment in which Burns breathed his last is much as it was during his life. The poet's youngest son, Colonel William Nicol Burns, purchased the property on his return from India. The poet's widow and family resided in this house until her death in 1834.

Although more Burns relics are to be found in the private homes of Dumfries than anywhere, a very interesting collection may be seen in Burns's House. The original fireplace and breakfast table remain, while a blue punchbowl, a copper toddy kettle, and the bread basket of " Bonnie Jean," are domestic articles carefully preserved. A silver snuff-box gifted to the poet by the Earl of Glencairn, on whom he penned an imperishable lament, a masonic apron gifted by Burns to Gordon of Kenmuir, and several scripts are relics worthy of more than a passing interest. One pathetic exhibit which arrests attention is the cast of the poet's skull obtained for phrenological purposes on the eve of the interment of the poet's widow in 1834.

THE MIDSTEEPLE, built 1705, was, until 1867, Courthouse, Municipal Buildings, Prison, and Storehouse for the town's arms and ammunition. Burns's funeral took place from the Midsteeple on 25th July, 1796, the remains having been removed overnight from his house in Mill Street (now Burns Street).

THE GLOBE INN (High Street, known as Burns's Howff). His punchbowl and toddy ladle are still preserved, and the chair he occupied when a visitor. In a room upstairs a pane of glass with two verses of poetry inscribed by the poet may be seen.

BURNS MAUSOLEUM. The place of pilgrimage in Dumfries is the Mausoleum in the ancient churchyard of St. Michael's which was erected in 1815. Designed in the form of a Grecian temple by T. F. Hunt of London, the original relief sculpture by Turnerelli depicting the genius of Coila finding Burns at the plough was replaced in 1936 by a new panel designed by Hermon Cawthra, R.B.S. The unveiling of the new statuary was performed by the Right Hon. J. Ramsay MacDonald in the presence of a large assembly. The cost of the renewal was £3000, contributed by admirers from all over the world. The preservation of the grave is in the charge of the Dumfries Burns Club, and annually, on the 25th of January, a floral tribute is laid on the poet's tomb by the Provost, magistrates, and members of the club. Burns's " Bonnie Jean " is interred in the same grave, and nearby rests in her long sleep the Jessie Lewars who nursed the poet tenderly to the end.

THE BURNS FEDERATION

The anniversary of Robert Burns's birthday, the 25th of January, is celebrated throughout the civilised world. This form of hero-worship as Carlyle expresses it, has been fostered mainly by the founding of Burns Clubs in Scotland which began within five years of the poet's death in 1796. It was a natural corollary that a co-ordinating institution would arise and this took form in The Burns Federation which was founded in Kilmarnock in 1885, the first president being Peter Sturrock, provost of that famous town. Stretching out a beneficent and guiding hand to Burns Clubs far and near, the objects of the Federation may be summarised thus:

To achieve by universal affiliation a bond of fellowship among members of Burns Clubs and kindred Societies. To secure and preserve manuscripts and other Burns relics. To mark with suitable inscriptions the locale of incidents associated with Burns in his lifetime. To encourage all movements and institutions in honour of Burns, and in general of Scottish literature, Art and Music.

There are over 300 clubs and societies on the roll of the Burns Federation and at the annual conference reports are submitted to the delegates who represent the various clubs, both at home and overseas. The first conferences were held at Kilmarnock (1885-93) but since that time the annual meeting has been held alternately in Aberdeen and London. The scope of the work of the Federation is extensive and is set forth in excellent form in the *Burns*

Chronicle, published annually by the Burns Federation, Kilmarnock, under the editorship of Mr. J. C. Ewing, of Glasgow. It is a scholarly and authoritative magazine with a wide world circulation.

J. MacKenna.

PICTORIAL
SECTION

★

*A selection of thirty
illustrations of special
interest to lovers of
Burnsiana*

COLLINS
LONDON & GLASGOW

Whatever mitigates the woes or increases the happiness of others, this is my criterion of goodness ; and whatever injures society at large, or any individual in it, this is my measure of iniquity.

Burns.

ROBERT BURNS
Drawing by Archibald Skirving

William Burnes was Born 11 nov: 1721

Agnes Brown was born 17 march 1732

was married together 15 Dec: 1757

had a son Robert 25 Jan: 1759

had a son Gilbert 28 Sept: 1760

had a daughter Agnes 30 Sept: 1762

had a daughter Anabella 14 Nov: 1764

had a son William 30 July 1767

had a son John 12 July 1769

had a daughter Isbel 27 June 1771

William Burness departed this life 13 Feb: 1784

Aged 63 years 2 months ane 22 days

Agnes Brown departed, this life on Monday 14th Jan.y 1820
Aged 87 years & 10 months, and was interred in the Church
yard of the parish of Bolton East Lothian

FAMILY REGISTER OF WILLIAM BURNES

BURNS' COTTAGE, ALLOWAY

BURNS' COTTAGE: INTERIOR

BURNS' COTTAGE: KITCHEN

BURNS' COTTAGE; INTERIOR

BURNS' FAMILY BIBLE

KILMARNOCK EDITION OF BURNS' POEMS

ALLOWAY KIRK AND GRAVEYARD

BURNS' MONUMENT, ALLOWAY

THE AULD BRIG O' DOON

THE AULD AND NEW BRIGS, AYR

MOUNT OLIPHANT FARM (1766-77)

LOCHLEA FARM (1774-84)

JEAN ARMOUR AND GRANDDAUGHTER

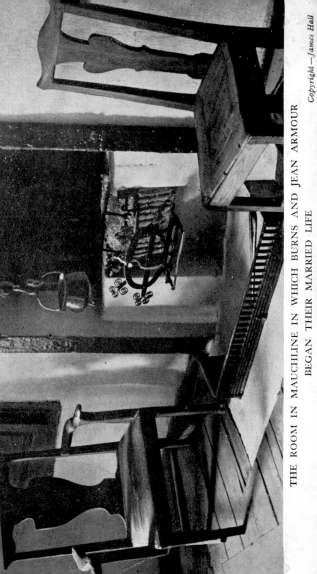

THE ROOM IN MAUCHLINE IN WHICH BURNS AND JEAN ARMOUR
BEGAN THEIR MARRIED LIFE

MOSSGIEL FARM (1781-86)

POOSIE NANSIE'S HOSTELRY, MAUCHLINE

BURNS' MONUMENT, KILMARNOCK

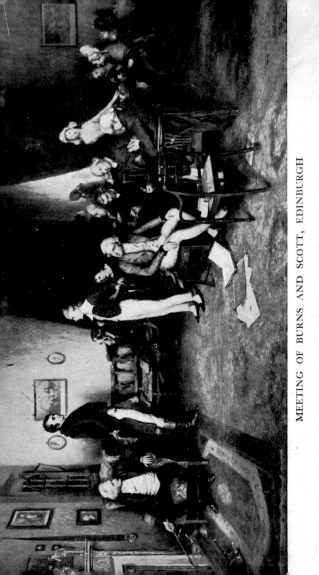

MEETING OF BURNS AND SCOTT, EDINBURGH

ELLISLAND FARM (1788-91)

BURNS' WALK BY THE NITH, DUMFRIES

Dear Brother,

It will be no very pleasing news to you to be told that I am dangerously ill, & not likely to get better — An inveterate rheumatism has reduced me to such a state of debility, & my appetite is totally gone, so that I can scarce stand on my legs. — I have been a week at sea-bathing, & I will continue there or in a friend's house in the country all the summer. God help my wife & children, if I am taken from their head! They will be poor indeed. — I have contracted one or two serious debts, partly from my illness these many months & partly from too much thoughtlessness as to expense when I came to town that will cut in too much on the little I leave them in your hands.

Remember me to my Mother. — Yours.

July 10th 1796.

R BURNS

BURNS' LAST LETTER

BURNS' LAST HOME, DUMFRIES

INAUGURATION OF BURNS AS POET LAUREATE OF LODGE

Men & Brethren,

I am truly sorry it is not

in my power to be at your quarterly meeting.— If I must
be absent in body, believe me I shall be present in spirit.
I suppose those who are as monies by bill or otherwise will
appear; I mean those we summoned.— If you please, I wish
you would delay prosecuting defaulters till I come home.—
The Court is up, and I will be home before it sits down
in the mean time to take a note of who appear and who do not
of our faulty debtors, will be right in my humble
opinion; and those who confess debt and crave days, I
think we should spare them.— Farewell!

Within your dear Mansion may wayward Contention
Or withered Envy ne'er enter;
May Secrecy round be the mystical bound,
And brotherly Love be the Centre! ‖

[Tarbolton 23d Aug.]   Robt Burn

DEPUTY MASTER'S APRON WORN BY BURNS

BURNS' MONUMENT, DUMFRIES: EXTERIOR

BURNS' MONUMENT, DUMFRIES: EXTERIOR

CONTENTS

CONTENTS

CONTENTS

PAGE

CONTENTS

CONTENTS

CONTENTS

CONTENTS

CONTENTS

POEMS AND SONGS

BY

ROBERT BURNS

HANDSOME NELL

Tune—'I am a man unmarried.'

O ONCE I lov'd a bonie lass,
  Aye, and I love her still;
And whilst that virtue warms my breast,
  I'll love my handsome Nell.

As bonie lasses I hae seen,
  And mony full as braw;
But, for a modest gracefu' mien,
  The like I never saw.

A bonie lass, I will confess,
  Is pleasant to the e'e;
But, without some better qualities,
  She's no a lass for me.

But Nelly's looks are blythe and sweet,
  And what is best of a',
Her reputation is complete,
  And fair without a flaw.

She dresses ay sae clean and neat,
  Both decent and genteel;
And then there's something in her gait
  Gars ony dress look weel.

A gaudy dress and gentle air
  May slightly touch the heart ;
But it's innocence and modesty
  That polishes the dart.

'Tis this in Nelly pleases me,
  'Tis this enchants my soul ;
For absolutely in my breast
  She reigns without control.

O TIBBIE, I HAE SEEN THE DAY

Tune—'Invercauld's Reel, or Strathspey.'

Chorus.—O Tibbie, I hae seen the day,
    Ye wadna been sae shy ;
  For laik o' gear ye lightly me,
    But, trowth, I care na by.

YESTREEN I met you on the moor,
Ye spak na, but gaed by like stoure ;
Ye geck at me because I'm poor,
  But fient a hair care I.
      O Tibbie, I hae seen the day, etc.

When comin' hame on Sunday last,
Upon the road as I cam past,
Ye snufft and gae your head a cast—
  But trowth I care't na by.
      O Tibbie, I hae seen the day, etc.

I doubt na, lass, but ye may think,
Because ye hae the name o' clink,
That ye can please me at a wink,
  Whene'er ye like to try.
      O Tibbie, I hae seen the day, etc.

But sorrow tak him that's sae mean,
Altho' his pouch o' coin were clean,
Wha follows ony saucy quean,
    That looks sae proud and high.
        O Tibbie, I hae seen the day, etc.

Altho' a lad were e'er sae smart,
If that he want the yellow dirt,
Ye'll cast your head anither airt,
    And answer him fu' dry.
        O Tibbie, I hae seen the day, etc.

But if he hae the name o' gear,
Ye'll fasten to him like a brier,
Tho' hardly he, for sense or lear,
    Be better than the kye.
        O Tibbie, I hae seen the day, etc.

But, Tibbie, lass, tak my advice :
Your daddie's gear maks you sae nice ;
The deil a ane wad spier your price,
    Were ye as poor as I.
        O Tibbie, I hae seen the day, etc.

There lives a lass beside yon park,
I'd rather hae her in her sark,
Than you wi' a' your thousand mark ;
    That gars you look sae high.
        O Tibbie, I hae seen the day, etc.

I DREAM'D I LAY

I DREAM'D I lay where flowers were springing
    Gaily in the sunny beam ;
List'ning to the wild birds singing,
    By a falling crystal stream :

Straight the sky grew black and daring;
   Thro' the wood the whirlwinds rave;
Trees with aged arms were warring,
   O'er the swelling drumlie wave.

Such was my life's deceitful morning,
   Such the pleasures I enjoyed:
But lang or noon, loud tempests storming,
   A' my flowery bliss destroy'd.
Tho' fickle fortune has deceiv'd me—
   She promis'd fair, and perform'd but ill,
Of mony a joy and hope bereaved me—
   I bear a heart shall support me still.

THE RUINED FARMER.

Tune—'Go from my window, Love, do.'

THE sun he is sunk in the west,
All creatures retirèd to rest,
While here I sit, all sore beset,
      With sorrow, grief, and woe:
And it's O, fickle Fortune, O!

The prosperous man is asleep,
Nor hears how the whirlwinds sweep;
But Misery and I must watch
      The surly tempest blow:
And it's O, fickle Fortune, O!

There lies the dear partner of my breast;
Her cares for a moment at rest:
Must I see thee, my youthful pride,
      Thus brought so very low!
And it's O, fickle Fortune, O!

There lie my sweet babes in her arms;
No anxious fear their hearts alarms;
But for their sake my heart does ache,
      With many a bitter throe:
And it's O, fickle Fortune, O!

I once was by Fortune carest:
I once could relieve the distrest:
Now life's poor pittance hardly earn'd,
      My fate will scarce bestow:
And it's O, fickle Fortune, O!

No comfort, no comfort I have!
How welcome to me were the grave!
But then my wife and children dear—
      O, whither would they go!
And it's O, fickle Fortune, O!

O whither, O where shall I turn!
All friendless, forsaken, forlorn!
For, in this world, Rest or Peace
      I never more shall know!
And it's O, fickle Fortune, O!

TRAGIC FRAGMENT

ALL villain as I am—a damnèd wretch,
A hardened, stubborn, unrepenting sinner,
Still my heart melts at human wretchedness;
And with sincere but unavailing sighs
I view the helpless children of distress:
With tears indignant I behold the oppressor
Rejoicing in the honest man's destruction,
Whose unsubmitting heart was all his crime.—
Ev'n you, ye hapless crew! I pity you;
Ye, whom the seeming good think sin to pity;

Ye poor, despised, abandoned vagabonds,
Whom Vice, as usual, has turn'd o'er to ruin.
Oh! but for friends and interposing Heaven,
I had been driven forth like you forlorn,
The most detested, worthless wretch among you!
O injured God! Thy goodness has endow'd me
With talents passing most of my compeers,
Which I in just proportion have abused—
As far surpassing other common villains
As Thou in natural parts has given me more.

THE TARBOLTON LASSES

IF ye gae up to yon hill-tap,
 Ye'll there see bonie Peggy;
She kens her father is a laird,
 And she forsooth's a leddy.

There's Sophy tight, a lassie bright,
 Besides a handsome fortune:
Wha canna win her in a night,
 Has little art in courtin'.

Gae down by Faile, and taste the ale,
 And tak a look o' Mysie;
She's dour and din, a deil within,
 But aiblins she may please ye.

If she be shy, her sister try,
 Ye'll maybe fancy Jenny;
If ye'll dispense wi' want o' sense—
 She kens herself she's bonie.

As ye gae up by yon hillside,
 Speer in for bonie Bessy;
She'll gie ye a beck, and bid ye light,
 And handsomely address ye.

There's few sae bonie, nane sae guid,
 In a' King George' dominion ;
If ye should doubt the truth o' this—
 It's Bessy's ain opinion !

AH, WOE IS ME, MY MOTHER DEAR

Paraphrase of Jeremiah, 15th chap., 10th verse

Ah, woe is me, my Mother dear !
 A man of strife ye've borne me
For sair contention I maun bear ;
 They hate, revile, and scorn me.

I ne'er could lend on bill or band,
 That five per cent. might blest me ;
And borrowing, on the tither hand,
 The de'il a ane wad trust me.

Yet I, a coin-denièd wight,
 By Fortune quite discarded ;
Ye see how I am, day and night,
 By lad and lass blackguarded !

MONTGOMERIE'S PEGGY

Altho' my bed were in yon muir,
 Amang the heather, in my plaidie ;
Yet happy, happy would I be,
 Had I my dear Montgomerie's Peggy.

When o'er the hill beat surly storms,
 And winter nights were dark and rainy ;
I'd seek some dell, and in my arms
 I'd shelter dear Montgomerie's Peggy.

Were I a Baron proud and high,
    And horse and servants waiting ready;
Then a' 'twad gie o' joy to me,—
    The sharin't with Montgomerie's Peggy.

THE PLOUGHMAN'S LIFE

As I was a-wand'ring ae morning in spring,
I heard a young ploughman sae sweetly to sing;
And as he was singin', thir words he did say,—
There's nae life like the ploughman's in the month o'
    sweet May.

The lav'rock in the morning she'll rise frae her nest,
And mount i' the air wi' the dew on her breast,
And wi' the merry ploughman she'll whistle and sing,
And at night she'll return to her nest back again.

THE RONALDS OF THE BENNALS

In Tarbolton, ye ken, there are proper young men,
    And proper young lasses an a', man;
But ken ye the Ronalds that live in the Bennals,
    They carry the gree frae them a', man.

Their father's a laird, and weel he can spare't,
    Braid money to tocher them a', man;
To proper young men, he'll clink in the hand
    Gowd guineas a hunder or twa, man.

There's ane they ca' Jean, I'll warrant ye've seen
    As bonie a lass or as braw, man;
But for sense and guid taste she'll vie wi' the best,
    And a conduct that beautifies a', man.

The charms o' the min', the langer they shine,
    The mair admiration they draw, man ;
While peaches and cherries, and roses and lilies,
    They fade and they wither awa' man.

If ye be for Miss Jean, tak this frae a frien',
    A hint o' a rival or twa, man ;
The Laird o' Blackbyre wad gang through the fire
    If that wad entice her awa', man.

The Laird o' Braehead has been on his speed,
    For mair than a towmond or twa, man ;
The Laird o' the Ford will straught on a board,
    If he canna get her at a', man.

Then Anna comes in, the pride o' her kin,
    The boast of our bachelors a', man :
Sae sonsy and sweet, sae fully complete,
    She steals our affections awa', man.

If I should detail the pick and the wale
    O' lasses that live here awa', man,
The fau't wad be mine if they didna shine
    The sweetest and best o' them a', man.

I lo'e her mysel, but darena weel tell,
    My poverty keeps me in awe, man ;
For making o' rhymes, and working at times,
    Does little or naething at a', man.

Yet I wadna choose to let her refuse,
    Nor hae't in her power to say na, man ;
For though I be poor, unnoticed, obscure,
    My stomach's as proud as them a', man.

Though I canna ride in weel-booted pride,
    And flee o'er the hills like a craw, man,
I can haud up my head wi' the best o' the breed,
    Though fluttering ever so braw, man.

My coat and my vest, they are Scotch o' the best,
O' pairs o' guid breeks I hae twa, man;
And stockings and pumps to put on my stumps,
And ne'er a wrang steek in them a', man.

My sarks they are few, but five o' them new,
Twal' hundred, as white as the snaw, man.
A ten shillings hat, a Holland cravat;
There are no mony poets sae braw, man.

I never had freens weel stockit in means,
To leave me a hundred or twa, man;
Nae weel-tocher'd aunts, to wait on their drants,
And wish them in hell for it a', man.

I never was cannie for hoarding o' money,
Or claughtin 't together at a', man;
I've little to spend, and naething to lend,
But deevil a shilling I awe, man.

HERE'S TO THY HEALTH

HERE's to thy health, my bonie lass,
Gude night and joy be wi' thee;
I'll come nae mair to thy bower-door,
To tell thee that I lo'e thee.
O dinna think, my pretty pink,
But I can live without thee:
I vow and swear I dinna care,
How lang ye look about ye.

Thou'rt ay sae free informing me,
Thou hast nae mind to marry;
I'll be as free informing thee,
Nae time hae I to tarry:

I ken thy freens try ilka means
    Frae wedlock to delay thee ;
Depending on some higher chance,
    But fortune may betray thee.

I ken they scorn my low estate,
    But that does never grieve me ;
For I'm as free as any he ;
    Sma' siller will relieve me.
I'll count my health my greatest wealth,
    Sae lang as I'll enjoy it ;
I'll fear nae scant, I'll bode nae want,
    As lang's I get employment.

But far off fowls hae feathers fair,
    And, ay until ye try them,
Tho' they seem fair, still have a care ;
    They may prove as bad as I am.
But at twal' at night, when the moon shines
      bright
    My dear, I'll come and see thee ;
For the man that loves his mistress weel,
    Nae travel makes him weary.

THE LASS OF CESSNOCK BANKS

On Cessnock banks a lassie dwells ;
    Could I describe her shape and mien ;
Our lasses a' she far excels,
    An' she has twa sparkling rogueish een.

She's sweeter than the morning dawn,
    When rising Phœbus first is seen ;
And dew-drops twinkle o'er the lawn ;
    An' she has twa sparkling rogueish een.

She's stately like yon youthful ash,
   That grows the cowslip braes between,
And drinks the stream with vigour fresh ;
   An' she has twa sparkling rogueish een.

She's spotless like the flow'ring thorn,
   With flow'rs so white and leaves so green,
When purest in the dewy morn ;
   An' she has twa sparkling rogueish een.

Her looks are like the vernal May,
   When ev'ning Phœbus shines serene ;
While birds rejoice on every spray ;
   An' she has twa sparkling rogueish een.

Her hair is like the curling mist,
   That climbs the mountain-sides at e'en,
When flow'r-reviving rains are past ;
   An' she has twa sparkling rogueish een.

Her forehead's like the show'ry bow,
   When gleaming sunbeams intervene
And gild the distant mountain's brow ;
   An' she has twa sparkling rogueish een.

Her cheeks are like yon crimson gem,
   The pride of all the flowery scene,
Just opening on its thorny stem ;
   An' she has twa sparkling rogueish een.

Her bosom's like the nightly snow,
   When pale the morning rises keen ;
While hid the murm'ring streamlets flow ;
   An' she has twa sparkling rogueish een.

Her lips are like yon cherries ripe,
   That sunny walls from Boreas screen ;
They tempt the taste and charm the sight ;
   An' she has twa sparkling rogueish een.

Her teeth are like a flock of sheep,
  With fleeces newly washen clean ;
That slowly mount the rising steep ;
  An' she has twa sparkling rogueish een.

Her breath is like the fragrant breeze,
  That gently stirs the blossom'd bean ;
When Phœbus sinks behind the seas ;
  An' she has twa sparkling rogueish een.

Her voice is like the ev'ning thrush,
  That sings on Cessnock banks unseen ;
While his mate sits nestling in the bush ;
  An' she has twa sparkling rogueish een.

But it's not her air, her form, her face,
  Tho' matching beauty's fabled queen ;
'Tis the mind that shines in ev'ry grace.
  An' chiefly in her rogueish een.

BONIE PEGGY ALISON.

Tune—'The Braes o' Balquhidder.'

Chorus.—And I'll kiss thee yet, yet,
      And I'll kiss thee o'er again ;
  And I'll kiss thee yet, yet,
      My bonie Peggy Alison.

ILK care and fear, when thou art near
  I ever mair defy them, O !
Young kings upon their hansel throne
  Are no sae blest as I am, O !
      And I'll kiss thee yet, yet, etc.

When in my arms, wi' a' thy charms,
 I clasp my countless treasure, O !
I seek nae mair o' Heav'n to share
 Than sic a moment's pleasure, O !
   And I'll kiss thee yet, yet, etc.

And by thy een sae bonie blue,
 I swear I'm thine for ever, O !
And on thy lips I seal my vow,
 And break it shall I never, O !
   And I'll kiss thee yet, yet, etc.

MARY MORISON.

O MARY, at thy window be,
 It is the wish'd, the trysted hour !
Those smiles and glances let me see,
 That make the miser's treasure poor :
How blythely wad I bide the stoure,
 A weary slave frae sun to sun,
Could I the rich reward secure,
 The lovely Mary Morison.

Yestreen, when to the trembling string
 The dance gaed thro' the lighted ha',
To thee my fancy took its wing,
 I sat, but neither heard nor saw :
Tho' this was fair, and that was braw,
 And yon the toast of a' the town,
I sigh'd, and said among them a',
 ' Ye are na Mary Morison.'

Oh, Mary, canst thou wreck his peace,
 Wha for thy sake wad gladly die ?
Or canst thou break that heart of his,
 Whase only faut is loving thee ?

If love for love thou wilt na gie,
　　At least be pity to me shown;
A thought ungentle canna be
　　The thought o' Mary Morison.

WINTER: A DIRGE

THE wintry west extends his blast,
　　And hail and rain does blaw;
Or, the stormy north sends driving forth
　　The blinding sleet and snaw:
While, tumbling brown, the burn comes down,
　　And roars frae bank to brae;
And bird and beast in covert rest,
　　And pass the heartless day.

'The sweeping blast, the sky o'ercast,'
　　The joyless winter day
Let others fear, to me more dear
　　Than all the pride of May:
The tempest's howl, it soothes my soul,
　　My griefs it seems to join;
The leafless trees my fancy please,
　　Their fate resembles mine!

Thou Power Supreme whose mighty scheme
　　These woes of mine fulfil,
Here, firm I rest; they must be best,
　　Because they are *Thy* will!
Then all I want—O do Thou grant
　　This one request of mine!—
Since to *enjoy* Thou dost deny,
　　Assist me to *resign*.

A PRAYER UNDER THE PRESSURE OF VIOLENT ANGUISH

O THOU Great Being! what Thou art
　　Surpasses me to know;
Yet sure I am, that known to Thee
　　Are all Thy works below.

Thy creature here before Thee stands,
　　All wretched and distrest;
Yet sure those ills that wring my soul
　　Obey Thy high behest.

Sure Thou, Almighty, canst not **act**
　　From cruelty or wrath!
O, free my weary eyes from tears,
　　Or close them fast in death!

But, if I must afflicted be,
　　To suit some wise design;
Then man my soul with firm resolves,
　　To bear and not repine!

PARAPHRASE OF THE FIRST PSALM

THE man, in life wherever plac'd,
　　Hath happiness in store,
Who walks not in the wicked's way,
　　Nor learns their guilty lore!

Nor from the seat of scornful pride
　　Casts forth his eyes abroad,
But with humility and awe
　　Still walks before his God.

That man shall flourish like the trees,
  Which by the streamlets grow ;
The fruitful top is spread on high,
  And firm the root below.

But he whose blossom buds in guilt
  Shall to the ground be cast,
And, like the rootless stubble, tost
  Before the sweeping blast.

For why ? that God the good adore,
  Hath giv'n them peace and rest,
But hath decreed that wicked men
  Shall ne'er be truly blest

THE FIRST SIX VERSES OF THE NINETIETH PSALM VERSIFIED

O Thou, at first, the greatest friend
  Of all the human race !
Whose strong right hand has ever been
  Their stay and dwelling place !

Before the mountains heav'd their heads
  Beneath Thy forming hand,
Before this ponderous globe itself,
  Arose at Thy command ;

That Pow'r which rais'd and still upholds
  This universal frame,
From countless, unbeginning time
  Was ever still the same.

Those mighty periods of years
  Which seems to us so vast,
Appear no more before Thy sight
  Than yesterday that's past.

B.P.   B

Thou giv'st the word : Thy creature, man,
　　Is to existence brought ;
Again Thou say'st, 'Ye sons of men,
　　Return ye into nought !'

Thou layest them, with all their cares,
　　In everlasting sleep ;
As with a flood Thou tak'st them off
　　With overwhelming sweep.

They flourish like the morning flow'r,
　　In beauty's pride array'd ;
But long ere night—cut down, it lies
　　All wither'd and decay'd.

A PRAYER IN THE PROSPECT OF DEATH

O THOU unknown, Almighty Cause
　　Of all my hope and fear !
In whose dread presence, ere an hour,
　　Perhaps I must appear !

If I have wander'd in those paths
　　Of life I ought to shun—
As something, loudly, in my breast,
　　Remonstrates I have done—

Thou know'st that Thou hast formed me
　　With passions wild and strong ;
And list'ning to their witching voice
　　Has often led me wrong.

Where human weakness has come short,
　　Or frailty stept aside,
Do Thou, All-Good—for such Thou art—
　　In shades of darkness hide.

Where with intention I have err'd,
    No other plea I have,
But, Thou art good ; and Goodness still
    Delighteth to forgive.

STANZAS, ON THE SAME OCCASION

Why am I loth to leave this earthly scene ?
    Have I so found it full of pleasing charms—
Some drops of joy with draughts of ill between—
    Some gleams of sunshine 'mid renewing storms ?
Is it departing pangs my soul alarms ?
    Or death's unlovely, dreary, dark abode ?
For guilt, for guilt, my terrors are in arms :
    I tremble to approach an angry God,
And justly smart beneath His sin-avenging rod.

Fain would I say, 'Forgive my foul offence !'
    Fain promise never more to disobey ;
But, should my Author health again dispense,
    Again I might desert fair virtue's way ;
Again in folly's path might go astray ;
    Again exalt the brute and sink the man ;
Then how should I for heavenly mercy pray,
    Who act so counter heavenly mercy's plan ?
Who sin so oft have mourn'd, yet to temptation ran ?

O Thou great Governor of all below !
    If I may dare a lifted eye to Thee,
Thy nod can make the tempest cease to blow,
    Or still the tumult of the raging sea :
With that controlling pow'r assist ev'n me,
    Those headlong furious passions to confine,
For all unfit I feel my pow'rs to be,
    To rule their torrent in th' allowed line ;
O, aid me with Thy help, Omnipotence Divine !

FICKLE FORTUNE

THOUGH fickle Fortune has deceived me,
  She promis'd fair and perform'd but ill ;
Of mistress, friends, and wealth bereav'd me,
  Yet I bear a heart shall support me still.—

I'll act with prudence as far as I'm able,
  But if success I must never find,
Then come misfortune, I bid thee welcome,
  I'll meet thee with an undaunted mind.

RAGING FORTUNE

O RAGING Fortune's withering blast
  Has laid my leaf full low !
O raging Fortune's withering blast
  Has laid my leaf full low !

My stem was fair, my bud was green,
  My blossom sweet did blow ;
The dew fell fresh, the sun rose mild,
  And made my branches grow ;

But luckless Fortune's northern storms
  Laid a' my blossoms low !
But luckless Fortune's northern storms
  Laid a' my blossoms low !

I'LL GO AND BE A SODGER

O WHY the deuce should I repine,
  And be an ill foreboder ?
I'm twenty-three, and five feet nine,
  I'll go and be a sodger !

I gat some gear wi' mickle care,
  I held it weel .hegither ;
But now it's gane, and something mair—
  I'll go and be a sodger !

NO CHURCHMAN AM I

Tune—'Prepare, my dear Brethren.'

No churchman am I for to rail and to write,
No statesman nor soldier to plot or to fight,
No sly man of business contriving a snare,
For a big-belly'd bottle's the whole of my care.

The peer I don't envy, I give him his bow ;
I scorn not the peasant, tho' ever so low ;
But a club of good fellows, like those that are here,
And a bottle like this, are my glory and care.

Here passes the squire on his brother—his horse ;
There centum per centum, the cit with his purse ;
But see you the *Crown* how it waves in the air ?
There a big-belly'd bottle still eases my care.

The wife of my bosom, alas ! she did die ;
For sweet consolation to church I did fly ;
I found that old Solomon provèd it fair,
That a big belly'd bottle's a cure for all care.

I once was persuaded a venture to make ;
A letter inform'd me that all was to wreck ;
But the pursy old landlord just waddl'd upstairs,
With a glorious bottle that ended my cares.

'Life's cares they are comforts'—a maxim laid down
By the Bard, what d'ye call him ? that wore the black
    gown ;
And faith I agree with th' old prig to a hair ;
For a big-belly'd bottle's a heav'n of a care.

A STANZA ADDED IN A MASON LODGE

Then fill up a bumper and make it o'erflow,
And honours masonic prepare for to throw ;
May ev'ry true Brother of the Compass and Square
Have a big belly'd bottle when harass'd with care.

MY FATHER WAS A FARMER

Tune—'The Weaver and his Shuttle, O.'

My father was a farmer upon the Carrick border,
And carefully he bred me in decency and order ;
He bade me act a manly part, though I had ne'er a
    farthing ;
For without an honest manly heart, no man was worth
    regarding.

Then out into the world my course I did determine ;
Tho' to be rich was not my wish, yet to be great was
    charming :
My talents they were not the worst, nor yet my
    education.
Resolv'd was I, at least to try, to mend my situation.

In many a way, and vain essay, I courted Fortune's
    favour ;
Some cause unseen still stept between, to frustrate
    each endeavour ;
Sometimes by foes I was o'erpower'd, sometimes by
    friends forsaken ;
And when my hope was at the top, I still was worst
    mistaken.

Then sore harass'd, and tir'd at last, with Fortune's
    vain delusion,
I dropt my schemes, like idle dreams, and came to
    this conclusion :
The past was bad, and the future hid, its good or ill
    untrièd ;
But the present hour was in my pow'r, and so I would
    enjoy it.

No help, nor hope, nor view had I, nor person to
    befriend me ;
So I must toil, and sweat, and moil, and labour to
    sustain me ;
To plough and sow, to reap and mow, my father bred
    me early ;
For one, he said, to labour bred, was a match for
    Fortune fairly.

Thus all obscure, unknown, and poor, thro' life I'm
    doom'd to wander,
Till down my weary bones I lay in everlasting slumber ;
No view nor care, but shun whate'er might breed me
    pain or sorrow ;
I live to-day as well's I may, regardless of to-morrow.

But cheerful still, I am as well as a monarch in his
    palace,
Tho' Fortune's frown still hunts me down, with all her
    wonted malice :
I make indeed my daily bread, but ne'er can make it
    farther :
But as daily bread is all I need, I do not much regard her.

When sometimes by my labour, I earn a little money,
Some unforeseen misfortune comes gen'rally upon me ;
Mischance, mistake, or by neglect, or my good-natur'd
    folly :
But come what will, I've sworn it still, I'll ne'er be
    melancholy.

All you who follow wealth and power with unremitting
 ardour,
The more in this you look for bliss, you leave your
 view the farther :
Had you the wealth Potosi boasts, or nations to adore
 you,
A cheerful honest-hearted clown I will prefer before
 you.

JOHN BARLEYCORN: A BALLAD

THERE was three kings into the east,
 Three kings both great and high,
And they hae sworn a solemn oath
 John Barleycorn should die.

They took a plough and plough'd him down,
 Put clods upon his head,
And they hae sworn a solemn oath
 John Barleycorn was dead.

But the cheerful Spring came kindly on,
 And show'rs began to fall ;
John Barleycorn got up again,
 And sore surpris'd them all.

The sultry suns of Summer came,
 And he grew thick and strong ;
His head weel arm'd wi' pointed spears,
 That no one should him wrong.

The sober Autumn enter'd mild,
 When he grew wan and pale ;
His bending joints and drooping head
 Show'd he began to fail.

His colour sicken'd more and more,
 He faded into age ;
And then his enemies began
 To show their deadly rage.

They've taen a weapon, long and sharp,
 And cut him by the knee ;
Then ty'd him fast upon a cart,
 Like a rogue for forgerie.

They laid him down upon his back,
 And cudgell'd him full sore ;
They hung him up before the storm,
 And turn'd him o'er and o'er.

They fillèd up a darksome pit
 With water to the brim,
They heavèd in John Barleycorn—
 There, let him sink or swim.

They laid him out upon the floor,
 To work him farther woe ;
And still, as signs of life appear'd,
 They toss'd him to and fro.

They wasted, o'er a scorching flame,
 The marrow of his bones ;
But a miller us'd him worst of all,
 For he crush'd him between two stones.

And they hae taen his very heart's blood,
 And drank it round and round ;
And still the more and more they drank,
 Their joy did more abound.

John Barleycorn was a hero bold,
 Of noble enterprise ;
For if you do but taste his blood,
 'Twill make your courage rise.

'Twill make a man forget his woe ;
    'Twill heighten all his joy :
'Twill make the widow's heart to sing,
    Tho' the tear were in her eye.

Then let us toast John Barleycorn,
    Each man a glass in hand ;
And may his great posterity
    Ne'er fail in old Scotland !

THE DEATH AND DYING WORDS OF POOR MAILIE

THE AUTHOR'S ONLY PET YOWE—AN UNCO MOURNFU TALE

As Mailie, an' her lambs thegither,
Was ae day nibblin' on the tether,
Upon her cloot she coost a hitch,
An' owre she warsl'd in the ditch :
There, groanin', dying, she did lie,
When *Hughoc* he cam doytin' by.

    Wi' glowerin' een, and lifted han's
Poor *Hughoc* like a statue stan's ;
He saw her days were near-hand ended,
But, wae's my heart ! he could na mend it !
He gapèd wide, but naething spak ;
At length poor Mailie silence brak.

    'O thou, whase lamentable face
Appears to mourn my woefu' case !
My dying words attentive hear,
An' bear them to my Master dear.

'Tell him, if e'er again he keep
As muckle gear as buy a sheep—
O, bid him never tie them mair,
Wi' wicked strings o' hemp or hair!
But ca' them out to park or hill,
An' let them wander at their will:
So may his flock increase, an' grow
To scores o' lambs, and packs o' woo'!

'Tell him, he was a Master kin',
An' ay was guid to me an' mine;
An' now my dying charge I gie him,
My helpless lambs, I trust them wi' him.

'O, bid him save their harmless lives,
Frae dogs, an' tods, an' butchers' knives!
But gie them guid cow-milk their fill,
Till they be fit to fend themsel;
An' tent them duly, e'en an' morn,
Wi' taets o' hay an' ripps o' corn.

'An' may they never learn the gaets,
Of ither vile, wanrestfu' pets—
To slink thro' slaps, an' reave an' steal.
At stacks o' pease, or stocks o' kail!
So may they, like their great forbears,
For monie a year come thro' the sheers:
So wives will gie them bits o' bread,
An' bairns greet for them when they're dead.

'My poor toop-lamb, my son an' heir,
O, bid him breed him up wi' care!
An' if he live to be a beast,
To pit some havins in his breast!

'An' warn him—what I winna name,
To stay content wi' yowes at hame;
An' no to rin an' wear his cloots,
Like ither menseless, graceless brutes.

'An' niest, my yowie, silly thing,
Gude keep thee frae a tether string !
O, may thou ne'er forgather up,
Wi' ony blastit, moorland toop;
But ay keep mind to moop an' mell,
Wi' sheep o' credit like thysel !

'And now, my bairns, wi' my last breath,
I lea'e my blessing wi' you baith :
An' when you think upo' your mither,
Mind to be kind to ane anither.

'Now, honest *Hughoc*, dinna fail,
To tell my master a' my tale ;
An' bid him burn this cursed tether,
An' for thy pains thou'se get my blather.'

This said, poor Mailie turn'd her head,
An' clos'd her een amang the dead !

POOR MAILIE'S ELEGY

LAMENT in rhyme, lament in prose,
Wi' saut tears trickling down your nose;
Our bardie's fate is at a close,
                        Past a' remead !
The last, sad cape-stane o' his woes
                        Poor Mailie's dead !

It's no the loss o' warl's gear,
That could sae bitter draw the tear,
Or mak our bardie, dowie, wear
                        The mournin' weed :
He's lost a friend an' neebor dear,
                        In Mailie dead.

Thro' a' the town she trotted by him;
A lang half-mile she could descry him;
Wi' kindly bleat, when she did spy him,
          She ran wi' speed:
A friend mair faithfu' ne'er cam nigh him,
           Than Mailie dead.

I wat she was a sheep o' sense,
An' could behave hersel wi' mense:
I'll say't she never brak a fence,
          Thro' thievish greed.
Our bardie, lanely, keeps the spence
         Sin' Mailie's dead.

Or, if he wanders up the howe,
Her living image in her yowe
Comes bleatin' till him, owre the knowe,
          For bits o' bread;
An' down the briny pearls rowe
         For Mailie dead.

She was nae get o' moorland tips,
Wi' tauted ket, an' hairy hips;
For her forbears were brought in ships,
          Frae 'yont the Tweed:
A bonier fleesh ne'er cross'd the clips
         Than Mailie's—dead.

Wae worth that man wha first did shape
That vile, wanchancie thing—a raep!
It maks guid fellows girn an' gape,
          Wi' chokin' dread;
An' Robin's bonnet wave wi' crape
         For Mailie dead.

O, a' ye bards on bonie Doon!
An' wha on Ayr your chanters tune!
Come, join the melancholious croon
         O' Robin's reed!
His heart will never get aboon—
         His Mailie's dead!

THE RIGS O' BARLEY

It was upon a Lammas night,
    When corn rigs are bonie,
Beneath the moon's unclouded light,
    I held awa' to Annie;
The time flew by, wi' tentless heed;
    Till, 'tween the late and early,
Wi' sma' persuasion she agreed
    To see me thro' the barley.

    Corn rigs, an' barley rigs,
        An' corn rigs are bonie:
    I'll ne'er forget that happy night,
        Amang the rigs wi' Annie.

The sky was blue, the wind was still,
    The moon was shining clearly;
I set her down, wi' right goodwill,
    Amang the rigs o' barley:
I ken't her heart was a' my ain;
    I lov'd her most sincerely;
I kiss'd her owre and owre again,
    Amang the rigs o' barley.
        Corn rigs, an' barley rigs, etc.

I lock'd her in my fond embrace;
    Her heart was beating rarely:
My blessings on that happy place,
    Amang the rigs o' barley!
But by the moon and stars so bright,
    That shone that hour so clearly!
She ay shall bless that happy night
    Amang the rigs o' barley.
        Corn rigs, an' barley rigs, etc.

I hae been blythe wi' comrades dear;
    I hae been merry drinking;
I hae been joyfu' gath'rin' gear;
    I hae been happy thinking:
But a' the pleasures e'er I saw,
    Tho' three times doubl'd fairly—
That happy night was worth them a',
     Amang the rigs o' barley.
        Corn rigs, an' barley rigs, etc.

NOW WESTLIN WINDS

Now westlin winds and slaught'ring guns
    Bring Autumn's pleasant weather;
The moorcock springs on whirring wings,
    Amang the blooming heather:
Now waving grain, wide o'er the plain,
    Delights the weary farmer;
And the moon shines bright, when I rove at night,
    To muse upon my charmer.

The partridge loves the fruitful fells,
    The plover loves the mountains;
The woodcock haunts the lonely dells,
    The soaring hern the fountains:
Thro' lofty groves the cushat roves,
    The path of man to shun it;
The hazel bush o'erhangs the thrush,
    The spreading thorn the linnet.

Thus ev'ry kind their pleasure find,
    The savage and the tender;
Some social join, and leagues combine,
    Some solitary wander:

Avaunt, away, the cruel sway!
    Tyrannic man's dominion;
The sportsman's joy, the murd'ring cry,
    The flutt'ring, gory pinion!

But, Peggy dear, the evening's clear,
    Thick flies the skimming swallow;
The sky is blue, the fields in view,
    All fading-green and yellow:
Come let us stray our gladsome way,
    And view the charms of Nature;
The rustling corn, the fruited thorn,
    And ev'ry happy creature.

We'll gently walk, and sweetly talk,
    Till the silent moon shine clearly;
I'll grasp thy waist, and, fondly prest,
    Swear how I love thee dearly:
Not vernal show'rs to budding flow'rs,
    Not Autumn to the farmer,
So dear can be as thou to me,
    My fair, my lovely charmer!

MY NANIE, O

BEHIND yon hills where Lugar flows,
    'Mang moors an' mosses many, O,
The wintry sun the day has clos'd,
    And I'll awa' to Nanie, O.

The westlin wind blaws loud an' shrill;
    The night's baith mirk and rainy, O;
But I'll get my plaid an' out I'll steal,
    An' owre the hill to Nanie, O.

My Nanie's charming, sweet, an' young;
    Nae artfu' wiles to win ye, O:
May ill befa' the flattering tongue
    That wad beguile my Nanie, O.

Her face is fair, her heart is true;
　　As spotless as she's bonie, O;
The op'ning gowan, wat wi' dew,
　　Nae purer is than Nanie, O.

A country lad is my degree,
　　An' few there be that ken me, O;
But what care I how few they be,
　　I'm welcome ay to Nanie, O.

My riches a's my penny-fee,
　　An' I maun guide it cannie, O;
But warl's gear ne'er troubles me,
　　My thoughts are a'—my Nanie, O.

Our auld guidman delights to view
　　His sheep an' kye thrive bonie, O;
But I'm as blythe that hauds his pleugh,
　　An' has nae care but Nanie, O.

Come weel, come woe, I care na by;
　　I'll tak what Heav'n will sen' me, O:
Nae ither care in life have I,
　　But live, an' love my Nanie, O.

GREEN GROW THE RASHES

Chorus.—Green grow the rashes, O;
　　　　Green grow the rashes, O;
　　　　The sweetest hours that e'er I spend,
　　　　Are spent among the lasses, O.

THERE's nought but care on ev'ry han',
　　In every hour that passes, O.
What signifies the life o' man,
　　An' 'twere na for the lasses, O:
　　　　　　　Green grow, etc.

The warl'y race may riches chase,
    An' riches still may fly them, O;
An' tho' at last they catch them fast,
    Their hearts can ne'er enjoy them, O.
                 Green grow, etc.

But gie me a cannie hour at e'en,
    My arms about my dearie, O;
An' warl'y cares, an' warl'y men,
    May a' gae tapsalteerie, O !
                 Green grow, etc.

For you sae douce, ye sneer at this;
    Ye're nought but senseless asses, O:
The wisest man the warl' e'er saw,
    He dearly lov'd the lasses, O.
                 Green grow, etc.

Auld Nature swears, the lovely dears
    Her noblest work she classes, O:
Her prentice han' she try'd on man,
    An' then she made the lasses, O.
                 Green grow, etc.

'INDEED WILL I,' QUO' FINDLAY

Tune—'Lass, an I come near thee.

'Wha is that at my bower-door?'
    "O wha is it but Findlay!"
'Then gae your gate, ye'se nae be here:'
    "Indeed maun I," quo' Findlay.
'What make ye, sae like a thief?'
    "O come and see," quo' Findlay;
'Before the morn ye'll work mischief'—
    "Indeed will I," quo' Findlay.

'Gif I rise and let you in'—
  "Let me in," quo' Findlay,
'Ye'll keep me waukin' wi' your din'—
  "Indeed will I," quo' Findlay.
'In my bower if you should stay'—
  "Let me stay," quo' Findlay;
'I fear ye'll bide till break o' day'—
  "Indeed will I," quo' Findlay.

'Here this night if ye remain'—
  "I'll remain," quo' Findlay;
'I dread ye'll learn the gate again'—
  "Indeed will I," quo' Findlay.
'What may pass within this bower'—
  "Let it pass," quo' Findlay;
'Ye maun conceal till your last hour'—
  "Indeed will I," quo' Findlay.

REMORSE—A FRAGMENT

Of all the numerous ills that hurt our peace—
That press the soul, or wring the mind with anguish,
Beyond comparison the worst are those
By our own folly, or our guilt brought on:
In ev'ry other circumstance, the mind
Has this to say, 'it was no deed of mine':
But, when to all the evil of misfortune
This sting is added, 'blame thy foolish self!'
Or worser far, the pangs of keen remorse,
The torturing, gnawing consciousness of guilt—
Of guilt, perhaps, where we've involvèd others,
The young, the innocent, who fondly lov'd us;
Nay more, that very love their cause of ruin!
O burning hell! in all thy store of torments
There's not a keener lash!

Lives there a man so firm, who, while his heart
Feels all the bitter horrors of his crime,
Can reason down its agonising throbs;
And, after proper purpose of amendment,
Can firmly force his jarring thoughts to peace ?
O happy, happy, enviable man !
O glorious magnanimity of soul !

EPITAPH ON JAMES GRIEVE, LAIRD OF BOGHEAD, TARBOLTON

HERE lies Boghead amang the dead,
In hopes to get salvation;
But if such as he in Heav'n may be,
Then welcome—hail ! damnation.

EPITAPH ON A CELEBRATED RULING ELDER

HERE Souter Hood in death does sleep;
To hell if he's gane thither,
Satan, gie him thy gear to keep;
He'll haud it weel thegither.

EPITAPH ON MY OWN FRIEND AND MY FATHER'S FRIEND, WM. MUIR IN TARBOLTON MILL

AN honest man here lies at rest,
As e'er God with his image blest;
The friend of man, the friend of truth,
The friend of age, and guide of youth :

Few hearts like his—with virtue warm'd,
   Few heads with knowledge so informed :
If there's another world, he lives in bliss;
   If there is none, he made the best of this.

EPITAPH ON MY EVER HONOURED FATHER

O YE whose cheek the tear of pity stains,
   Draw near with pious rev'rence, and attend !
Here lie the loving husband's dear remains,
   The tender father, and the gen'rous friend;
The pitying heart that felt for human woe,
   The dauntless heart that fear'd no human pride;
The friend of man—to vice alone a foe;
   For 'ev'n his failings lean'd to virtue's side.'

BALLAD ON THE AMERICAN WAR

Tune—'Killiecrankie.'

WHEN Guildford good our pilot stood,
   An' did our hellim thraw, man;
Ae night, at tea, began a plea,
   Within America, man :
Then up they gat the maskin'-pat,
   And in the sea did jaw, man;
An' did nae less, in full congress,
   Than quite refuse our law, man.

Then thro' the lakes Montgomery takes,
   I wat he was na slaw, man;
Down Lowrie's Burn he took a turn,
   And Carleton did ca', man :

But yet, whatreck, he, at Quebec,
    Montgomery-like did fa', man,
Wi' sword in hand, before his band,
    Amang his en'mies a', man.

Poor Tammy Gage within a cage
    Was kept at Boston-ha', man;
Till Willie Howe took o'er the knowe
    For Philadelphia, man;
Wi' sword an' gun he thought a sin
    Guid Christian bluid to draw, man;
But at New-York, wi' knife an' fork,
    Sir-Loin he hacked sma', man.

Burgoyne gaed up, like spur an' whip,
    Till Fraser brave did fa', man;
Then lost his way, ae misty day,
    In Saratoga shaw, man.
Cornwallis fought as lang's he dought,
    An' did the buckskin's claw, man;
But Clinton's glaive frae rust to save,
    He hung it to the wa', man.

Then Montague, an' Guildford too,
    Began to fear a fa', man;
And Sackville dour, wha stood the stoure,
    The German chief to thraw, man :
For Paddy Burke, like ony Turk,
    Nae mercy had at a', man;
An' Charlie Fox threw by the box,
    An' lows'd his tinkler jaw, man.

Then Rockingham took up the game;
    Till death did on him ca', man;
When Shelburne meek held up his cheek,
    Conform to gospel law, man :
Saint Stephen's boys, wi' jarring noise,
    They did his measures thraw, man;
For North an' Fox united stocks,
    An' bore him to the wa', man.

Then clubs an' hearts were Charlie's cartes,
  He swept the stakes awa', man,
Till the diamond's ace, of Indian race,
  Led him a sair *faux pas*, man :
The Saxon lads, wi' loud placads,
  On Chatham's boy did ca', man;
An' Scotland drew her pipe an' blew,
  'Up, Willie, waur them a', man !'

Behind the throne then Granville's gone,
  A secret word or twa, man;
While slee Dundas arous'd the class
  Be-north the Roman wa', man :
An' Chatham's wraith, in heav'nly graith,
  (Inspirèd bardies saw, man,)
Wi' kindling eyes, cry'd, 'Willie, rise !
  Would I hae fear'd them a', man' ?

But, word an' blow, North, Fox, and Co.
  Gowff'd Willie like a' ba', man;
Till Suthron raise, an' coost their claise
  Behind him in a raw, man :
An' Caledon threw by the drone,
  An' did her whittle draw, man;
An' swoor fu' rude, thro' dirt an' bluid,
  To mak it guid in law, man.

REPLY TO AN ANNOUNCEMENT BY
JOHN RANKINE

I AM a keeper of the law
  In some sma' points, altho' not a';
Some people tell me gin I fa',
    Ae way or ither,
The breaking of ae point, tho' sma'
    Breaks a' thegither.

I hae been in for't ance or twice,
And winna say o'er far for thrice;
Yet never met wi' that surprise
      That broke my rest;
But now a rumour's like to rise—
      A whaup's i' the nest !

EPISTLE TO JOHN RANKINE

ENCLOSING SOME POEMS

O ROUGH, rude, ready-witted Rankine,
The wale o' cocks for fun an' drinking !
There's mony godly folks are thinking,
      Your dreams and tricks
Will send you Korah-like a-sinkin,'
      Straught to auld Nick's.

Ye hae sae mony cracks an' cants,
And in your wicked, drucken rants,
Ye mak a devil o' the saunts,
      An' fill them fou;
And then their failings, flaws, an' wants,
      Are a' seen thro'.

Hipocrisy, in mercy spare it !
That holy robe, O dinna tear it !
Spare't for their sakes, wha aften wear it—
      The lads in black;
But your curst wit, when it comes near it,
      Rives't aff their back.

Think, wicked Sinner, wha ye're skaithing :
It's just the 'Blue-gown' badge an' claithing
O' saunts; tak that, ye lea'e them naething
      To ken them by,
Frae ony unregenerate heathen,
      Like you or I.

I've sent you here some rhymin' ware,
A' that I bargain'd for, an' mair;
Sae, when ye hae an hour to spare,
   I will expect,
Yon sang ye'll sen't, wi' cannie care,
    And no neglect.

Tho' faith, sma' heart hae I to sing!
My muse dow scarcely spread her wing;
I've play'd mysel a bonie spring,
    An' danc'd my fill!
I'd better gaen an' sair't the king,
    At Bunker's Hill.

'Twas ae night lately, in my fun,
I gaed a rovin' wi' the gun,
An' brought a paitrick to the grun'—
    A bonie hen;
And, as the twilight was begun,
    Thought nane wad ken.

The poor, wee thing was little hurt;
I straiket it a wee for sport,
Ne'er thinking they wad fash me for't;
    But Deil-ma-care!
Somebody tells the poacher-court,
    The hale affair.

Some auld, us'd hands had taen a note,
That sic a hen had got a shot;
I was suspected for the plot;
    I scorn'd to lie;
So gat the whissle o' my groat,
    An' pay't the fee.

It pits me ay as mad's a hare;
So I can rhyme nor write nae mair;
But pennyworths again is fair,
    When time's expedient:
Meanwhile I am, respected Sir,
    Your most obedient.

A POET'S WELCOME TO HIS LOVE-BEGOTTEN DAUGHTER

THOU's welcome, wean; mishanter fa' me,
If thoughts o' thee, or yet thy mamie,
Shalt ever daunton me or awe me,
  My bonie lady,
Or if I blush when thou shalt ca' me
  Tyta or daddie.

Tho' now they ca' me fornicator,
An' tease my name in kintry clatter,
The mair they talk, I'm kent the better,
  E'en let them clash;
An auld wife's tongue's a feckless matter
  To gie ane fash.

Welcome! my bonie, sweet, wee dochter,
Tho' ye come here a wee unsought for,
And tho' your comin' I hae fought for,
  Baith kirk and quier;
Yet, by my faith, ye're no unwrought for,
  That I shall swear!

Wee image o' my bonie Betty,
As fatherly I kiss and daut thee,
As dear, and near my heart I set thee
  Wi' as gude will
As a' the priests had seen me get thee
  That's out o' h—ll.

Sweet fruit o' mony a merry dint,
My funny toil is now a' tint,
Sin' thou cam to the warl' asklent,
  Which fools may scoff at;
In my last plack thy part's be in't
  The better ha'f o't.

Tho' I should be the waur bestead,
Thou's be as braw and bienly clad,
And thy young years as nicely bred
                    Wi' education,
As ony brat o' wedlock's bed,
                    In a' thy station.

Lord grant that thou may ay inherit
Thy mither's person, grace, an' merit,
An' thy poor, worthless daddy's spirit,
                    Without his failin's,
'Twill please me mair to see thee heir it,
                    Than stocket mailens.

For if thou be what I wad hae thee,
And tak the counsel I shall gie thee,
I'll never rue my trouble wi' thee—
                    The cost nor shame o't,
But be a loving father to thee,
                    And brag the name o't.

O LEAVE NOVELS

O LEAVE novels, ye Mauchline belles,
    Ye're safer at your spinning-wheel;
Such witching books are baited hooks
    For rakish rooks like Rob Mossgiel;
Your fine Tom Jones and Grandisons,
    They make your youthful fancies reel;
They heat your brains, and fire your veins,
    And then you're prey for Rob Mossgiel.

Beware a tongue that's smoothly hung,
    A heart that warmly seems to feel;
That feeling heart but acts a part—
    'Tis rakish art in Rob Mossgiel.

> The frank address, the soft caress,
>   Are worse than poisoned darts of steel;
> The frank address, and politesse,
>   Are all finesse in Rob Mossgiel.

THE MAUCHLINE LADY

WHEN first I came to Stewart Kyle,
  My mind it was na steady;
Where'er I gaed, where'er I rade,
  A mistress still I had ay:

But when I came roun' by Mauchline toun,
  Not dreadin' anybody,
My heart was caught, before I thought,
  And by a Mauchline lady.

MY GIRL SHE'S AIRY

Tune—'Black Jock.'

My girl she's airy, she's buxom and gay;
Her breath is as sweet as the blossoms in May;
  A touch of her lips it ravishes quite:
She's always good natur'd, good humour'd, and free
She dances, she glances, she smiles upon me;
  I never am happy when out of her sight.

THE BELLES OF MAUCHLINE

IN Mauchline there dwells six proper young belles,
  The pride of the place and its neighbourhood a'
Their carriage and dress, a stranger would guess,
  In London or Paris, they'd gotten it a'.

Miss Miller is fine, Miss Markland's divine,
  Miss Smith she has wit, and Miss Betty is braw:
There's beauty and fortune to get wi' Miss Morton,
  But Armour's the jewel for me o' them a'.

EPITAPH ON A NOISY POLEMIC

BELOW thir stanes lie Jamie's banes;
  O Death, it's my opinion,
Thou ne'er took such a bleth'rin' b-tch
  Into thy dark dominion!

EPITAPH ON A HENPECKED SQUIRE

As father Adam first was fool'd
  (A case that's still too common),
Here lies a man a woman ruled—
  The devil ruled the woman.

EPIGRAM ON SAID OCCASION

O DEATH, hadst thou but spar'd his life,
  Whom we this day lament!
We freely wad exchanged the wife,
  And a' been weel content.
Ev'n as he is, cauld in his graff,
  The swap we yet will do't;
Tak thou the carlin's carcase aff,
  Thou'se get the saul o' boot.

ANOTHER

ONE Queen Artemisa, as old stories tell,
When deprived of her husband she lovèd so well,
In respect for the love and affection he showed her
She reduc'd him to dust and she drank up the powder
But Queen Netherplace, of a diff'rent complexion,
When called on to order the fun'ral direction,
Would have ate her dear lord, on a slender pretence
Not to show her respect, but—to save the expence

ON TAM THE CHAPMAN

As Tam the chapman on a day,
Wi' Death forgather'd by the way,
Weel pleas'd, he greets a wight so famous,
And Death was nae less pleas'd wi' Thomas,
Wha cheerfully lays down his pack,
And there blaws up a hearty crack:
His social, friendly, honest heart
Sae tickled Death, they could na part;
Sae, after viewing knives and garters,
Death taks him hame to gie him quarters.

EPITAPH ON JOHN RANKINE

AE day, as Death, that gruesome carl,
Was driving to the tither warl'
A mixtie-maxtie motley squad,
And mony a guilt-bespotted lad—
Black gowns of each denomination,
And thieves of every rank and station,
From him that wears the star and garter,
To him that wintles in a halter:

Ashamed himself to see the wretches,
He mutters, glowrin' at the bitches,
'By G—d I'll not be seen behint them,
Nor 'mang the sp'ritual core present them,
Without, at least, ae honest man,
To grace this d—d infernal clan!'
By Adamhill a glance he threw,
'L—d God!' quoth he, 'I have it now;
There's just the man I want, i' faith!'
And quickly stoppit Rankine's breath.

MAN WAS MADE TO MOURN—A DIRGE

WHEN chill November's surly blast
  Made fields and forests bare,
One ev'ning, as I wander'd forth
  Along the banks of Ayr,
I spied a man, whose aged step
  Seem'd weary, worn with care;
His face was furrow'd o'er with years,
  And hoary was his hair.

'Young stranger, whither wand'rest thou?'
  Began the rev'rend sage;
'Does thirst of wealth thy step constrain,
  Or youthful pleasure's rage?
Or haply, prest with cares and woes,
  Too soon thou hast began
To wander forth, with me to mourn
  The miseries of man.

'The sun that overhangs yon moors,
  Out-spreading far and wide,
Where hundreds labour to support
  A haughty lordling's pride;—

I've seen yon weary winter-sun
   Twice forty times return;
And ev'ry time has added proofs,
   That man was made to mourn.

'O man ! while in thy early years,
   How prodigal of time !
Mis-spending all thy precious hours—
   Thy glorious youthful prime !
Alternate follies take the sway;
   Licentious passions burn;
Which tenfold force gives Nature's law,
   That man was made to mourn.

'Look not alone on youthful prime,
   Or manhood's active might;
Man then is useful to his kind,
   Supported is his right :
But see him on the edge of life,
   With cares and sorrows worn;
Then Age and Want—oh ! ill-match'd pair—
   Show man was made to mourn.

'A few seem favourites of fate,
   In pleasure's lap carest;
Yet, think not all the rich and great
   Are likewise truly blest :
But oh ! what crowds in ev'ry land,
   All wretched and forlorn,
Thro' weary life this lesson learn,
   That man was made to mourn.

'Many and sharp the num'rous ills
   Inwoven with our frame !
More pointed still we make ourselves,
   Regret, remorse, and shame !

And man, whose heav'n-erected face
  The smiles of love adorn,—
Man's inhumanity to man
  Makes countless thousands mourn!

'See yonder poor, o'er-labour'd wight,
  So abject, mean, and vile,
Who begs a brother of the earth
  To give him leave to toil;
And see his lordly fellow-worm
  The poor petition spurn,
Unmindful, tho' a weeping wife
  And helpless offspring mourn.

'If I'm design'd yon lordling's slave—
  By Nature's law design'd—
Why was an independent wish
  E'er planted in my mind?
If not, why am I subject to
  His cruelty, or scorn?
Or why has man the will and pow'r
  To make his fellow mourn?

'Yet, let not this too much, my son,
  Disturb thy youthful breast:
This partial view of human-kind
  Is surely not the best!
The poor, oppressèd, honest man
  Had never, sure, been born,
Had there not been some recompense
  To comfort those that mourn!

'O Death! the poor man's dearest friend,
  The kindest and the best!
Welcome the hour my aged limbs
  Are laid with thee at rest!

B.P.   C.

The great, the wealthy fear thy blow,
From pomp and pleasure torn;
But, oh ! a blest relief for those
That weary-laden mourn !'

THE TWA HERDS ; OR, THE HOLY TULYIE

AN UNCO MOURNFU' TALE

Blockheads with reason, wicked wits abhor,
But fool with fool is barbarous civil war.—POPE

O A' ye pious godly flocks,
Weel fed on pastures orthodox,
Wha now will keep ye frae the fox,
  Or worrying tykes ?
Or wha will tent the waifs an' crocks,
  About the dykes ?

The twa best herds in a' the wast,
That e'er ga'e gospel horn a blast
These five an' twenty simmers past—
  Oh, dool to tell !
Hae had a bitter black out-cast
  Atween themsel.

O, Moodie, man, an' wordy Russell,
How could you raise so vile a bustle;
Ye'll see how 'new-light' herds will whistle,
  An' think it fine !
The L—'s cause ne'er gat sic a twistle,
  Sin' I hae min'.

O, Sirs ! whae'er wad hae expeckit
Your duty ye wad sae negleckit,
Ye wha were ne'er by lairds respeckit
  To wear the plaid;
But by the brutes themselves eleckit,
  To be their guide.

What flock wi' Moodie's flock could rank
Sae hale and hearty every shank,
Nae poison'd soor Arminian stank
  He let them taste;
Frae Calvin's well, ay clear they drank,---
  O, sic a feast!

The thummart, willcat, brock, an' tod,
Weel kend his voice thro' a' the wood,
He smell'd their ilka hole an' road,
  Baith out an' in;
An' weel he lik'd to shed their bluid,
  An' sell their skin.

What herd like Russell tell'd his tale;
His voice was heard thro' muir and dale,
He kenn'd the L—'s sheep, ilka tail,
  Owre a' the height;
An' saw gin they were sick or hale,
  At the first sight.

He fine a mangy sheep could scrub,
Or nobly fling the gospel club,
And 'new-light' herds could nicely drub
  Or pay their skin;
Could shake them o'er the burning dub,
  Or heave them in.

Sic twa—O! do I live to see't,
Sic famous twa should disagree't,
And names, like 'villain,' 'hypocrite,'
  Ilk ither gi'en,
While 'new-light' herds, wi' laughin' spite,
  Say neither's lien!

A' ye wha tent the gospel fauld,
There's Duncan deep, an' Peebles shaul',
But chiefly thou, apostle Auld,
  We trust in thee,
That thou wilt work them, hot an' cauld,
  Till they agree.

Consider, sirs, how we're beset;
There's scarce a new herd that we get,
But comes frae 'mang that cursèd set,
   I winna name;
I hope frae heav'n to see them yet
   In fiery flame.

Dalrymple has been lang our fae,
M:Gill has wrought us meikle wae,
An' that curs'd rascal ca'd M'Quhae,
   And baith the Shaws:
That aft hae made us black an' blae,
   Wi' vengefu' paws.

Auld Wodrow lang has hatch'd mischief;
We thought ay death wad bring relief,
But he has gotten, to our grief,
   Ane to succeed him,
A chield wha'll soundly buff our beef;
   I meikle dread him.

And mony a ane that I could tell,
Wha fain would openly rebel,
Forby turn-coats amang oursel,
   There's Smith for ane;
I doubt he's but a grey nick quill,
   An' that ye'll fin'.

O! a' ye flocks o'er a' the hills,
By mosses, meadows, moors, and fells,
Come, join your counsel and your skills
   To cowe the lairds,
An' get the brutes the power themsels
   To chuse their herds.

Then Orthodoxy yet may prance,
An' Learning in a woody dance,
An' that fell cur ca'd 'common-sense,'
   That bites sae sair,
Be banished o'er the sea to France:
   Let him bark there.

Then Shaw's an' Dalrymple's eloquence,
M'Gill's close nervous excellence,
M'Quhae's pathetic manly sense,
      An' guid M'Math,
Wi' Smith, wha thro' the heart can glance,
      May a' pack aff.

EPISTLE TO DAVIE, A BROTHER POET

JANUARY

WHILE winds frae off Ben-Lomond blaw,
An' bar the doors wi' drivin' snaw,
   An' hing us owre the ingle,
I set me down to pass the time,
An' spin a verse or twa o' rhyme,
   In hamely, westlin jingle :
While frosty winds blaw in the drift
   Ben to the chimla lug,
I grudge a wee the great-folk's gift,
   That live sae bien an' snug :
     I tent less, and want less
      Their roomy fire-side;
     But hanker, and canker,
      To see their cursed pride.

It's hardly in a body's pow'r,
To keep, at times, frae being sour,
   To see how things are shar'd;
How best o' chiels are whyles in want,
While coofs on countless thousands rant,
   And ken na how to ware't;
But, Davie, lad, ne'er fash your head,
   Tho' we hae little gear;
We're fit to win our daily bread,
   As lang's we're hale and fier :

'Mair spier na, nor fear na,'
  Auld age ne'er mind a feg;
The last o't, the warst o't,
  Is only but to beg.

To lye in kilns and barns at e'en,
When banes are craz'd, and bluid is thin,
  Is, doubtless, great distress!
Yet then content could make us blest;
Ev'n then, sometimes, we'd snatch a taste
  Of truest happiness.
The honest heart that's free frae a'
  Intended fraud or guile,
However Fortune kick the ba',
  Has ay some cause to smile;
    An' mind still, you'll find still,
      A comfort this nae sma';
    Nae mair then, we'll care then,
      Nae farther we can fa'.

What tho', like commoners of air,
We wander out, we know not where,
  But either house or hal',
Yet nature's charms, the hills and woods,
The sweeping vales, and foaming floods,
  Are free alike to all.
In days when daisies deck the ground,
  And blackbirds whistle clear,
With honest joy our hearts will bound
  To see the coming year:
    On braes when we please then,
      We'll sit an' sowth a tune;
    Syne rhyme till't, we'll time till't,
      An' sing't when we hae done.

It's no in titles nor in rank;
It's no in wealth like Lon'on bank,
  To purchase peace and rest:

It's no in makin' muckle, mair;
It's no in books, it's no in lear,
  To make us truly blest:
If happiness hae not her seat
  An' centre in the breast,
We may be wise, or rich, or great,
    But never can be blest;
      Nae treasures nor pleasures
        Could make us happy lang;
      The heart ay's the part ay
        That makes us right or wrang.

Think ye, that sic as you and I,
Wha drudge an' drive thro' wet and dry,
  Wi' never ceasing toil;
Think ye, are we less blest than they,
Wha scarcely tent us in their way,
  As hardly worth their while?
Alas! how oft in haughty mood
  God's creatures they oppress!
Or else, neglecting a' that's good,
  They riot in excess!
    Baith careless and fearless
      Of either heaven or hell;
    Esteeming, and deeming
      It a' an idle tale!

Then let us cheerfu' acquiesce,
Nor make our scanty pleasures less,
  By pining at our state:
And, even should misfortunes come,
I, here wha sit, hae met wi' some—
  An's thankfu' for them yet,
They gie the wit of age to youth;
  They let us ken oursel;
They make us see the naked truth—
  The real guid and ill:

Tho' losses an' crosses
　　Be lessons right severe,
There's wit there, ye'll get there,
　　Ye'll find nae other where.

But tent me, Davie, ace o' hearts !
(To say aught less wad wrang the cartes,
　　And flatt'ry I detest)
This life has joys for you and I;
An' joys that riches ne'er could buy,
　　An' joys the very best.
There's a' the pleasures o' the heart,
　　The lover an' the frien';
Ye hae your Meg, your dearest part,
　　And I my darling Jean !
　　　It warms me, it charms me,
　　　　To mention but her name :
　　　It heats me, it beets me,
　　　　An' sets me a' on flame !

O all ye Pow'rs who rule above !
O Thou whose very self art love !
　　Thou know'st my words sincere !
The life-blood streaming thro' my heart,
Or my more dear immortal part,
　　Is not more fondly dear !
When heart-corroding care and grief
　　Deprive my soul of rest,
Her dear idea brings relief,
　　And solace to my breast.
　　　Thou Being, All-seeing,
　　　　O hear my fervent pray'r;
　　　Still take her, and make her
　　　　Thy most peculiar care !

All hail; ye tender feelings dear !
The smile of love, the friendly tear.
　　The sympathetic glow !

Long since, this world's thorny ways
Had number'd out my weary days,
   Had it not been for you !
Fate still has blest me with a friend,
   In ev'ry care and ill;
And oft a more endearing band—
   A tie more tender still.
     It lightens, it brightens
      The tenebrific scene,
     To meet with, an' greet with
      My Davie, or my Jean !

O, how that *Name* inspires my style !
The words come skelpin, rank an' file,
   Amaist before I ken !
The ready measure rins as fine,
As Phœbus an' the famous Nine
   Were glowrin' owre my pen.
My spavet Pegasus will limp,
   Till ance he's fairly het;
And then he'll hilch, and stilt, an' jimp,
   And rin an unco fit :
     But least then the beast then
      Should rue this hasty ride,
     I'll light now, and dight now
      His sweaty, wizen'd hide.

HOLY WILLIE'S PRAYER

And send the godly in a pet to pray.—POPE.

O THOU, who in the heavens does dwell,
Who, as it pleases best Thysel,
Sends ane to heaven, an' ten to hell,
     A' for thy glory,
And no for ony gude or ill
      They've done afore Thee !

I bless and praise Thy matchless might,
When thousands Thou hast left in night,
That I am here afore Thy sight,
   For gifts an' grace
A burning and a shining light
  To a' this place.

What was I, or my generation,
That I should get sic exaltation,
I wha deserve most just damnation
   For broken laws,
Five thousand years ere my creation,
  Thro' Adam's cause.

When frae my mither's womb I fell,
Thou might hae plungèd me in hell,
To gnash my gums, to weep and wail,
   In burnin' lakes,
Where damned devils roar and yell,
  Chain'd to their stakes.

Yet I am here a chosen sample,
To show Thy grace is great and ample:
I'm here a pillar o' Thy temple,
   Strong as a rock,
A guide, a buckler, and example,
  To a' Thy flock.

O L—d, Thou kens what zeal I bear,
When drinkers drink, an' swearers swear,
An' singin' there, an' dancin' here,
   Wi' great and sma';
For I am keepit by Thy fear
  Free frae them a'.

But yet, O L—d! confess I must,
At times I'm fashed wi' fleshly lust:
An' sometimes, too, in warldly trust,
   Vile self gets in;
But Thou remembers we are dust,
  Defil'd wi' sin.

O L—d! yestreen, Thou kens, wi' Meg—
Thy pardon I sincerely beg,
O! may't ne'er be a livin' plague
   To my dishonour,
An' I'll ne'er lift a lawless leg
   Again upon her.

Besides, I farther maun allow,
Wi' Leezie's lass three times I trow—
But L—d, that Friday I was fou,
   When I cam near her;
Or else, Thou kens, Thy servant true
   Wad never steer her.

Maybe Thou lets this fleshly thorn
Buffet Thy servant e'en and morn,
Lest he owre proud and high shou'd turn,
   That he's sae gifted:
If sae, Thy han' maun e'en be borne,
   Until Thou lift it.

L—d, bless Thy chosen in this place,
For here Thou hast a chosen race:
But G—d confound their stubborn face,
   An' blast their name,
Wha bring Thy elders to disgrace
   An' public shame.

L—d, mind Gaw'n Hamilton's deserts;
He drinks, an' swears, an' plays at cartes,
Yet has sae mony takin' arts,
   Wi' great and sma',
Frae G—d's ain priest the people's hearts
   He steals awa'.

An' when we chasten'd him therefor,
Thou kens how he bred sic a splore,
An' set the warld in a roar
   O' laughing at us;—
Curse Thou his basket and his store,
   Kail an' potatoes.

L—d, hear my earnest cry and pray'r,
Against that Presbyt'ry o' Ayr;
Thy strong right hand, L—d, make it bare
        Upo' their heads;
L—d, visit them, an' dinna spare,
        For their misdeeds.

O L—d, my G—d! that glib-tongu'd Aiken,
My vera heart and flesh are quakin',
To think how we stood sweatin', shakin',
        An' p—d wi' dread,
While Auld, wi' hingin' lip, gaed sneakin',
        And hid his head.

L—d, in Thy day o' vengeance try him,
L—d, visit them wha did employ him,
And pass not in Thy mercy by them,
        Nor hear their pray'r,
But for Thy people's sake destroy them,
        An' dinna spare.

But, L—d, remember me an' mine
Wi' mercies temporal an' divine,
That I for grace an' gear may shine,
        Excell'd by nane,
And a' the glory shall be Thine,
        Amen, Amen!

EPITAPH ON HOLY WILLIE

HERE Holy Willie's sair worn clay
    Taks up its last abode;
His saul has ta'en some other way,
    I fear, the left-hand road.

Stop! there he is, as sure's a gun,
    Poor, silly body, see him;
Nae wonder he's as black's the grun,
    Observe wha's standing wi' him.

Your brunstane devilship, I see
    Has got him there before ye;
But haud your nine-tail cat a wee,
    Till ance you've heard my story.

Your pity I will not implore,
    For pity ye have nane;
Justice, alas! has gi'en him o'er,
    And mercy's day is gane.

But hear me, Sir, deil as ye are,
    Look something to your credit;
A coof like him wad stain your name,
    If it were kent ye did it.

DEATH AND DOCTOR HORNBOOK

A TRUE STORY

SOME books are lies frae end to end,
And some great lies were never penn'd;
Ev'n ministers they hae been kenn'd;
            In holy rapture,
A rousing whid at times to vend,
            And nail't wi' Scripture.

But this that I am gaun to tell,
Which lately on a night befel,
Is just as true's the Deil's in hell
            Or Dublin city:
That e'er he nearer comes oursel
            'S a muckle pity.

The clachan yill had made me canty,
I was na fou, but just had plenty;
I stacher'd whyles, but yet took tent ay
      To free the ditches;
An' hillocks, stanes, an' bushes, kenn'd ay
      Frae ghaists an' witches.

The rising moon began to glowre
The distant *Cumnock* hills out-owre:
To count her horns, wi' a' my pow'r,
      I set mysel;
But whether she had three or four,
      I cou'd na tell.

I was come round about the hill,
An' toddlin' doon on *Willie's mill*,
Setting my staff wi' a' my skill,
      To keep me sicker;
Tho' leeward whyles, against my will,
      I took a bicker.

I there wi' *Something* did forgather,
That pat me in an eerie swither;
An' awfu' scythe, out-owre ae shouther,
      Clear-dangling, hang;
A three-tae'd leister on the ither
      Lay, large an' lang.

Its stature seem'd lang Scotch ells twa,
The queerest shape that e'er I saw,
For fient a wame it had ava;
      And then its shanks,
They were as thin, as sharp an' sma'
      As cheeks o' branks.

'Guid-een,' quo' I; 'Friend! hae ye been mawin',
'When ither folk are busy sawin!'
It seem'd to mak a kind o' stan',
      But naething spak;
At length, says I, 'Friend! whare ye gaun?
      'Will ye go back?'

It spak right howe,—'My name is *Death*,
'But be na' fley'd'.—Quoth I, 'Guid faith,
'Ye're maybe come to stap my breath;
   'But tent me, billie;
'I red ye weel, tak care o' skaith,
    'See, there's a gully!'

'Gudeman,' quo' he, 'put up your whittle,
'I'm no designed to try its mettle;
'But if I did, I wad be kittle
   'To be mislear'd;
'I wad na mind it, no that spittle
   'Out-owre my beard.'

'Weel, weel!' says I, 'a bargain be't;
'Come, gies your hand, an' sae we're gree't;
'We'll ease our shanks and tak a seat—
   'Come, gies your news;
'This while ye hae been mony a gate,
   'At mony a house.'

'Ay, ay!' quo' he, and shook his head,
'It's e'en a lang, lang time indeed
'Sin' I began to nick the thread,
   'An' choke the breath:
'Folk maun do something for their bread,
   'An' sae maun *Death*.

'Sax thousand years are near-hand fled
'Sin I was to the butching bred,
'An' mony a scheme in vain's been laid,
   'To stap or scar me;
'Till ane *Hornbook's* ta'en up the trade,
   'And faith! he'll waur me.

'Ye ken *Jock Hornbook* i' the Clachan,
'Deil mak his king's-hood in a spleuchan!
'He's grown sae weel acquaint wi' *Buchan*
   'And ither chaps,
'The weans haud out their fingers laughin',
   'An' pouk my hips.

'See, here's a scythe, an' there's a dart,
'They hae pierc'd mony a gallant heart;
'But Doctor *Hornbook* wi' his art
        'An' cursed skill,
'Has made them baith no worth a f—t,
         'D—n'd haet they'll kill!

''Twas but yestreen, nae farther gane,
'I threw a noble throw at ane;
'Wi' less, I'm sure, I've hundreds slain;
        'But deil-ma' care,
'It just play'd dirl on the bane,
        'But did nae mair.

'*Hornbook* was by, wi' ready art,
'An' had sae fortify'd the part,
'That when I lookèd to my dart,
        'It was sae blunt,
'Fient haet o't wad hae pierc'd the heart
        'Of a kail-runt.

'I drew my scythe in sic a fury,
'I near-hand cowpit wi' my hurry,
'But yet the bauld *Apothecary*
        'Withstood the shock;
'I might as weel hae try'd a quarry
        'O' hard whin rock.

'Ev'n them he canna get attended,
'Altho' their face he ne'er had kend it,
'Just ——— in a kail-blade, an' send it,
        'As soon's he smells 't,
'Baith their disease, and what will mend it,
        'At once he tells 't.

'And then a ' doctor's saws an' whittles,
'Of a' dimensions, shapes, an' mettles,
'A' kinds o' boxes, mugs, an' bottles,
        'He's sure to hae;
'Their Latin names as fast he rattles
        'As A B C.

'Calces o' fossils, earths, and trees;
'True sal-marinum o' the seas;
'The farina of beans an' pease,
   'He has't in plenty;
'Aqua-fontis, what you please,
   'He can content ye.

'Forbye some new, uncommon weapons,
'Urinus spiritus of capons;
'Or mite-horn shavings, filings, scrapings,
   'Distill'd *per se;*
'Sal-alkali o' midge-tails-clippings,
   'And mony mae.'

'Waes me for *Johnie Ged's Hole* now,
Quoth I, 'if that thae news be true!
'His braw calf-ward whare gowans grew,
   'Sae white and bonie,
'Nae doubt they'll rive it wi' the plew;
   'They'll ruin *Johnie!*'

The creature grain'd an eldritch laugh,
And says, 'Ye needna yoke the pleugh,
'Kirkyards will soon be till'd enough,
   'Tak ye nae fear:
'They'll a' be trench'd wi' mony a sheugh,
   'In twa-three year.

'Whare I kill'd ane, a fair strae death,
'By loss o' blood or want of breath,
'This night I'm free to tak my aith,
   'That *Hornbook's* skill
'Has clad a score i' their last claith,
   'By drap an' pill.

'An honest wabster to his trade,
'Whase wife's twa nieves were scarce weel-bred,
'Gat tippence-worth to mend her head,
   'When it was sair;
'The wife slade cannie to her bed,
   'But ne'er spak mair.

'A country laird had ta'en the batts,
'Or some curmurring in his guts,
'His only son for *Hornbook* sets,
   'An' pays him well:
'The lad, for twa guid gimmer-pets
   'Was laird himsel.

'A bonie lass—ye kend her name—
'Some ill-brewn drink had hov'd her wame;
'She trusts hersel, to hide the shame,
   'In *Hornbook's* care;
'*Horn* sent her aff to her lang hame.
   'To hide it there.

'That's just a swatch o' *Hornbook's* way;
'Thus goes he on from day to day,
'Thus does he poison, kill, an' slay,
   'An's weel paid for't;
'Yet stops me o' my lawfu' prey,
   'Wi' his d—n'd dirt:

'But, hark! I'll tell you of a plot,
'Tho' dinna ye be speakin' o't;
'I'll nail the self-conceited sot,
   'As dead's a herrin';
'Niest time we meet, I'll wad a groat,
   'He gets his fairin'!'

But just as he began to tell,
The auld kirk-hammer strak the bell
Some wee short hour ayont the *twal*,
   Which rais'd us baith:
I took the way that pleas'd mysel,
   And sae did *Death*.

EPISTLE TO J. LAPRAIK

AN OLD SCOTTISH BARD—APRIL 1, 1785

WHILE briers an' woodbines budding green,
An' paitricks scraichin' loud at e'en,
An' morning poussie whiddin seen,
   Inspire my muse,
This freedom, in an unknown frien',
   I pray excuse.

On Fasten-e'en we had a rockin',
To ca' the crack and weave our stockin';
And there was muckle fun and jokin',
   Ye need na doubt;
At length we had a hearty yokin',
   At 'sang about.'

There was ae sang, amang the rest,
Aboon them a' it pleas'd me best,
That some kind husband had addrest
   To some sweet wife;
It thirl'd the heart-strings thro' the breast,
   A' to the life.

I've scarce heard ought describ'd sae weel,
What gen'rous, manly bosoms feel;
Thought I, 'can this be Pope, or Steele,
   Or Beattie's wark?'
They tauld me 'twas an odd kind chiel
   About Muirkirk.

It pat me fidgin-fain to hear't,
An' sae about him there I speir't;
Then a' that kent him round declar'd
   He had *ingine;*
That nane excell'd it, few cam near't,
   It was sae fine :

That, set him to a pint of ale,
An' either douce or merry tale,
Or rhymes an' sangs he'd made himsel,
    Or witty catches—
'Tween Inverness an' Teviotdale,
    He had few matches.

Then up I gat, an' swoor an aith,
Tho' I should pawn my pleugh an' graith,
Or die a cadger pownie's death,
    At some dyke-back,
A pint an' gill I'd gie them baith,
    To hear your crack.

But, first an' foremost, I should tell,
Amaist as soon as I could spell,
I to the crambo-jingle fell;
    Tho' rude an' rough—
Yet crooning to a body's sel,
    Does weel eneugh.

I am nae poet, in a sense;
But just a rhymer like by chance.
An' hae to learning nae pretence;
    Yet, what the matter?
Whene'er my muse does on me glance,
    I jingle at her.

Your critic-folk may cock their nose,
And say, 'how can you e'er propose,
You wha ken hardly verse frae prose,
    To mak a sang?'
But, by your leave, my learned foes,
    Ye're maybe wrang.

What's a' your jargon o' your schools—
Your Latin names for horns an' stools?
If honest Nature made you fools,
    What sairs your grammars?
Ye'd better taen up spades and shools,
    Or knappin-hammers.

A set o' dull, conceited hashes
Confuse their brains in college-classes!
They gang in stirks, and come out asses,
   Plain truth to speak;
An' syne they think to climb Parnassus
   By dint o' Greek!

Gie me ae spark o' nature's fire,
That's a' the learning I desire;
Then tho' I drudge thro' dub an' mire
   At pleugh or cart,
My muse, tho' hamely in attire,
   May touch the heart.

O for a spunk o' Allan's glee,
Or Fergusson's, the bauld an' slee,
Or bright Lapraik's, my friend to be,
   If I can hit it!
That would be lear eneugh for me,
   If I could get it.

Now, sir, if ye hae friends enow,
Tho' real friends I b'lieve are few;
Yet, if your catalogue be fu',
   I'se no insist:
But, gif ye want ae friend that's true,
   I'm on your list.

I winna blaw about mysel,
As ill I like my fauts to tell;
But friends, an' folk that wish me well,
   They sometimes roose me;
Tho' I maun own, as mony still
   As far abuse me.

There's ae wee faut they whiles lay to me,
I like the lasses—Gude forgie me!
For mony a plack they wheedle frae me
   At dance or fair;
Maybe some ither thing they gie me
   They weel can spare.

But Mauchline Race or Mauchline Fair,
I should be proud to meet you there:
We'se gie ae night's discharge to care,
    If we forgather;
An' hae a swap o' rhymin'-ware
    Wi' ane anither.

The four-gill chap, we'se gar him clatter,
An' kirsen him wi' reekin water;
Syne we'll sit down an' tak our whitter,
    To cheer our heart;
An' faith, we'se be acquainted better
    Before we part.

Awa' ye selfish, warl'y race,
Wha think that havins, sense, an' grace,
Ev'n love an' friendship should give place
    To catch-the-plack!
I dinna like to see your face,
    Nor hear your crack.

But ye whom social pleasure charms,
Whose hearts the tide of kindness warms,
Who hold your being on the terms,
    'Each aid the others,'
Come to my bowl, come to my arms,
    My friends, my brothers!

But, to conclude my lang epistle,
As my auld pen's worn to the gristle,
Twa lines frae you would gar me fissle,
    Who am most fervent,
While I can either sing or whistle,
    Your friend and servant.

SECOND EPISTLE TO J. LAPRAIK

APRIL 21, 1785

WHILE new-ca'd kye rowte at the stake
An' pownies reek in pleugh or braik,
This hour on e'enin's edge I take,
   To own I'm debtor
To honest-hearted, auld Lapraik,
   For his kind letter.

Forjesket sair, with weary legs,
Rattlin' the corn out-owre the rigs,
Or dealing thro' amang the naigs
   Their ten-hours' bite,
My awkwart Muse sair pleads and begs
   I would na write.

The tapetless, ramfeezl'd hizzie,
She's saft at best an' something lazy:
Quo' she, 'ye ken we've been sae busy
   This month an' mair,
That trowth, my head is grown right dizzie,
   An' something sair.'

Her dowff excuses pat me mad;
'Conscience,' says I, 'ye thowless jade!
I'll write, an' that a hearty blaud,
   This vera night;
So dinna ye affront your trade,
   But rhyme it right.

'Shall bauld Lapraik, the king o' hearts,
Tho' mankind were a pack o' cartes,
Roose ye sae weel for your deserts,
   In terms sae friendly;
Yet ye'll neglect to shaw your parts
   An' thank him kindly?'

Sae I gat paper in a blink,
An' down gaed stumpie in the ink :
Quoth I, 'before I sleep a wink,
   I vow I'll close it ;
An' if ye winna mak it clink,
    By Jove, I'll prose it !'

Sae I've begun to scrawl, but whether
In rhyme, or prose, or baith thegither ;
Or some hotch-potch that's rightly neither,
   Let time mak proof ;
But I shall scribble down some blether
   Just clean aff-loof.

My worthy friend, ne'er grudge an' carp,
Tho' fortune use you hard an' sharp ;
Come, kittle up your moorland harp
   Wi' gleesome touch !
Ne'er mind how Fortune waft and warp ;
   She's but a b–tch.

She's gien me mony a jirt an' fleg,
Sin' I could striddle owre a rig ;
But, by the L—d, tho' I should beg
   Wi' lyart pow,
I'll laugh an' sing, an' shake my leg,
   As lang's I dow !

Now comes the sax-an-twentieth simmer
I've seen the bud upo' the timmer,
Still persecuted by the limmer
   Frae year to year ;
But yet, despite the kittle kimmer,
   I, Rob, am here.

Do ye envy the city gent,
Behind a kist to lie an' sklent ;
Or purse-proud, big wi' cent. per cent.
   An' muckle wame,
In some big brugh to represent
   A baillie's name ?

Or is't the paughty feudal thane,
Wi' ruffl'd sark an' glancing cane,
Wha thinks himself nae sheep-shank bane,
   But lordly stalks;
While caps and bonnets aff are taen,
   As by he walks?

'O Thou wha gies us each guid gift!
Gie me o' wit an' sense a lift,
Then turn me, if Thou please adrift,
   Thro' Scotland wide;
Wi' cits nor lairds I wadna shift,
   In a' their pride!'

Were this the charter of our state,
'On pain o' hell be rich an' great,'
Damnation then would be our fate,
   Beyond remead;
But, thanks to heaven, that's no the gate
   We learn our creed.

For thus the royal mandate ran,
When first the human race began;
'The social, friendly, honest man,
   Whate'er he be—
'Tis *he* fulfils great Nature's plan,
   And none but he.'

O mandate glorious and divine!
The followers o' the ragged nine—
Poor, thoughtless devils—yet may shine
   In glorious light;
While sordid sons o' Mammon's line
   Are dark as night!

Tho' here they scrape, an' squeeze, an' growl,
Their worthless nievefu' of a soul
May in some future carcase howl,
   The forest's fright;
Or in some day-detesting owl
   May shun the light.

Then may Lapraik and Burns arise,
To reach their native, kindred skies,
And sing their pleasures, hopes an' joys
      In some mild sphere;
Still closer knit in friendship's ties,
      Each passing year.

EPISTLE TO WILLIAM SIMSON

SCHOOLMASTER, OCHILTREE—MAY 1785

I GAT your letter, winsome Willie;
Wi' gratefu' heart I thank you brawlie;
Tho' I maun say't, I wad be silly,
      And unco vain,
Should I believe, my coaxin' billie,
      Your flatterin' strain.

But I'se believe ye kindly meant it:
I sud be laith to think ye hinted
Ironic satire, sidelins sklented
      On my poor musie;
Tho' in sic phraisin' terms ye've penn'd it,
      I scarce excuse ye.

My senses wad be in a creel,
Should I but dare a hope to speel,
Wi' Allan, or wi' Gilbertfield,
      The braes o' fame;
Or Fergusson, the writer-chiel,
      A deathless name.

(O Fergusson! thy glorious parts
Ill suited law's dry, musty arts!
My curse upon your whunstane hearts,
      Ye E'nbrugh gentry!
The tythe o' what ye waste at cartes
      Wad stow'd his pantry!)

Yet when a tale comes i' my head,
Or lasses gie my heart a screed—
As whiles they're like to be my dead,
    (O sad disease !)
I kittle up my rustic reed;
    It gies me ease.

Auld Coila, now, may fidge fu' fain,
She's gotten poets o' her ain;
Chiels wha their chanters winna hain,
    But tune their lays,
Till echoes a' resound again
    Her weel-sung praise.

Nae poet thought her worth his while,
To set her name in measur'd style;
She lay like some unkenn'd-of isle
    Beside New Holland,
Or whare wild-meeting oceans boil
    Besouth Magellan.

Ramsay an' famous Fergusson
Gied Forth an' Tay a lift aboon;
Yarrow an' Tweed, to monie a tune
    Owre Scotland rings;
While Irwin, Lugar, Ayr, an' Doon
    Naebody sings.

Th' Illissus, Tiber, Thames, an' Seine
Glide sweet in monie a tunefu' line :
But, Willie, set your fit to mine,
    An' cock your crest;
We'll gar our streams an' burnies shine
    Up wi' the best !

We'll sing auld Coila's plains an' fells,
Her moors red-brown wi' heather bells,
Her banks an' braes, her dens and dells,
    Whare glorious Wallace
Aft bure the gree, as story tells,
    Frae Suthron billies.

At Wallace' name, what Scottish blood
But boils up in a spring-tide flood !
Oft have our fearless fathers strode
   By Wallace' side,
Still pressing onward, red-wat-shod,
   Or glorious dy'd !

O sweet are Coila's haughs an' woods,
Where lintwhites chant amang the buds,
And jinkin' hares, in amorous whids,
   Their loves enjoy;
While thro' the braes the cushat croods
   With wailfu' cry !

Ev'n winter bleak has charms to me,
When winds rave thro' the naked tree;
Or frosts on hills of Ochiltree
   Are hoary gray;
Or blinding drifts wild-furious flee,
   Dark'ning the day !

O Nature ! a' thy shews an' forms
To feeling, pensive hearts hae charms !
Whether the summer kindly warms,
   Wi' life an' light;
Or winter howls, in gusty storms,
   The lang, dark night !

The muse, nae poet ever fand her,
Till by himsel he learn'd to wander,
Adown some trottin' burn's meander,
   An' no think lang :
O sweet to stray, an' pensive ponder
   A heart-felt sang !

The warly race may drudge an' drive,
Hog-shouther, jundie, stretch, an' strive;
Let me fair Nature's face descrive,
   And I, wi' pleasure,
Shall let the busy, grumbling hive
   Bum owre their treasure.

Fareweel, 'my rhyme-composing' brither!
We've been owre lang unkenn'd to ither:
Now let us lay our heads thegither,
      In love fraternal:
May envy wallop in a tether,
        Black fiend, infernal!

While Highlandmen hate tolls an' taxes;
While moorlan' herds like guid, fat braxies;
While terra firma, on her axis,
      Diurnal turns;
Count on a friend, in faith an' practice,
        In Robert Burns.

POSTSCRIPT

My memory's no worth a preen;
I had amaist forgotten clean,
Ye bade me write you what they mean
      By this 'new-light,'
'Bout which our herds sae aft hae been
      Maist like to fight.

In days when mankind were but callans
At grammar, logic, an' sic talents,
They took nae pains their speech to balance,
      Or rules to gie;
But spak their thoughts in plain, braid lallans,
      Like you or me.

In thae auld times, they thought the moon,
Just like a sark, or pair o' shoon,
Wore by degrees, till her last roon
      Gaed past their viewin';
An' shortly after she was done
      They gat a new ane.

This passed for certain, undisputed;
It ne'er cam i' their heads to doubt it,
Till chiels gat up an' wad confute it,
          An' ca'd it wrang;
An' muckle din there was about it,
          Baith loud an' lang.

Some herds, weel learn'd upo' the beuk,
Wad threap auld folk the thing misteuk;
For 'twas the auld moon turn'd a neuk
          An' out o' sight,
An' blacklins-comin' to the leuk,
          She grew mair bright.

This was deny'd, it was affirm'd;
The herds and hissels were alarm'd;
The rev'rend gray-beards rav'd an' storm'd,
          That beardless laddies
Should think they better were inform'd,
          Than their auld daddies.

Frae less to mair, it gaed to sticks;
Frae words an' aiths, to clours an' nicks;
An' monie a fallow gat his licks,
          Wi' hearty crunt;
An' some, to learn them for their tricks,
          Were hang'd an' brunt.

This game was play'd in mony lands,
An' 'auld-light' caddies bure sic hands,
That faith, the youngsters took the sands
          Wi' nimble shanks;
Till lairds forbad, by strict commands,
          Sic bluidy pranks.

But 'new-light' herds gat sic a cowe,
Folk thought them ruin'd stick-an-stowe;
Till now, amaist on ev'ry knowe
          Ye'll find ane plac'd;
An' some, their 'new-light' fair avow,
          Just quite barefac'd.

Nae doubt the 'auld-light' flocks are bleatin';
Their zealous herds are vex'd and sweatin';
Mysel, I've even seen them greetin
   Wi' girnin' spite,
To hear the moon sae sadly lie'd on
    By word an' write.

But shortly they will cowe the louns!
Some 'auld-light' herds in neebor touns
Are mind't, in things they ca' balloons,
   To tak a flight;
An' stay ae month amang the moons
    An' see them right.

Guid observation they will gie them;
An' when the auld moon's gaun to lea'e them,
The hindmost shaird, they'll fetch it wi' them,
   Just i' their pouch;
An' when the 'new-light' billies see them,
    I think they'll crouch!

Sae, ye observe that a' this clatter
Is naething but a 'moonshine-matter';
But tho' dull prose-folk Latin splatter
   In logic tulyie,
I hope we bardies ken some better
    Than mind sic brulyie.

ONE NIGHT AS I DID WANDER

A FRAGMENT

ONE night as I did wander,
  When corn begins to shoot,
I sat me down to ponder,
  Upon an auld tree-root:

Auld Ayr ran by before me,
    And bicker'd to the seas;
A cushat crooded o'er me,
    That echoed through the braes.

THO' CRUEL FATE

THO' cruel fate should bid us part,
    Far as the pole and line,
Her dear idea round my heart,
    Should tenderly entwine.
Tho' mountains rise, and deserts howl,
    And oceans roar between;
Yet, dearer than my deathless soul,
    I still would love my Jean.

RANTIN', ROVIN' ROBIN

THERE was a lad was born in Kyle,
But whatna day o' whatna style,
I doubt it's hardly worth the while
    To be sae nice wi' Robin.

Chorus.—Robin was a rovin' boy,
        Rantin', rovin', rantin', rovin',
    Robin was a rovin' boy,
        Rantin', rovin' Robin !

Our monarch's hindmost year but ane
Was five-and-twenty days begun,
'Twas then a blast o' Janwar' win'
    Blew hansel in on Robin.
            Robin was, etc.

The gossip keekit in his loof,
Quo' scho, 'Wha lives will see the proof,
This waly boy will be nae coof:
    I think we'll ca' him Robin.'
             Robin was, etc.

'He'll hae misfortunes great an' sma',
  But ay a heart aboon them a',
He'll be a credit till us a'—
    We'll a' be proud o' Robin.'
             Robin was, etc.

'But sure as three times three mak nine,
I see by ilka score and line,
This chap will dearly like our kin',
    So leeze me on thee! Robin.'
             Robin was, etc.

ELEGY ON THE DEATH OF ROBERT RUISSEAUX

Now Robin lies in his last lair,
He'll gabble rhyme, nor sing nae mair;
Cauld poverty, wi' hungry stare,
        Nae mair shall fear him;
Nor anxious fear, nor cankert care,
        E'er mair come near him.

To tell the truth, they seldom fash'd him,
Except the moment that they crush'd him;
For sune as chance or fate had hush'd 'em,
        Tho' e'er sae short,
Then wi' a rhyme or sang he hash'd 'em,
        And thought it sport.

Tho' he was bred to kintra-wark,
And counted was baith wight and stark
Yet that was never Robin's mark
　　　　To mak a man;
But tell him, he was learn'd and clark,
　　　　Ye roos'd him then!

EPISTLE TO JOHN GOLDIE, IN KILMARNOCK

AUTHOR OF THE GOSPEL RECOVERED—AUGUST 1785

O GOWDIE, terror o' the whigs,
Dread o' blackcoats and reverend wigs!
Sour Bigotry on his last legs
　　　　Girns an' looks back,
Wishing the ten Egyptian plagues
　　　　May seize you quick.

Poor gapin', glowrin' Superstition!
Wae's me, she's in a sad condition:
Fye! bring *Black Jock*, her state physician,
　　　　To see her water:
Alas, there's ground for great suspicion
　　　　She'll ne'er get better.

Enthusiasm's past redemption,
Gane in a gallopin' consumption:
Not a' her quacks, wi' a' their gumption,
　　　　Can ever mend her;
Her feeble pulse gies strong presumption,
　　　　She'll soon surrender.

Auld Orthodoxy lang did grapple,
For every hole to get a stapple;
But now she fetches at the thrapple,
　　　　An' fights for breath;
Haste, gie her name up in the chapel,
　　　　Near unto death.

It's you an' *Taylor* are the chief
To blame for a' this black mischief;
But could the L—d's ain folk get leave,
    A toom tar barrel
An' twa red peats wad bring relief,
    And end the quarrel.

For me, my skill's but very sma',
An' skill in prose I've nane ava';
But quietlenswise, between us twa,
    Weel may ye speed !
And tho' they sud you sair misca',
    Ne'er fash your head.

E'en swinge the dogs, and thresh them sicker !
The mair they squeel ay chap the thicker;
An' still 'mang hands a hearty bicker
    O' something stout;
It gars an owthor's pulse beat quicker,
    And helps his wit.

There's naething like the honest nappy;
Whare'll ye e'er see men sae happy,
Or women sonsie, saft an' sappy,
    'Tween morn and morn,
As them wha like to taste the drappie,
    In glass or horn ?

I've seen me daez't upon a time,
I scarce could wink or see a styme;
Just ae half-mutchkin does me prime,
    (Ought less, is little,)
Then back I rattle on the ryhme,
    As gleg's a whittle.

THIRD EPISTLE TO J. LAPRAIK

Guid speed and furder to you, Johnie,
Guid health, hale han's an' weather bonie;
Now, when ye're nickin' down fu' cannie
      The staff o' bread,
May ye ne'er want a stoup o' bran'y
      To clear your head.

May Boreas never thresh your rigs,
Nor kick your rickles aff their legs,
Sendin' the stuff o'er muirs an' haggs
      Like drivin' wrack;
But may the tapmost grain that wags
      Come to the sack.

I'm bizzie, too, an' skelpin' at it,
But, bitter, daudin showers hae wat it;
Sae my auld stumpie pen I gat it
      Wi' muckle wark,
An' took my jocteleg an' whatt it,
      Like ony clark.

It's now twa month that I'm your debtor,
For your braw, nameless, dateless letter,
Abusing me for harsh ill-nature
      On holy men,
While deil a hair yoursel ye're better,
      But mair profane.

But let the kirk-folk ring their bells,
Let's sing about our noble sel's :
We'll cry nae jads frae heathen hills
      To help, or roose us;
But browster wives an' whisky stills,
      They are the muses.

Your friendship, sir, I winna quat it,
An' if ye mak objections at it,
Then hand in nieve some day we'll knot it,
    An' witness take,
And when wi' usquabae we've wat it,
      It winna break.

But if the beast and branks be spar'd
Till kye be gaun without the herd,
And a' the vittel in the yard,
    And theekit right,
I mean your ingle-side to guard
    Ae winter night.

Then muse-inspirin' aquavitæ
Shall mak us baith sae blythe and witty,
Till ye forget ye're auld an' gatty,
    And be as canty
As ye were nine years less than thretty—
    Sweet ane an' twenty!

But stooks are cowpet wi' the blast,
And now the sinn keeks in the west,
Then I maun rin amang the rest,
    An' quat my chanter;
Sae I subscribe mysel in haste,
    Yours, Rab the Ranter.

Sept. 13, 1785.

EPISTLE TO THE REV. JOHN M'MATH

ENCLOSING A COPY OF 'HOLY WILLIE'S PRAYER,' WHICH
HE HAD REQUESTED, SEPT. 17, 1785

WHILE at the stook the shearers cow'r
To shun the bitter blaudin' show'r,
Or in gulravage rinnin' scowr;
    To pass the time,
To you I dedicate the hour
    In idle rhyme.

My musie, tir'd wi' mony a sonnet,
On gown, an' ban', an' douse black bonnet,
Is grown right eerie now she's done it,
       Lest they shou'd blame her,
An' rouse their holy thunder on it
       And anathem her.

I own 'twas rash, an' rather hardy,
That I a simple, country bardie,
Shou'd meddle wi' a pack sae sturdy,
       Wha, if they ken me,
Can.easy, wi' a single wordie,
       Louse h—ll upon me.

But I gae mad at their grimaces,
Their sighin' cantin', grace-proud faces,
Their three-mile prayers, an' half-mile graces,
       Their raxin conscience,
Whase greed, revenge, and pride disgraces
       Waur nor their nonsense.

There's Gaw'n, misca'd waur than a beast,
Wha has mair honor in his breast
Than mony scores as guid's the priest
       Wha sae abused him :
And may a bard no crack his jest
       What way they've us'd him ?

See him, the poor man's friend in need,
The gentleman in word an' deed—
An' shall his fame an' honor bleed
       By worthless skellums,
An' not a muse erect her head
       To cowe the blellums ?

O Pope, had I thy satire's darts
To gie the rascals their deserts,
I'd rip their rotten, hollow hearts,
       An' tell aloud
Their jugglin' hocus-pocus arts
       To cheat the crowd.

God knows, I'm no the thing I shou'd be,
Nor am I even the thing I cou'd be,
But twenty times I rather would be
   An atheist clean,
Than under gospel colours hid be
   Just for a screen.

An honest man may like a glass,
An honest man may like a lass,
But mean revenge, an' malice fause
   He'll still disdain,
An' then cry zeal for gospel laws,
   Like some we ken.

They take religion in their mouth;
They talk o' mercy, grace, an' truth,
For what ? to gie their malice skouth
   On some puir wight,
An' hunt him down, owre right and ruth,
   To ruin streicht.

All hail, Religion ! maid divine !
Pardon a muse sae mean as mine,
Who in her rough imperfect line
   Thus daurs to name thee;
To stigmatise false friends of thine
   Can ne'er defame thee.

Tho' blotch't and foul wi' mony a stain,
An' far unworthy of thy train,
With trembling voice I tune my strain,
   To join with those
Who boldly dare thy cause maintain
   In spite of foes :

In spite o' crowds, in spite o' mobs,
In spite o' undermining jobs,
In spite o' dark banditti stabs
   At worth an' merit,
By scoundrels, even wi' holy robes,
   But hellish spirits.

O Ayr! my dear, my native ground,
Within thy presbyterial bound
A candid liberal band is found
       Of public teachers,
As men, as christians too, renown'd,
       An' manly preachers.

Sir, in that circle you are nam'd;
Sir, in that circle you are fam'd;
An' some, by whom your doctrine's blam'd
       (Which gies ye honour)
Even, sir, by them your heart's esteem'd,
       An' winning manner.

Pardon this freedom I have ta'en,
An' if impertinent I've been,
Impute it not, good sir, in ane
       Whase heart ne'er wrang'd ye,
But to his utmost would befriend
       Ought that belang'd ye.

SECOND EPISTLE TO DAVIE

A BROTHER POET

AULD NEIBOUR,
    I'm three times doubly o'er your debtor,
For your auld-farrant, frien'ly letter;
Tho' I maun say't I doubt ye flatter,
       Ye speak sae fair;
For my puir, silly, rhymin' clatter
       Some less maun sair.

Hale be your heart, hale be your fiddle,
Lang may your elbuck jink an' diddle,
To cheer you thro' the weary widdle
       O' warl'y cares;
Till bairns' bairns kindly cuddle
       Your auld gray hairs.

But Davie, lad, I'm rede ye're glaikit;
I'm tauld the muse ye hae negleckit;
An' gif it's sae, ye sud be licket
   Until ye fyke;
Sic hauns as you sud ne'er be faiket,
  Be hain't what like.

For me, I'm on Parnassus' brink,
Rivin' the words to gar them clink;
Whyles daez't wi' love, whyles daez't wi' drink,
   Wi' jads or masons;
An' whyles, but aye owre late, I think
  Braw sober lessons.

Of a' the thoughtless sons o' man,
Commen' to me the bardie clan;
Except it be some idle plan
   O' rhymin' clink—
The devil-haet, that I sud ban—
  They ever think.

Nae thought, nae view, nae scheme o' livin',
Nae cares to gie us joy or grievin'.
But just the pouchie put the nieve in,
   An' while ought's there,
Then, hiltie, skiltie, we gae scrievin',
  An' fash nae mair.

Leeze me on rhyme! it's ay a treasure,
My chief, amaist my only pleasure;
At hame, a-fiel', at wark, or leisure,
   The muse, poor hizzie!
Tho' rough an' raploch be her measure,
  She's seldom lazy.

Haud to the muse, my dainty Davie:
The warl' may play you monie a shavie:
But for the muse, she'll never leave ye,
   Tho' e'er sae puir,
Na, even tho' limpin' wi' the spavie
  Frae door to door.

YOUNG PEGGY

YOUNG Peggy blooms our boniest lass,
  Her blush is like the morning,
The rosy dawn, the springing grass,
  With early gems adorning.
Her eyes outshine the radiant beams
  That gild the passing shower,
And glitter o'er the crystal streams,
  And cheer each fresh'ning flower.

Her lips, more than the cherries bright,
  A richer dye has graced them;
They charm th' admiring gazer's sight,
  And sweetly tempt to taste them;
Her smile is as the evening mild,
  When feather'd pairs are courting,
And little lambkins wanton wild,
  In playful bands disporting.

Were Fortune lovely Peggy's foe,
  Such sweetness would relent her;
As blooming spring unbends the brow
  Of surly savage winter.
Detraction's eye no aim can gain,
  Her winning pow'rs to lessen;
And fretful Envy grins in vain
  The poison'd tooth to fasten.

Ye Pow'rs of Honor, Love, and Truth
  From ev'ry ill defend her !
Inspire the highly-favour'd youth
  The destinies intend her :
Still fan the sweet connubial flame
  Responsive in each bosom;
And bless the dear parental name
  With many a filial blossom.

FAREWELL TO BALLOCHMYLE

THE Catrine woods were yellow seen,
  The flowers decay'd on Catrine lee,
Nae lav'rock sang on hillock green,
  But nature sicken'd on the e'e.
Thro' faded groves Maria sang,
  Hersel in beauty's bloom the while;
And ay the wild-wood echoes rang,
  Fareweel the braes o' Ballochmyle.

Low in your wintry beds, ye flowers,
  Again ye'll flourish fresh and fair;
Ye birdies dumb, in with'ring bowers,
  Again ye'll charm the vocal air.
But here, alas! for me nae mair
  Shall birdie charm, or floweret smile;
Fareweel the bonie banks of Ayr,
  Fareweel, fareweel! sweet Ballochmyle!

FRAGMENTS—HER FLOWING LOCKS

HER flowing locks, the raven's wing,
Adown her neck and bosom hing;
How sweet unto that breast to cling,
  And round that neck entwine her!

Her lips are roses wat wi' dew,
O, what a feast, her bonie mou!
Her cheeks a mair celestial hue,
  A crimson still diviner!

HALLOWE'EN

Yes ! let the rich deride, the proud disdain,
The simple pleasures of the lowly train;
To me more dear, congenial to my heart,
One native charm, than all the gloss of art.—GOLDSMITH.

UPON that night, when fairies light
　　On Cassilis Downans dance,
Or owre the lays, in splendid blaze,
　　On sprightly coursers prance;
Or for Colean the route is ta'en,
　　Beneath the moon's pale beams;
There, up the Cove, to stray an' rove,
　　Amang the rocks and streams
　　　　　To sport that night :

Amang the bonie winding banks,
　　Where Doon rins, wimplin', clear;
Where Bruce ance ruled the martial ranks,
　　An' shook his Carrick spear;
Some merry, friendly, country-folks
　　Together did convene,
To burn their nits, an' pou their stocks,
　　An' haud their Hallowe'en
　　　　　Fu' blythe that night.

The lasses feat, an' cleanly neat,
　　Mair braw than when they're fine;
Their faces blythe, fu' sweetly kythe,
　　Hearts leal, an' warm, an' kin' :
The lads sae trig, wi' wooer-babs
　　Weel-knotted on their garten;
Some unco blate, an' some wi' gabs
　　Gar lasses' hearts gang startin'
　　　　　Whyles fast at night.

Then, first an' foremost, thro' the kail,
  Their 'stocks' maun a' be sought ance;
They steek their een, an' grape an' wale
  For muckle anes, an' straught anes.
Poor hav'rel Will fell aft the drift,
  An' wandered thro' the 'bow-kail,'
An' pou't for want o' better shift,
  A runt, was like a sow-tail
        Sae bow't that night.

Then, straught or crooked, yird or nane,
  They roar an' cry a' throw'ther;
The vera wee-things, toddlin, rin,
  Wi' stocks out owre their shouther:
An' gif the custok's sweet or sour,
  Wi' joctelegs they taste them;
Syne coziely, aboon the door,
  Wi' cannie care, they've plac'd them
        To lie that night.

The lasses staw frae 'mang them a',
  To pou their stalks o' corn;
But Rab slips out, an' jinks about,
  Behint the muckle thorn:
He grippet Nelly hard an' fast;
  Loud skirl'd a' the lasses;
But her tap-pickle maist was lost,
  Whan kiutlin' in the 'fause-house'
        Wi' him that night.

The auld guid-wife's weel-hoordet nits
  Are round an' round divided,
An' mony lads an' lasses' fates
  Are there that night decided:
Some kindle couthie, side by side,
  An' burn thegither trimly;
Some start awa' wi' saucy pride,
  An' jump out owre the chimlie
        Fu' high that night.

Jean slips in twa, wi' tentie e'e;
 Wha 'twas, she wadna tell;
But this is *Jock*, and this is *me*,
 She says in to hersel:
He bleez'd owre her, an' she owre him,
 As they wad never mair part;
Till fuff! he started up the lum,
 And Jean had e'en a sair heart
   To see't that night.

Poor Willie, wi' his bow-kail runt,
 Was brunt wi' primsie Mallie;
An' Mary, nae doubt, took the drunt,
 To be compared to Willie:
Mall's nit lap out, wi' pridefu' fling,
 An' her ain fit, it brunt it;
While Willie lap, an' swoor by 'jing,'
 'Twas just the way he wanted
   To be that night.

Nell had the 'fause-house' in her min',
 She pits hersel an' Rob in;
In loving bleeze they sweetly join,
 Till white in ase they're sobbin':
Nell's heart was dancin' at the view;
 She whisper'd Rob to leuk for't:
Rob, stownins, prie'd her bonie mou',
 Fu' cozie in the neuk for't,
   Unseen that night.

But Merran sat behint their backs,
 Her thoughts on Andrew Bell;
She lea'es them gashin' at their cracks,
 An' slips out-by hersel:
She thro' the yard the nearest taks,
 An' for the kiln she goes then,
An' darklins grapet for the 'bauks,'
 And in the 'blue clue' throws then,
   Right fear't that night.

An' ay she win't, an' ay she swat—
   I wat she made nae jaukin';
Till something held within the pat,
   Guid L—d! but she was quaukin'!
But whether 'twas the deil himsel,
   Or whether 'twas a bauk-en',
Or whether it was Andrew Bell,
   She did na wait on talkin'
         To spier that night.

Wee Jenny to her graunie says,
   'Will ye go wi' me, graunie?
I'll eat the apple at the glass,
   I gat frae uncle Johnie:'
She fuff't her pipe wi' sic a lunt,
   In wrath she was sae vap'rin',
She notic't na an aizle brunt
   Her braw, new, worset apron
         Out thro' that night.

'Ye little skelpie-limmer's-face!
   I daur you try sic sportin',
As seek the foul thief ony place,
   For him to spae your fortune:
Nae doubt but ye may get a sight!
   Great cause ye hae to fear it;
For mony a ane has gotten a fright,
   An' liv'd an' died deleeret,
         On sic a night.

'Ae hairst afore the Sherra-moor,
   I mind't as weel's yestreen—
I was a gilpey then, I'm sure
   I was na past fyfteen:
The simmer had been cauld an' wat,
   An' stuff was unco green;
An' ay a rantin' kirn we gat,
   An' just on Hallowe'en
         It fell that night.

'Our "stibble-rig" was Rab M'Graen,
    A clever, sturdy fallow;
His sin gat Eppie Sim wi' wean,
    That liv'd in Achmacalla:
He gat hemp-seed, I mind it weel,
    An' he made unco light o't;
But mony a day was by himsel,
    He was sae sairly frighted
            That vera night.'

Then up gat fechtin' Jamie Fleck,
    An' he swoor by his conscience,
That he could saw hemp-seed a peck;
    For it was a' but nonsense :
The auld guidman raught doon the pock,
    An' out a handfu' gied him;
Syne bad him slip frae 'mang the folk,
    Sometime when nae ane see'd him,
            An' try't that night.

He marches thro' amang the stacks,
    Tho' he was something sturtin';
The graip he for a harrow taks,
    An' haurls at his curpin :
And ev'ry now an' then, he says,
    'Hemp-seed I saw thee,
An' her that is to be my lass
    Come after me, an' draw thee
            As fast this night.'

He whistl'd up 'Lord Lennox' March,
    To keep his courage cheery;
Altho' his hair began to arch,
    He was sae fley'd an' eerie :
Till presently he hears a squeak,
    An' then a grane an' gruntle;
He by his shouther gae a keek,
    An' tumbled wi' a wintle
            Out-owre that night.

He roar'd a horrid murder-shout,
  In dreadfu' desperation !
An' young an' auld come rinnin' out,
  An' hear the sad narration :
He swoor 'twas hilchin Jean M'Craw,
  Or crouchie Merran Humphie—
Till stop ! she trotted thro' them a';
  And wha was it but grumphie
        Asteer that night ?

Meg fain wad to the barn gaen,
  To winn three wechts o' naething;
But for to meet the deil her lane,
  She pat but little faith in :
She gies the herd a pickle nits,
  An' twa red cheekit apples,
To watch, while for the barn she sets,
  In hopes to see Tam Kipples
        That vera night.

She turns the key wi' cannie thraw,
  An' owre the threshold ventures;
But first on Sawnie gies a ca',
  Syne bauldly in she enters :
A ratton rattl'd up the wa',
  An' she cry'd L—d preserve her !
An' ran thro' midden-hole an' a',
  An' pray'd wi' zeal and fervour,
        Fu' fast that night.

They hoy't out Will, wi' sair advice;
  They hecht him some fine braw ane;
It chanc'd the stack he faddom't thrice,
  Was timmer-propt for thrawin':
He taks a swirlie auld moss-oak
  For some black, grousome carlin;
An' loot a winze, an' drew a stroke,
  Till skin in blypes cam haurlin'
        Aff's nieves that night.

A wanton widow Leezie was,
    As cantie as a kittlen;
But och! that night, amang the shaws,
    She gat a fearful settlin'!
She thro' the whins, an' by the cairn,
    An' owre the hill gaed scrievin';
Whare three lairds' lan's meet at a burn,
    To dip her left sark sleeve in,
                Was bent that night.

Whyles owre a linn the burnie plays,
    As thro' the glen it wimpl't;
Whyles round a rocky scaur it strays,
    Whyles in a wiel it dimpl't;
Whyles glitter'd to the nightly rays,
    Wi' bickerin,' dancin' dazzle;
Whyles cookit underneath the braes,
    Below the spreading hazle
                Unseen that night.

Amang the brachens, on the brae,
    Between her an' the moon,
The deil, or else an outler quey,
    Gat up an' ga'e a croon:
Poor Leezie's heart maist lap the hool;
    Near lav'rock-height she jumpet,
But mist a fit, an' in the pool
    Out-owre the lugs she plumpet,
                Wi' a plunge that night.

In order, on the clean hearth-stane,
    The 'luggies' three are ranged;
An' ev'ry time great care is ta'en
    To see them duly changed:
Auld uncle John, wha wedlock's joys
    Sin' 'Mar's-year' did desire,
Because he gat the toom dish thrice,
    He heaved them on the fire,
                In wrath that night.

Wi' merry sangs, an' friendly cracks,
    I wat they did na weary;
And unco tales, an' funnie jokes—
    Their sports were cheap an' cheery:
Till butter'd sowens, wi' fragrant lunt,
    Set a' their gabs a-steerin';
Syne, wi' a social glass o' strunt,
    They parted aff careerin'
            Fu' blythe that night.

TO A MOUSE

ON TURNING HER UP IN HER NEST WITH THE PLOUGH
NOVEMBER, 1785

WEE sleeket, cowrin' tim'rous beastie,
O, what a panic's in thy breastie!
Thou need na start awa' sae hasty,
            Wi' bickerin' brattle!
I wad be laith to rin an' chase thee,
            Wi' murderin' pattle!

I'm truly sorry man's dominion,
Has broken nature's social union,
An' justifies that ill opinion,
            Which makes thee startle
At me, thy poor, earth-born companion,
            An' fellow-mortal!

I doubt na, whyles, but thou may thieve;
What then? poor beastie, thou maun live!
A daimen icker in a thrave
            'S a sma' request;
I'll get a blessin' wi' the lave,
            An' never miss't!

Thy wee bit housie, too, in ruin !
Its silly wa's the win's are strewin' !
An' naething, now, to big a new ane,
        O' foggage green !
An' bleak December's winds ensuin',
        Baith snell an' keen !

Thou saw the fields laid bare an' waste,
An' weary winter comin' fast,
An' cozie here, beneath the blast,
        Thou thought to dwell—
Till crash ! the cruel coulter past
        Out thro' thy cell.

That wee bit heap o' leaves an' stibble,
Has cost thee mony a weary nibble !
Now thou's turn'd out, for a' thy trouble,
        But house or hald,
To thole the winter's sleety dribble,
        An' cranreuch cauld !

But Mousie, thou art no thy lane,
In proving foresight may be vain;
The best-laid schemes o' mice an' men
        Gang aft agley,
An' lea'e us nought but grief an' pain,
        For promis'd joy !

Still thou art blest, compar'd wi' me !
The present only toucheth thee :
But och ! I backward cast my e'e,
        On prospects drear !
An' forward, tho' I canna see,
        I guess an' fear !

EPITAPH ON JOHN DOVE, INNKEEPER

> HERE lies Johnie Pigeon;
> What was his religion
>   Whaever desires to ken,
> To some other warl'
> Maun follow the carl,
>   For here Johnie Pigeon had nane!
>
> Strong ale was ablution—
> Small beer—persecution,
>   A dram was '*memento mori*';
> But a full-flowing bowl
> Was the saving his soul,
>   And port was celestial glory.

EPITAPH FOR A WAG IN MAUCHLINE

> LAMENT him, Mauchline husbands a',
>   He aften did assist ye;
> For had ye staid hale weeks awa',
>   Your wives they ne'er had miss'd ye.
>
> Ye Mauchline bairns, as on ye press
>   To school in bands thegither,
> O tread ye lightly on his grass,—
>   Perhaps he was your father!

ADAM ARMOUR'S PRAYER

> GUDE pity me, because I'm little!
> For though I am an elf o' mettle,
> An' can, like ony wabster's shuttle,
>   Jink there or here,
> Yet, scarce as lang's a gude kail-whittle,
>   I'm unco queer.

An' now Thou kens our woefu' case;
For Geordie's 'jurr' we're in disgrace,
Because we 'stang'd' her through the place,
    An' hurt her spleuchan;
For whilk we daurna show our face
    Within the clachan.

An' now we're dernd in dens and hollows,
And hunted, as was William Wallace,
Wi' constables—thae blackguard fallows,
    An' sodgers baith;
But Gude preserve us frae the gallows,
    That shamefu' death!

Auld grim black-bearded Geordie's sel'—
O shake him owre the mouth o' hell!
There let him hing, an' roar, an' yell
    Wi' hideous din,
And if he offers to rebel,
    Then heave him in.

When Death comes in wi' glimmerin' blink,
An' tips auld drucken Nanse the wink,
May Sautan gie her doup a clink
    Within his yett,
An' fill her up wi' brimstone drink,
    Red-reekin' het.

Though Jock an' hav'rel Jean are merry—
Some devil seize them in a hurry,
An' waft them in th' infernal wherry
    Straught through the lake,
An' gie their hides a noble curry
    Wi' oil of aik!

As for the 'jurr'—puir worthless body!
She's got mischief enough already;
Wi' stanget hips, and buttocks bluidy,
    She's suffer'd sair;
But, may she wintle in a woody,
    If she wh—e mair!

THE JOLLY BEGGARS—A CANTATA

Recitativo.

When lyart leaves bestrow the yird,
Or wavering like the bauckie-bird,
 Bedim cauld Boreas' blast;
When hailstanes drive wi' bitter skyte,
And infant frosts begin to bite,
 In hoary crancreuch drest;
Ae night at e'en a merry core
 O' randie, gangrel bodies,
In Poosie-Nansie's held the splore,
 To drink their orra duddies :
  Wi' quaffing and laughing,
   They ranted an' they sang,
  Wi' jumping an' thumping,
   The vera girdle rang.

First, niest the fire, in auld red rags,
Ane sat, weel brac'd wi' mealy bags,
 And knapsack a' in order;
His doxy lay within his arm;
Wi' usquebae an' blankets warm
 She blinket on her sodger :
An' ay he gies the tozie drab
 The tither skelpin' kiss,
While she held up her greedy gab,
 Just like an aumous dish :
  Ilk smack still did crack still,
   Just like a cadger's whip;
  Then staggering an' swaggering,
   He roar'd this ditty up—

Air.

Tune—'Soldier's Joy.'

I am a son of Mars who have been in many wars,
　And show my cuts and scars wherever I come;
This here was for a wench, and that other in a trench
　When welcoming the French at the sound of the
　　drum.

　　　Lal de daudle, etc.

My prenticeship I past where my leader breath'd his
　last,
　When the bloody die was cast on the heights of
　　Abram :
And I servèd out my trade when the gallant game was
　play'd
　And the Moro low was laid at the sound of the drum.

I lastly was with Curtis among the floating batt'ries
　And there I left for witness an arm and a limb;
Yet let my country need me, with Elliot to head me,
　I'd clatter on my stumps at the sound of a drum.

And now tho' I must beg, with a wooden arm and leg,
　And many a tatter'd rag hanging over my bum,
I'm as happy with my wallet, my bottle and my callet,
　As when I used in scarlet to follow a drum.

What tho', with hoary locks, I must stand the winter
　shocks,
　Beneath the woods and rocks, oftentimes for a home,
When the tother bag I sell, and the tother bottle tell,
　I could meet a troop of hell, at the sound of a drum.

Recitativo.

He ended; and the kebars sheuk,
    Aboon the chorus roar;
While frighted rattons backward leuk,
    An' seek the benmost bore :
A fairy fiddler frae the neuk,
    He skirl'd out, encore !
But up arose the martial chuck,
    An' laid the loud uproar.

Air.

Tune—'Sodger Laddie.'

I once was a maid, tho' I cannot tell when,
And still my delight is in proper young men :
Some one of a troop of dragoons was my daddie,
No wonder I'm fond of a sodger laddie.
        Sing, lal de dal, etc.

The first of my loves was a swaggering blade,
To rattle the thundering drum was his trade;
His leg was so tight, and his cheek was so ruddy,
Transported I was with my sodger laddie.

But the godly old chaplain left him in the lurch;
The sword I forsook for the sake of the church :
He ventur'd the soul, and I risket the body,
'Twas then I prov'd false to my sodger laddie.

Full soon I grew sick of my sanctified sot,
The regiment at large for a husband I got;
From the gilded spontoon to the fife I was ready,
I askèd no more but a sodger laddie.

But the peace it reduc'd me to beg in despair,
Till I met my old boy in a Cunningham fair;
His rags regimental, they flutter'd so gaudy,
My heart it rejoic'd at a sodger laddie.

And now I have liv'd—I know not how long,
And still I can join in a cup and a song;
But whilst with both hands I can hold the glass
      steady,
Here's to thee, my hero, my sodger laddie.

Recitativo.

Poor Merry-Andrew, in the neuk,
    Sat guzzling wi' a tinkler-hizzie;
They mind't na wha the chorus teuk,
    Between themselves they were sae busy :
At length, wi' drink an' courting dizzy,
    He stoiter'd up an' made a face;
Then turn'd an' laid a smack on Grizzie,
    Syne tun'd his pipes wi' grave grimace.

Air.

Tune—'Auld Sir Symon.'

Sir Wisdom's a fool when he's fou;
    Sir Knave is a fool in a session;
He's there but a prentice I trow,
    But I am a fool by profession.

My grannie she bought me a beuk,
    An' I held awa' to the school;
I fear I my talent misteuk,
    But what will ye hae of a fool?

For drink I would venture my neck;
  A hizzie's the half of my craft;
But what could ye other expect,
  Of ane that's avowedly daft?

I'ance was tyed up like a stirk,
  For civilly swearing and quaffing;
I ance was abus'd i' the kirk,
  For towsing a lass i' my daffin.

Poor Andrew that tumbles for sport,
  Let naebody name wi' a jeer;
There's even, I'm tauld, i' the Court
  A tumbler ca'd the Premier.

Observ'd ye yon reverend lad
  Mak faces to tickle the mob;
He rails at our mountebank squad—
  It's rivalship just i' the job.

And now my conclusion I'll tell,
  For faith I'm confoundedly dry;
The chiel that's a fool for himsel,
  Guid L—d! he's far dafter than I.

Recitativo.

Then niest outspak a raucle carlin,
Wha kent fu' weel to cleek the sterlin;
For monie a pursie she had hooked,
An' had in mony a well been douked:
Her love had been a Highland laddie,
But weary fa' the waefu' woodie;
Wi' sighs an' sobs she thus began
To wail her braw John Highlandman.

Air.

Tune—'O an ye were dead, Gudeman.'

A Highland lad my love was born,
The lalland laws he held in scorn;
But he still was faithfu' to his clan,
My gallant, braw John Highlandman.

Chorus.

Sing hey my braw John Highlandman!
Sing ho my braw John Highlandman!
There's not a lad in a' the lan'
Was match for my John Highlandman.

With his philibeg an' tartan plaid,
An' guid claymore down by his side,
The ladies' hearts he did trepan,
My gallant, braw John Highlandman.
          Sing hey, etc.

We rangèd a' from Tweed to Spey,
An' liv'd like lords an' ladies gay;
For a lalland face he fearèd none—
My gallant, braw John Highlandman.
          Sing hey, etc.

They banish'd him beyond the sea,
But ere the bud was on the tree,
Adown my cheeks the pearls ran,
Embracing my John Highlandman.
          Sing hey, etc.

But, och! they catch'd him at the last,
And bound him in a dungeon fast:
My curse upon them every one,
They've hang'd my braw John Highlandman!
          Sing hey, etc.

And now a widow I must mourn
The pleasures that will ne'er return;
No comfort but a hearty can,
When I think on John Highlandman.
      Sing hey, etc.

Recitativo.

A pigmy scraper wi' his fiddle,
Wha us'd at trysts an' fairs to driddle,
Her strappin' limb and gausy middle
      (He reach'd nae higher)
Had hol'd his heartie like a riddle,
      An' blawn't on fire.

Wi' hand on hainch, and upward e'e,
He croon'd his gamut, one, two, three,
Then in an arioso key,
      The wee Apollo
Set off wi' allegretto glee
      His giga solo.

Air.

Tune—'Whistle owre the lave o't.'

Let me ryke up to dight that tear,
An' go wi' me an' be my dear;
An' then your every care an' fear
    May whistle owre the lave o't.

Chorus.

I am a fiddler to my trade,
An' a' the tunes that e'er I played,
The sweetest still to wife or maid,
    Was whistle owre the lave o't.

At kirns an' weddin's we'se be there,
An' O sae nicely's we will fare !
We'll bowse about till Daddie Care
    Sing whistle owre the lave o't.
                I am, etc.

Sae merrily's the banes we'll pyke,
An' sun oursel's about the dyke;
An' at our leisure, when ye like,
    We'll whistle owre the lave o't.
                I am, etc.

But bless me wi' your heav'n o' charms,
An' while I kittle hair on thairms,
Hunger, cauld, an' a' sic harms,
    May whistle owre the lave o't.
                I am, etc.

Recitativo.

Her charms had struck a sturdy caird,
    As weel as poor gut-scraper;
He taks the fiddler by the beard,
    An' draws a roosty rapier—
He swoor by a' was swearing worth,
    To speet him like a pliver,
Unless he would from that time forth
    Relinquish her for ever.

Wi' ghastly e'e, poor tweedle-dee
    Upon his hunkers bended,
An' pray'd for grace, wi' ruefu' face,
    An' so the quarrel ended.
But tho' his little heart did grieve
    When round the tinkler prest her,
He feign'd to snirtle in his sleeve,
    When thus the caird address'd her :

Air.

Tune—'Clout the Cauldron.'

My bonie lass, I work in brass,
  A tinkler is my station;
I've travell'd round all Christian ground
  In this my occupation;
I've taen the gold, an' been enrolled
  In many a noble squadron;
But vain they search'd when off I march'd
  To go an' clout the cauldron.
                    I've taen the gold, etc.

Despise that shrimp, that wither'd imp,
  With a' his noise an' cap'rin';
An' take a share with those that bear
  The budget and the apron !
And *by* that stowp ! my faith an' houpe,
  And *by* that dear Kilbaigie,
If e'er ye want, or meet wi' scant,
  May I ne'er weet my craigie.
                    And by that stowp, etc.

Recitativo.

The caird prevail'd—th' unblushing fair
  In his embraces sank;
Partly wi' love o'ercome sae sair,
  An' partly she was drunk :
Sir Violino, with an air,
  That show'd a man o' spunk,
Wish'd unison between the pair,
  An' made the bottle clunk
                    To their health that night.

But hurchin' Cupid shot a shaft,
    That play'd a dame a shavie—
The fiddler rak'd her, fore and aft,
    Behint the chicken cavie.
Her lord, a wight o' Homer's craft,
    Tho' limpin' wi' the spavie,
He hirpl'd up, an' lap like daft,
    An' shor'd them *Dainty Davie*
                O' boot that night.

He was a care-defying blade
    As ever Bacchus listed !
Tho' Fortune sair upon him laid,
    His heart, she ever miss'd it.
He had no wish but—to be glad,
    Nor want but—when he thirsted;
He hated nought but—to be sad,
    An' thus the muse suggested
                His sang that night.

Air.

Tune—'For a' that, an a' that.

I am a Bard of no regard,
    Wi' gentle folks an' a' that;
But Homer-like, the glowrin' byke,
    Frae town to town I draw that.

Chorus.

For a' that, an' a' that,
    An' twice as muckle's a' that;
I've lost but ane, I've twa behin',
    I've wife eneugh for a' that.

I never drank the Muses' stank,
    Castalia's burn, an' a' that;
But there it streams an' richly reams,
    My Helicon I ca' that.
              For a' that, etc.

Great love I bear to a' the fair,
　　Their humble slave, an' a' that;
But lordly will, I hold it still,
　　A mortal sin to thraw that.
　　　　　　　　For a' that, etc.

In raptures sweet, this hour we meet,
　　Wi' mutual love, an' a' that;
But for how lang the flie may stang,
　　Let inclination law that.
　　　　　　　　For a' that, etc.

Their tricks an' craft hae put me daft,
　　They've taen me in, an' a' that;
But clear your decks, an' here's the Sex!
　　I like the jads for a' that.

Chorus.

For a' that, an' a' that,
　　An' twice as muckle's a' that;
My dearest bluid, to do them guid,
　　They're welcome till't for a' that.

Recitativo.

So sang the bard—and Nansie's wa's
Shook with a thunder of applause,
　　Re-echo'd from each mouth!
They toom'd their pocks, they pawn'd their
　　duds,
They scarcely left to co'or their fuds,
　　To quench their lowin' drowth:
Then owre again, the jovial thrang
　　The poet did request
To lowse his pack and wale a sang
　　A ballad o' the best;

He rising, rejoicing,
   Between his twa Deborahs,
Looks round him, an' found them
   Impatient for the chorus.

Air.

Tune—'Jolly Mortals, fill your Glasses.'

See the smoking bowl before us,
   Mark our jovial ragged ring!
Round and round take up the chorus,
   And in raptures let us sing.

Chorus.

A fig for those by law protected!
   Liberty's a glorious feast!
Courts for cowards were erected,
   Churches built to please the priest.

What is title, what is treasure,
   What is reputation's care?
If we lead a life of pleasure,
   'Tis no matter how or where!
         A fig for, etc.

With the ready trick and fable,
   Round we wander all the day;
And at night in barn or stable,
   Hug our doxies on the hay.
         A fig for, etc.

Does the train-attended carriage
   Thro' the country lighter rove?
Does the sober bed of marriage
   Witness brighter scenes of love?
         A fig for, etc.

Life is all a variorum
    We regard not how it goes;
Let them cant about decorum,
    Who have character to lose.
                    A fig for, etc.

Here's to budgets, bags, and wallets !
    Here's to all the wandering train,
Here's our ragged brats and callets,
    One and all cry out, Amen !

Chorus.

A fig for those by law protected !
    Liberty's a glorious feast !
Courts for cowards were erected,
    Churches built to please the priest.

THO' WOMEN'S MINDS

THO' women's minds, like winter winds,
    May shift and turn, an' a' that,
The noblest breast adores them maist—
    A consequence I draw that.

Chorus.—For a' that, an' a' that,
            And twice as meikle's a' that;
        The bonie lass that I loe best,
            She'll be my ain for a' that.

Great love I bear to a' the fair,
    Their humble slave, an' a' that;
But lordly will, I hold it still
    A mortal sin to thraw that.
                    For a' that, etc.

But there is ane aboon the lave,
　　Has wit, and sense, an' a' that;
A bonie lass, I like her best,
　　And wha a crime dare ca' that?
　　　　　　　　For a' that, etc.

In rapture sweet this hour we meet,
　　Wi' mutual love, an' a' that,
But for how lang the flie may stang,
　　Let inclination law that.
　　　　　　　　For a' that, etc.

Their tricks an' craft hae put me daft,
　　They've taen me in, an' a' that;
But clear your decks, and—here's 'The sex!
　　I like the jads for a' that.
　　　　　　　　For a' that, etc.

KISSIN' MY KATIE

Tune—'The bob o' Dumblane.'

O MERRY hae I been teethin' a heckle
　　An' merry hae I been shapin' a spoon;
O merry hae I been cloutin' a kettle,
　　An kissin' my Katie when a' was done.
O a' the lang day I ca' at my hammer,
　　An' a' the lang day I whistle and sing;
O a' the lang night I cuddle my kimmer,
　　An' a' the lang night as happy's a king.

Bitter in dool I lickit my winnins
　　O' marrying Bess, to gie her a slave:
Blest be the hour she cool'd in her linnens,
　　And blythe be the bird that sings on her
　　　　grave!

Come to my arms, my Katie, my Katie;
O come to my arms and kiss me again !
Drucken or sober, here's to thee Katie !
An' blest be the day I did it again.

THE COTTAR'S SATURDAY NIGHT

INSCRIBED TO R. AIKEN, ESQ.

Let not Ambition mock their useful toil,
 Their homely joys, and destiny obscure;
Nor Grandeur hear, with a disdainful smile,
 The short and simple annals of the poor.—GRAY.

My lov'd my honor'd, much respected friend !
 No mercenary bard his homage pays;
With honest pride, I scorn each selfish end,
 My dearest meed, a friend's esteem and praise :
To you I sing, in simple Scottish lays,
 The lowly train in life's sequester'd scene;
 The native feelings strong, the guileless ways;
What Aiken in a cottage would have been;
Ah ! though his worth unknown, far happier there
 I ween !

November chill blaws loud wi' angry sugh;
 The short'ning winter-day is near a close;
The miry beasts retreating frae the pleugh;
 The black'ning trains o' craws to their repose :
 The toil-worn Cottar frae his labor goes—
This night his weekly moil is at an end,
 Collects his spades, his mattocks, and his hoes,
Hoping the morn in ease and rest to spend,
And weary o'er the moor, his course does hame-
 ward bend.

At length his lonely cot appears in view,
    Beneath the shelter of an aged tree;
Th' expectant wee-things, toddlin', stacher through
    To meet their 'dad,' wi' flichterin' noise and glee.
His wee bit ingle, blinkin' bonilie,
His clean hearth-stane, his thrifty wifie's smile,
    The lisping infant, prattling on his knee,
Does a' his weary kiaugh and care beguile,
An' makes him quite forget his labour and his toil.

Belyve, the elder bairns come drapping in,
    At service out, amang the farmers roun';
Some ca' the pleugh, some herd, some tentie rin
    A cannie errand to a neibor town :
    Their eldest hope, their Jenny, woman-grown,
In youthfu' bloom—love sparkling in her e'e—
    Comes hame; perhaps, to show a brave new gown,
Or deposite her sair-worn penny fee,
To help her parents dear, if they in hardship be.

With joy unfeign'd, brothers and sisters meet,
    And each for other's welfare kindly spiers :
The social hours, swift-wing'd, unnotic'd fleet;
    Each tells the uncos that he sees or hears.
    The parents partial eye their hopeful years;
Anticipation forward points the view;
    The mother, wi' her needle and her sheers
Gars auld claes look amaist as weel's the new;
The father mixes a' wi' admonition due.

Their master's and their mistress's command,
    The younkers a' are warned to obey;
And mind their labors wi' an eydent hand,
    And ne'er tho' out o' sight, to jauk or play;
    'And O ! be sure to fear the Lord alway,
And mind your duty, duly, morn and night;
    Lest in temptation's path you gang astray,
Implore His counsel and assisting might :
They never sought in vain that sought the Lord
    aright.'

But hark ! a rap comes gently to the door;
   Jenny, wha kens the meaning o' the same,
Tells how a neibor lad came o'er the moor,
   To do some errands, and convoy her hame.
   The wily mother sees the conscious flame
Sparkle in Jenny's e'e, and flush her cheek;
   With heart-struck anxious care, inquires his name,
While Jenny hafflins is afraid to speak;
Weel-pleased the mother hears, it's nae wild, worth-
    less rake.

Wi' kindly welcome, Jenny brings him ben;
   A strappin' youth, he takes the mother's eye;
Blythe Jenny sees the visit's no ill taen;
   The father cracks of horses, pleughs, and kye.
   The youngster's artless heart o'erflows wi' joy,
But blate and laithfu', scarce can weel behave;
   The mother, wi' a woman's wiles, can spy
What makes the youth sae bashfu' and sae grave;
Weel-pleas'd to think her bairn's respected like the
    lave.

O happy love ! where love like this is found :
   O heart-felt raptures ! bliss beyond compare !
I've pacèd much this weary, mortal round,
   And sage experience bids me this declare—
   'If Heaven a draught of heavenly pleasure spare—
One cordial in this melancholy vale,
   'Tis when a youthful, loving, modest pair,
In other's arms, breathe out the tender tale,
Beneath the milk-white thorn that scents the
    evening gale.'

Is there, in human form, that bears a heart,
   A wretch ! a villain ! lost to love and truth !
That can, with studied, sly, ensnaring art,
   Betray sweet Jenny's unsuspecting youth ?
   Curse on his perjur'd arts ! dissembling, smooth !

Are honor, virtue, conscience, all exil'd?
   Is there no pity, no relenting ruth,
Points to the parents fondling o'er their child!
Then paints the ruin'd maid, and their distraction
    wild?

But now the supper crowns their simple board,
   The halesome parritch, chief of Scotia's food;
The sowpe their only hawkie does afford,
   That, 'yont the hallan snugly chows her cood:
The dame brings forth, in complimental mood,
To grace the lad, her well-hain'd kebbuck, fell;
   And aft he's prest, and aft he ca's it guid:
The frugal wifie, garrulous, will tell
How 'twas a twomond auld, sin' lint was i' the
    bell.

The cheerfu' supper done, wi' serious face,
   They, round the ingle, form a circle wide;
The sire turns o'er, with patriarchal grace,
   The big ha'-bible, ance his father's pride:
   His bonnet rev'rently is laid aside,
His lyart haffets wearing thin and bare;
   Those strains that once did sweet in Zion glide,
He wales a portion with judicious care;
And 'Let us worship God!' he says with solemn
    air.

They chant their artless notes in simple guise,
   They tune their hearts, by far the noblest aim;
Perhaps 'Dundee's' wild-warbling measures rise,
   Or plaintive 'Martyrs,' worthy of the name;
   Or noble 'Elgin' beets the heavenward flame,
The sweetest far of Scotia's holy lays:
   Compar'd with these, Italian trills are tame;
The tickled ears no heart-felt raptures raise;
Nae unison hae they, with our Creator's praise.

The priest-like father reads the sacred page,
　　How Abram was the friend of God on high;
Or, Moses bade eternal warfare wage
　　With Amalek's ungracious progeny;
Or, how the royal bard did groaning lie
　　Beneath the stroke of Heaven's avenging ire;
　　Or Jacob's pathetic plaint, and wailing cry;
Or rapt Isaiah's wild, seraphic fire;
Or other sacred seers that tune the sacred lyre.

Perhaps the Christian volume is the theme,
　　How guiltless blood for guilty man was shed;
How He, who bore in Heaven the second name,
　　Had not on earth whereon to lay His head:
　　How His first followers and servants sped;
The precepts sage they wrote to many a land:
　　How he, who lone in Patmos banishèd,
Saw in the sun a mighty angel stand,
And heard great Bab'lon's doom pronounc'd by
　　Heaven's command.

Then kneeling down to Heaven's Eternal King,
　　The saint, the father, and the husband prays:
Hope 'springs exulting on triumphant wing,'
　　That thus they all shall meet in future days,
　　There, ever bask in uncreated rays,
No more to sigh, or shed the bitter tear,
　　Together hymning their Creator's praise,
In such society, yet still more dear;
While circling Time moves round in an eternal sphere.

Compar'd with this, how poor Religion's pride,
　　In all the pomp of method, and of art;
When men display to congregations wide
　　Devotion's ev'ry grace, except the heart!
The Power, incens'd, the pageant will desert,

The pompous strain, the sacerdotal stole;
  But haply, in some cottage far apart,
May hear, well-pleas'd, the language of the soul;
And in His Book of Life the inmates poor enroll.

Then homeward all take off their sev'ral way;
  The youngling cottagers retire to rest:
The parent pair their secret homage pay,
  And proffer up to Heaven the warm request,
  That He who stills the raven's clam'rous nest,
And decks the lily fair in flow'ry pride,
  Would, in the way His wisdom sees the best,
For them and for their little ones provide;
But chiefly, in their hearts with grace divine pre-
    side.

From scenes like these, old Scotia's grandeur springs,
  That makes her lov'd at home, rever'd abroad:
Princes and lords are but the breath of kings,
  'An honest man's the noblest work of God';
  And certes, in fair virtue's heavenly road,
The cottage leaves the palace far behind;
  What is a lordling's pomp? a cumbrous load,
Disguising oft the wretch of human kind,
Studied in arts of hell, in wickedness refin'd.

O Scotia! my dear, my native soil!
  For whom my warmest wish to Heaven is sent,
Long may thy hardy sons of rustic toil
  Be blest with health, and peace, and sweet
    content!
  And O! may Heaven their simple lives prevent
From luxury's contagion, weak and vile!
  Then, howe'er crowns and coronets be rent,
A virtuous populace may rise the while,
And stand a wall of fire around their much-lov'd
    isle.

O Thou! who pour'd the patriotic tide,
   That stream'd thro' Wallace's undaunted heart,
Who dar'd to, nobly, stem tyrannic pride,
   Or nobly die, the second glorious part:
   (The patriot's God, peculiarly Thou art,
His friend, inspirer, guardian, and reward!)
   O never, never Scotia's realm desert;
But still the patriot, and the patriot bard
In bright succession raise, her ornament and guard!

ADDRESS TO THE DEIL

> O Prince! O chief of many thronèd pow'rs
> That led th' embatt'd seraphim to war.—MILTON.

O Thou! whatever title suit thee—
Auld 'Hornie,' 'Satan,' 'Nick,' or 'Clootie,'
Wha in yon cavern grim and sootie,
    Clos'd under hatches,
Spairges about the brunstane cootie,
    To scaud poor wretches!

Hear me, auld 'Hangie,' for a wee,
And let poor damnèd bodies be;
I'm sure sma' pleasure it can gie,
    Ev'n to a deil,
To skelp an' scaud poor dogs like me,
    An' hear us squeel!

Great is thy pow'r an' great thy fame;
Far kenn'd an' noted is thy name;
An' tho' yon lowin' heuch's thy hame,
    Thou travels far;
An' faith! thou's neither lag nor lame,
    Nor blate, nor scaur.

Whyles, ranging like a roarin' lion,
For prey, a' holes an' corners tryin';
Whyles, on the strong-wing'd tempest flyin'
    Tirlin' the kirks;
Whyles, in the human bosom pryin',
    Unseen thou lurks.

I've heard my rev'rend grannie say,
In lanely glens ye like to stray;
Or where auld ruin'd castles gray
    Nod to the moon,
Ye fright the nightly wand'rer's way,
    Wi' eldritch croon.

When twilight did my grannie summon,
To say her pray'rs, douse, honest woman !
Aft 'yont the dyke she's heard you bummin',
    Wi' eerie drone;
Or, rustlin' thro' the boortrees comin',
    Wi' heavy groan.

Ae dreary, windy, winter night,
The stars shot down wi' sklentin' light,
Wi' you mysel, I gat a fright,
    Ayont the lough;
Ye, like a rash-buss, stood in sight,
    Wi' waving sough.

The cudgel in my neive did shake,
  Each bristl'd hair stood like a stake,
When wi' an eldritch, stoor 'quaick,
    quaick,'
    Amang the springs,
Awa' ye squatter'd like a drake,
    On whistlin' wings.

Let warlocks grim, an' wither'd hags.
Tell how wi' you, on ragweed nags,
They skim the muirs an' dizzy crags,
        Wi' wicked speed;
And in kirkyards renew their leagues,
        Owre howket dead.

Thence, countra wives, wi' toil an' pain,
May plunge an' plunge the kirn in vain;
For oh ! the yellow treasure's taen
        By witchin' skill;
An' dawtet, twal-pint 'hawkie's' gane
        As yell's the bill.

Thence, mystic knots mak great abuse
On young guidmen, fond, keen an' croose;
When the best wark-lume i' the house,
        By cantraip wit,
Is instant made no worth a louse,
        Just at the bit.

When thowes dissolve the snawy hoord,
An' float the jinglin' icy boord,
Then, water-kelpies haunt the foord,
        By your direction,
And 'nighted trav'llers are allur'd
        To their destruction.

And aft your moss-traversin' 'Spunkies'
Decoy the wight that late an' drunk is :
The bleezin', curst, mischievous monkies
        Delude his eyes,
Till in some miry slough he sunk is,
        Ne'er mair to rise.

When masons' mystic word an' grip
In storms an' tempests raise you up,
Some cock or cat your rage maun stop,
        Or, strange to tell !
The youngest 'brither' ye wad whip
        Aff straught to hell.

Lang syne in Eden's bonie yard,
When youthfu' lovers first were pair'd,
An' all the soul of love they shar'd,
  The raptur'd hour—
Sweet on the fragrant flow'ry swaird,
  In shady bow'r;

Then you, ye auld, snick-drawing dog!
Ye came to Paradise incog,
An' play'd on man a cursed brogue,
  (Black be your fa'!)
An' gied the infant warld a shog,
  'Maist ruin'd a'.

D'ye mind that day when in a bizz
Wi' reeket duds, an' reestet gizz,
Ye did present your smootie phiz
  'Mang better folk,
An' sklented on the man of Uzz
  Your spitefu' joke?

An' how ye gat him i' your thrall,
An' brak him out o' house an' hal',
While scabs an' botches did him gall,
  Wi' bitter claw;
An' lows'd his ill-tongu'd wicked scaull—
  Was warst ava?

But a' your doings to rehearse,
Your wily snares an' fechtin' fierce,
Sin' that day Michael did you pierce,
  Down to this time,
Wad ding a Lallan tongue, or Erse,
  In prose or rhyme.

An' now, auld 'Cloots,' I ken ye're thinkin',
A certain bardie's rantin', drinkin',
Some luckless hour will send him linkin'
  To your black pit;
But, faith! he'll turn a corner jinkin',
  An' cheat you yet.

But fare-you-weel, auld 'Nickie-ben!'
O wad ye tak a thought an' men'!
Ye aiblins might—I dinna ken—
      Still hae a stake:
I'm wae to think upo' yon den,
      Ev'n for your sake!

SCOTCH DRINK

Gie him strong drink until he wink,
  That's sinking in despair;
An' liquor guid to fire his bluid,
  That's prest wi' grief and care:
There let him bowse, an' deep carouse,
  Wi' bumpers flowing o'er,
Till he forgets his loves or debts,
  An' minds his griefs no more.
            SOLOMON'S PROVERBS, xxxi. 6, 7.

LET other poets raise a fracas
'Bout vines, and wines, an' drucken Bacchus,
An' crabbet names an' stories wrack us,
      An' grate our lug:
I sing the juice Scotch bere can mak us,
      In glass or jug.

O thou, my muse! guid auld Scotch drink!
Whether thro' wimplin' worms thou jink,
Or, richly brown, ream owre the brink,
      In glorious faem,
Inspire me, till I lisp an' wink,
      To sing thy name!

Let husky wheat the haughs adorn,
An' aits set up their awnie horn,
An' pease and beans, at e'en or morn,
      Perfume the plain:
Leeze me on thee, John Barleycorn,
      Thou king o' grain!

On thee aft Scotland chows her cood,
In souple scones, the wale o' food !
Or tumblin' in the boiling flood
      Wi' kail an' beef;
But when thou pours thy strong heart's blood,
      There thou shines chief.

Food fills the wame, an' keeps us leevin';
Tho' life's a gift no worth receivin',
When heavy-dragg'd wi' pine an' grievin';
      But oil'd by thee,
The wheels o' life gae down-hill, scrievin',
      Wi' rattlin' glee.

Thou clears the head o' doited Lear;
Thou cheers the heart o' drooping Care;
Thou strings the nerves o' Labor sair,
      At 's weary toil;
Thou ev'n brightens dark Despair
      Wi' gloomy smile.

Aft, clad in massy siller weed,
Wi' gentles thou erects thy head;
Yet, humbly kind in time o' need,
      The poor man's wine;
His wee drap parritch, or his bread;
      Thou kitchens fine.

Thou art the life o' public haunts;
But thee, what were our fairs and rants ?
Ev'n godly meetings o' the saunts,
      By thee inspir'd,
When, gaping, they besiege the tents,
      Are doubly fir'd.

That merry night we get the corn in,
O sweetly, then, thou reams the horn in !
Or reekin' on a New-year mornin'
      In cog or bicker,
An' just a wee drap sp'ritual burn in,
      An' gusty sucker !

When Vulcan gies his bellows breath,
An' ploughman gather wi' their graith,
O rare ! to see the fizz an' freath
   I' th' lugget caup !
Then Burnewin comes on like death
   At every chaup.

Nae mercy, then, for airn or steel;
The brawnie, bainie, ploughman chiel,
Brings hard owrehip, wi' sturdy wheel,
   The strong forehammer,
Till block an' studdie ring an' reel,
   Wi' dinsome clamour.

When skirlin' weanies see the light,
Thou maks the gossips clatter bright,
How fumblin' cuifs their dearies slight;
   Wae worth the name !
Nae howdie gets a social night,
   Or plack frae them.

When neibors anger at a plea,
An' just as wud as wud can be,
How easy can the barley brie
   Cement the quarrel !
It's aye the cheapest lawyer's fee,
   To taste the barrel.

Alake ! that e'er my muse has reason,
To wyte her countrymen wi' treason !
But mony daily weet their weason
   Wi' liquors nice,
An' hardly, in a winter season,
   E'er spier her price.

Wae worth that brandy, burnin' trash !
Fell source o' mony a pain an' brash !
Twins mony a poor, doylt, drucken hash,
   O' half his days;
An' sends, beside, auld Scotland's cash
   To her warst faes.

Ye Scots, wha wish auld Scotland well!
Ye chiefs, to you my tale I tell,
Poor, plackless devils like mysel!
    It sets you ill,
Wi' bitter, dearthfu' wines to mell,
      Or foreign gill.

May gravels round his blather wrench,
An' gouts torment him, inch by inch,
Wha twists his gruntle wi' a glunch
    O' sour disdain,
Out owre a glass o' whisky-punch
      Wi' honest men!

O whisky! soul o' plays an' pranks!
Accept a bardie's gratefu' thanks!
When wanting thee, what tuneless cranks
    Are my poor verses!
Thou comes—they rattle i' their ranks,
      At ither's a—s!

Thee, Ferintosh! O sadly lost!
Scotland lament frae coast to coast!
Now colic grips, an' barkin' hoast
    May kill us a';
For loyal Forbes' charter'd boast
      Is taen awa'!

Thae curst horse-leeches o' th' Excise,
Wha mak the whisky stells their prize!
Haud up thy han', Deil! ance, twice, thrice!
    There, seize the blinkers!
An' bake them up in brunstane pies
      For poor d—n'd drinkers.

Fortune! if thou'll but gie me still
Hale breeks, a scone, an' whisky gill,
An' rowth o' rhyme to rave at will,
    Tak a' the rest,
An' deal't about as thy blind skill
      Directs thee best.

THE AULD FARMER'S NEW-YEAR MORNING SALUTATION TO HIS AULD MARE, MAGGIE

ON GIVING HER THE ACCUSTOMED RIPP OF CORN TO HANSEL IN THE NEW-YEAR

A GUID New-year I wish thee, Maggie!
Hae, there's a ripp to thy auld baggie:
Tho' thou's howe-backit now, an' knaggie,
     I've seen the day
Thou could hae gaen like ony staggie,
     Out-owre the lay.

Tho' now thou's dowie, stiff an' crazy,
An' thy auld hide as white's a daisie,
I've seen thee dappl't, sleek an' glaizie,
     A bonie gray:
He should been tight that daur't to raize thee,
     Ance in a day.

Thou ance was i' the foremost rank,
A filly buirdly, steeve an' swank;
An' set weel down a shapely shank,
     As e'er tread yird;
An' could hae flown out-owre a stank,
     Like ony bird.

It's now some nine-an'-twenty year,
Sin' thou was my guid-father's meere;
He gied me thee, o' tocher clear,
     An' fifty mark;
Tho' it was sma', 'twas weel-won gear,
     An' thou was stark.

When first I gaed to woo my Jenny,
Ye then were trottin' wi' your minnie :
Tho' ye was trickie, slee, an' funnie,
  Ye ne'er was donsie;
But hamely, tawie, quiet, an' cannie,
  An' unco sonsie.

That day, ye pranc'd wi' muckle pride,
When ye bure hame my bonie bride :
An' sweet an' gracefu' she did ride,
  Wi' maiden air !
Kyle-Stewart I could bragget wide,
  For sic a pair.

Tho' now ye dow but hoyte and hobble,
An' wintle like a saumont-coble,
That day, ye was a jinker noble,
  For heels an' win' !
An' ran them till they a' did wauble,
  Far, far, behin' !

When thou an' I were young an' skeigh,
An' stable-meals at fair, were dreigh,
How thou wad prance, an' snore, an' skriegh,
  An' tak the road !
Town's bodies ran, an' stood abiegh,
  An' ca't thee mad.

When thou was corn't, an' I was mellow,
We took the road ay like a swallow :
At brooses thou had ne'er a fellow,
  For pith an' speed;
But ev'ry tail thou pay't them hollow,
  Where'er thou gaed.

The sma', droop-rumpl't, hunter cattle
Might aiblins waur't thee for a brattle;
But sax Scotch mile, thou try't their mettle,
  An' gar't them whaizle :
Nae whip nor spur, but just a wattle
  O' saugh or hazle.

Thou was a noble 'fittie-lan',
As e'er in tug or tow was drawn!
Aft thee an' I, in aught hours' gaun,
  On guid March-weather,
Hae turn'd sax rood beside our han',
  For days thegither.

Thou never braing't, an' fetch't, an' flisket;
But thy auld tail thou wad hae whisket,
An' spread abreed thy well-fill'd brisket,
  Wi' pith an' power;
Till sprittie knowes wad rair't an' risket
  An' slypet owre.

When frosts lay lang, an' snaws were deep,
An' threaten'd labour back to keep,
I gied thy cog a wee bit heap
  Aboon the timmer:
I ken'd my Maggie wad na sleep,
  For that, or simmer.

In cart or car thou never reested;
The steyest brae thou wad hae fac't it;
Thou never lap, an' stenned, and breastet,
  Then stood to blaw;
But just thy step a wee thing hastet,
  Thou snoov't awa'.

My 'pleugh' is now thy bairn-time a',
Four gallant brutes as e'er did draw;
Forbye sax mae I've sell't awa',
  That thou has nurst:
They drew me thretteen pund an' twa,
  The vera warst.

Mony a sair daurg we twa hae wrought,
An' wi' the weary warl' fought!
An' mony an anxious day, I thought
  We wad be beat!
Yet here to crazy age wer'e brought,
  Wi' something yet.

An' think na, my auld trusty servan',
That now perhaps thou's less deservin',
An' my auld days may end in starvin';
    For my last fow,
A heapet stimpart, I'll reserve ane
    Laid by for you.

We've worn to crazy years thegither;
We'll toyte about wi' ane anither;
Wi' tentie care I'll flit thy tether
    To some hain'd rig,
Whare ye may nobly rax your leather,
    Wi' sma' fatigue.

THE TWA DOGS

A TALE

'TWAS in that place o' Scotland's isle,
That bears the name o' auld 'King Coil,'
Upon a bonie day in June,
When wearin' thro' the afternoon,
Twa dogs, that were na thrang at hame,
Forgather'd ance upon a time.
    The first I'll name, they ca'd him 'Cæsar,'
Was keepet for 'his Honor's' pleasure:
His hair, his size, his mouth, his lugs,
Shew'd he was nane o' Scotland's dogs;
But whalpet some place far abroad,
Whare sailors gang to fish for cod.
    His lockèd, letter'd, braw brass collar
Shew'd him the gentleman an' scholar;
But tho' he was o' high degree,
The fient a pride, nae pride had he;
But wad hae spent an hour caressin',
Ev'n wi' a tinkler-gipsey's messan:

At kirk or market, mill or smiddie,
Nae tawted tyke, tho' e'er sae duddie,
But he wad stand, as glad to see him,
An' stroan'd on stanes an' hillocks wi' him.

　　The tither was a ploughman's collie—
A rhyming, ranting, raving billie,
Wha for his friend an' comrade had him,
And in his freaks had 'Luath' ca'd him,
After some dog in Highland sang,
Was made lang syne—Lord knows how lang.

　　He was a gash an' faithfu' tyke,
As ever lap a sheugh or dyke.
His honest, sonsie, baws'nt face
Ay gat him friends in ilka place;
　　His breast was white, his tousie back
Weel clad wi' coat o' glossy black;
His gawsie tail, wi' upward curl,
Hung owre his hurdies wi' a swirl.

　　Nae doubt but they were fain o' ither,
And unco pack an' thick thegither;
Wi' social nose whyles snuff'd an' snowket;
Whyles mice an' moudieworts they howket;
Whyles scour'd awa' in lang excursion,
An' worry'd ither in diversion;
Till tir'd at last wi' mony a farce,
They set them down upon their arse,
An' there began a lang digression
About the 'lords o' the creation.'

CÆSAR

　　I've aften wonder'd, honest Luath,
What sort o' life poor dogs like you have;
An' when the gentry's life I saw,
What way poor bodies liv'd ava.
　　Our laird gets in his rackèd rents,
His coals, his kane, an' a' his stents:

He rises when he likes himsel;
His flunkies answer at the bell;
He ca's his coach; he ca's his horse;
He draws a bonie silken purse,
As lang's my tail, where, thro' the steeks,
The yellow letter'd Geordie keeks.

Frae morn to e'en it's nought but toiling,
At baking, roasting, frying, boiling;
An' tho' the gentry first are stechin',
Yet ev'n the ha' folk fill their pechan
Wi' sauce, ragouts, an' sic like trashtrie
That's little short o' downright wastrie.
Our whipper-in, wee, blasted wonner,
Poor, worthless elf, it eats a dinner,
Better than ony tenant-man
His Honour has in a' the lan':
An' what poor cot-folk pit their painch in,
I own it's past my comprehension.

LUATH

Trowth, Cæsar, whyles they're fash't eneugh:
A cottar howkin' in a sheugh,
Wi' dirty stanes biggin' a dyke,
Baring a quarry, an' sic like;
Himsel, a wife, he thus sustains,
A smytrie o' wee duddie weans,
An' nought but his han'-daurg, to keep
Them right an' tight in thack an' raep.

An' when they meet wi' sair disasters,
Like loss o' health, or want o' masters,
Ye maist wad think, a wee touch langer,
An' they maun starve o' cauld an' hunger:
But how it comes, I never kent yet,
They're maistly wonderfu' contented;
An' buirdly chiels, an' clever hizzies,
Are bred in sic a way as this is.

CÆSAR

But then to see how ye're neglecket,
How huff'd, an' cuff'd, an' disrespecket!
L——d man, our gentry care as little
For delvers, ditchers, an' sic cattle;
They gang as saucy by poor folk,
As I wad by a stinking brock.

I've notic'd, on our laird's court-day—
An' mony a time my heart's been wae—
Poor tenant bodies, scant o' cash,
How they maun thole a factor's snash;
He'll stamp an' threaten, curse an' swear
He'll apprehend them, poind their gear;
While they maun stan', wi' aspect humble,
An' hear it a', an' fear an' tremble!

I see how folk live that hae riches;
But surely poor-folk maun be wretches!

LUATH

They're no sae wretched's ane wad think.
Tho' constantly on poortith's brink,
They're sae accustom'd wi' the sight,
The view o't gies them little fright.

Then chance and fortune are sae guided,
They're ay in less or mair provided;
An' tho' fatigu'd wi' close employment,
A blink o' rest's a sweet enjoyment.

The dearest comfort o' their lives,
Their grushie weans an' faithfu' wives;
The prattling things are just their pride,
That sweetens a' their fireside.

An' whyles twalpennie worth o' nappy
Can mak the bodies unco happy:
They lay aside their private cares,
To mind the Kirk and State affairs;

They'll talk o' patronage an' priests,
Wi' kindling fury i' their breasts,
Or tell what new taxation's comin',
An' ferlie at the folk in Lon'on.

As bleak-fac'd Hallowmass returns,
They get the jovial, rantin' kirns,
When rural life, of ev'ry station,
Unite in common recreation;
Love blinks, Wit slaps, an' social Mirth
Forgets there's Care upo' the earth.

That merry day the year begins,
They bar the door on frosty win's;
The nappy reeks wi' mantling ream,
An' sheds a heart-inspiring steam;
The luntin' pipe, an' sneeshin' mill,
Are handed round wi' right guid will;
The cantie auld folks crackin' crouse,
The young anes ranting thro' the house—
My heart has been sae fain to see them,
That I for joy hae barket wi' them.

Still it's owre true that ye hae said,
Sic game is now owre aften play'd;
There's mony a creditable stock
O' decent, honest, fawsont folk,
Are riven out baith root an' branch,
Some rascal's pridefu' greed to quench,
Wha thinks to knit himsel' the faster
In favour wi' some gentle master,
Wha, aiblins thrang a parliamentin',
For Britain's guid his saul indentin'—

CÆSAR

Haith, lad, ye little ken about it:
For Britain's guid! guid faith! I doubt it.
Say rather, gaun as Premiers lead him:
An' saying aye or no's they bid him:

At operas an' plays parading,
Mortgaging, gambling, masquerading :
Or maybe, in a frolic daft,
To Hague or Calais takes a waft,
To mak a tour an' tak a whirl,
To learn *bon ton*, an' see the worl',
　　There, at Vienna, or Versailles,
He rives his father's auld entails;
Or by Madrid he takes the rout,
To thrum guitars an' fecht wi' nowt;
Or down Italian vista startles,
Wh–re-hunting amang groves o' myrtles :
Then bowses drumlie German-water,
To mak himsel' look fair an' fatter,
An' clear the consequential sorrows,
Love-gifts of Carnival signoras.
　　For Britain's guid ! for her destruction !
Wi' dissipation, feud an' faction.

LUATH

　Hech man ! dear sirs ! is that the gate
They waste sae mony a braw estate !
Are we sae foughten an' harass'd
For gear to gang that gate at last ?
　O would they stay aback frae courts,
An' please themsels wi' countra sports,
It wad for ev'ry ane be better,
The laird, the tenant, an' the cottar !
For thae frank, rantin', ramblin' billies,
Feint haet o' them's ill-hearted fellows;
Except for breakin' o' their timmer,
Or speakin' lightly o' their limmer,
Or shootin' o' a hare or moor-cock,
The ne'er-a-bit they're ill to poor folk,
　　But will ye tell me, master Cæsar,
Sure great folk's life's a life o' pleasure ?
Nae cauld nor hunger e'er can steer them,
The very thought o't need na fear them.

CÆSAR

L—d, man, were ye but whyles whare I am
The gentles, ye wad ne'er envy them !
  It's true, they need na starve or sweat,
Thro' winter's cauld, or simmer's heat;
They've nae sair-wark to craze their banes,
An' fill auld age wi' grips an' granes;
But human bodies are sic fools,
For a' their colleges an' schools,
That when nae real ills perplex them,
They mak enow themsels to vex them;
An' aye the less they hae to sturt them,
In like proportion, less will hurt them.
  A country fellow at the pleugh,
His acre's till'd, he's right eneugh;
A country girl at her wheel,
Her dizzen's dune, she's unco weel;
But gentlemen, an' ladies warst,
Wi' ev'n-down want o' wark are curst.
They loiter, lounging, lank an' lazy;
Tho' deil-haet ails them, yet uneasy :
Their days insipid, dull an' tasteless;
Their nights unquiet, lang an' restless.
  An' ev'n their sports, their balls an' races,
Their galloping through public places,
There's sic parade, sic pomp an' art,
The joy can scarcely reach the heart.
  The men cast out in party-matches,
Then sowther a' in deep debauches.
Ae night they're mad wi' drink an wh–ring,
Niest day their life is past enduring.
  The ladies arm-in-arm in clusters,
As great an' gracious a' as sisters;
But hear their absent thoughts o' ither,
They're a' run deils an' jads thegither.
Whyles, owre the wee bit cup an' plaitie,
They sip the scandal-potion pretty;

Or lee-lang nights, wi' crabbet leuks
Pore owre the devil's pictur'd beuks;
Stake on a chance a farmer's stackyard,
An' cheat like ony unhanged blackguard.
    There's some exceptions, man an' woman;
But this is gentry's life in common.

By this, the sun was out of sight,
An' darker gloamin' brought the night;
The bum-clock humm'd wi' lazy drone;
The kye stood rowtin' i' the loan;
When up they gat an' snook their lugs,
Rejoic'd they were na *men* but *dogs*;
An' each took aff his several way,
Resolv'd to meet some ither day.

THE AUTHOR'S EARNEST CRY AND PRAYER

TO THE SCOTCH REPRESENTATIVES IN THE HOUSE OF COMMONS

Dearest of distillation! last and best—
. . How art thou lost!—PARODY ON MILTON.

YE Irish lords, ye knights an' squires,
Wha represent our brughs an' shires,
An' doucely manage our affairs
          In parliament,
To you a simple poet's pray'rs
           Are humbly sent.

Alas! my roupet muse is hearse!
Your Honors' hearts wi' grief 'twad pierce,
To see her sittin' on her arse
          Low i' the dust,
And scriechin' out prosaic verse,
          An' like to burst!

Tell them wha hae the chief direction,
Scotland an' me's in great affliction,
E'er sin' they laid that curst restriction
  On aqua-vitæ;
An' rouse them up to strong conviction,
   An' move their pity.

Stand forth, an' tell yon Premier youth
The honest, open, naked truth :
Tell him o' mine an' Scotland's drouth,
   His servants humble :
The muckle deevil blaw you south,
   If ye dissemble !

Does ony great man glunch an' gloom ?
Speak out, an' never fash your thumb !
Let posts an' pensions sink or soom
   Wi' them wha grant them;
If honestly they canna come,
   Far better want them.

In gath'rin' votes you were na slack;
Now stand as tightly by your tack :
Ne'er claw your lug, an' fidge your back,
   An' hum an' haw;
But raise your arm, an' tell your crack
   Before them a'.

Paint Scotland greetin' owre her thrissle;
Her mutchkin stowp as toom's a whissle;
An' d—mn'd excisemen in a bussle,
   Seizin' a stell,
Triumphant, crushin't like a mussel,
   Or limpet shell !

Then, on the tither hand, present her—
A blackguard smuggler right behint her,
An' cheek-for-chow, a chuffie vintner
   Colleaguing join,
Pickin' her pouch as bare as winter
   Of a' kind coin.

Is there, that bears the name o' Scot,
But feels his heart's bluid rising hot,
To see his poor auld mither's pot
    Thus dung in staves,
An' plunder'd o' her hindmost groat,
    By gallows knaves?

Alas! I'm but a nameless wight,
Trode i' the mire out o' sight?
But could I like Montgomeries fight,
    Or gab like Boswell,
There's some sark-necks I wad draw tight,
    An' tie some hose well.

God bless your Honors! can ye see't—
The kind, auld, cantie carlin greet,
An' no get warmly to your feet,
    An' gar them hear it,
An' tell them wi' a patriot-heat,
    Ye winna bear it?

Some o' you nicely ken the laws,
To round the period an' pause,
An' with rhetòric clause on clause
    To mak harangues;
Then echo thro' Saint Stephen's wa's
    Auld Scotland's wrangs.

Dempster, a true blue Scot I'se warran;
Thee, aith-detesting, chaste Kilkerran;
An' that glib-gabbet Highland baron,
    The Laird o' Graham;
An' ane, a chap that's d—mn'd auldfarran,
    Dundas his name:

Erskine, a spunkie Norland billie;
True Campbell's, Frederick and Ilay;
An' Livistone, the bauld Sir Willie;
    An' mony ithers,
Whom auld Demosthenes or Tully
    Might own for brithers.

See, sodger Hugh, my watchman stented,
If poets e'er are represented;
I ken if that your sword were wanted,
      Ye'd lend a hand;
But when there's ought to say anent it,
      Ye're at a stand.

Arouse, my boys! exert your mettle,
To get auld Scotland back her kettle;
Or faith! I'll wad my new pleugh-pettle,
      Ye'll see't or lang,
She'll teach you, wi' a reekin' whittle,
      Anither sang.

This while she's been in crankous mood,
Her lost Militia fir'd her bluid;
(Deil nor they never mair do guid,
      Play'd her that pliskie!)
An' now she's like to rin red wud
      About her whisky.

An' L—d! if ance they pit her till't,
Her tartan petticoat she'll kilt,
An' durk an' pistol at her belt,
      She'll tak the streets,
An' rin her whittle to the hilt,
      I' the first she meets!

For G—d-sake, sirs! then speak her fair,
An' straik her cannie wi' the hair,
An' to the muckle house repair,
      Wi' instant speed,
An' strive, wi' a' your wit an' lear,
      To get remead.

Yon ill-tongu'd tinkler, Charlie Fox,
May taunt you wi' his jeers and mocks;
But gie him't het, my hearty cocks!
      E'en cowe the cadie!
An' send him to his dicing box
      An' sportin' lady.

Tell yon guid bluid o' auld Boconnock's,
I'll be his debt twa mashlum bonnocks,
An' drink his health in auld Nanse Tinnock's
                    Nine times a-week,
If he some scheme, like tea an' winnocks,
                    Wad kindly seek.

Could he some commutation broach,
I'll pledge my aith in guid braid Scotch,
He needna fear their foul reproach
                    Nor erudition,
Yon mixtie-maxtie, queer hotch-potch,
                    The 'Coalition.'

Auld Scotland has a raucle tongue;
She's just a devil wi' a rung;
An' if she promise auld or young
                    To tak their part,
Tho' by the neck she would be strung,
                    She'll no desert.

And now, ye chosen Five-and-Forty,
May still your mither's heart support ye;
Then, tho' a minister grow dorty,
                    An' kick your place,
Ye'll snap your fingers, poor an' hearty,
                    Before his face.

God bless your Honors, a' your days,
Wi' sowps o' kail and brats o' claise,
In spite o' a' the thievish kaes,
                    That haunt St Jamie's!
Your humble poet sings an' prays,
                    While Rab his name is.

POSTSCRIPT

Let half-starv'd slaves in warmer skies
See future wines, rich-clust'ring rise;

Their lot auld Scotland ne'er envies,
   But, blythe and frisky,
She eyes her freeborn, martial boys
   Tak aff their whisky.

What tho' their Phœbus kinder warms,
While fragrance blooms and beauty charms,
When wretches range, in famish'd swarms,
   The scented groves;
Or, hounded forth, dishonor arms
   In hungry droves!

Their gun's a burden on their shouther;
They downa bide the stink o' powther;
Their bauldest thought's a hank'ring swither
   To stand or rin,
Till skelp—a shot—they're aff, a' throw'ther
   To save their skin.

But bring a Scotsman frae his hill,
Clap in his cheek a Highland gill,
Say, such is royal George's will,
   An' there's the foe!
He has nae thought but how to kill
   Twa at a blow.

Nae cauld, faint-hearted doubtings tease him
Death comes, wi' fearless eye he sees him;
Wi' bluidy hand a welcome gies him;
   An' when he fa's,
His latest draught o' breathin' lea'es him
   In faint huzzas.

Sages their solemn een may steek,
An' raise philosophic reek,
An' physically causes seek,
   In clime an' season;
But tell me whisky's name in Greek,
   I'll tell the reason.

Scotland, my auld, respected mither!
Tho' whiles ye moistify your leather,
Till, whare ye sit on craps o' heather,
    Ye tine your dam;
Freedom an' whisky gang thegither!
    Tak aff your dram.

THE ORDINATION

For sense, they little owe to frugal Heav'n—
To please the mob they hide the little giv'n.'

KILMARNOCK wabsters, fidge and claw,
 An' pour your creeshie nations;
An' ye wha leather rax an' draw,
 Of a' denominations;
Swith! to the Laigh Kirk, ane an' a',
 An' there tak up your stations;
Then aff to Begbie's in a raw,
 An' pour divine libations
   For joy this day.

Curst 'Common-sense,' that imp o' h-ll,
 Cam in wi' Maggie Lauder:
But Oliphant aft made her yell,
 An' Russell sair misca'd her:
This day Mackinlay taks the flail,
 An' he's the boy will blaud her!
He'll clap a shangan on her tail,
 An' set the bairns to daud her
   Wi' dirt this day.

Mak haste an' turn King David owre,
 And lilt wi' holy clangor;
O' double verse come gie us four,
 An' skirl up 'the Bangor':

This day the kirk kicks up a stoure,
    Nae mair the knaves shall wrang her;
For Heresy is in her pow'r,
    And gloriously she'll whang her,
        Wi' pith this day.

Come, let a proper text be read,
    An' touch it aff wi' vigour,
How graceless Ham leugh at his dad,
    Which made Canaan a nigger;
Or Phineas drove the murdering blade,
    Wi' whore-abhorring rigour;
Or Zipporah, the scauldin' jad,
    Was like a bluidy teeger,
        I' th' inn that day.

There, try his mettle on the creed,
    And bind him down wi' caution,
That stipend is a carnal weed
    He taks but for the fashion;
And gie him o'er the flock to feed,
    And punish each transgression;
Especial, rams that cross the breed,
    Gie them sufficient threshin';
        Spare them nae day.

Now auld Kilmarnock, cock thy tail,
    An' toss thy horns fu' canty;
Nae mair thou'lt rowte out-owre the dale,
    Because thy pasture's scanty;
For lapfu's large o' gospel kail
    Shall fill thy crib in plenty,
An' runts o' grace the pick an' wale,
    No gi'en by way o' dainty,
        But ilka day.

Nae mair by 'Babel's streams' we'll weep,
    To think upon our 'Zion';
And hing our fiddles up to sleep,
    Like baby-clouts a-dryin'!

Come, screw the pegs wi' tunefu' cheep,
    And o'er the thairms be tryin';
Oh, rare! to see our elbuck's wheep,
    And a' like lamb-tails flyin',
          Fu' fast this day!

Lang Patronage, wi' rod o' airn,
    Has shor'd the Kirk's undoin';
As lately Fenwick, sair forfairn,
    Has proven to its ruin:
Our patron, honest man! Glencairn,
    He saw mischief was brewin';
An' like a godly, elect bairn,
    He's waled us out a true ane,
          And sound this day.

Now Robertson, harangue nae mair,
    But steek your gab for ever;
Or try the wicked town of Ayr,
    For there they'll think you clever;
Or, nae reflection on your lear,
    Ye may commence a shaver;
Or to the Netherton repair,
    An' turn a carpet weaver,
          Aff-hand this day.

Mu'trie and you were just a match,
    We never had sic twa drones;
Auld 'Hornie' did the Laigh Kirk watch,
    Just like a winkin' baudrons,
And ay he catch'd the tither wretch,
    To fry them in his caudrons;
But now his Honor maun detach,
    Wi' a' his brimstone squadrons,
          Fast, fast this day.

See, see auld Orthodoxy's faes,
    She's swingein' thro' the city!
Hark, how the nine-tail'd cat she plays!
    I vow it's unco pretty:

There, Learning, with his Greekish face,
　　Grunts out some Latin ditty;
And 'Common-sense' is gaun, she says,
　　To mak to Jamie Beattie
　　　　　　Her plaint this day.

But there's Morality himsel
　　Embracing all opinions;
Hear, how he gies the tither yell,
　　Between his twa companions!
See, how she peels the skin an' fell,
　　As ane was peelin' onions!
Now there, they're packèd aff to h-ll,
　　An' banish'd our dominions,
　　　　　　Henceforth this day.

O happy day! rejoice, rejoice!
　　Come bouse about the porter!
Morality's demure decoys
　　Shall here nae mair find quarter:
Mackinlay, Russell, are the boys
　　That heresy can torture;
They'll gie her on a rape a hoyse,
　　And cowe her measure shorter
　　　　　　By th' head some day.

Come, bring the tither mutchkin in,
　　And here's—for a conclusion—
To ev'ry 'new-light' mother's son,
　　From this time forth, confusion!
If mair they deave us wi' their din,
　　Or patronage intrusion,
We'll light a spunk, and ev'ry skin,
　　We'll rin them aff in fusion,
　　　　　　Like oil some day.

EPISTLE TO JAMES SMITH

Friendship, mysterious cement of the soul !
Sweet'ner of Life, and solder of Society !
I owe thee much——   BLAIR.

DEAR SMITH, the slee'st, pawkie thief,
That e'er attempted stealth or rief !
Ye surely hae some warlock-breef
          Owre human hearts :
For ne'er a bosom yet was prief
          Against your arts.

For me, I swear by sun an' moon,
An' ev'ry star that blinks aboon,
Ye've cost me twenty pair o' shoon,
          Just gaun to see you;
An' ev'ry ither pair that's done,
          Mair taen I'm wi' you.

That auld, capracious carlin, Nature,
To mak amends for scrimpet stature,
She's turn'd you aff, a human-creature
          On her first plan,
And in her freaks, on ev'ry feature
          She's wrote the Man.

Just now I've taen the fit o' rhyme,
My barmie noddle's working prime.
My fancy yerket up sublime,
          Wi' hasty summon;
Hae ye a leisure-moment's time
          To hear what's comin' ?

Some rhyme a neibor's name to lash;
Some rhyme (vain thought !) for needfu' cash;
Some rhyme to court the countra clash,
          An' raise a din;
For me, an aim I never fash;
          I rhyme for fun.

The star that rules my luckless lot,
Has fated me the russet coat,
An' damn'd my fortune to the groat;
    But, in requit,
Has blest me with a random-shot
    O' countra wit.

This while my notion's taen a sklent,
To try my fate in guid, black prent;
But still the mair I'm that way bent,
    Something cries 'Hoolie!
I red you, honest man, tak tent!
    Ye'll shaw your folly;

There's ither poets, much your betters,
Far seen in Greek, deep men o' letters,
Hae thought they had ensur'd their debtors,
    A' future ages;
Now moths deform, in shapeless tatters,
    Their unknown pages.'

Then farewell hopes of laurel-boughs,
To garland my poetic brows!
Henceforth I'll rove where busy ploughs
    Are whistlin' thrang,
An' teach the lanely heights an' howes
    My rustic sang.

I'll wander on, wi' tentless heed
How never-halting moments speed,
Till fate shall snap the brittle thread;
    Then, all unknown,
I'll lay me with th' inglorious dead,
    Forgot and gone!

But why o' death begin a tale?
Just now we're living sound an' hale;
Then top and maintop crowd the sail,
    Heave Care o'er-side!
And large, before Enjoyment's gale,
    Let's tak the tide.

This life, sae far's I understand,
Is a' enchanted fairy-land,
Where Pleasure is the magic-wand,
  That wielded right,
Maks hours like minutes, hand in hand,
  Dance by fu' light.

The magic-wand then let us wield;
For ance that five-an'-forty's speel'd,
See, crazy, weary, joyless eild,
  Wi' wrinkl'd face,
Comes hostin', hirplin' owre the field,
  Wi' creepin' pace.

When ance life's day draws near the gloamin',
Then fareweel vacant, careless roamin';
An' fareweel cheerfu' tankards foamin',
  An' social noise :
An' fareweel dear, deluding woman,
  The joy of joys !

O Life ! how pleasant, in thy morning,
Young Fancy's rays the hills adorning !
Cold-pausing Caution's lesson scorning,
  We frisk away,
Like school-boys, at th' expected warning,
  To joy an' play.

We wander there, we wander here,
We eye the rose upon the brier,
Unmindful that the thorn is near,
  Among the leaves;
And tho' the puny wound appear,
  Short while it grieves.

Some, lucky, find a flow'ry spot,
For which they never toil'd nor swat;
They drink the sweet and eat the fat,
  But care or pain;
And haply eye the barren hut
  With high disdain.

With steady aim, some fortune chase,
Keen hope does ev'ry sinew brace;
Thro' fair, thro' foul, they urge the race,
    An' seize the prey :
Then cannie, in some cozie place,
    They close the day.

And others, like your humble servan',
Poor wights! nae rules nor roads observin',
To right or left eternal swervin',
    They zig-zag on;
Till, curst with age, obscure an' starvin',
    They aften groan.

Alas! what bitter toil an' straining—
But truce with peevish, poor complaining!
Is fortune's fickle *Luna* waning?
    E'en let her gang!
Beneath what light she has remaining,
    Let's sing our sang.

My pen I here fling to the door,
And kneel, ye Pow'rs! and warm implore,
'Tho' I should wander *Terra* o'er,
    In all her climes,
Grant me but this, I ask no more,
    Ay rowth o' rhymes.

'Gie dreepin' roasts to countra lairds,
Till icicles hing frae their beards;
Gie fine braw claes to fine life-guards,
    And maids of honor ;
An' yill an' whisky gie to cairds,
    Until they sconner.

'A title, Dempster merits it;
A garter gie to Willie Pitt;
Gie wealth to some be-ledger'd cit,
    In cent. per cent.;
But give me real, sterling wit,
    And I'm content.

'While ye are pleas'd to keep me hale,
I'll sit down o'er my scanty meal,
Be't water brose or muslin-kail,
   Wi' cheerfu' face,
As lang's the Muses dinna fail
   To say the grace.'

An anxious e'e I never throws
Behint my lug, or by my nose;
I jouk beneath Misfortune's blows
   As weel's I may;
Sworn foe to sorrow, care, and prose,
   I rhyme away.

O ye douce folk that live by rule,
Grave, tideless-blooded, calm an' cool,
Compar'd wi' you—O fool! fool! fool!
   How much unlike!
Your hearts are just a standing pool,
   Your lives, a dyke!

Nae hare-brain'd, sentimental traces
In your unletter'd, nameless faces!
In *arioso* trills and graces
   Ye never stray;
But *gravissimo*, solemn basses
   Ye hum away.

Ye are sae grave, nae doubt ye're wise;
Nae ferly tho' ye do despise
The hairum-scairum, ram-stam boys,
   The rattling squad:
I see ye upward cast your eyes—
   Ye ken the road!

Whilst I—but I shall haud me there,
Wi' you I'll scarce gang ony where—
Then, Jamie, I shall say nae mair,
   But quat my sang,
Content wi' you to mak a pair,
   Whare'er I gang.

THE VISION

DUAN FIRST

THE sun had clos'd the winter day,
The curlers quat their roarin' play,
And hunger'd maukin' taen her way,
　　　　To kail-yards green,
While faithless snaws ilk step betray
　　　　Whare she has been.

The thresher's weary flingin'-tree,
The lee-lang day had tirèd me;
And when the day had clos'd his e'e,
　　　　Far i' the west,
Ben i' the spence, right pensivelie,
　　　　I gaed to rest.

There, lanely by the ingle-cheek,
I sat and ey'd the spewing reek,
That fill'd, wi' hoast-provoking smeek,
　　　　The auld clay biggin';
An' heard the restless rattons squeak
　　　　About the riggin'.

All in this mottie, misty clime,
I backward mus'd on wasted time,
How I had spent my youthfu' prime,
　　　　An' done naething,
But stringing blethers up in rhyme,
　　　　For fools to sing.

Had I to guid advice but harket,
I might, by this, hae led a market,
Or strutted in a bank and clarket
　　　　My cash-account;
While here, half-mad, half-fed, half-sarket,
　　　　Is a' th' amount.

I started, mutt'ring 'blockhead! coof!'
And heav'd on high my wauket loof,
To swear by a' yon starry roof,
  Or some rash aith,
That I henceforth wad be rhyme-proof
  Till my last breath—

When click! the string the snick did draw;
An' jee! the door gaed to the wa';
An' by my ingle-lowe I saw,
  Now bleezin' bright,
A tight, outlandish hizzie, braw,
  Come full in sight.

Ye need na doubt, I held my whisht;
The infant aith, half-form'd, was crusht;
I glowr'd, as eerie's I'd been dusht,
  In some wild glen;
When sweet, like modest Worth, she blusht,
  An' steppèd ben.

Green, slender, leaf-clad holly-boughs
Were twisted, gracefu' round her brows;
I took her for some Scottish Muse,
  By that same token;
And come to stop those reckless vows,
  Would soon be broken.

A 'hare-brain'd, sentimental trace'
Was strongly marked in her face;
A wildly-witty, rustic grace
  Shone full upon her;
Her eye, ev'n turn'd on empty space,
  Beam'd keen with honor.

Down flow'd her robe, a tartan sheen,
Till half a leg was scrimply seen;
An' such a leg! my bonie Jean
  Could only peer it;
Sae straught, sae taper, tight an' clean—
  Nane else came near it.

Her mantle large, of greenish hue,
My gazing wonder chiefly drew;
Deep lights and shades, bold-mingling, threw
    A lustre grand;
And seem'd, to my astonish'd view,
    A well-known land.

Here, rivers in the sea were lost;
There, mountains to the skies were toss't :
Here, tumbling billows mark'd the coast,
    With surging foam;
There, distant shone Art's lofty boast,
    The lordly dome.

Here, Doon pour'd down his far-fetch'd floods;
There, well-fed Irwine stately thuds :
Auld hermit Ayr staw thro' his woods,
    On to the shore ;
And many a lesser torrent scuds,
    With seeming roar.

Low, in a sandy valley spread,
An ancient borough rear'd her head;
Still, as in Scottish story read,
    She boasts a race
To ev'ry nobler virtue bred,
    And polish'd grace.

By stately tow'r, or palace fair,
Or ruins pendent in the air,
Bold stems of heroes, here and there,
    I could discern;
Some seem'd to muse, some seem'd to dare,
    With feature stern.

My heart did glowing transport feel,
To see a race heroic wheel,
And brandish round the deep-dyed steel,
    In sturdy blows;
While, back-recoiling, seem'd to reel
    Their Suthron foes.

His Country's Saviour, mark him well!
Bold Richardton's heroic swell;
The chief, on Sark who glorious fell
       In high command;
And he whom ruthless fates expel
       His native land.

There, where a sceptr'd Pictish shade
Stalk'd round his ashes lowly laid,
I mark'd a martial race, pourtray'd
       In colours strong :
Bold, soldier-featur'd, undismay'd,
       They strode along.

Thro' many a wild, romantic grove,
Near many a hermit-fancied cove
(Fit haunts for friendship or for love,
       In musing mood),
An aged Judge, I saw him rove,
       Dispensing good.

With deep-struck, reverential awe,
The learned Sire and Son I saw :
To Nature's God, and Nature's law,
       They gave their lore;
This, all its source and end to draw,
       That, to adore.

Brydon's brave ward I well could spy,
Beneath old Scotia's smiling eye;
Who call'd on Fame, low standing by,
       To hand him on,
Where many a patriot-name on high,
       And hero shone.

DUAN SECOND

With musing-deep, astonish'd stare,
I view'd the heavenly-seeming Fair;

A whispering throb did witness bear
Of kindred sweet,
When with an elder sister's air
She did me greet.

'All hail! my own inspirèd bard!
In me thy native Muse regard;
Nor longer mourn thy fate is hard,
Thus poorly low;
I come to give thee such reward,
As we bestow!

'Know, the great genius of this land
Has many a light aerial band,
Who, all beneath his high command
Harmoniously,
As arts or arms they understand,
Their labours ply.

'They Scotia's race among them share:
Some fire the soldier on to dare;
Some rouse the patriot up to bare
Corruption's heart:
Some teach the bard—a darling care—
The tuneful art.

''Mong swelling floods of reeking gore,
They, ardent, kindling spirits pour;
Or, 'mid the venal senate's roar,
They, sightless, stand,
To mend the honest patriot-lore,
And grace the hand.

'And when the bard, or hoary sage,
Charm or instruct the future age,
They bind the wild poetic rage
In energy,
Or point the inconclusive page
Full on the eye.

'Hence, Fullarton, the brave and young;
Hence, Dempster's zeal-inspirèd tongue;
Hence, sweet, harmonious Beattie sung
  His "Minstrel" lays;
Or tore, with noble ardour stung,
  The sceptic's bays.

'To lower orders are assign'd
The humbler ranks of human-kind,
The rustic bard, the laboring hind,
  The artisan;
All chuse, as various they're inclin'd,
  The various man.

'When yellow waves the heavy grain,
The threat'ning storm some strongly rein;
Some teach to meliorate the plain,
  With tillage-skill;
And some instruct the shepherd-train,
  Blythe o'er the hill.

'Some hint the lover's harmless wile;
Some grace the maiden's artless smile;
Some soothe the laborer's weary toil
  For humble gains,
And make his cottage-scenes beguile
  His cares and pains.

'Some, bounded to a district-space,
Explore at large man's infant race,
To mark the embryotic trace
  Of rustic bard;
And careful note each opening grace,
  A guide and guard.

'Of these am I—Coila my name:
And this district as mine I claim,
Where once the Campbells, chiefs of fame,
  Held ruling pow'r:
I mark'd thy embryo-tuneful flame,
  Thy natal hour.

'With future hope I oft would gaze
Fond, on thy little early ways,
Thy rudely caroll'd chiming phrase,
    In uncouth rhymes;
Fir'd at the simple, artless lays
    Of other times.

'I saw thee seek the sounding shore,
Delighted with the dashing roar;
Or when the North his fleecy store
    Drove thro' the sky,
I saw grim Nature's visage hoar
    Struck thy young eye.

'Or when the deep green-mantled earth
Warm cherish'd ev'ry floweret's birth,
And joy and music pouring forth
    In ev'ry grove;
I saw thee eye the general mirth
    With boundless love.

'When ripen'd fields and azure skies
Call'd forth the reapers' rustling noise,
I saw thee leave their ev'ning joys,
    And lonely stalk,
To vent thy bosom's swelling rise,
    In pensive walk.

'When youthful love, warm-blushing, strong,
Keen-shivering, shot thy nerves along,
Those accents grateful to thy tongue,
    Th' adorèd *Name*,
I taught thee how to pour in song,
    To soothe thy flame.

'I saw thy pulse's maddening play,
Wild send thee Pleasure's devious way,
Misled by Fancy's meteor-ray,
    By passion driven;
But yet the light that led astray
    Was light from Heaven.

'I taught thy manners-painting strains,
The loves, the ways of simple swains,
Till now, o'er all my wide domains
   Thy fame extends;
And some, the pride of Coila's plains,
   Become thy friends.

'Thou canst not learn, nor I can show,
To paint with Thomson's landscape glow;
Or wake the bosom-melting throe,
   With Shenstone's art;
Or pour, with Gray, the moving flow
   Warm on the heart.

'Yet, all beneath th' unrivall'd rose,
The lowly daisy sweetly blows;
Tho' large the forest's monarch throws
   His army-shade,
Yet green the juicy hawthorn grows,
   Adown the glade.

'Then never murmur nor repine;
Strive in thy humble sphere to shine;
And trust me, not Potosi's mine,
   Nor king's regard,
Can give a bliss o'ermatching thine,
   A rustic bard.

'To give my counsels all in one,
Thy tuneful flame still careful fan:
Preserve the dignity of Man,
   With soul erect;
And trust the Universal Plan
   Will all protect.

'And wear thou *this*'—she solemn said,
And bound the holly round my head:
The polish'd leaves and berries red
   Did rustling play;
And, like a passing thought, she fled
   In light away.

THE RANTIN' DOG, THE DADDIE O'T

Tune—'Whare'll our gudeman lie.'

O WHA my babie-clouts will buy ?
O wha will tend me when I cry ?
Wha will kiss me where I lie ?
   The rantin' dog, the daddie o't.

O wha will own he did the faut ?
O wha will buy the groanin' maut ?
O wha will tell me how to ca't ?
   The rantin' dog, the daddie o't.

When I mount the creepie-chair,
Wha will sit beside me there ?
Gie me Rob, I'll seek nae mair,
   The rantin' dog, the daddie o't.

Wha will crack to me my lane ?
Wha will mak me fidgin' fain ?
Wha will kiss me o'er again ?
   The rantin' dog, the daddie o't.

HERE'S HIS HEALTH IN WATER

Tune—'The Job of Journey-work.'

ALTHO' my back be at the wa',
   And tho' he be the fautor;
Altho' my back be at the wa',
   Yet, here's his health in water.
O wae gae by his wanton sides,
   Sae brawlie's he could flatter;

Till for his sake I'm slighted sair,
    And dree the kintra clatter:
But tho' my back be at the wa',
    Yet, here's his health in water.

ADDRESS TO THE UNCO GUID

OR THE RIGIDLY RIGHTEOUS

My Son, these maxims make a rule,
    An' lump them ay thegither;
The *Rigid Righteous* is a fool,
    The *Rigid Wise* anither:
The cleanest corn that e'er was dight
    May hae some pyles o' caff in;
So ne'er a fellow-creature slight
    For random fits o' daffin.
        SOLOMON.—Eccles. ch. vii. verse 16

O YE wha are sae guid yoursel,
    Sae pious and sae holy,
Ye've nought to do but mark and tell
    Your neibours' fauts and folly!
Whase life is like a weel-gaun mill,
    Supplied wi' store o' water;
The heapet happer's ebbing still,
    An' still the clap plays clatter.

Hear me, ye venerable core,
    As counsel for poor mortals
That frequent pass douce Wisdom's door
    For glakit Folly's portals:
I, for their thoughtless, careless sakes,
    Would here propone defences—
Their donsie tricks, their black mistakes,
    Their failings and mischances.

Ye see your state wi' theirs compared,
　　And shudder at the niffer;
But cast a moment's fair regard,
　　What maks the mighty differ?
Discount what scant occasion gave,
　　That purity ye pride in;
And (what's aft mair than a' the lave)
　　Your better art o' hidin'.

Think, when your castigated pulse
　　Gies now and then a wallop!
What ragings must his veins convulse,
　　That still eternal gallop!
Wi' wind and tide fair i' your tail,
　　Right on ye scud your sea-way;
But in the teeth o' baith to sail,
　　It maks an unco lee-way.

See Social Life and Glee sit down,
　　All joyous and unthinking,
Till, quite transmugrify'd, they're grown
　　Debauchery and Drinking:
O would they stay to calculate
　　Th' eternal consequences;
Or your more dreaded hell to state,
　　Damnation of expenses!

Ye high, exalted, virtuous dames,
　　Tied up in godly laces,
Before ye gie poor Frailty names,
　　Suppose a change o' cases;
A dear-lov'd lad, convenience snug,
　　A treach'rous inclination;
But, let me whisper i' your lug,
　　Ye're aiblins nae temptation.

Then gently scan your brother man,
　　Still gentler sister woman;
Tho' they may gang a kennin wrang,
　　To step aside is human:

One point must still be greatly dark,
  The moving *Why* they do it;
And just as lamely can ye mark,
  How far perhaps they rue it.

Who made the heart, 'tis He alone
  Decidedly can try us;
He knows each chord, its various tone,
  Each spring, its various bias :
Then at the balance let's be mute,
  We never can adjust it;
What's done we partly may compute,
  But know not what's resisted.

THE INVENTORY

IN ANSWER TO A MANDATE BY THE SURVEYOR OF THE TAXES

SIR, as your mandate did request,
I send you here a faithfu' list,
O' gudes an' gear, an' a' my graith,
To which I'm clear to gie my aith.

  Imprimis, then, for carriage cattle,
I hae four brutes o' gallant mettle,
As ever drew before a pettle.
My *Land-afore's* a guid auld 'has been,'
An' wight an' wilfu' a' his days been :
My *Land-ahin's* a weel gaun fillie,
That aft has borne me hame frae Killie,
An' your auld borough mony a time,
In days when riding was nae crime,
But ance, when in my wooing pride
I, like a blockhead, boost to ride,
The wilfu' creature sae I pat to,
(L—d pardon a' my sins, an' that too !)

I play'd my fillie sic a shavie,
She's a' bedevil'd wi' the spavie.
My *Furr-ahin's* a wordy beast,
As e'er in tug or tow was traced.
The fourth's a Highland Donald hastie,
A d—n'd red-wud Kilburnie blastie!
Foreby a cowt, o' cowts the wale,
As ever ran before a tail :
Gin he be spar'd to be a beast,
He'll draw me fifteen pund at least.
Wheel-carriages I hae but few,
Three carts, an' twa are feckly new;
An auld wheelbarrow, mair for token,
Ae leg an' baith the trams are broken;
I made a poker o' the spin'le,
An' my auld mither brunt the trin'le.

For men, I've three mischievous boys,
Run-deils for rantin' an' for noise;
A gaudsman ane, a thrasher t' other :
Wee Davock hauds the nowt in fother.
I rule them as I ought, discreetly,
An' aften labour them completely;
An' ay on Sundays duly, nightly,
I on the 'Questions' *targe* them tightly;
Till, faith! wee Davock's grown sae gleg,
Tho' scarcely langer than your leg,
He'll screed you aff Effectual Calling,
As fast as ony in the dwalling.
I've nane in female servan' station,
(L—d keep me ay frae a' temptation!)
I hae nae wife—and that my bliss is,
An' ye have laid nae tax on misses;
An' then, if kirk folk dinna clutch me,
I ken the deevils darena touch me.
Wi' weans I'm mair than weel contented,
Heav'n sent me ane mair than I wanted :
My sonsie, smirking, dear-bought Bess,

She stares the daddy in her face,
Enough of ought ye like but grace :
But her, my bonie, sweet wee lady,
I've paid enough for her already;
An' gin ye tax her or her mither,
By the L——d, ye'se get them a' thegither !

And now, remember, Mr Aiken,
Nae kind o' licence out I'm takin' :
Frae this time forth, I do declare
I'se ne'er ride horse nor hizzie mair;
Thro' dirt and dub for life I'll paidle,
Ere I sae dear pay for a saddle;
My travel a', on foot I'll shank it,
I've sturdy bearers, Gude be thankit !
The kirk and you may tak you that,
It puts but little in your pat;
Sae dinna put me in your beuk,
Nor for my ten white shillings leuk.

This list, wi' my ain hand I wrote it,
The day and date as under noted;
Then know all ye whom it concerns,
Subscripsi huic,   ROBERT BURNS.

MOSSGIEL, *February* 22, 1786.

TO JOHN KENNEDY, DUMFRIES HOUSE

Now, Kennedy, if foot or horse
E'er bring you in by Mauchlin corse,
(Lord, man, there's lasses there wad force
    A hermit's fancy;
An' down the gate in faith they're worse,
    An' mair unchancy).

But as I'm sayin', please step to Dow's,
An' taste sic gear as Johnie brews,

Till some bit callan brings me news
   That ye are there;
An' if we dinna hae a bouze,
   I'se ne'er drink mair.

It's no I like to sit an' swallow,
Then like a swine to puke an' wallow;
But gie me just a true good fallow,
   Wi' right ingine,
And spunkie ance to mak us mellow,
   An' then we'll shine.

Now if ye're ane o' warl's folk,
Wha rate the wearer by the cloak,
An' sklent on poverty their joke,
   Wi' bitter sneer,
Wi' you nae friendship I will troke,
   Nor cheap nor dear.

But if, as I'm informèd weel, .
Ye hate as ill's the vera deil
The flinty heart that canna feel—
   Come, sir, here's to you!
Hae, there's my haun', I wiss ye weel,
   An' gude be wi' you.
       ROBT. BURNESS.

MOSSGIEL, 3rd March, 1786.

TO MR M'ADAM, OF CRAIGEN-GILLAN,

IN ANSWER TO AN OBLIGING LETTER HE SENT IN THE COMMENCEMENT OF MY POETIC CAREER

SIR, o'er a gill I gat your card,
  I trow it made me proud;
'See wha taks notice o' the bard!'
  I lap and cry'd fu' loud.

Now deil-ma-care about their jaw,
　　The senseless, gawky million;
I'll cock my nose aboon them a',
　　I'm roos'd by Craigen-Gillan !

'Twas noble, sir; 'twas like yoursel,
　　To grant your high protection :
A great man's smile, ye ken fu' well,
　　Is ay a blest infection.

Tho' by his banes wha in a tub
　　Match'd Macedonian Sandy !
On my ain legs thro' dirt and dub,
　　I independent stand ay,—

And when those legs to gude, warm kail,
　　Wi' welcome canna bear me,
A lee dyke-side, a sybow-tail,
　　An' barley-scone shall cheer me.

Heaven spare you lang to kiss the breath
　　O' mony flow'ry simmers !
An' bless your bonie lasses baith,
　　I'm tauld they're loosome kimmers !

An' God bless young Dunaskin's laird,
　　The blossom of our gentry !
An' may he wear an auld man's beard,
　　A credit to his country.

TO A LOUSE

ON SEEING ONE ON A LADY'S BONNET AT CHURCH

Ha ! whaur ye gaun, ye crowlin' ferlie ?
Your impudence protects you sairlie;
I canna say but ye strunt rarely,
　　　　Owre gauze and lace;
Tho' faith ! I fear, ye dine but sparely
　　　　On sic a place.

Ye ugly, creepin', blasted wonner,
Detested, shunn'd by saunt an' sinner,
How daur ye set your fit upon her—
     Sae fine a lady ?
Gae somewhere else, and seek your dinner
      On some poor body.

Swith ! in some beggar's haffet squattle,
Wi' ither kindred, jumping cattle;
There ye may creep, and sprawl, and sprattle,
     In shoals and nations;
Whaur horn nor bane ne'er daur unsettle
      Your thick plantations.

Now haud you there, ye're out o' sight,
Below the fatt'rels, snug and tight,
Na, faith ye yet ! ye'll no be right,
     Till ye've got on it—
The verra tapmost, tow'rin' height
      O' Miss's bonnet.

My sooth ! right bauld ye set your nose out,
As plump an' gray as ony groset :
O for some rank, mercurial rozet,
     Or fell, red smeddum,
I'd gie you sic a hearty dose o't,
      Wad dress your droddum.

I wad na been surpris'd to spy
You on an auld wife's flannen toy;
Or aiblins some bit duddie boy,
     On's wyliecoat;
But Miss's fine Lunardi ! fye !
      How daur ye do't ?

O Jenny, dinna toss your head,
An' set your beauties a' abread !
Ye little ken what cursed speed
     The blastie's makin' :
Thae winks an' finger-ends, I dread,
      Are notice takin'.

O wad some Power the giftie gie us,
To see oursels as ithers see us!
It wad frae mony a blunder free us,
        An' foolish notion:
What airs in dress an' gait wad lea'e us,
        An' ev'n devotion!

INSCRIBED ON A WORK OF HANNAH MORE'S

PRESENTED TO THE AUTHOR BY A LADY

THOU flatt'ring mark of friendship kind,
Still may thy pages call to mind
    The dear, the beauteous, donor;
Tho' sweetly female ev'ry part,
Yet such a head, and more—the heart
    Does both the sexes honor:
She show'd her taste refin'd and just,
    When she selected thee;
Yet deviating, own I must,
    For sae approving me:
        But kind still I'll mind still
        The *giver* in the gift;
        I'll bless her, an' wiss her
        A Friend aboon the lift.

THE HOLY FAIR

A robe of seeming truth and trust
    Hid crafty observation;
And secret hung, with poison'd crust,
    The dirk of Defamation:
A mask that like the gorget show'd
    Dye-varying on the pigeon;
And for a mantle large and broad,
    He wrapt him in *Religion.*
                        HYPOCRISY A-LA-MODE.

UPON a simmer Sunday morn,
    When Nature's face is fair,
I walkèd forth to view the corn,
    An' snuff the caller air.

The rising sun owre Galston muirs
  Wi' glorious light was glintin';
The hares were hirplin' down the furrs,
  The lav'rocks they were chantin'
        Fu' sweet that day.

As lightsomely I glowr'd abroad,
  To see a scene sae gay,
Three hizzies, early at the road,
  Cam skelpin' up the way.
Twa had manteeles o' dolefu' black,
  But ane wi' lyart lining;
The third, that gaed a wee a-back,
  Was in the fashion shining,
        Fu' gay that day.

The twa appear'd like sisters twin,
  In feature, form, an' claes;
Their visage wither'd, lang an' thin,
  An' sour as ony slaes :
The third cam up, hap-stap-an'-lowp,
  As light as ony lambie,
An' wi' a curchie low did stoop,
  As soon as e'er she saw me,
        Fu' kind that day.

Wi' bonnet aff, quoth I, 'Sweet lass,
  I think ye seem to ken me;
I'm sure I've seen that bonie face,
  But yet I canna name ye.'
Quo' she, an' laughin' as she spak,
  An' taks me by the hands,
'Ye, for my sake, hae gien the feck
  Of a' the ten commands
        A screed some day.'

'My name is Fun—your cronie dear,
  The nearest friend ye hae;
An' this is Superstition here,
  An' that's Hypocrisy.

I'm gaun to Mauchline "holy fair,"
  To spend an' hour in daffin':
Gin ye'll go there, yon runkl'd pair,
  We will get famous laughin'
        At them this day.'

Quoth I, 'Wi' a' my heart, I'll do't;
  I'll get my Sunday's sark on,
An' meet you on the holy spot;
  Faith, we'se hae fine remarkin'!'
Then I gaed hame at crowdie-time,
  An' soon I made me ready;
For roads were clad, frae side to side,
  Wi' mony a wearie body,
        In droves that day.

Here farmers gash, in ridin' graith,
  Gaed hoddin by their cottars:
There swankies young, in braw braid-claith,
  Are springin' owre the gutters.
The lasses, skelpin' barefit, thrang,
  In silks an' scarlets glitter;
Wi' sweet-milk cheese, in mony a whang,
  An' farls, bak'd wi' butter,
        Fu' crump that day.

When by the 'plate' we set our nose,
  Weel heapèd up wi' ha'pence,
A greedy glow'r 'black-bonnet' throws,
  An' we maun draw our tippence.
Then in we go to see the show:
  On ev'ry side they're gath'rin';
Some carrying dails, some chairs and stools,
  An' some are busy bleth'rin'
        Right loud that day.

Here stands a shed to fend the show'rs,
  An' screen our countra gentry;
There 'Racer Jess,' an' twa-three wh–res,
  Are blinkin' at the entry.

Here sits a raw o' tittlin' jads,
    Wi' heavin' breasts an' bare neck;
An' there a batch o' wabster lads,
    Blackguardin' frae Kilmarnock,
            For fun this day.

Here some are thinkin' on their sins,
    An' some upo' their claes;
Ane curses feet that fyl'd his shins,
    Anither sighs an' prays :
On this hand sits a chosen swatch,
    Wi' screw'd-up, grace-proud faces;
On that a set o' chaps, at watch,
    Thrang winkin' on the lasses
            To chairs that day.

O happy is that man, an' blest !
    Nae wonder that it pride him !
Whase ain dear lass, that he likes best,
    Comes clinkin' down beside him !
Wi' arm repos'd on the chair back,
    He sweetly does compose him;
Which, by degrees, slips round her neck,
    An's loof upon her bosom,
            Unkend that day.

Now a' the congregation o'er
    Is silent expectation;
For Moodie speels the holy door,
    Wi' tidings o' damnation :
Should *Hornie*, as in ancient days,
    'Mang sons o' God present him,
The vera sight o' Moodie's face,
    To 's ain het hame had sent him
            Wi' fright that day.

Hear how he clears the points o' Faith
    Wi' rattlin' and wi' thumpin' !
Now meekly calm, now wild in wrath,
    He's stampin', an' he's jumpin';

His lengthen'd chin, his turned-up snout,
　　His eldritch squeel an' gestures,
O how they fire the heart devout,
　　Like cantharidian plaisters
　　　　　　On sic a day!

But hark! the tent has chang'd its voice;
　　There's peace an' rest nae langer;
For a' the real judges rise,
　　They canna sit for anger,
Smith opens out his cauld harangues,
　　On practice and on morals;
An' aff the godly pour in thrangs,
　　To gie the jars an' barrels
　　　　　　A lift that day.

What signifies his barren shine,
Of moral powers an' reason?
His English style, an' gesture fine
　　Are a' clean out o' season.
Like Socrates or Antonine,
　　Or some auld pagan heathen,
The *moral man* he does define,
　　But ne'er a word o' *faith* in
　　　　　　That's right that day.

In guid time comes an antidote
　　Against sic poison'd nostrum;
For Peebles, frae the water-fit,
　　Ascends the holy rostrum:
See, up he's got the word o' God,
　　An' meek an' mim has view'd it,
While 'Common-sense' has taen the road
　　An' aff, an' up the Cowgate
　　　　　　Fast, fast that day.

Wee Miller niest, the Guard relieves,
　　An' Orthodoxy raibles,
Tho' in his heart he weel believes,
　　An' thinks it auld wives' fables:

But faith! the birkie wants a manse,
   So, cannilie he hums them;
Altho' his carnal wit an' sense
   Like hafflins-wise o'ercomes him
          At times that day.

Now butt an' ben the change-house fills,
   Wi' yill-caup commentators;
Here's cryin' out for bakes and gills,
   An' there the pint-stowp clatters;
While thick an' thrang, an' loud an' lang,
   Wi' logic an' wi' scripture,
They raise a din, that in the end
   Is like to breed a rupture
          O' wrath that day.

Leeze me on drink! it gies us mair
   Than either school or college;
It ken'les wit, it waukens lear,
   It pangs us fou o' knowledge:
Be't whisky-gill or penny-wheep,
   Or ony stronger potion,
It never fails, on drinkin' deep,
   To kittle up our notion,
          By night or day.

The lads an' lasses, blythely bent
   To mind baith saul an' body,
Sit round the table, weel content,
   An' steer about the toddy:
On this ane's dress, an' that ane's leuk,
   They're makin' observations;
While some are cozie i' the neuk,
   An' forming assignations
          To meet some day.

But now the L—'s ain trumpet touts,
   Till a' the hills are rairin',
And echoes back-return the shouts;
   Black Russell is na sparin':

His piercin' words, like Highlan' swords,
  Divide the joints an' marrow;
His talk o'. Hell, whare devils dwell,
  Our vera 'sauls does harrow'
            Wi' fright that day!

A vast, unbottom'd, boundless pit,
  Fill'd fou o' lowin' brunstane,
Whase ragin' flame, an' scorching heat,
  Wad melt the hardest whun-stane!
The half-asleep start up wi' fear,
  An' think they hear it roarin';
When presently it does appear,
  'Twas but some neibor snorin'
            Asleep that day.

'Twad be owre lang a tale to tell,
  How mony stories past;
An' how they crouded to the yill,
  When they were a' dismist;
How drink gaed round, in cogs an' caups,
  Amang the furms an' benches;
An' cheese an' bread, frae women's laps,
  Was dealt about in lunches,
            An' dawds that day.

In comes a gawsie, gash guidwife,
  An' sits down by the fire,
Syne draws her kebbuck an' her knife;
  The lasses they are shyer:
The auld guidmen, about the grace,
  Frae side to side they bother;
Till some ane by his bonnet lays,
  An' gies them't like a tether,
            Fu' lang that day.

Waesucks! for him that gets nae lass,
  Or lasses that hae naething!
Sma' need has he to say a grace,
  Or melvie his braw claithing!

O wives, be mindfu' ance yoursel
How bonie lads ye wanted;
An' dinna, for a kebbuck-heel,
Let lasses be affronted
On sic a day!

Now 'Clinkumbell,' wi' rattlin' tow,
Begins to jow an' croon;
Some swagger hame the best they dow,
Some wait the afternoon.
At slaps the billies halt a blink,
Till lasses strip their shoon:
Wi' faith an' hope, an' love an' drink,
They're a' in famous tune
For crack that day.

How mony hearts this day converts,
O' sinners and o' lasses!
Their hearts o' stane, gin night, are gane,
As saft as ony flesh is:
There's some are fou o' love divine;
There's some are fou o' brandy;
An' mony jobs that day begin,
May end in 'houghmagandie'
Some ither day.

AND MAUN I STILL ON MENIE DOAT

Tune—'Johnny's Gray Breeks.'

AGAIN rejoicing Nature sees
Her robe assume its vernal hues:
Her leafy locks wave in the breeze,
All freshly steep'd in morning dews.

Chorus.—And maun I still on Menie doat,
    And bear the scorn that's in her e'e ?
For it's jet, jet-black, an' it's like a hawk,
    An' it winna let a body be.

In vain to me the cowslips blaw,
    In vain to me the vi'lets spring;
In vain to me in glen or shaw,
    The mavis and the lintwhite sing,
              And maun I still, etc.

The merry ploughboy cheers his team,
    Wi' joy the tentie seedsman stalks;
But life's to me a weary dream,
    A dream of ane that never wauks.
              And maun I still, etc.

The wanton coot the water skims,
    Amang the reeds the ducklings cry,
The stately swan majestic swims,
    And ev'ry thing is blest but I.
              And maun I still, etc.

The sheep-herd steeks his faulding slap,
    And o'er the moorland whistles shrill;
Wi' wild, unequal, wand'ring step,
    I meet him on the dewy hill.
              And maun I still, etc.

And when the lark, 'tween light and dark,
    Blythe waukens by the daisy's side,
And mounts and sings on flittering wings,
    A woe-worn ghaist I hameward glide.
              And maun I still, etc.

Come winter, with thine angry howl,
    And raging, bend the naked tree;
Thy gloom will soothe my cheerless soul,
    When nature all is sad like me.!
              And maun I still, etc.

TO A MOUNTAIN DAISY

ON TURNING ONE DOWN WITH THE PLOUGH, IN APRIL, 1786

WEE, modest, crimson-tipped flow'r,
Thou's met me in an evil hour;
For I maun crush amang the stoure
   Thy slender stem :
To spare thee now is past my pow'r,
   Thou bonie gem.

Alas ! it's no thy neibor sweet,
The bonie lark, companion meet,
Bending thee 'mang the dewy weet,
   Wi' spreckl'd breast !
When upward-springing, blythe, to greet
   The purpling east.

Cauld blew the bitter-biting north
Upon thy early, humble birth;
Yet cheerfully thou glinted forth
   Amid the storm,
Scarce rear'd above the parent earth
   Thy tender form.

The flaunting flow'rs our gardens yield,
High shelt'ring woods and wa's maun shield;
But thou, beneath the random bield
   O' clod or stane,
Adorns the histie stibble field,
   Unseen, alane.

There, in thy scanty mantle clad,
Thy snawie bosom sun-ward spread,
Thou lifts thy unassuming head
   In humble guise;
But now the share uptears thy bed,
   And low thou lies !

Such is the fate of artless maid,
Sweet flow'ret of the rural shade !
By love's simplicity betray'd,
        And guileless trust;
Till she, like thee, all soil'd, is laid
        Low i' the dust.

Such is the fate of simple bard,
On life's rough ocean luckless starr'd !
Unskilful he to note the card
        Of prudent lore,
Till billows rage, and gales blow hard,
        And whelm him o'er !

Such fate to suffering worth is giv'n,
Who long with wants and woes has striv'n,
By human pride or cunning driv'n
        To mis'ry's brink;
Till wrench'd of ev'ry stay but Heav'n,
        He, ruin'd, sink !

Ev'n thou who mourn'st the Daisy's fate,
That fate is thine—no distant date;
Stern Ruin's plough-share drives elate,
        Full on thy bloom,
Till crush'd beneath the furrow's weight,
        Shall be thy doom !

TO RUIN

ALL hail, inexorable lord !
At whose destruction-breathing word,
   The mightiest empires fall !
Thy cruel, woe-delighted train,
The ministers of grief and pain.
   A sullen welcome, all !

With stern-resolv'd, despairing eye,
　　I see each aimèd dart;
For one has cut my dearest tie,
　　And quivers in my heart.
　　　　Then low'ring, and pouring,
　　　　　The storm no more I dread;
　　　　Tho' thick'ning, and black'ning,
　　　　　Round my devoted head.

And thou grim Pow'r by life abhorr'd,
While life a pleasure can afford,
　　Oh! hear a wretch's pray'r!
No more I shrink appall'd, afraid;
I court, I beg thy friendly aid,
　　To close this scene of care!
When shall my soul, in silent peace,
　　Resign life's joyless day—
My weary heart its throbbings cease,
　　Cold mould'ring in the clay?
　　　　No fear more, no tear more,
　　　　　To stain my lifeless face,
　　　　Enclaspèd, and grasped,
　　　　　Within thy cold embrace!

THE LAMENT

OCCASIONED BY THE UNFORTUNATE ISSUE OF A FRIEND'S AMOUR

Alas! how oft does goodness wound itself,
And sweet affection prove the spring of woe!—HOME.

O THOU pale orb that silent shines,
　　While care-untroubled mortals sleep!
Thou seest a wretch who inly pines,
　　And wanders here to wail and weep!

With woe I nightly vigils keep,
　　Beneath thy wan, unwarming beam;
And mourn, in lamentation deep,
　　How life and love are all a dream!

I joyless view thy rays adorn
　　The faintly-marked, distant hill;
I joyless view thy trembling horn,
　　Reflected in the gurgling rill:
My fondly-fluttering heart, be still!
　　Thou busy pow'r, remembrance, cease!
Ah! must the agonising thrill
　　For ever bar returning peace!

No idly-feign'd, poetic pains,
　　My sad, love-lorn lamentings claim:
No shepherd's pipe—Arcadian strains;
　　No fabled tortures, quaint and tame.
The plighted faith, the mutual flame,
　　The oft-attested pow'rs above,
The promis'd father's tender name;
　　These were the pledges of my love!

Encircled in her clasping arms,
　　How have the raptur'd moments flown!
How have I wish'd for fortune's charms,
　　For her dear sake, and her's alone!
And, must I think it! is she gone,
　　My secret heart's exulting boast?
And does she heedless hear my groan?
　　And is she ever, ever lost?

Oh! can she bear so base a heart,
　　So lost to honour, lost to truth,
As from the fondest lover part,
　　The plighted husband of her youth?
Alas! life's path may be unsmooth!
　　Her way may lie thro' rough distress!
Then, who her pangs and pains will soothe,
　　Her sorrows share, and make them less?

Ye winged hours that o'er us pass'd,
  Enraptur'd more, the more enjoy'd,
Your dear remembrance in my breast
  My fondly-treasur'd thoughts employ'd:
That breast, how dreary now, and void,
  For her too scanty once of room!
Ev'n ev'ry ray of hope destroy'd,
  And not a wish to gild the gloom!

The morn that warns th' approaching day,
  Awakes me up to toil and woe;
I see the hours in long array,
  That I must suffer, lingering slow:
Full many a pang, and many a throe,
  Keen recollection's direful train,
Must wring my soul, ere Phœbus, low,
  Shall kiss the distant western main.

And when my nightly couch I try,
  Sore harass'd out with care and grief,
My toil-beat nerves, and tear-worn eye,
  Keep watchings with the nightly thief:
Or if I slumber, fancy, chief,
  Reigns, haggard-wild, in sore affright:
Ev'n day, all-bitter, brings relief
  From such a horror-breathing night.

O thou bright queen, who, o'er th' expanse
  Now highest reign'st, with boundless sway!
Oft has thy silent-marking glance
  Observ'd us, fondly-wand'ring, stray!
The time, unheeded, sped away,
  While love's luxurious pulse beat high,
Beneath thy silver-gleaming ray,
  To mark the mutual-kindling eye.

Oh! scenes in strong remembrance set!
  Scenes, never, never to return!
Scenes, if in stupor I forget,
  Again I feel, again I burn!

From ev'ry joy and pleasure torn,
  Life's weary vale I'll wander thro';
And hopeless, comfortless, I'll mourn
  A faithless woman's broken vow!

DESPONDENCY—AN ODE

OPPRESS'D with grief, oppress'd with care,
A burden more than I can bear,
  I set me down and sigh;
O life! thou art a galling load,
Along a rough, a weary road,
  To wretches such as I!
Dim-backward as I cast my view,
  What sick'ning scenes appear!
What sorrows yet may pierce me through,
  Too justly I may fear!
    Still caring, despairing,
      Must be my bitter doom;
    My woes here shall close ne'er
      But with the closing tomb!

Happy! ye sons of busy life,
Who, equal to the bustling strife,
  No other view regard!
Ev'n when the wishèd end's denied,
Yet while the busy means are plied,
  They bring their own reward:
Whilst I, a hope-abandon'd wight,
  Unfitted with an aim,
Meet ev'ry sad returning night,
  And joyless morn the same!
    You, bustling and justling,
      Forget each grief an' pain;
    I, listless, yet restless,
      Find ev'ry prospect vain.

How blest the solitary's lot,
Who, all-forgetting, all-forgot,
   Within his humble cell,
The cavern, wild with tangling roots,
Sits o'er his newly gather'd fruits,
   Beside his crystal well!
Or haply, to his ev'ning thought,
   By unfrequented stream,
The ways of men are distant brought,
   A faint, collected dream;
     While praising, and raising,
       His thoughts to Heav'n on high,
     As wand'ring, meand'ring,
       He views the solemn sky.

Than I, no lonely hermit plac'd
Where never human footstep trac'd,
   Less fit to play the part;
The lucky moment to improve,
And just to stop, and just to move,
   With self-respecting art:
But ah! those pleasures, loves, and joys,
   Which I too keenly taste,
The solitary can despise—
   Can want, and yet be blest!
     He needs not, he heeds not,
       Or human love or hate;
     Whilst I here must cry here
       At perfidy ingrate!

O enviable early days,
When dancing thoughtless pleasure's maze,
   To care, to guilt unknown!
How ill exchang'd for riper times,
To feel the follies, or the crimes,
   Of others, or my own!
Ye tiny elves that guiltless sport,
   Like linnets in the bush,
Ye little know the ills ye court,
   When manhood is your wish!

The losses, the crosses,
   That active man engage;
The fears all, the tears all,
   Of dim declining Age!

TO GAVIN HAMILTON, ESQ., MAUCHLINE

RECOMMENDING A BOY

MOSSGAVILLE, *May* 3, 1786.

I HOLD it, sir, my bounden duty
To warn you how that 'Master Tootie,'
   Alias 'Laird M'Gaun,'
Was here to hire yon lad away
'Bout whom ye spak the tither day,
   An' wad hae done't aff han';
But lest he learn the callan tricks—
   An' faith I muckle doubt him—
Like scrapin' out auld Crummie's nicks,
   An' tellin' lies about them;
      As lieve then, I'd have then,
         Your clerkship he should sair,
      If sae be ye may be
         Not fitted otherwhere.

Altho' I say't, he's gleg enough,
An' 'bout a house that's rude an' rough,
   The boy might learn to swear;
But then wi' *you* he'll be sae taught,
An' get sic fair example straught,
   I hae na ony fear.
Ye'll catechise him, every quirk,
   An' shore him weel wi' 'hell';
An' gar him follow to the kirk—
   Ay when ye gang yoursel.

If ye then, maun be then
    Frae hame this comin' Friday,
Then please, sir, to lea'e, sir,
    The orders wi' your lady.

My word of honour I hae gi'en,
In Paisley John's, that night at e'en,
    To meet the 'warld's worm';
To try to get the twa to 'gree,
An' name the airles an' the fee,
    In legal mode an' form :
I ken he weel a *snick* can draw,
    When simple bodies let him;
An' if a Devil be at a',
    In faith he's sure to get him.
    To phrase you an' praise you,
      Ye ken your Laureat scorns :
    The pray'r still, you share still,
      Of grateful MINSTREL BURNS.

VERSIFIED REPLY TO AN INVITATION

SIR,
    Yours this moment I unseal,
      And faith I'm gay and hearty !
To tell the truth and shame the deil,
    I am as fou as Bartie :
But Foorsday, sir, my promise leal,
      Expect me o' your partie,
If on a beastie I can speil,
    Or hurl in a cartie.

        Yours,

          ROBERT BURNS.

MAUCHLIN, *Monday night,* 10 *o'clock.*

WILL YE GO TO THE INDIES, MY MARY?

Tune—'Ewe-Bughts, Marion.'

WILL ye go to the Indies, my Mary,
 And leave auld Scotia's shore?
Will ye go to the Indies, my Mary,
 Across th' Atlantic's roar?

O sweet grows the lime and the orange,
 And the apple on the pine;
But a' the charms o' the Indies
 Can never equal thine.

I hae sworn by the Heavens to my Mary,
 I hae sworn by the Heavens to be true;
And sae may the Heavens forget me,
 When I forget my vow!

O plight me your faith, my Mary,
 And plight me your lily-white hand;
O plight me your faith, my Mary,
 Before I leave Scotia's strand.

We hae plighted our troth, my Mary,
 In mutual affection to join;
And curst be the cause that shall part us!
 The hour and the moment o' time!

MY HIGHLAND LASSIE, O

NAE gentle dames, tho' ne'er sae fair,
 Shall ever be my muse's care:
Their titles a' are empty show;
 Gie me my Highland lassie, O.

Chorus.—Within the glen sae bushy, O.
Aboon the plain sae rashy, O.
I set me down wi' right guid will,
To sing my Highland lassie, O.

O were yon hills and vallies mine,
Yon palace and yon gardens fine!
The world then the love should know
I bear my Highland lassie, O.

But fickle fortune frowns on me,
And I maun cross the raging sea;
But while my crimson currents flow,
I'll love my Highland lassie, O.

Altho' thro' foreign climes I range,
I know her heart will never change,
For her bosom burns with honour's glow,
My faithful Highland lassie, O.

For her I'll dare the billow's roar,
For her I'll trace a distant shore,
That Indian wealth may lustre throw
Around my Highland lassie, O.

She has my heart, she has my hand,
By secret troth and honor's band!
'Till the mortal stroke shall lay me low,
I'm thine, my Highland lassie, O.

Farewell the glen sae bushy, O!
Farewell the plain sae rashy, O!
To other lands I now must go,
To sing my Highland lassie, O.

EPISTLE TO A YOUNG FRIEND

May ——, 1786.

I LANG hae thought, my youthfu' friend,
   A something to have sent you,
Tho' it should serve nae ither end
   Than just a kind memento :
But how the subject-theme may gang,
   Let time and chance determine;
Perhaps it may turn out a sang;
   Perhaps, turn out a sermon.

Ye'll try the world soon, my lad;
   And, Andrew dear, believe me,
Ye'll find mankind an unco squad,
   And muckle they may grieve ye .
For care and trouble set your thought
   Ev'n when your end's attained;
And a' your views may come to nought,
   Where ev'ry nerve is strained.

I'll no say men are villains a';
   The real, harden'd wicked,
Wha hae nae check but human law,
   Are to a few restricked;
But, och ! mankind are unco weak,
   An' little to be trusted;
If *self* the wavering balance shake,
   It's rarely right adjusted !

Yet they wha fa' in fortune's strife,
   Their fate we shouldna censure;
For still, th' important end o' life
   They equally may answer;
A man may hae an honest heart,
   Tho' poortith hourly stare him;
A man may tak a neibor's part,
   Yet hae nae cash to spare him.

Ay free, aff han', your story tell,
　When wi' a bosom crony;
But still keep something to yoursel
　Ye scarcely tell to ony :
Conceal yoursel as weel's ye can
　Frae critical dissection;
But keek thro' ev'ry other man,
　Wi' sharpen'd sly inspection.

The sacred lowe o' weel-plac'd love,
　Luxuriantly indulge it;
But never tempt th' illicit rove
　Tho' naething should divulge it :
I wave the quantum o' the sin,
　The hazard of concealing;
But, och ! it hardens a' within,
　And petrifies the feeling !

To catch Dame Fortune's golden smile,
　Assiduous wait upon her;
And gather gear by ev'ry wile
　That's justify'd by honor;
Not for to hide it in a hedge,
　Nor for a train attendant;
But for the glorious privilege
　Of being independent.

The fear o' Hell's a hangman's whip,
　To haud the wretch in order;
But where you feel your honour grip,
　Let that ay be your border :
Its slightest touches, instant pause—
　Debar a' side-pretences;
And resolutely keeps its laws,
　Uncaring consequences.

The great Creator to revere,
　Must sure become the creature;
But still the preaching cant forbear,
　And ev'n the rigid feature :

Yet ne'er with wits profane to range,
  Be complaisance extended;
An atheist-laugh's a poor exchange
  For Deity offended!

When ranting round in pleasure's ring,
  Religion may be blinded;
Or if she gie a random sting,
  It may be little minded;
But when on life we're tempest-driv'n—
  A conscience but a canker—
A correspondence fix'd wi' Heav'n,
  Is sure a noble anchor!

Adieu, dear, amiable youth!
  Your heart can ne'er be wanting!
May prudence, fortitude, and truth,
  Erect your brow undaunting!
In ploughman phrase, 'God send you speed,'
  Still daily to grow wiser;
And may you better reck the rede,
  Than ever did th' adviser!

ADDRESS OF BEELZEBUB

To the Right Honorable the Earl of Breadalbane,
President of the Right Honorable and Honorable the Highland Society, which met on the 23rd of May last, at the
Shakespeare, Covent Garden, to concert ways and means to
frustrate the designs of five hundred Highlanders who, as
the Society were informed by Mr M'Kenzie of Applecross,
were so audacious as to attempt an escape from their lawful
lords and masters whose property they are, by emigrating
from the lands of Mr Macdonald of Glengary to the wilds
of Canada, in search of that fantastic thing—LIBERTY.

Long life, my lord, an' health be yours,
Unskaith'd by hunger'd Highland boors;
Lord grant nae duddie, desperate beggar,
Wi' dirk, claymore, and rusty trigger,
May twin auld Scotland o' a life
She likes—as lambkins like a knife.

Faith, you and Applecross were right,
To keep the Highland hounds in sight :
I doubt na ! they wad bid nae better,
Than let them ance out owre the water,
Then up amang thae lakes and seas,
They'll mak what rules and laws they please :
Some daring Hancocke, or a Franklin,
May set their Highland bluid a-ranklin' ;
Some Washington again may head them,
Or some Montgomery, fearless, lead them ;
Till (God knows what may be effected
When by such heads and hearts directed),
Poor dunghill sons of dirt and mire
May to Patrician rights aspire !
Nae sage North now, nor sager Sackville,
To watch and premier o'er the pack vile,—
An' whare will ye get Howes and Clintons
To bring them to a right repentance—
To cowe the rebel generation,
An' save the honor o' the nation ?
They, an' be d—d ! what right hae they
To meat, or sleep, or light o' day ?
Far less—to riches, pow'r, or freedom,
But what your lordship likes to gie them ?

But hear, my lord ! Glengary, hear !
Your hand's owre light on them, I fear ;
Your factors, grieves, trustees, and bailies,
I canna say but they do gaylies ;
They lay aside a' tender mercies,
An' tirl the hallions to the birses ;
Yet while they're only poind't and herriet,
They'll keep their stubborn Highland spirit :
But smash them ! crash them a' to spails,
An' rot the dyvors i' the jails !
The young dogs, swinge them to the labour :
Let wark an' hunger mak them sober !

The hizzies, if they're aughtlins fawsont,
Let them in Drury-lane be lesson'd !
An' if the wives an' dirty brats
Come thiggin' at your doors an' yetts,
Flaffin' wi' duds, an' gray wi' beas',
Frightin' away your ducks an' geese ;
Get out a horsewhip or a jowler,
The langest thong, the fiercest growler,
An' gar the tatter'd gypsies pack
Wi' a' their bastards on their back !

Go on, my Lord ! I lang to meet you,
An' in my 'house at hame' to greet you,
Wi' common lords ye shanna mingle,
The benmost neuk beside the ingle,
At my right han' assigned your seat,
'Tween Herod's hip an' Polycrate ;
Or (if you on your station tarrow),
Between Almagro and Pizarro,
A seat, I'm sure ye're well deservin't ;
An' till ye come—your humble servant,
                                    BEELZEBUB.

June 1st, Anno Mundi 5790.

A DREAM

Thoughts, words, and deeds, the Statute blames with reason ;
But surely Dreams were ne'er indicted Treason.

On reading, in the public papers, the Laureate's Ode, with
the other parade of June 4, 1786, the Author was no sooner
dropt asleep, than he imagined himself transported to the
Birthday Levee ; and, in his dreaming fancy, made the following Address :—

GUID-MORNIN' to your Majesty !
    May Heaven augment your blisses
On ev'ry new birthday ye see,
    A humble poet wishes.

My bardship here, at your Levee
   O sic a day as this is,
Is sure an uncouth sight to see,
   Amang thae birthday dresses
          Sae fine this day.

I see ye're complimented thrang,
   By mony a lord an' lady;
'God save the King' 's a cuckoo sang
   That 's unco easy said ay :
The poets, too, a venal gang,
   Wi' rhymes weel-turn'd an' ready,
Wad gar you trow ye ne'er do wrang,
   But ay unerring steady,
          On sic a day.

For me ! before a monarch's face,
   Ev'n there I winna flatter;
For neither pension, post, nor place,
   Am I your humble debtor :
So, nae reflection on your Grace,
   Your Kingship to bespatter;
There's mony waur been o' the race,
   And aiblins ane been better
          Than you this day.

'Tis very true, my sovereign King,
   My skill may weel be doubted;
But facts are chiels that winna ding,
   An' downa be disputed :
Your royal nest, beneath your wing,
   Is e'en right reft an' clouted,
And now the third part o' the string,
   An' less, will gang about it
          Than did ae day.

Far be't frae me that I aspire
   To blame your legislation,
Or say, ye wisdom want, or fire
   To rule this mighty nation :

But faith! I muckle doubt, my sire,
    Ye've trusted ministration
To chaps wha in a barn or byre
    Wad better fill'd their station,
                Than courts yon day.

And now ye've gien auld Britain peace,
    Her broken shins to plaister;
Your sair taxation does her fleece,
    Till she has scarce a tester :
For me, thank God, my life's a lease,
    Nae bargain wearin' faster,
Or faith! I fear, that, wi' the geese,
    I shortly boost to pasture
                I' the craft some day.

I'm no mistrusting Willie Pitt,
    When taxes he enlarges,
(An' Will's a true guid fallow's get,
    A name not envy spairges),
That he intends to pay your debt,
    An' lessen a' your charges;
But, G—d sake! let nae saving fit
    Abridge your bonie barges
                An' boats this day.

Adieu, my Liege! may Freedom geck
    Beneath your high protection;
An' may ye rax Corruption's neck,
    And gie her for dissection!
But since I'm here, I'll no neglect,
    In loyal, true affection,
To pay your Queen, wi' due respect,
    My fealty an' subjection
                This great birthday.

Hail, Majesty most Excellent!
    While nobles strive to please ye,
Will ye accept a compliment,
    A simple poet gies ye?

Thae bonie bairntime, Heav'n has lent,
   Still higher may they heeze ye
In bliss, till fate some day is sent,
   For ever to release ye
         Frae care that day.

For you, young Potentate o' Wales,
   I tell your Highness fairly,
Down Pleasure's stream, wi' swelling sails,
   I'm tauld ye're driving rarely;
But some day ye may gnaw your nails,
   An' curse your folly sairly,
That e'er ye brak' Diana's pales,
   Or rattl'd dice wi' Charlie
         By night or day.

Yet aft a ragged cowt's been known,
   To mak a noble aiver;
So, ye may doucely fill a throne,
   For a' their clish-ma-claver:
There, him at Agincourt wha shone,
   Few better were or braver;
And yet, wi' funny, queer Sir John,
   He was an unco shaver
         For mony a day.

For you, right rev'rend Osnaburg,
   Nane sets the lawn-sleeve sweeter,
Altho' a ribban at your lug
   Wad been a dress completer:
As ye disown yon paughty dog,
   That bears the keys of Peter,
Then swith! an' get a wife to hug,
   Or trowth, ye'll stain the mitre
         Some luckless day!

Young, royal 'tarry-breeks,' I learn,
   Ye've lately come athwart her—
A glorious galley, stem and stern,
   Well rigg'd for Venus' barter;

But first hang out that she'll discern
   Your hymeneal charter;
Then heave aboard your grapple-airn,
   An' 'large upon her quarter,
          Come full that day.

Ye, lastly, bonie blossoms a',
   Ye royal lasses dainty,
Heav'n mak ye guid as weel as braw,
   An' gie ye lads a-plenty!
But sneer na British boys awa'!
   For kings are unco scant ay,
An' German gentles are but sma',
   They're better just than want ay
          On ony day.

God bless you a'! consider now,
   Ye're unco muckle dautet;
But ere the course o' life be through.
   It may be bitter sautet:
An' I hae seen their coggie fou,
   That yet hae tarrow't at it.
But or the day was done, I trow,
   The leggen they hae clautet
          Fu' clean that day.

A DEDICATION

TO GAVIN HAMILTON, ESQ.

EXPECT na, sir, in this narration,
A fleechin', fleth'rin' Dedication,
To roose you up, an' ca' you guid,
An' sprung o' great an' noble bluid,
Because ye're surnam'd like His Grace—
Perhaps related to the race:

Then, when I'm tir'd—and sae are ye,
Wi' mony a fulsome, sinfu' lie,
Set up a face how I stop short,
For fear your modesty be hurt.

This may do—maun do, sir, wi' them wha
Maun please the great-folk for a wamefou;
For me! sae laigh I need na bow,
For, Lord be thanket, I can plough;
And when I downa yoke a naig,
Then, Lord be thanket, I can beg;
Sae I shall say—an' that's nae flatt'rin'—
It's just sic poet an' sic' patron.

The Poet, some guid angel help him,
Or else, I fear, some ill ane skelp him!
He may do weel for a' he's done yet,
But only—he's no just begun yet.

The Patron (sir, ye maun forgie me;
I winna lie, come what will o' me),
On ev'ry hand it will allow'd be,
He's just—nae better than he shou'd be.

I readily and freely grant
He downa see a poor man want;
What's no his ain, he winna tak it;
What ance he says, he winna break it;
Ought he can lend he'll no refus't,
Till aft his guidness is abus'd;
And rascals whyles that do him wrang,
Ev'n that, he does na mind it lang;
As master, landlord, husband, father,
He does na fail his part in either.

But then, nae thanks to him for a' that;
Nae godly symptom ye can ca' that;
It's naething but a milder feature
Of our poor, sinfu' corrupt nature:

Ye'll get the best o' moral works,
'Mang black Gentoos, and pagan Turks,
Or hunters wild on Ponataxi,
Wha never heard of orthodoxy.
That he's the poor man's friend in need,
The gentleman in word and deed,
It's no thro' terror of d—mn-t-n;
It's just a carnal inclination.

Morality, thou deadly bane,
Thy tens o' thousands thou hast slain!
Vain is his hope, whase stay an' trust is
In moral mercy, truth, and justice!

No—stretch a point to catch a plack;
Abuse a brother to his back;
Steal thro' the winnock frae a whore,
But point the rake that taks the door;
Be to the poor like onie whunstane,
And haud their noses to the grunstane;
Ply ev'ry art o' legal thieving;
No matter—stick to sound believing.

Learn three-mile pray'rs, an' half-mile
    graces,
Wi' weel-spread looves, an' lang, wry faces;
Grunt up a solemn, lengthen'd groan,
And damn a' parties but your own;
I'll warrant, then ye're nae deceiver,
A steady, sturdy, staunch believer.

O ye wha leave the springs o' Calvin,
For gumlie dubs of your ain delvin'!
Ye sons of Heresy and Error,
Ye'll some day squeel in quaking terror,
When Vengeance draws the sword in wrath,
And in the fire throws the sheath;

When Ruin, with his sweeping besom,
Just frets till Heav'n commission gies him;
While o'er the harp pale Misery moans,
And strikes the ever deep'ning tones,
Still louder shrieks, and heavier groans!

Your pardon, sir, for this digression:
I maist forgat my Dedication;
But when Divinity comes 'cross me,
My readers still are sure to lose me.

So, sir, you see 'twas nae daft vapour;
But I maturely thought it proper,
When a' my works I did review,
To dedicate them, sir, to you:
Because (ye need na tak it ill),
I thought them something like yoursel.

Then patronize them wi' your favour,
And your petitioner shall ever ——
I had amaist said, ever pray,
But that's a word I need na say;
For prayin' I hae little skill o't;
I'm baith dead-sweer, an' wretched ill o't;
But I'se repeat each poor man's pray'r,
That kens or hears about you, Sir ——

'May ne'er Misfortune's growling bark,
Howl thro' the dwelling o' the clerk!
May ne'er his gen'rous, honest heart,
For that same gen'rous spirit smart!
May Kennedy's far-honor'd name
Lang beet his hymeneal flame,
Till Hamiltons, at least a dizzen,
Are frae their nuptial labors risen:
Five bonie lasses round their table,
And sev'n braw fellows, stout an' able,
To serve their king an' country weel,
By word, or pen, or pointed steel!

May health and peace, with mutual rays,
Shine on the ev'ning o' his days;
Till his wee, curlie John's ier-oe,
When ebbing life nae mair shall flow,
The last, sad, mournful rites bestow!'

I will not wind a lang conclusion,
With complimentary effusion;
But whilst your wishes and endeavours
Are blest with Fortune's smiles and favours,
I am, dear sir, with zeal most fervent,
Your much indebted, humble servant.

But if (which Pow'rs above prevent)
That iron-hearted carl, Want,
Attended, in his grim advances,
By sad mistakes, and black mischances,
While hopes, and joys, and plesasures fly him,
Make you as poor a dog as I am,
Your 'humble servant'; then no more;
For who would humbly serve the poor?
But, by a poor man's hopes in Heav'n
While recollection's pow'r is giv'n—
If, in the vale of humble life,
The victim sad of fortune's strife,
I, thro' the tender gushing tear,
Should recognise my master dear;
If friendless, low, we meet together,
Then, sir, your hand—my friend and brother!

VERSIFIED NOTE TO DR MACKENZIE, MAUCHLINE

FRIDAY first's the day appointed
By the Right Worshipful anointed,
    To hold our grand procession;
To get a blad o' Johnie's morals,
And taste a swatch o' Manson's barrels
    I' the way of our profession.

The Master and the Brotherhood
Would a' be glad to see you;
For me I wad be mair than proud
To share the mercies wi' you.
If Death, then, wi' skaith, then,
Some mortal heart is hechtin',
Inform him, and storm him,
That Saturday you'll fecht him.

ROBERT BURNS.

MOSSGIEL, *An. M.* 5790.

THE FAREWELL

TO THE BRETHREN OF ST JAMES'S LODGE, TARBOLTON

Tune—'Good-night, and joy be wi' you a'.'

ADIEU! a heart-warm, fond adieu;
Dear brothers of the *mystic tye* !
Ye favoured, ye *enlighten'd* few,
Companions of my social joy;
Tho' I to foreign lands must hie,
Pursuing Fortune's slidd'ry ba';
With melting heart, and brimful eye,
I'll mind you still, tho' far awa'.

Oft have I met your social band,
And spent the cheerful, festive night :
Oft, honour'd with supreme command,
Presided o'er the *sons of light* :
And by that *hieroglyphic* bright,
Which none but *Craftsmen* ever saw !
Strong Mem'ry on my heart shall write
Those happy scenes, when far awa'.

May Freedom, Harmony, and Love,
    Unite you in the *grand Design*,
Beneath th' Omniscient Eye above—
    The glorious *Architect* Divine,
That you may keep th' *unerring line*,
    Still rising by the *plummet's law*,
Till *Order* bright completely shine,
    Shall be my pray'r when far awa'.

And *you*, farewell! whose merits claim
    Justly that *highest badge* to wear:
Heav'n bless your honour'd, noble name,
    To *Masonry* and *Scotia* dear!
A last request permit me here—
    When yearly ye assemble a',
One *round*, I ask it with a *tear*,
    To him, *the Bard that's far awa'.*

ON A SCOTCH BARD

GONE TO THE WEST INDIES

A' ye wha live by sowps o' drink,
A' ye wha live by crambo-clink,
A' ye wha live and never think,
        Come, mourn wi' me!
Our billie's gien us a' a jink,
        An' owre the sea!

Lament him a' ye rantin' core,
Wha dearly like a random-splore;
Nae mair he'll join the merry roar,
        In social key;
For now he's taen anither shore,
        An' owre the sea!

The bonie lasses weel may wiss him,
And in their dear petitions place him :
The widows, wives, an' a' may bless him
        Wi' tearfu' e'e;
For weel I wat they'll sairly miss him
        That's owre the sea !

O Fortune, they hae room to grumble !
Hadst thou taen aff some drowsy bummle,
Wha can do nought but fyke an' fumble,
        'Twad been nae plea;
But he was gleg as onie wumble,
        That's owre the sea !

Auld, cantie Kyle, may weepers wear,
An' stain them wi' the saut, saut tear :
'Twill mak her poor auld heart, I fear,
        In flinders flee :
He was her Laureat monie a year,
        That's owre the sea.

He saw Misfortune's cauld nor-west
Lang mustering up a bitter blast;
A jillet brak his heart at last,
        Ill may she be !
So, took a berth afore the mast,
        An' owre the sea.

To tremble under Fortune's cummock,
On scarce a bellyfu' o' drummock,
Wi' his proud, independent stomach,
        Could ill agree;
So, row't his hurdies in a hammock,
        An' owre the sea.

He ne'er was gien to great misguidin',
Yet coin his pouches wad na bide in;
Wi' him it ne'er was under hidin';
        He dealt it free :
The Muse was a' that he took pride in,
        That's owre the sea.

Jamaica bodies, use him weel,
An' hap him in a cozie biel:
Ye'll find him ay a dainty chiel,
          An' fou o' glee:
He wad na wrang'd the vera deil,
          That's owre the sea.

Fareweel my rhyme-composing billie!
Your native soil was right ill-willie;
But may ye flourish like a lily,
          Now bonilie!
I'll toast you in my hindmost gillie,
          Tho' owre the sea!

FAREWELL TO ELIZA

Tune—'Gilderoy.'

FROM thee, Eliza, I must go,
   And from my native shore;
The cruel fates between us throw
   A boundless ocean's roar:
But boundless oceans, roaring wide,
   Between my love and me,
They never, never can divide
   My heart and soul from thee.

Farewell, farewell, Eliza dear,
   The maid that I adore!
A boding voice is in mine ear,
   We part to meet no more!
But the latest throb that leaves my heart,
   While Death stands victor by—
That throb, Eliza, is thy part,
   And thine that latest sigh!

B.P.   H

A BARD'S EPITAPH

Is there a whim-inspirèd fool,
Owre fast for thought, owre hot for rule,
Owre blate to seek, owre proud to snool,
          Let him draw near;
And owre this grassy heap sing dool,
          And drap a tear.

Is there a bard of rustic song,
Who, noteless, steals the crowds among,
That weekly this area throng,
          O, pass not by!
But, with a frater-feeling strong,
          Here, heave a sigh.

Is there a man, whose judgment clear
Can others teach the course to steer,
Yet runs, himself, life's mad career,
          Wild as the wave,
Here, pause—and, thro' the starting tear,
          Survey this grave.

The poor inhabitant below
Was quick to learn and wise to know,
And keenly felt the friendly glow,
          And softer flame;
But thoughtless follies laid him low,
          And stain'd his name!

Reader, attend! whether thy soul
Soars fancy's flights beyond the pole,
Or darkling grubs this earthly hole,
          In low pursuit;
Know, prudent, cautious, self-control
          Is wisdom's root.

EPITAPH FOR ROBERT AIKEN, ESQ.

KNOW thou, O stranger to the fame
Of this much lov'd, much honoured name !
(For none that knew him need be told)
A warmer heart death ne'er made cold.

EPITAPH FOR GAVIN HAMILTON, ESQ.

THE poor man weeps—here Gavin sleeps,
    Whom canting wretches blam'd;
But with such as he, where'er he be,
    May I be sav'd or d—d !

EPITAPH ON 'WEE JOHNIE'

Hic Jacet wee Johnie

WHOE'ER thou art, O reader, know
    That Death has murder'd Johnie;
An' here his *body* lies fu' low;
    For *saul* he ne'er had ony.

THE LASS O' BALLOCHMYLE

Tune—'Ettrick Banks.'

'TWAS even—the dewy fields were green,
    On every blade the pearls hang;
The zephyr wanton'd round the bean,
    And bore its fragrant sweets alang :

In ev'ry glen the mavis sang,
    All nature list'ning seem'd the while,
Except where greenwood echoes rang,
    Amang the braes o' Ballochmyle.

With careless step I onward stray'd,
    My heart rejoic'd in nature's joy,
When, musing in a lonely glade,
    A maiden fair I chanc'd to spy:
Her look was like the morning's eye,
    Her air like nature's vernal smile;
Perfection whisper'd, passing by,
    'Behold the lass o' Ballochmyle!'

Fair is the morn in flowery May,
    And sweet is night in autumn mild;
When roving thro' the garden gay,
    Or wand'ring in the lonely wild:
But woman, nature's darling child!
    There all her charms she does compile;
Even there her other works are foil'd
    By the bonie lass o' Ballochmyle.

O had she been a country maid,
    And I the happy country swain,
Tho' shelter'd in the lowest shed
    That ever rose on Scotland's plain!
Thro' weary winter's wind and rain,
    With joy, with rapture, I would toil;
And nightly to my bosom strain
    The bonie lass o' Ballochmyle.

Then pride might climb the slipp'ry steep,
    Where fame and honors lofty shine;
And thirst of gold might tempt the deep,
    Or downward seek the Indian mine:
Give me the cot below the pine,
    To tend the flocks or till the soil;
And ev'ry day have joys divine
    With the bonie lass o' Ballochmyle.

LINES TO MR JOHN KENNEDY

FAREWELL, dear friend ! may gude luck hit you,
And 'mang her favourites admit you :
If e'er Detraction shore to smit you,
      May nane believe him,
And ony deil that thinks to get you,
      Good Lord, deceive him !

LINES TO AN OLD SWEETHEART

ONCE fondly lov'd, and still remember'd dear,
    Sweet early object of my youthful vows,
Accept this mark of friendship, warm, sincere,
    Friendship ! 'tis all cold duty now allows.

And when you read the simple, artless rhymes,
    One friendly sigh for him—he asks no more,
Who, distant, burns in flaming, torrid climes,
    Or haply lies beneath th' Atlantic roar.

LINES WRITTEN ON A BANK-NOTE

WAE worth thy power, thou cursed leaf,
Fell source o' a' my woe and grief ;
For lack o' thee I've lost my lass,
For lack o' thee I scrimp my glass :
I see the children of affliction
Unaided, through thy curst restriction :
I've seen the oppressor's cruel smile
Amid his hapless victim's spoil ;

And for thy potence vainly wished,
To crush the villain in the dust :
For lack o' thee, I leave this much-lov'd shore,
Never, perhaps, to greet auld Scotland more.

R. B.

KYLE.

STANZAS ON NAETHING

EXTEMPORE EPISTLE TO GAVIN HAMILTON, ESQ.

To you, sir, this summons I've sent,
    Pray, whip till the pownie is fraething;
But if you demand what I want,
    I honestly answer you—naething.

Ne'er scorn a poor Poet like me,
    For idly just living and breathing,
While people of every degree
    Are busy employed about—naething.

Poor Centum-per-centum may fast,
    And grumble his hurdies their claithing,
He'll find, when the balance is cast,
    He's gane to the devil for—naething.

The courtier cringes and bows,
    Ambition has likewise its plaything;
A coronet beams on his brows;
    And what is a coronet—naething.

Some quarrel the Presbyter gown,
    Some quarrel Episcopal graithing;
But every good fellow will own
    The quarrel is a' about—naething.

The lover may sparkle and glow,
    Approaching his bonie bit gay thing;
But marriage will soon let him know
    He's gotten—a buskit up naething.

The Poet may jingle and rhyme,
    In hopes of a laureate wreathing,
And when he has wasted his time,
    He's kindly rewarded wi'—naething.

The thundering bully may rage,
    And swagger and swear like a heathen;
But collar him fast, I'll engage,
    You'll find that his courage is—naething.

Last night wi' a feminine whig—
    A poet she couldna put faith in;
But soon we grew lovingly big,
    I taught her, her terrors were naething.

Her whigship was wonderful pleased,
    But charmingly tickled wi' ae thing;
Her fingers I lovingly squeezed,
    And kissed her, and promised her—naething.

The priest anathèmas may threat—
    Predicament, sir, that we're baith in;
But when honor's reveillè is beat,
    The holy artillery's naething.

And now I must mount on the wave—
    My voyage perhaps there is death in;
But what is a watery grave?
    The drowning a Poet is naething.

And now, as grim death's in my thought,
    To you, sir, I make this bequeathing;
My service as long as ye've ought,
    And my friendship, by God, when ye've
        naething.

THE FAREWELL

The valiant, in himself, what can he suffer,
Or what does he regard his single woes?
But when, alas! he multiplies himself,
To dearer selves, to the lov'd tender fair,
To those whose bliss, whose beings hang upon him,
To helpless children—then, oh then he feels
The point of misery festering in his heart,
And weakly weeps his fortunes like a coward:
Such, such am I—undone!
                    THOMSON'S *Edward and Eleanora.*

FAREWELL, old Scotia's bleak domains,
Far dearer than the torrid plains,
    Where rich ananas blow!
Farewell, a mother's blessing dear!
A brother's sigh! a sister's tear!
    My Jean's heart-rending throe!
Farewell, my Bess! tho' thou'rt bereft
    Of my paternal care,
A faithful brother I have left,
    My part in him thou'lt share!
        Adieu, too, to you too,
            My Smith, my bosom frien';
        When kindly you mind me,
            O then befriend my Jean!

What bursting anguish tears my heart;
From thee, my Jeany, must I part?
    Thou, weeping, answ'rest—'No!'
Alas! misfortune stares my face,
And points to ruin and disgrace,
    I for thy sake must go!
Thee, Hamilton, and Aiken dear,
    A grateful, warm adieu:
I, with a much-indebted tear,
    Shall still remember you!

All hail then, the gale then,
    Wafts me from thee, dear shore !
It rustles, and whistles,
    I'll never see thee more !

THE CALF

To the Rev. JAMES STEVEN, on his text, MALACHI, chap. iv.
ver. 2—'And ye shall go forth, and grow up as CALVES of the
stall '

RIGHT, sir ! your text I'll prove it true,
    Tho' heretics may laugh;
For instance, there's yoursel just now,
    God knows, an unco *calf*.

And should some patron be so kind,
    As bless you wi' a kirk,
I doubt na, sir, but then we'll find,
    Ye're still as great a *stirk*.

But if the lover's raptur'd hour,
    Shall ever be your lot,
Forbid it, ev'ry heavenly Power,
    You e'er should be a *stot !*

Tho', when some kind connubial dear
    Your but-an'-ben adorns,
The like has been that—you may wear
    A noble head of *horns*.

And, in your lug, most reverend James,
    To hear you roar and rowte,
Few men o' sense will doubt your claims
    To rank amang the *nowte*.

And when ye're number'd wi' the dead,
  Below a grassy hillock,
With justice they may mark your head—
  'Here lies a famous *bullock!*'

NATURE'S LAW—A POEM

HUMBLY INSCRIBED TO GAVIN HAMILTON, ESQ.

Great Nature spoke; observant man obey'd.—POPE.

LET other heroes boast their scars,
  The marks of strut and strife;
And other poets sing of wars,
  The plagues of human life;
Shame fa' the fun; wi' sword and gun
  To slap mankind like lumber!
I sing his name, and nobler fame,
  Wha multiplies our number.

Great Nature spoke, with air benign,
  'Go on, ye human race;
This lower world I you resign;
  Be fruitful and increase.
The liquid fire of strong desire
  I've poured it in each bosom;
Here, on this hand, does Mankind stand,
  And there is Beauty's blossom.'

The Hero of these artless strains,
  A lowly bard was he,
Who sung his rhymes in Coila's plains,
  With meikle mirth an' glee;
Kind Nature's care had given his share
  Large, of the flaming current;
And, all devout, he never sought
  To stem the sacred torrent.

He felt the powerful, high behest
   Thrill, vital, thro' and thro';
And sought a correspondent breast,
   To give obedience due :
Propitious Powers screen'd the young flow'rs,
   From mildews of abortion;
And lo ! the bard—a great reward—
   Has got a double portion !

Auld cantie Coil may count the day,
   As annual it returns,
The third of Libra's equal sway,
   That gave another Burns,
With future rhymes, an' other times,
   To emulate his sire;
To sing auld Coil in nobler style,
   With more poetic fire.

Ye Powers of peace, and peaceful song,
   Look down with gracious eyes ;
And bless auld Coila, large and long,
   With multiplying joys;
Lang may she stand to prop the land,
   The flow'r of ancient nations;
And Burnses spring, her fame to sing.
   To endless generations !

WILLIE CHALMERS

Wi' braw new branks in mickle pride,
   And eke a braw new brechan,
My Pegasus I'm got astride,
   And up Parnassus pechin';
Whiles owre a bush wi' downward crush,
   The doited beastie stammers;
Then up he gets, and off he sets,
   For sake o' Willie Chalmers.

I doubt na, lass, that weel kenn'd name
   May cost a pair o' blushes;
I am nae stranger to his fame,
   Nor his warm urgèd wishes.
Your bonie face, sae mild and sweet,
   His honest heart enamours,
And faith ye'll no be lost a whit,
   Tho' wair'd on Willie Chalmers.

Auld Truth hersel might swear ye're fair,
   And Honour safely back her;
And Modesty assume your air,
   And ne'er a ane mistak her :
And sic twa love-inspiring een
   Might fire even holy palmers;
Nae wonder then they've fatal been
   To honest Willie Chalmers.

I doubt na fortune may you shore
   Some mim-mou'd pouther'd priestie,
Fu' lifted up wi' Hebrew lore,
   And band upon his breastie :
But oh ! what signifies to you
   His lexicons and grammars;
The feeling heart's the royal blue,
   And that's wi' Willie Chalmers.

Some gapin', glowrin' countra laird
   May warsle for your favour;
May claw his lug, and straik his beard,
   And hoast up some palaver : .
My bonie maid, before ye wed
   Sic clumsy-witted hammers,
Seek Heaven for help, and barefit skelp
   Awa' wi' Willie Chalmers.

Forgive the Bard ! my fond regard
   For ane that shares my bosom,
Inspires my Muse to gie 'm his dues,
   For deil a hair I roose him.

May powers aboon unite you soon,
　And fructify your amours,
And every year come in mair dear
　To you and Willie Chalmers.

REPLY TO A TRIMMING EPISTLE RECEIVED
FROM A TAILOR

WHAT ails ye now, ye lousie bitch,
To thresh my back at sic a pitch?
Losh, man! hae mercy wi' your natch,
　　　　Your bodkin's bauld;
I didna suffer half sae much
　　　　Frae Daddie Auld.

What tho' at times, when I grow crouse,
I gie their wames a random pouse,
Is that enough for you to souse
　　　　Your servant sae?
Gae mind your seam, ye prick-the-louse,
　　　　An' jag-the-flea!

King David, o' poetic brief,
Wrocht 'mang the lasses sic mischief
As fill'd his after-life wi' grief,
　　　　An' bluidy rants,
An' yet he's rank'd amang the chief
　　　　O' lang-syne saunts.

And maybe, Tam, for a' my cants,
My wicked rhymes, an' drucken rants,
I'll gie auld cloven Clootie's haunts;
　　　　An unco slip yet,
An' snugly sit amang the saunts,
　　　　At Davie's hip yet!

But, fegs ! the Session says I maun
Gae fa' upo' anither plan
Than garrin' lasses coup the cran,
    Clean heels owre body,
An' sairly thole their mother's ban
    Afore the howdy.

This leads me on to tell for sport,
How I did wi' the Session sort;
Auld Clinkum, at the inner port,
    Cried three times, 'Robin !
Come hither lad, and answer for't,
    Ye're blam'd for jobbin' !'

Wi' pinch I put a Sunday's face on,
An' snoov'd awa' before the Session :
I made an open, fair confession—
    I scorn'd to lee,
An' syne Mess John, beyond expression,
    Fell foul o' me.

A fornicator-loun he call'd me,
An' said my faut frae bliss expell'd me;
I own'd the tale was true he tell'd me,
    'But, what the matter ?
(Quo' I) I fear unless ye geld me,
    I'll ne'er be better !'

'Geld you ! (quo' he) an' what for no ?
If that your right hand, leg, or toe
Should ever prove your spiritual foe,
    You should remember
To cut it aff—an' what for no ?—
    Your dearest member !'

'Na, na (quo' I), I'm no for that,
Gelding's nae better than 'tis ca't;
I'd rather suffer for my faut,
    A hearty flewit,
As sair owre hip as ye can draw't,
    Tho' I should rue it.'

'Or, gin ye like to end the bother,
To please us a'—I've just ae ither—
When next wi' yon lass I forgather,
        Whate'er betide it,
I'll frankly gie her 't a' thegither,
        An' let her guide it.'

But, sir, this pleas'd them warst of a',
An' therefore, Tam, when that I saw,
I said 'Gude night,' an' cam awa',
        An' left the Session;
I saw they were resolvèd a'
        On my oppression.

THE BRIGS OF AYR

INSCRIBED TO JOHN BALLANTINE, ESQ., AYR

THE simple Bard, rough at the rustic plough,
Learning his tuneful trade from ev'ry bough;
The chanting linnet, or the mellow thrush,
Hailing the setting sun, sweet, in the green thorn
    bush;
The soaring lark, the perching red-breast shrill,
Or deep-ton'd plovers grey, wild-whistling o'er the
    hill;
Shall he—nurst in the peasant's lowly shed,
To hardy independence bravely bred,
By early poverty to hardship steel'd,
And train'd to arms in stern Misfortune's field—
Shall he be guilty of their hireling crimes,
The servile, mercenary Swiss of rhymes?
Or labour hard the panegyric close,
With all the venal soul of dedicating prose?
No! though his artless strains he rudely sings,
And throws his hand uncouthly o'er the strings,
He glows with all the spirit of the Bard,
Fame, honest fame, his great, his dear reward.

Still, if some patron's gen'rous care he trace,
Skill'd in the secret to bestow with grace;
When Ballantine befriends his humble name,
And hands the rustic stranger up to fame,
With heartfelt throes his grateful bosom swells,
The godlike bliss, to give, alone excels.

'Twas when the stacks get on their winter hap,
And thack and rape secure the toil-won crap:
Potato bings are snuggèd up frae skith
O' coming Winter's biting, frosty breath;
The bees, rejoicing o'er their summer toils,
Unnumber'd buds an' flow'rs' delicious spoils,
Seal'd up with frugal care in massive waxen piles,
Are doom'd by Man, that tyrant o'er the weak,
The death o' devils, smoor'd wi' brimstone reek:
The thundering guns are heard on ev'ry side,
The wounded coveys, reeling, scatter wide;
The feather'd field-mates, bound by Nature's tie,
Sires, mothers, children, in one carnage lie:
(What warm, poetic heart but inly bleeds,
And execrates man's savage, ruthless deeds!)
Nae mair the flow'r in field or meadow springs,
Nae mair the grove with airy concert rings,
Except perhaps the Robin's whistling glee,
Proud o' the height o' some bit half-lang tree:
The hoary morns precede the sunny days,
Mild, calm, serene, wide spreads the noontide blaze,
While thick the gossamour waves wanton in the rays.

'Twas in that season, when a simple Bard,
Unknown and poor—simplicity's reward!—
Ae night, within the ancient brugh of Ayr,
By whim inspir'd, or haply prest wi' care,
He left his bed, and took his wayward route,
And down by *Simpson's* wheel'd the left about:
(Whether impell'd by all-directing Fate,
To witness what I after shall narrate;

Or whether, rapt in meditation high,
He wander'd out, he knew not where nor why :)
The drowsy Dungeon-clock had number'd two,
And Wallace Tower had sworn the fact was true :
The tide-swoln firth, with sullen-sounding roar,
Through the still night dash'd hoarse along the
    shore.
All else was hush'd as Nature's closèd e'e;
The silent moon shone high o'er tower and tree;
The chilly frost, beneath the silver beam,
Crept gently, crusting-o'er the glittering stream—

When, lo ! on either hand the list'ning Bard,
The clanging sugh of whistlings wings is heard;
Two dusky forms dart thro' the midnight air,
Swift as the gos drives on the wheeling hare;
Ane on the Auld Brig his airy shape uprears,
The ither flutters o'er the rising piers :
Our warlock Rhymer instantly descried
The Sprites that o'er the Brigs of Ayr preside.
(That Bards are second-sighted is nae joke,
And ken the lingo of the sp'ritual folk;
Fays, Spunkies, Kelpies, a', they can explain them,
And ev'n the vera deils they brawly ken them).
'Auld Brig' appear'd of ancient Pictish race,
The very wrinkles Gothic in his face;
He seem'd as he wi' Time had warstl'd lang,
Yet, teughly doure, he bade an unco bang.
'New Brig' was buskit in a braw new coat,
That he, at Lon'on, frae ane Adams got;
In's hand five taper staves as smooth's a bead,
Wi' virls an' whirlygigums at the head.
The Goth was stalking round with anxious search,
Spying the time-worn flaws in ev'ry arch;
It chanc'd his new-come neibor took his e'e,
And e'en a vex'd and angry heart had he !
Wi' thieveless sneer to see his modish mien,
He, down the water, gies him this guid-een :—

AULD BRIG

I doubt na, frien', ye'll think ye're nae sheepshank,
Ance ye were streekit owre frae bank to bank!
But gin ye be a brig as auld as me—
Tho' faith, that date, I doubt, ye'll never see—
There'll be, if that day come, I'll wad a boddle,
Some fewer whigmaleeries in your noddle.

NEW BRIG

Auld Vandal! ye but show your little mense,
Just much about it wi' your scanty sense :
Will your poor, narrow foot-path of a street,
Where twa wheel-barrows tremble when they meet,
Your ruin'd, formless bulk o' stane and lime,
Compare wi' bonie brigs o' modern time ?
There's men o' taste wou'd tak the Ducat stream,
Tho' they should cast the vera sark and swim,
E'er they would grate their feelings wi' the view
O' sic an ugly, Gothic hulk as you.

AULD BRIG

Conceited gowk! puff'd up wi' windy pride!
This mony a year I've stood the flood an' tide;
And tho' wi' crazy eild I'm sair forfairn,
I'll be a brig when ye're a shapeless cairn!
As yet ye little ken about the matter,
But twa-three winters will inform ye better.
When heavy, dark, continued, a'-day rains,
Wi' deepening deluges o'erflow the plains;
When from the hills where springs the brawling Coil,
Or stately Lugar's mossy fountains boil;
Or where the Greenock winds his moorland course,
Or haunted Garpal draws his feeble source,
Arous'd by blustering winds an' spotting thowes,
In mony a torrent down the snaw-broo rowes;

While crashing ice, borne on the roaring spate,
Sweeps dams, an' mills, an' brigs, a' to the gate;
And from Glenbuck, down to the Ratton-key,
Auld Ayr is just one lengthen'd, tumbling sea—
Then down ye'll hurl (deil nor ye never rise !)
And dash the gumlie jaups up to the pouring skies !
A lesson sadly teaching, to your cost,
That Architecture's noble art is lost !

NEW BRIG

Fine architecture, trowth, I needs must say't o't,
The L—d be thankit that we've tint the gate o't !
Gaunt, ghastly, ghaist-alluring edifices;
Hanging with threat'ning jut like precipices;
O'er-arching, mouldy, gloom-inspiring coves,
Supporting roofs, fantastic, stony groves;
Windows and doors in nameless sculptures drest,
With order, symmetry, or taste unblest;
Forms like some bedlam Statuary's dream,
The craz'd creations of misguided whim;
Forms might be worshipp'd on the bended knee,
And still the second dread command be free;
Their likeness is not found on earth, in air, or sea !
Mansions that would disgrace the building taste
Of any mason reptile, bird or beast :
Fit only for a doited monkish race,
Or frosty maids forsworn the dear embrace,
Or cuifs of later times, wha held the notion,
That sullen gloom was sterling true devotion :
Fancies that our guid Brugh denies protection,
And soon may they expire, unblest wi' resurrection !

AULD BRIG

O ye, my dear-remember'd, ancient yealings,
Were ye but here to share my wounded feelings !
Ye worthy Proveses, an' mony a Bailie,
Wha in the paths o' righteousness did toil ay;

Ye dainty Deacons, an' ye douce Conveeners,
To whom our moderns are but causey-cleaners;
Ye godly Councils, wha hae blest this town;
Ye godly Brethren o' the sacred gown,
Wha meekly gie your hurdies to the smiters;
And (what would now be strange), ye godly Writers
A' ye douce folk I've borne aboon the broo,
Were ye but here, what would ye say or do?
How would your spirits groan in deep vexation,
To see each melancholy alteration;
And, agonising, curse the time and place
When ye begat the base degenerate race!
Nae langer rev'rend men, their country's glory,
In plain braid Scots hold forth a plain, braid story;
Nae langer thrifty citizens, an' douce,
Meet owre a pint, or in the Council-house;
But staumrel, corky-headed, graceless *Gentry*,
The herryment and ruin of the country;
Men, three-parts made by tailors and by barbers,
Wha waste your weel-hain'd gear on d—'d new brigs
    and harbours!

NEW BRIG

Now haud you there! for faith ye've said enough
And muckle mair than ye can mak to through.
As for your Priesthood, I shall say but little,
Corbies and *Clergy* are a shot right kittle:
But, under favour o' your langer beard,
Abuse o' Magistrates might weel be spared;
To liken them to your auld-warld squad,
I must needs say, comparisons are odd.
In Ayr, *wag-wits* nae mair can hae a handle
To mouth 'a Citizen' a term o' scandal;
Nae mair the Council waddles down the street,
In all the pomp of ignorant conceit;
Men wha grew wise priggin' owre hops an' raisins,
Or gather'd lib'ral views in Bonds and Seisins:

If haply Knowledge, on a random tramp,
Had shor'd them with a glimmer of his lamp,
And would to Common-sense for once betray'd them,
Plain, dull Stupidity stept kindly in to aid them.

What farther clish-ma-claver might been said,
What bloody wars, if Sprites had blood to shed,
No man can tell; but, all before their sight,
A fairy train appear'd in order bright;
Adown the glittering stream they featly danc'd;
Bright to the moon their various dresses glanc'd:
They footed o'er the wat'ry glass so neat,
The infant ice scarce bent beneath their feet:
While arts of Minstrelsy among them rung,
And soul-ennobling Bards heroic ditties sung.

O had M'Lauchlan, thairm-inspiring sage,
Been there to hear this heavenly band engage,
When thro' his dear strathspeys they bore with
    Highland rage;
Or when they struck old Scotia's melting airs,
The lover's raptured joys or bleeding cares;
How would his Highland lug been nobler fir'd,
And ev'n his matchless hand with finer touch
    inspir'd!
No guess could tell what instrument appear'd,
But all the soul of Music's self was heard;
Harmonious concert rung in every part,
While simple melody pour'd moving on the heart.

The Genius of the Stream in front appears,
A venerable Chief advanc'd in years;
His hoary head with water-lilies crown'd,
His manly leg with garter-tangle bound.
Next came the loveliest pair in all the ring,
Sweet female Beauty hand in hand with Spring;
Then, crown'd with flow'ry hay, came Rural Joy,
And Summer, with his fervid-beaming eye;

All-cheering Plenty, with her flowing horn,
Led yellow Autumn wreath'd with nodding corn;
Then Winter's time-bleach'd locks did hoary show,
By Hospitality with cloudless brow :
Next followed Courage with his martial stride,
From where the Feal wild-woody coverts hide;
Benevolence, with mild, benignant air,
A female form, came from the tow'rs of Stair;
Learning and Worth in equal measures strode,
From simple Catrine, their long-lov'd abode;
Last, white-rob'd Peace, crown'd with a hazel
    wreath,
To rustic Agriculture did bequeath
The broken, iron instruments of death :
At sight of whom our Sprites forgat their kindling
    wrath.

THE NIGHT WAS STILL

THE night was still, and o'er the hill
    The moon shone on the castle wa',
The mavis sang, while dew-drops hang
    Around her on the castle wa',
Sae merrily they danced the ring
    Frae e'enin' till the cock did craw;
And ay the o'erword o' the spring
    Was Irvine's bairns are bonnie a'.

EPIGRAM ON ROUGH ROADS

I'M now arrived—thanks to the gods !—
    Thro' pathways rough and muddy,
A certain sign that makin' roads
    Is no this people's study :

Altho' I'm not wi' Scripture cram'd,
   I'm sure the Bible says
That heedless sinners shall be damn'd,
   Unless they mend their *ways*.

PRAYER—O THOU DREAD POWER

O Thou dread Power, who reign'st above,
   I know thou wilt me hear,
When for this scene of peace and love,
   I make my prayer sincere.

The hoary Sire—the mortal stroke,
   Long, long be pleas'd to spare;
To bless his little filial flock,
   And show what good men are.

She, who her lovely offspring eyes
   With tender hopes and fears,
O bless her with a mother's joys,
   But spare a mother's tears!

Their hope, their stay, their darling youth,
   In manhood's dawning blush,
Bless him, Thou God of love and truth,
   Up to a parent's wish.

The beauteous, seraph sister-band—
   With earnest tears I pray—
Thou know'st the snares on ev'ry hand,
   Guide Thou their steps alway.

When, soon or late, they reach that coast,
   O'er Life's rough ocean driven,
May they rejoice, no wand'rer lost,
   A family in Heaven!

FAREWELL TO THE BANKS OF AYR

Tune—'Roslin Castle.'

THE gloomy night is gath'ring fast,
Loud roars the wild, inconstant blast,
Yon murky cloud is foul with rain,
I see it driving o'er the plain;
The hunter now has left the moor,
The scatt'red coveys meet secure;
While here I wander, prest with care,
Along the lonely banks of Ayr.

The Autumn mourns her rip'ning corn
By early Winter's ravage torn;
Across her placid, azure sky,
She sees the scowling tempest fly:
Chill runs my blood to hear it rave;
I think upon the stormy wave,
Where many a danger I must dare,
Far from the bonie banks of Ayr.

'Tis not the surging billow's roar,
'Tis not that fatal, deadly shore,
Tho' death in ev'ry shape appear,
The wretched have no more to fear:
But round my heart the ties are bound,
The heart transpierc'd with many a wound;
These bleed afresh, those ties I tear,
To leave the bonie banks of Ayr.

Farewell, old Coila's hills and dales,
Her heathy moors and winding vales;
The scenes where wretched Fancy roves,
Pursuing past, unhappy loves!
Farewell, my friends! farewell, my foes!
My peace with these, my love with those:
The bursting tears my heart declare—
Farewell, the bonie banks of Ayr!

ON MEETING WITH LORD DAER

THIS wot ye all whom it concerns,
I, Rhymer Robin, alias Burns,
   October twenty-third,
A ne'er-to-be-forgotten day,
Sae far I sprackl'd up the brae,
   I dinner'd wi' a Lord.

I've been at drucken writers' feasts,
Nay, been bitch-fou 'mang godly priests—
   Wi' rev'rence be it spoken !—
I've even join'd the honor'd jorum,
When mighty Squireships of the quorum,
   Their hydra drouth did sloken.

But wi' a Lord !—stand out my shin,
A Lord—a Peer—an Earl's son !
   Up higher yet, my bonnet !
An' sic a Lord !—lang Scotch ells twa,
Our Peerage he o'erlooks them a',
   As I look o'er my sonnet.

But O for Hogarth's magic pow'r !
To show Sir Bardie's willyart glow'r,
   An' how he star'd an' stammer'd,
When, goavin', as if led wi' branks,
An' stumpin' on his ploughman shanks,
   He in the parlour hammer'd.

I sidling shelter'd in a nook,
An' at his Lordship steal't a look,
   Like some portentous omen;
Except good sense and social glee,
An' (what surpris'd me) modesty
   I markèd nought uncommon.

I watch'd the symptoms o' the Great,
The gentle pride, the lordly state,
  The arrogant assuming;
The fient a pride, nae pride had he,
Nor sauce, nor state, that I could see,
   Mair than an honest ploughman.

Then from his Lordship I shall learn,
Henceforth to meet with unconcern
  One rank as weel's another;
Nae honest, worthy man need care
To meet with noble, youthful Daer,
   For he but meets a brother.

MASONIC SONG

Tune—'Shawn-boy'; or, 'Over the water to Charlie.'

YE sons of old Killie, assembled by Willie,
 To follow the noble vocation;
Your thrifty old mother has scarce such another
 To sit in that honourèd station.
I've little to say, but only to pray,
 As praying's the *ton* of your fashion;
A prayer from the Muse you well may excuse,
 'Tis seldom her favourite passion.

Ye powers who preside o'er the wind and the tide,
 Who markèd each element's border;
Who formed this frame with beneficent aim,
 Whose sovereign statute is order :—
Within this dear mansion, may wayward Contention
 Or witherèd Envy ne'er enter;
May secrecy round be the mystical bound,
 And brotherly love be the centre !

TAM SAMSON'S ELEGY

An honest man's the noblest work of God.—POPE.

HAS auld Kilmarnock seen the deil?
Or great Mackinlay thrawn his heel?
Or Robertson again grown weel,
   To preach an' read?
'Na, waur than a'!' cries ilka chiel,
    'Tam Samson's dead!'

Kilmarnock lang may grunt an' graen,
An' sigh, an' sab, an' greet her lane,
An' cleed her bairns, man, wife, an' wean,
   In mourning weed;
To Death she's dearly pay'd the kane—
   Tam Samson's dead!

The Brethren o' the mystic 'level'
May hing their head in woefu' bevel,
While by their nose the tears will revel,
   Like ony bead;
Death's gien the Lodge an unco devel—
   Tam Samson's dead!

When Winter muffles up his cloak,
And binds the mire like a rock;
When to the loughs the curlers flock,
   Wi' gleesome speed,
Wha will they station at the 'cock'?—
   Tam Samson's dead!

He was the king o' a' the core,
To guard, or draw, or wick a bore,
Or up the rink like Jehu roar,
   In time o' need;
But now he lags on Death's 'hog-score'—
   Tam Samson's dead!

Now safe the stately sawmont sail,
And trouts bedropp'd wi' crimson hail,
And eels, weel-ken'd for souple tail,
   And geds for greed,
Since, dark in Death's 'fish-creel, we wail'
   Tam Samson dead!

Rejoice, ye birring paitricks a';
Ye cootie muircocks, crousely craw;
Ye maukins, cock your fud fu' braw,
   Withouten.dread;
Your mortal fae is now awa'—
   Tam Samson's dead!

That woefu' morn be ever mourn'd,
Saw him in shootin' graith adorn'd,
While pointers round impatient burn'd,
   Frae couples free'd;
But, och! he gaed and ne'er return'd!
   Tam Samson's dead!

In vain auld age his body batters,
In vain the gout his ankles fetters,
In vain the burns cam down like waters,
   An acre braid!
Now ev'ry auld wife, greetin', clatters
   'Tam Samson's dead!'

Owre mony a weary hag he limpit,
An' ay the tither shot he thumpit,
Till coward Death behint him jumpit,
   Wi' deadly feide;
Now he proclaims wi' tout o' trumpet,
   'Tam Samson's dead!'

When at his heart he felt the dagger,
He reel'd his wonted bottle-swagger,
But yet he drew the mortal trigger,
   Wi' weel-aimed heed;
'L—d, five!' he cry'd, an' owre did stagger—
   Tam Samson's dead!

Ilk hoary hunter mourn'd a brither;
Ilk sportsman-youth bemoan'd a father;
Yon auld gray stane, amang the heather,
      Marks out his head;
Whare Burns has wrote, in rhyming blether,
      'Tam Samson's Dead!'

There, low he lies in lasting rest;
Perhaps upon his mould'ring breast
Some spitefu' muirfowl bigs her nest,
      To hatch and breed:
Alas! nae mair he'll them molest!
      Tam Samson's dead!

When August winds the heather wave,
And sportsmen wander by yon grave,
Three volleys let his memory crave,
      O' pouther an' lead,
Till Echo answer frae her cave,
      'Tam Samson's dead!'

Heav'n rest his saul whare'er he be!
Is th' wish o' mony mae than me:
He had twa fauts, or maybe three,
      Yet what remead?
Ae social, honest man want we:
      Tam Samson's dead!

THE EPITAPH

'Tam Samson's' weel-worn clay here lies,
  Ye canting zealots, spare him!
If honest worth in Heaven rise!
  Ye'll mend or ye win near him.

PER CONTRA

Go Fame, an' canter like a filly
Thro' a' the streets an' neuks o' Killie;
Tell ev'ry social honest billie
      To cease his grievin';
For, yet unskaith'd by Death's gleg gullie,
      Tam Samson's leevin'!

EPISTLE TO MAJOR LOGAN

HAIL, thairm-inspirin', rattlin' Willie!
Tho' fortune's road be rough an' hilly
To every fiddling, rhyming billie,
   We never heed,
But take it like the unback'd filly,
    Proud o' her speed.

When, idly goavin', whyles we saunter;
Yirr! fancy barks, awa' we canter,
Up hill, down brae, till some mischanter,
   Some black bog-hole,
Arrests us, then the scathe an' banter
    We're forced to thole.

Hale be your heart! hale be your fiddle!
Lang may your elbuck jink and diddle,
To cheer you through the weary widdle
   O' this wild warl',
Until you on a crummock driddle,
    A gray-hair'd carl.

Come wealth, come poortith, late or soon,
Heaven send your heart-strings ay in tune,
And screw your temper-pins aboon
   (A fifth or mair),
The melancholious, lazy croon
    O' cankrie care.

May still your life from day to day
Nae 'lente largo' in the play,
But 'allegretto forte' gay,
   Harmonious flow,
A sweeping, kindling, bauld strathspey—
    Encore! Bravo!

A blessing on the cheery gang
Wha dearly like a jig or sang,
An' never think o' right an' wrang
        By square an' rule,
But as the clegs o' feeling stang,
        Are wise or fool.

My hand-waled curse keep hard in chase
The harpy, hoodock, purse-proud race,
Wha count on poortith as disgrace;
        Their tuneless hearts,
May fireside discords jar a base
        To a' their parts!

But come, your hand, my careless brither,
I' th' ither warl', if there's anither,
An' that there is, I've little swither
        About the matter;
We, cheek for chow, shall jog thegither,
        I'se ne'er bid better.

We've faults and failings—granted clearly,
We're frail backsliding mortals merely,
Eve's bonie squad, priests wyte them sheerly
        For our grand fa';
But still, but still, I like them dearly—
        God bless them a'!

Ochon for poor Castalian drinkers,
When they fa' foul o' earthly jinkers!
The witching, curs'd, delicious blinkers
        Hae put me hyte,
And gart me weet my waukrife winkers,
        Wi' girnin' spite.

But by yon moon—and that's high swearin'—
An' every star within my hearin'!
An' by her een wha was a dear ane!
        I'll ne'er forget;
I hope to gie the jads a clearin',
        In fair play yet.

My loss I mourn, but not repent it;
I'll seek my pursie whare I tint it;
Ance to the Indies I were wonted,
   Some cantraip hour,
By some sweet elf I'll yet be dinted;
   Then *vive l'amour!*

Faites mes baissemains respectueusè,
To sentimental sister Susie,
An' honest Lucky; no to roose you,
   Ye may be proud,
That sic a couple fate allows ye,
   To grace your blood.

Nae mair at present can I measure,
An' trowth my rhymin' ware's nae treasure;
But when in Ayr, some half-hour's leisure,
   Be't light, be't dark,
Sir Bard will do himself the pleasure
   To call at Park.

       ROBERT BURNS.

MOSSGIEL, 30*th October*, 1786.

ON SENSIBILITY

RUSTICITY's ungainly form
 May cloud the highest mind;
But when the heart is nobly warm,
 The *good* excuse will find.
Propriety's cold, cautious rules
 Warm fervour may o'erlook;
But spare poor sensibility
 Th' ungentle, harsh rebuke.

A WINTER NIGHT

Poor naked wretches, wheresoe'er you are,
That bide the pelting of this pityless storm !
How shall your houseless heads, and unfed sides,
Your loop'd and window'd raggedness, defend you
From seasons such as these ?—SHAKESPEARE.

WHEN biting Boreas, fell and doure,
Sharp shivers thro' the leafless bow'r;
When Phœbus gies a short-liv'd glow'r,
   Far south the lift,
Dim-dark'ning thro' the flaky show'r,
   Or whirling drift :

Ae night the storm the steeples rocked,
Poor Labour sweet in sleep was locked,
While burns, wi' snawy wreaths up-choked,
   Wild-eddying swirl;
Or, thro' the mining outlet bocked,
   Down headlong hurl :

List'ning the doors an' winnocks rattle,
I thought me on the ourie cattle,
Or silly sheep, wha bide this brattle
   O' winter war,
And thro' the drift, deep-lairing, sprattle
   Beneath a scaur.

Ilk happing bird,—wee, helpless thing !
That, in the merry months o' spring,
Delighted me to hear thee sing,
   What comes o' thee ?
Whare wilt thou cow'r thy chittering wing,
   An' close thy e'e ?

Ev'n you, on murdering errands toil'd,
Lone from your savage homes exil'd,
The blood-stain'd roost, and sheep-cote spoil'd
    My heart forgets,
While pityless the tempest wild
      Sore on you beats!

Now Phœbe, in her midnight reign,
Dark-muffl'd, view'd the dreary plain;
Still crowding thoughts, a pensive train,
    Rose in my soul,
When on my ear this plaintive strain,
      Slow, solemn, stole :—

'Blow, blow, ye winds, with heavier gust!
And freeze, thou bitter-biting frost!
Descend, ye chilly, smothering snows!
Not all your rage, as now united, shows
    More hard unkindness, unrelenting,
    Vengeful malice, unrepenting,
Than heaven-illumin'd Man on brother Man bestow

'See stern Oppression's iron grip,
    Or mad Ambition's gory hand,
Sending, like blood-hounds from the slip,
    Woe, Want, and Murder o'er the land!
Ev'n in the peaceful rural vale,
    Truth, weeping, tells the mournful tale,
How pamper'd Luxury, Flatt'ry by her side,
    The parasite empoisoning her ear,
    With all the servile wretches in the rear,
Looks o'er proud Property, extended wide;
    And eyes the simple rustic hind,
Whose toil upholds the glitt'ring show—
    A creature of another kind,
    Some coarser substance, unrefin'd—
Plac'd for her lordly use, thus far, thus vile, below

'Where, where is Love's fond, tender throe,
With lordly Honor's lofty brow,
      The pow'rs you proudly own ?
Is there, beneath Love's noble name,
Can harbour, dark, the selfish aim,
      To bless himself alone !
   Mark maiden-innocence a prey
      To love-pretending snares :
   This boasted Honor turns away,
   Shunning soft Pity's rising sway,
Regardless of the tears and unavailing pray'rs !
   Perhaps this hour, in Misery's squalid nest,
   She strains your infant to her joyless breast,
And with a mother's fears shrinks at the rocking
      blast !

'Oh ye ! who, sunk in beds of down,
   Feel not a want but what yourselves create,
   Think, for a moment, on his wretched fate,
Whom friends and fortune quite disown !
Ill-satisfy'd keen nature's clamorous call,
   Stretch'd on his straw, he lays himself to sleep;
While thro' the ragged roof and chinky wall,
   Chill, o'er his slumbers, piles the drifty heap !
      Think on the dungeon's grim confine,
      Where Guilt and poor Misfortune pine !
      Guilt-erring man, relenting view,
      But shall thy legal rage pursue
      The wretch, already crushèd low
      By cruel Fortune's undeservèd blow ?
Affliction's sons are brothers in distress;
A brother to relieve, how exquisite the bliss !'

      I heard nae mair, for Chanticleer
         Shook off the pouthery snaw,
      And hail'd the morning with a cheer,
         A cottage-rousing craw.

But deep this truth impress'd my mind—
Thro' all His works abroad,
The heart benevolent and kind
The most resembles God.

YON WILD MOSSY MOUNTAINS.

Yon wild mossy mountains sae lofty and wide,
That nurse in their bosom the youth o' the Clyde,
Where the grouse lead their coveys thro' the heather to
feed,
And the shepherd tents his flock as he pipes on his reed.

Not Gowrie's rich valley, nor Forth's sunny shores,
To me hae the charms o' yon wild, mossy moors;
For there, by a lanely, sequesterèd stream,
Besides a sweet lassie, my thought and my dream.

Amang thae wild mountains shall still be my path,
Ilk stream foaming down its ain green, narrow strath,
For there, wi' my lassie, the day-lang I rove,
While o'er us unheeded flie the swift hours o' love.

She is not the fairest, altho' she is fair;
O' nice education but sma' is her share;
Her parentage humble as humble can be;
But I lo'e the dear lassie because she lo'es me.

To Beauty what man but maun yield him a prize,
In her armour of glances, and blushes, and sighs?
And when wit and refinement hae polish'd her darts,
They dazzle our een, as they flie to our hearts.

But kindness, sweet kindness, in the fond-sparkling e'e,
Has lustre outshining the diamond to me;
And the heart beating love as I'm clasp'd in her arms,
O, these are my lassie's all-conquering charms!

ADDRESS TO EDINBURGH

Edina! Scotia's darling seat!
　All hail thy palaces and tow'rs,
Where once, beneath a Monarch's feet,
　Sat Legislation's sovereign pow'rs:
From marking wildly-scatt'red flow'rs,
　As on the banks of Ayr I stray'd,
And singing, lone, the lingering hours,
　I shelter in thy honor'd shade.

Here Wealth still swells the golden tide,
　As busy Trade his labour plies;
There Architecture's noble pride
　Bids elegance and splendour rise:
Here Justice, from her native skies,
　High wields her balance and her rod;
There Learning, with his eagle eyes,
　Seeks Science in her coy abode.

Thy sons, Edina, social, kind,
　With open arms the stranger hail;
Their views enlarg'd, their liberal mind,
　Above the narrow, rural vale:
Attentive still to Sorrow's wail,
　Or modest Merit's silent claim;
And never may their sources fail!
　And never Envy blot their name!

Thy daughters bright thy walks adorn,
　Gay as the gilded summer sky,
Sweet as the dewy, milk-white thorn,
　Dear as the raptur'd thrill of joy!
Fair Burnet strikes th' adoring eye,
　Heaven's beauties on my fancy shine;
I see the Sire of Love on high,
　And own His work indeed divine!

There, watching high the least alarms,
  Thy rough, rude fortress gleams afar;
Like some bold veteran, gray in arms,
  And marked with many a seamy scar:
The pond'rous wall and massy bar,
  Grim-rising o'er the rugged rock,
Have oft withstood assailing war,
  And oft repell'd th' invader's shock.

With awe-struck thought, and pitying tears,
  I view that noble, stately Dome,
Where Scotia's kings of other years,
  Fam'd heroes! had their royal home:
Alas! how chang'd the times to come!
  Their royal name low in the dust!
Their hapless race wild-wand'ring roam!
  Tho' rigid Law cries out, "'twas just!"

Wild beats my heart to trace your steps,
  Whose ancestors, in days of yore,
Thro' hostile ranks and ruin'd gaps
  Old Scotia's bloody lion bore:
Ev'n I who sing in rustic lore,
  Haply my sires have left their shed,
And fac'd grim Danger's loudest roar,
  Bold-following where your fathers led!

Edina! Scotia's darling seat!
  All hail thy palaces and tow'rs;
Where once, beneath a Monarch's feet,
  Sat Legislation's sovereign pow'rs:
From marking wildly-scatt'red flow'rs,
  As on the banks of Ayr I stray'd,
And singing, lone, the lingering hours,
  I shelter in thy honor'd shade.

ADDRESS TO A HAGGIS

FAIR fa' your honest, sonsie face,
Great chieftain o' the puddin'-race !
Aboon them a' ye tak your place,
   Painch, tripe, or thairm :
Weel are ye wordy o' a grace
   As lang's my arm.

The groaning trencher there ye fill,
Your hurdies like a distant hill,
Your pin wad help to mend a mill
   In time o' need,
While thro' your pores the dews distil
   Like amber bead.

His knife see rustic Labour dight,
An' cut you up wi' ready sleight,
Trenching your gushing entrails bright,
   Like ony ditch;
And then, O what a glorious sight,
   Warm-reekin', rich !

Then, horn for horn, they stretch an' strive :
Deil tak the hindmost ! on they drive,
Till a' their weel-swall'd kytes belyve
   Are bent like drums;
Then auld Guidman, maist like to rive,
   'Bethanket !' hums.

Is there that owre his French *ragout*,
Or *olio* that wad staw a sow,
Or *fricassee* wad mak her spew
   Wi' perfect sconner,
Looks down wi' sneering, scornfu' view
   On sic a dinner ?

Poor devil! see him owre his trash,
As feckless as a wither'd rash,
His spindle shank, a guid whip-lash,
        His nieve a nit;
Thro' bloody flood or field to dash,
        O how unfit!

But mark the Rustic, haggis-fed,
The trembling earth resounds his tread,
Clap in his walie nieve a blade,
        He'll mak it whissle;
An' legs an' arms, an' heads will sned,
        Like taps o' thrissle.

Ye Pow'rs wha mak mankind your care,
And dish them out their bill o' fare,
Auld Scotland wants nae skinking ware
        That jaups in luggies;
But, if ye wish her gratefu' prayer,
        Gie her a Haggis!

TO MISS LOGAN

WITH BEATTIE'S POEMS FOR A NEW-YEAR'S GIFT
JANUARY 1, 1787

AGAIN the silent wheels of time
    Their annual round have driven,
And you, tho' scarce in maiden prime,
    Are so much nearer Heaven.

No gifts have I from Indian coasts
    The infant year to hail;
I send you more than India boasts,
    In Edwin's simple tale.

Our sex with guile, and faithless love,
  Is charg'd, perhaps too true;
But may, dear maid, each lover prove
  An Edwin still to you.

WILLIAM SMELLIE—A SKETCH

SHREWD Willie Smellie to Crochallan came;
The old cock'd hat, the gray surtout, the same;
His bristling beard just rising in its might,
'Twas four long nights and days to shaving night;
His uncomb'd, grizzly locks, wild staring, thatch'd
A head for thought profound and clear, unmatch'd;
Yet tho' his caustic wit was biting-rude,
His heart was warm, benevolent, and good.

RATTLIN', ROARIN' WILLIE

O RATTLIN', roarin' Willie,
  O, he held to the fair,
An' for to sell his fiddle,
  An' buy some other ware;
But parting wi' his fiddle,
  The saut tear blin't his e'e,
An' rattlin', roarin' Willie,
  Ye're welcome hame to me.

O Willie, come sell your fiddle,
  O sell your fiddle sae fine!
O Willie, come sell your fiddle,
  An' buy a pint o' wine!

If I should sell my fiddle,
    The warld would think I was mad;
For monie a rantin' day
    My fiddle an' I hae had.

As I cam by Crochallan,
    I cannilie keeket ben;
Rattlin', roarin' Willie
    Was sittin' at yon boord-en';
Sittin' at yon boord-en',
    And amang gude companie;
Rattlin', roarin' Willie,
    Ye're welcome hame to me!

BONIE DUNDEE

O WHAR gat ye that haver-meal bannock?
    Silly blin' booby, O dinna ye see;
I gat it frae a brisk young sodger laddie
    Atween Saint Johnstoun an' bonie Dundee.

O gin I saw the laddie that gae me't!
    Aft has he doudl't me upon his knee;
May Heaven protect my bonie Scots laddie,
    An' send him safe hame to his babie an' me.

My blessin's upon thy sweet wee lippie!
    My blessin's upon thy bonie e'e-brie!
Thy smiles are sae like my blythe sodger laddie,
    Thou's ay the dearer, and dearer to me!

But I'll big a bow'r on yon bonie banks,
    Whare Tay rins wimplin' by sae clear;
An' I'll cleed thee in the tartan sae fine,
    And mak thee a man like thy daddie dear.

EPIGRAMS

EXTEMPORE IN THE COURT OF SESSION

LORD ADVOCATE

HE clench'd his pamphlets in his fist,
    He quoted and he hinted,
Till, in a declamation-mist,
    His argument he tint it:
He gapèd for't, he grapèd for't,
    He fand it was awa', man;
But what his common sense came short,
    He ekèd out wi' law, man.

MR ERSKINE

Collected, Harry stood awee,
    Then open'd out his arm, man;
His Lordship sat wi' ruefu' e'e,
    And ey'd the gathering storm, man:
Like wind-driv'n hail it did assail,
    Or torrents owre a linn, man;
The BENCH sae wise lift up their eyes,
    Half-wauken'd wi' the din, man.

INSCRIPTION FOR THE HEADSTONE OF FERGUSSON THE POET

No sculptured marble here, nor pompous lay,
    'No storied urn nor animated bust';
This simple stone directs pale Scotia's way,
    To pour her sorrows o'er the Poet's dust.

ADDITIONAL STANZAS

She mourns, sweet tuneful youth, thy hapless fate
    Tho' all the powers of song thy fancy fired,
Yet Luxury and Wealth lay by in state,
    And, thankless, starv'd what they so much
      admired.

This tribute, with a tear, now gives
    A brother Bard—he can no more bestow;
But dear to fame thy Song immortal lives,
    A nobler monument than Art can show.

INSCRIBED UNDER FERGUSSON'S PORTRAIT

Curse on ungrateful man, that can be pleased,
And yet can starve the author of the pleasure.
O thou, my elder brother in misfortune,
By far my elder brother in the Muses,
With tears I pity thy unhappy fate!
Why is the Bard unpitied by the world,
Yet has so keen a relish of its pleasures?

EPISTLE TO MRS SCOTT

THE GUDEWIFE OF WAUCHOPE HOUSE, ROXBURGHSHIRE

I mind it weel in early date,
    When I was beardless, young, and blate,
      An' first could thresh the barn,
    Or haud a yokin' at the pleugh;
    An' tho' forfoughten sair eneugh,
      Yet unco proud to learn:

When first amang the yellow corn
　　A man I reckon'd was,
An' wi' the lave ilk merry morn
　　Could rank my rig and lass,
　　　　Still shearing, and clearing
　　　　　The tither stookèd raw,
　　　　Wi' claivers and haivers,
　　　　　Wearing the day awa'.

E'en then, a wish (I mind its pow'r),
A wish that to my latest hour
　　Shall strongly heave my breast,
That I for poor auld Scotland's sake
Some usefu' plan or book could make,
　　Or sing a sang at least.
The rough burr-thistle, spreading wide
　　Amang the bearded bear,
I turn'd the weeder-clips aside,
　　An' spar'd the symbol dear:
　　　　No nation, no station,
　　　　　My envy e'er could raise;
　　　　A Scot still, but blot still,
　　　　　I knew nae higher praise.

But still the elements o' sang,
In formless jumble, right an' wrang,
　　Wild floated in my brain;
'Till on that har'st I said before,
My partner in the merry core,
　　She rous'd the forming strain;
I see her yet, the sonsie quean
　　That lighted up my jingle,
Her witching smile, her pawky een
　　That gart my heart-strings tingle;
　　　　I firèd, inspirèd,
　　　　　At every kindling keek,
　　　　But bashing, and dashing,
　　　　　I fearèd ay to speak.

Health to the sex ! ilk guid chiel says :
Wi' merry dance in winter days,
  An' we to share in common;
The gust o' joy, the balm of woe,
The saul o' life, the heaven below,
  Is rapture-giving woman.
Ye surly sumphs, who hate the name,
  Be mindfu' o' your mither;
She, honest woman, may think shame
  That ye're connected wi' her :
    Ye're wae men, ye're nae men
      That slight the lovely dears;
    To shame ye, disclaim ye,
      Ilk honest birkie swears.

For you, no bred to barn and byre,
Wha sweetly tune the Scottish lyre,
  Thanks to you for your line :
The marled plaid ye kindly spare,
By me should gratefully be ware;
  'Twad please me to the nine.
I'd be mair vauntie o' my hap,
  Douce hingin' owre my curple,
Than ony ermine ever lap,
  Or proud imperial purple.
    Farewell then, lang hale then,
      An' plenty be your fa';
    May losses and crosses
      Ne'er at your hallan ca' !

March, 1787.   R. BURNS.

TO MISS ISABELLA MACLEOD

EDINBURGH, *March* 16, 1787.

THE crimson blossom charms the bee,
  The summer sun the swallow;
So dear this tuneful gift to me
  From lovely Isabella.

Her portrait fair upon my mind
  Revolving time shall mellow,
And mem'ry's latest effort find
  The lovely Isabella.

No Bard nor lover's rapture this
  In fancies vain and shallow!
She is, so come my soul to bliss,
  The lovely Isabella.

VERSES INTENDED TO BE WRITTEN BELOW A NOBLE EARL'S PICTURE

Whose is that noble, dauntless brow?
  And whose that eye of fire?
And whose that generous princely mien,
  E'en rooted foes admire?

Stranger! to justly show that brow,
  And mark that eye of fire,
Would take *His* hand, whose vernal tints
  His other works inspire.

Bright as a cloudless summer sun,
  With stately port he moves;
His guardian Seraph eyes with awe
  The noble Ward he loves.

Among the illustrious Scottish sons,
  That Chief thou mayst discern;
Mark Scotia's fond-returning eye,
  It dwells upon Glencairn.

PROLOGUE

SPOKEN BY MR WOODS ON HIS BENEFIT NIGHT, MONDAY,
16TH APRIL, 1787

When, by a generous Public's kind acclaim,
That dearest meed is granted—honest fame;
When *here* your favour is the actor's lot,
Nor even the *man* in *private life* forgot;
What breast so dead to heavenly Virtue's glow,
But heaves impassion'd with the grateful throe?

Poor is the task to please a barb'rous throng,
It needs no Siddons' powers in Southern's song;
But here an ancient nation fam'd afar
For genius, learning high, as great in war.
Hail, Caledonia! name for ever dear!
Before whose sons I'm honoured to appear?
Where every science, every noble art,
That can inform the mind, or mend the heart
Is known; as grateful nations oft have found,
Far as the rude barbarian marks the bound,
Philosophy, no idle pedant dream,
Here holds her search by heaven-taught Reason's
    beam;
Here history paints with elegance and force
The tide of Empire's fluctuating course;
Here Douglas forms wild Shakespeare into plan
And Harley rouses all the God in man.
When well-form'd taste and sparkling wit unite
With manly lore, or female beauty bright
(Beauty, where faultless symmetry and grace
    Can only charm us in the second place),
Witness, my heart, how oft with panting fear,
As on this night, I've met these judges here!
But still the hope Experience taught to live,
Equal to judge—you're candid to forgive.

No hundred-headed Riot here we meet,
With decency and law beneath his feet;
Nor Insolence assumes fair Freedom's name :
Like CALEDONIANS, you applaud or blame.

O Thou, dread Power! whose empire-giving hand
Has oft been stretch'd to shield the honour'd land!
Strong may she glow with all her ancient fire;
May every son be worthy of his sire;
Firm may she rise, with generous disdain
At Tyranny's , or direr Pleasure's chain;
Still Self-dependent in her native shore,
Bold may she brave grim Danger's loudest roar,
Till Fate the curtain drops on worlds to be no more.

THE BONIE MOOR-HEN

THE heather was blooming, the meadows were mawn,
Our lads gaed a-hunting ae day at the dawn,
O'er moors and o'er mosses and mony a glen,
At length they discovered a bonie moor-hen.

Chorus—I rede you, beware at the hunting, young men,
   I rede you, beware at the hunting, young men;
   Take some on the wing, and some as they
    spring,
   But cannily steal on a bonie moor-hen.

Sweet-brushing the dew from the brown heather
 bells,
Her colours betray'd her on yon mossy fells;
Her plumage outlustr'd the pride o' the spring,
And O! as she wanton'd sae gay on the wing.
    I rede you, etc.

Auld Phœbus himsel, as he peep'd o'er the hill,
In spite at her plumage he tryèd his skill;
He levell'd his rays where she bask'd on the brae—
His rays were outshone, and but mark'd where she
 lay.
   I rede you, etc.

They hunted the valley, they hunted the hill,
The best of our lads wi' the best o' their skill;
But still as the fairest she sat in their sight,
Then whirr! she was over, a mile at a flight.
   I rede you, etc.

MY LORD A-HUNTING

Chorus—My lady's gown, there's gairs upon't,
   And gowden flowers sae rare upon't;
   But Jenny's jimps and jirkinet,
   My lord thinks meikle mair upon't.

My lord a-hunting he is gane,
But hounds or hawks wi' him are nane;
By Colin's cottage lies his game,
If Colin's Jenny be at hame.
   My lady's gown, etc.

My lady's white, my lady's red,
And kith and kin o' Cassillis' blude;
But her ten-pund lands o' tocher gude
Were a' the charms his lordship lo'ed.
   My lady's gown, etc.

Out o'er yon muir, out o'er yon moss,
Whare gor-cocks thro' the heather pass,
There wons auld Colin's bonie lass,
A lily in a wilderness.
   My lady's gown, etc.

Sae sweetly move her genty limbs,
　Like music notes o' lovers' hymns :
The diamond-dew in her een sae blue,
　Where laughing love sae wanton swims.
　　　　My lady's gown, etc.

My lady's dink, my lady's drest,
　The flower and fancy o' the west;
But the lassie that a man lo'es best,
O that's the lass to mak him blest.
　　　　My lady's gown, etc.

EPIGRAM AT ROSLIN INN

My blessings on ye, honest wife !
　I ne'er was here before;
Ye've wealth o' gear for spoon and knife—
　Heart could not wish for more.
Heav'n keep you clear o' sturt and strife,
　Till far ayont fourscore,
And while I toddle on thro' life,
　I'll ne'er gae by your door !

EPIGRAM ADDRESSED TO AN ARTIST

WHOM THE POET FOUND ENGAGED ON A REPRESENTA-
TION OF JACOB'S DREAM

Dear ———, I'll gie ye some advice,
　You'll tak it no uncivil :
You shouldna paint at angels mair,
　But try and paint the devil.

To paint an Angel's kittle wark,
    Wi' Nick, there's little danger:
You'll easy draw a lang-kent face,
    But no sae weel a *Stranger.*—R. B.

THE BOOK-WORMS

THROUGH and through th' inspir'd leaves,
    Ye maggots, make your windings;
But O respect his lordship's taste,
    And spare the golden bindings.

ON ELPHINSTONE'S TRANSLATION OF MARTIAL'S EPIGRAMS

O THOU whom Poesy abhors,
Whom Prose has turnèd out of doors,
Heard'st thou yon groan?—proceed no
        further,
'Twas laurel'd Martial calling 'murther.'

BOTTLE AND FRIEND

There's nane that's blest of human kind,
    But the cheerful and the gay, man.

HERE's a bottle and an honest friend!
    What wad ye wish for mair, man?
Wha kens, before his life may end,
    What his share may be o' care, man?

Then catch the moments as they fly,
    And use them as they ought, man:
Believe me, happiness is shy,
    And comes not ay when sought, man.

LINES WRITTEN UNDER THE PICTURE OF THE CELEBRATED MISS BURNS

CEASE, ye prudes, your envious railing,
    Lovely Burns has charms—confess:
True it is, she had one failing,
    Had a woman ever less?

EPITAPH FOR WILLIAM NICOL, OF THE HIGH SCHOOL, EDINBURGH

YE maggots, feed on Nicol's brain,
    For few sic feasts you've gotten;
And fix your claws in Nicol's heart,
    For deil a bit o't's rotten.

EPITAPH FOR WILLIAM MICHIE

SCHOOLMASTER OF CLEISH PARISH, FIFESHIRE

HERE lie Willie Michie's banes,
    O Satan, when ye tak him,
Gie him the schulin' o' your weans,
    For clever deils he'll mak them!

HEY, CA' THRO'

Up wi' the carls o' Dysart,
    And the lads o' Buckhaven,
And the kimmers o' Largo,
    And the lasses o' Leven.

Chorus—Hey, ca' thro', ca' thro',
        For we hae mickle ado;
      Hey, ca' thro', ca' thro',
        For we hae mickle ado.

We hae tales to tell,
    An' we hae sangs to sing;
We hae pennies to spend,
    An' we hae pints to bring,
      Hey, ca' thro', etc. .

We'll live a' our days,
    And them that comes behin',
Let them do the like,
    An' spend the gear they win.
      Hey, ca' thro', etc.

ADDRESS TO WM. TYTLER, ESQ., OF WOODHOUSELEE

WITH AN IMPRESSION OF THE AUTHOR'S PORTRAIT

REVERED defender of beauteous Stuart,
    Of Stuart, a name once respected;
A name, which to love was the mark of a true heart
    But now 'tis despis'd and neglected.

Tho' something like moisture conglobes in my eye,
  Let no one misdeem me disloyal;
A poor friendless wand'rer may well claim a sigh,
  Still more, if that wand'rer were royal.

My fathers that name have rever'd on a throne :
  My fathers have died to right it;
Those fathers would spurn their degenerate son,
  That name should he scoffingly slight it.

Still in prayers for King George I most heartily join,
  The Queen, and the rest of the gentry :
Be they wise, be they foolish, is nothing of mine;
  Their title's avow'd by my country.

But why of that epocha make such a fuss,
  That gave us th' Electoral stem ?
If bringing them over was lucky for us,
  I'm sure 'twas as lucky for them.

But loyalty truce ! we're on dangerous ground;
  Who knows how the fashions may alter ?
The doctrine to-day, that is loyalty sound,
  To-morrow may bring us a halter !

I send you a trifle, a head of a bard,
  A trifle scarce worthy your care;
But accept it, good Sir, as a mark of regard,
  Sincere as a saint's dying prayer.

Now life's chilly evening dim shades on your eye,
  And ushers the long dreary night :
But you, like the star that athwart gilds the sky,
  Your course to the latest is bright.

EPIGRAM TO MISS AINSLIE IN CHURCH

FAIR maid, you need not take the hint,
 Nor idle texts pursue :
'Twas guilty sinners that he meant,
 Not *Angels* such as you.

BURLESQUE LAMENT FOR THE ABSENCE OF WILLIAM CREECH, PUBLISHER

AULD chuckie Reekie's sair distrest,
Down droops her ance weel burnish'd crest,
Nae joy her bonie buskit nest
 Can yield ava,
Her darling bird that she lo'es best—
 Willie's awa'.

O Willie was a witty wight,
And had o' things an unco sleight,
Auld Reekie ay he keepit tight,
 And trig an' braw :
But now they'll busk her like a fright,—
 Willie's awa' !

The stiffest o' them a' he bow'd,
The bauldest o' them a' he cow'd;
They durst nae mair than he allow'd,
 That was a law :
We've lost a birkie weel worth gowd;
 Willie's awa' !

Now gawkies, tawpies, gowks and fools,
Frae colleges and boarding schools,
May sprout like simmer puddock-stools
 In glen or shaw,
He wha could brush them down to mools—
 Willie's awa' !

The brethren o' the commerce-chaumer
May mourn their loss wi' doolfu' clamour;
He was a dictionar and grammar
      Among them a';
I fear they'll now mak mony a stammer;
        Willie's awa' !

Nae mair we see his levee door
Philosophers and Poets pour,
And toothy critics by the score,
      In bloody raw !
The adjutant o' a' the core—
        Willie's awa' !

Now worthy Gregory's Latin face,
Tytler's and Greenfield's modest grace;
M'Kenzie, Stewart, such a brace
      As Rome ne'er saw;
They a' maun meet some ither place,
        Willie's awa' !

Poor Burns ev'n 'Scotch Drink' canna quicken,
He cheeps like some bewilder'd chicken
Scar'd frae it's minnie and the cleckin',
      By hoodie-craw;
Grief's gien his heart an unco kickin',
        Willie's awa' !

Now ev'ry sour-mou'd girnin' blellum,
And Calvin's folk, are fit to fell him;
Ilk self-conceited critic skellum
      His quill may draw;
He wha could brawlie ward their bellum—
        Willie's awa' !

Up wimpling stately Tweed I've sped,
And Eden scenes on crystal Jed,
And Ettrick banks, now roaring red,
      While tempests blaw;
But every joy and pleasure's fled,
        Willie's awa' !

May I be Slander's common speech;
A text for Infamy to preach;
And lastly, streekit out to bleach
      In winter snaw,
When I forget thee, WILLIE CREECH,
      Tho' far awa'!

May never wicked Fortune touzle him!
May never wicked men bamboozle him!
Until a pow as auld's Methusalem
      He canty claw!
Then to the blessed new Jerusalem,
      Fleet wing awa'!

NOTE TO MR RENTON OF LAMERTON

YOUR billet, Sir, I grant receipt;
Wi' you I'll canter ony gate,
Tho' 'twere a trip to yon blue warl',
Whare birkies march on burning marl:
Then, Sir, God willing, I'll attend ye,
And to His goodness I commend ye.
              R. BURNS.

THE BARD AT INVERARAY

WHOE'ER he be that sojourns here,
   I pity much his case,
Unless he come to wait upon
   The lord *their* god, 'His Grace.'

There's naething here but Highland pride,
   And Highland scab and hunger:
If Providence has sent me here,
   'Twas surely in an anger.

EPIGRAM TO MISS JEAN SCOTT

O HAD each Scot of ancient times
    Been Jeanie Scott, as thou art;
The bravest heart on English ground
    Had yielded like a coward.

ON THE DEATH OF JOHN M'LEOD, ESQ.

ROTHER TO A YOUNG LADY, A PARTICULAR FRIEND OF
THE AUTHOR

SAD thy tale, thou idle page,
    And rueful thy alarms;
Death tears the brother of her love
    From Isabella's arms.

Sweetly deckt with pearly dew
    The morning rose may blow;
But cold successive noontide blasts
    May lay its beauties low.

Fair on Isabella's morn
    The sun propitious smil'd;
But, long ere noon, succeeding clouds
    Succeeding hopes beguil'd.

Fate oft tears the bosom chords
    That Nature finest strung;
So Isabella's heart was form'd,
    And so that heart was wrung.

Dread Omnipotence alone
    Can heal the wound He gave—
Can point the brimful care-worn eyes
    To scenes beyond the grave.

Virtue's blossoms there shall blow,
    And fear no withering blast;
There Isabella's spotless worth
    Shall happy be at last.

ELEGY ON THE DEATH OF SIR JAMES HUNTER BLAIR

THE lamp of day with ill-presaging glare,
    Dim, cloudy, sank beneath the western wave;
Th' inconstant blast howl'd thro' the darkening air
    And hollow whistled in the rocky cave.

Lone as I wander'd by each cliff and dell,
    Once the lov'd haunts of Scotia's royal train;
Or mus'd where limpid streams, once hallow'd, well
    Or mould'ring ruins mark the sacred fane.

Th' increasing blast roared round the beetling rocks
    The clouds, swift-wing'd, flew o'er the starry sky
The groaning trees untimely shed their locks,
    And shooting meteors caught the startled eye.

The paly moon rose in the livid east,
    And 'mong the cliffs disclos'd a stately form
In weeds of woe, that frantic beat her breast,
    And mix'd her wailings with the raving storm.

Wild to my heart the filial pulses glow,
    'Twas Caledonia's trophied shield I view'd:
Her form majestic droop'd in pensive woe,
    The lightning of her eye in tears imbued.

Revers'd that spear, redoubtable in war,
    Reclined that banner, erst in fields unfurl'd,
That like a deathful meteor gleam'd afar,
    And brav'd the mighty monarchs of the world.

'My patriot son fills an untimely grave!'
 With accents wild and lifted arms she cried:
'Low lies the hand that oft was stretch'd to save,
 Low lies the heart that swell'd with honest pride.

'A weeping country joins a widow's tear;
 The helpless poor mix with the orphan's cry;
The drooping Arts surround their patron's bier;
 And grateful Science heaves the heart-felt sigh!

'I saw my sons resume their ancient fire;
 I saw fair Freedom's blossoms richly blow:
But ah! how hope is born but to expire!
 Relentless Fate has laid their guardian low.

'My patriot falls, but shall he lie unsung,
 While empty greatness saves a worthless name?
No; every Muse shall join her tuneful tongue,
 And future ages hear his growing fame.

'And I will join a mother's tender cares,
 Thro' future times to make his virtues last;
That distant years may boast of other Blairs!'
 She said, and vanish'd with the sweeping blast.

TO MISS FERRIER

ENCLOSING THE ELEGY ON SIR J. H. BLAIR

NAE heathen name shall I prefix,
 Frae Pindus or Parnassus;
Auld Reekie dings them a' to sticks,
 For rhyme-inspiring lasses.

Jove's tunefu' dochters three times three
 Made Homer deep their debtor;
But, gien the body half an e'e,
 Nine Ferriers wad done better!

Last day my mind was in a bog,
　　Down George's Street I stoited;
A creeping, cauld, prosaic fog
　　My very senses doited.

Do what I dought to set her free,
　　My saul lay in the mire;
Ye turned a neuk—I saw your e'e—
　　She took the wing like fire.

The mournfu' sang I here enclose,
　　In gratitude I send you,
And pray, in rhyme as weel as prose,
　　A' guid things may attend you!

IMPROMPTU ON CARRON IRON WORKS

WE cam na here to view your warks,
　　In hopes to be mair wise,
But only, lest we gang to hell,
　　It may be nae surprise:
But when we tirl'd at your door
　　Your porter dought na hear us;
Sae may, shou'd we to Hell's yetts come,
　　Your billy Satan sair us!

WRITTEN BY SOMEBODY ON THE WINDOW

OF AN INN AT STIRLING, ON SEEING THE ROYAL PALACE IN RUIN

HERE Stuarts once in glory reigned,
And laws for Scotland's weal ordained;
But now unroof'd their palace stands,
Their sceptre's sway'd by other hands;

Fallen indeed, and to the earth
Whence grovelling reptiles take their birth.
The injured Stuart line is gone,
A race outlandish fills their throne;
An idiot race, to honour lost;
Who know them best despise them most.

VERSES WRITTEN WITH A PENCIL

OVER THE CHIMNEY-PIECE, IN THE PARLOUR OF THE
INN AT KENMORE, TAYMOUTH

ADMIRING Nature in her wildest grace,
These northern scenes with weary feet I trace;
O'er many a winding dale and painful steep,
Th' abodes of covey'd grouse and timid sheep,
My savage journey, curious, I pursue,
Till fam'd Breadalbane opens to my view.
The meeting cliffs each deep-sunk glen divides,
The woods, wild-scatter'd, clothe their ample sides;
Th' outstretching lake, imbosomed 'mong the hills,
The eye with wonder and amazement fills;
The Tay meand'ring sweet in infant pride,
The palace rising on his verdant side,
The lawns wood-fring'd in Nature's native taste,
The hillocks dropt in Nature's careless haste,
The arches striding o'er the new-born stream,
The village glittering in the noontide beam—

.   .   .   .   .

Poetic ardors in my bosom swell,
Lone wand'ring by the hermit's mossy cell;
The sweeping theatre of hanging woods,
Th' incessant roar of headlong tumbling floods—

.   .   .   .   .

Here Poesy might wake her heav'n-taught lyre,
And look through Nature with creative fire;

Here, to the wrongs of Fate half reconcil'd,
Misfortune's lighten'd steps might wander wild;
And Disappointment, in these lonely bounds,
Find balm to soothe her bitter rankling wounds :
Here heart-struck Grief might heav'nward stretch
    her scan,
And injur'd Worth forget and pardon man.

. . . . . .

THE BIRKS OF ABERFELDY

Chorus.—Bonie lassie, will ye go,
    Will ye go, will ye go,
    Bonie lassie, will ye go
      To the birks of Aberfeldy !

Now Simmer blinks on flowery braes,
And o'er the crystal streamlet plays;
Come, let us spend the lightsome days,
    In the birks of Aberfeldy.
      Bonie lassie, etc.

The little birdies blythely sing,
While o'er their heads the hazels hing,
Or lightly flit on wanton wing,
    In the birks of Aberfeldy.
      Bonie lassie, etc.

The braes ascend like lofty wa's,
The foamy stream deep-roaring fa's,
O'erhung wi' fragrant spreading shaws—
    The birks of Aberfeldy.
      Bonie lassie, etc.

The hoary cliffs are crown'd wi' flowers,
White o'er the linns the burnie pours,
And rising, weets wi' misty showers
  The birks of Aberfeldy.
   Bonie lassie, etc.

Let Fortune's gifts at random flee,
They ne'er shall draw a wish frae me;
Supremely blest wi' love and thee,
  In the birks of Aberfeldy.
   Bonie lassie, etc.

THE HUMBLE PETITION OF BRUAR WATER

TO THE NOBLE DUKE OF ATHOLE

My lord, I know your noble ear
  Woe ne'er assails in vain;
Embolden'd thus, I beg you'll hear
  Your humble slave complain,
How saucy Phœbus' scorching beams,
  In flaming summer-pride,
Dry-withering, waste my foamy streams,
  And drink my crystal tide.

The lightly-jumpin', glow'rin' trouts,
  That thro' my waters play,
If, in their random, wanton spouts,
  They near the margin stray;
If, hapless chance! they linger lang,
  I'm scorching up so shallow,
They're left the whitening stanes amang,
  In gasping death to wallow.

Last day I grat wi' spite and teen,
　　As poet Burns came by,
That, to a bard, I should be seen
　　Wi' half my channel dry;
A panegyric rhyme, I ween,
　　Ev'n as I was, he shor'd me;
But had I in my glory been,
　　He, kneeling, wad ador'd me.

Here, foaming down the skelvy rocks,
　　In twisting strength I rin;
There, high my boiling torrent smokes,
　　Wild-roaring o'er a linn:
Enjoying large each spring and well,
　　As Nature gave them me,
I am, altho' I say't mysel,
　　Worth gaun a mile to see.

Would then my noble master please
　　To grant my highest wishes,
He'll shade the banks wi' tow'ring trees,
　　And bonie spreading bushes.
Delighted doubly then, my lord,
　　You'll wander on my banks,
And listen mony a grateful bird
　　Return you tuneful thanks.

The sober lav'rock, warbling wild,
　　Shall to the skies aspire;
The gowdspink, Music's gayest child,
　　Shall sweetly join the choir;
The blackbird strong, the lintwhite clear,
　　The mavis mild and mellow;
The robin pensive Autumn cheer,
　　In all her locks of yellow.

This, too, a covert shall ensure,
　　To shield them from the storm;
And coward maukin sleep secure,
　　Low in her grassy form:

Here shall the shepherd make his seat,
　To weave his crown of flow'rs;
Or find a shelt'ring, safe retreat,
　From prone-descending show'rs.

And here, by sweet, endearing stealth,
　Shall meet the loving pair,
Despising worlds, with all their wealth,
　As empty, idle care;
The flow'rs shall vie in all their charms,
　The hour of heav'n to grace;
And birk extend their fragrant arms
　To screen the dear embrace.

Here, haply, too, at vernal dawn,
　Some musing bard may stray,
And eye the smoking, dewy lawn,
　And misty mountain gray;
Or, by the reaper's nightly beam,
　Mild-chequering thro' the trees,
Rave to my darkly dashing stream,
　Hoarse-swelling on the breeze.

Let lofty firs, and ashes cool,
　My lowly banks o'erspread,
And view, deep-bending in the pool,
　Their shadows' wat'ry-bed :
Let fragrant birks, in woodbines drest,
　My craggy cliffs adorn;
And, for the little songster's nest,
　The close embow'ring thorn.

So may, old Scotia's darling hope,
　Your little angel band
Spring, like their fathers, up to prop
　Their honour'd native land !
So may, thro' Albion's farthest ken,
　To social-flowing glasses,
The grace be—'Athole's honest men,
　And Athole's bonie lasses !'

LINES ON THE FALLS OF FYERS

NEAR LOCH-NESS

WRITTEN WITH A PENCIL ON THE SPOT

AMONG the heathy hills and ragged woods
The roaring Fyers pours his mossy floods;
Till full he dashes on the rocky mounds,
Where, thro' a shapeless-breach, his stream resounds,
As high in air the bursting torrents flow,
As deep recoiling surges foam' below,
Prone down the rock the whitening sheet descends,
And viewless Echo's ear, astonished, rends.
Dim-seen, through rising mists and ceaseless
    show'rs,
The hoary cavern, wide surrounding lours :
Still thro' the gap the struggling river toils,
And still, below, the horrid caldron boils—

  .   .   .   .   .

A HIGHLAND WELCOME

WRITTEN ON PARTING WITH A KIND HOST IN THE HIGHLANDS

WHEN Death's dark stream I ferry o'er,
    (A time that surely shall come),
In Heav'n itself I'll ask no more,
    Than just a Highland welcome.

STRATHALLAN'S LAMENT

THICKEST night, surround my dwelling !
    Howling tempests, o'er me rave !
Turbid torrents, wintry swelling,
    Roaring by my lonely cave !

Crystal streamlets gently flowing,
  Busy haunts of base mankind,
Western breezes softly blowing,
  Suit not my distracted mind.

In the cause of Right engagèd,
  Wrongs injurious to redress,
Honor's war we strongly wagèd,
  But the heavens deny'd success,
Ruin's wheel has driven o'er us,
  Not a hope that dare attend,
The wide world is all before us—
  But a world without a friend.

CASTLE GORDON

STREAMS that glide in orient plains,
Never bound by Winter's chains;
  Glowing here on golden sands,
There immixed with foulest stains
  From Tyranny's empurpled hands:
These, their richly gleaming waves,
I leave to tyrants and their slaves;
Give me the stream that sweetly laves
  The banks by Castle Gordon.

Spicy forests, ever gay,
Shading from the burning ray
  Hapless wretches sold to toil;
Or the ruthless native's way,
  Bent on slaughter, blood, and spoil:
Woods that ever verdant wave,
I leave the tyrant and the slave;
Give me the groves that lofty brave
  The storms, by Castle Gordon.

Wildly here without control,
Nature reigns and rules the whole;
   In that sober, pensive mood,
Dearest to the feeling soul,
   She plants the forest, pours the flood:
Life's poor day I'll musing rave,
And find at night a sheltering cave,
Where waters flow and wild woods wave,
    By bonie Castle Gordon.

LADY ONLIE, HONEST LUCKY

Tune—'The Ruffian's Rant.'

A' THE lads o' Thorniebank,
   When they gae to the shore o' Bucky,
They'll step in an' tak a pint,
   Wi' Lady Onlie, honest lucky.

Chorus.—Lady Onlie, honest lucky,
      Brews gude ale at shore o' Bucky;
   I wish her sale for her gude ale,
      The best on a' the shore o' Bucky.

Her house sae bien, her curch sae clean,
   I wat she is a dainty chuckie;
And cheery blinks the ingle-gleede
   O' Lady Onlie, honest lucky.
      Lady Onlie, etc.

THENIEL MENZIES' BONIE MARY

Air—'The Ruffian's Rant,' or 'Roy's Wife.'

IN comin' by the brig o' Dye,
   At Darlet we a blink did tarry;
As day was dawin' in the sky,
   We drank a health to bonie Mary.

Chorus.—Theniel Menzies' bonie Mary,
   Theniel Menzies' bonie Mary,
   Charlie Grigor tint his plaidie,
   Kissin' Theniel's bonie Mary.

Her een sae bright, her brow sae white,
 Her haffet locks as brown's a berry;
And ay they dimpl't wi' a smile,
 The rosy cheeks o' bonie Mary.
    Theniel Menzies' bonie Mary, etc.

We lap an' danc'd the lee-lang day,
 Till piper lads were wae and weary;
But Charlie gat the spring to pay,
 For kissin' Theniel's bonie Mary, etc.
    Theniel Menzies' bonie Mary, etc.

THE BONIE LASS OF ALBANY

Tune—'Mary's Dream.'

My heart is wae, and unco wae,
 To think upon the raging sea
That roars between her gardens green
 An' the bonie Lass of Albany.

This lovely maid's of royal blood
 That ruled Albion's kingdoms three,
But oh, alas ! for her bonie face,
 They've wrang'd the Lass of Albany.

In the rolling tide of spreading Clyde
 There sits an isle of high degree,
And a town of fame whose princely name
 Should grace the Lass of Albany.

But there's a youth, a witless youth,
 That fills the place where she should be;
We'll send him o'er to his native shore,
 And bring our ain sweet Albany.

Alas the day, and woe the day,
 A false usurper wan the gree,
Who now commands the towers and lands—
 The royal right of Albany.

We'll daily pray, we'll nightly pray,
 On bended knees most fervently,
The time may come, with pipe an' drum
 We'll welcome hame fair Albany.

ON SCARING SOME WATER-FOWL IN LOCH-TURIT

WHY, ye tenants of the lake,
For me your wat'ry haunt forsake?
Tell me, fellow-creatures, why
At my presence thus you fly?
Why disturb your social joys,
Parent, filial, kindred ties?—
Common friend to you and me,
Nature's gifts to all are free:
Peaceful keep your dimpling wave,
Busy feed, or wanton lave;
Or, beneath the sheltering rock,
Bide the surging billow's shock.

Conscious, blushing for our race,
Soon, too soon, your fears I trace.
Man, your proud usurping foe,
Would be lord of all below:
Plumes himself in freedom's pride,
Tyrant stern to all beside.

The eagle, from the cliffy brow,
Marking you his prey below,
In his breast no pity dwells,
Strong necessity compels :
But Man, to whom alone is giv'n
A ray direct from pitying Heav'n,
Glories in his heart humane—
And creatures for his pleasure slain !

In these savage, liquid plains,
Only known to wand'ring swains,
Where the mossy riv'let strays,
Far from human haunts and ways;
All on Nature you depend,
And life's poor season peaceful spend.

Or, if man's superior might
Dare invade your native right,
On the lofty ether borne,
Man with all his pow'rs you scorn;
Swiftly seek, on clanging wings,
Other lakes and other springs;
And the foe you cannot brave,
Scorn at least to be his slave.

BLYTHE WAS SHE

Tune—'Andro and his Cutty Gun.'

Chorus.—Blythe, blythe and merry was she,
        Blythe was she but and ben;
        Blythe by the banks of Earn,
        And blythe in Glenturit glen.

By Oughtertyre grows the aik,
    On Yarrow banks the birken shaw;
But Phemie was a bonier lass
    Than braes o' Yarrow ever saw.
        Blythe, blythe, etc.

Her looks were like a flow'r in May,
    Her smile was like a simmer morn :
She trippèd by the banks o' Earn,
    As light's a bird upon a thorn.
        Blythe, blythe, etc.

Her bonie face it was as meek
    As ony lamb upon a lea;
The evening sun was ne'er sae sweet,
    As was the blink o' Phemie's e'e.
        Blythe, blythe, etc.

The Highland hills I've wander'd wide,
    And o'er the Lowlands, I hae been;
But Phemie was the blythest lass
    That ever trode the dewy green.
        Blythe, blythe, etc.

A ROSE-BUD BY MY EARLY WALK

A ROSE-BUD by my early walk,
Adown a corn-inclosèd bawk,
Sae gently bent its thorny stalk,
    All on a dewy morning.
Ere twice the shades o' dawn are fled,
In a' its crimson glory spread,
And drooping rich the dewy head,
    It scents the early morning.

Within the bush her covert nest
A little linnet fondly prest;
The dew sat chilly on her breast,
    Sae early in the morning.
She soon shall see her tender brood,
The pride, the pleasure o' the wood,
Amang the fresh green leaves bedew'd,
    Awake the early morning.

So thou, dear bird, young Jeany fair,
On trembling string or vocal air,
Shall sweetly pay the tender care
    That tents thy early morning.
So thou, sweet Rose-bud, young and gay,
Shall beauteous blaze upon the day,
And bless the parent's evening ray
    That watch'd thy early morning.

EPITAPH FOR MR W. CRUICKSHANK

HONEST Will to Heaven's away,
    And mony shall lament him;
His fau'ts they a' in Latin lay,
    In English nane e'er kent them.

THE BANKS OF THE DEVON

How pleasant the banks of the clear winding Devon,
    With green spreading bushes and flow'rs blooming
      fair!
But the boniest flow'r on the banks of the Devon
    Was once a sweet bud on the braes of the Ayr.
Mild be the sun on this sweet blushing flower,
    In the gay rosy morn, as it bathes in the dew;
And gently the fall of the soft vernal shower,
    That steals on the evening each leaf to renew!

O spare the dear blossom, ye orient breezes,
    With chill hoary wing as ye usher the dawn;
And far be thou distant, thou reptile that seizes
    The verdure and pride of the garden or lawn!
Let Bourbon exult in his gay gilded lilies,
    And England triumphant display her proud rose:
A fairer than either adorns the green valleys,
    Where Devon, sweet Devon, meandering flows.

BRAVING ANGRY WINTER'S STORMS

Tune—'Neil Gow's Lament for Abercairny.'

WHERE, braving angry winter's storms,
　　The lofty Ochils rise,
Far in their shade my Peggy's charms
　　First blest my wondering eyes;
As one who by some savage stream
　　A lonely gem surveys,
Astonish'd, doubly marks its beam
　　With art's most polish'd blaze.

Blest be the wild, sequester'd shade,
　　And blest the day and hour,
Where Peggy's charms I first survey'd,
　　When first I felt their pow'r!
The tyrant Death, with grim controul,
　　May seize my fleeting breath;
But tearing Peggy from my soul
　　Must be a stronger death.

MY PEGGY'S CHARMS

MY Peggy's face, my Peggy's form,
The frost of hermit Age might warm;
My Peggy's worth, my Peggy's mind,
Might charm the first of human kind.

I love my Peggy's angel air,
Her face so truly, heavenly fair,
Her native grace, so void of art,
But I adore my Peggy's heart.

The lily's hue, the rose's dye,
The kindling lustre of an eye;
Who but owns their magic sway!
Who but knows they all decay!

The tender thrill, the pitying tear,
The generous purpose, nobly dear,
The gentle look that rage disarms—
These are all immortal charms.

THE YOUNG HIGHLAND ROVER

Tune—'Morag.'

LOUD blaws the frosty breezes,
    The snaws the mountains cover;
Like winter on me seizes,
    Since my young Highland rover
    Far wanders nations over.
Where'er he go, where'er he stray,
    May Heaven be his warden;
Return him safe to fair Strathspey,
    And bonie Castle-Gordon.

The trees now naked groaning,
    Shall soon wi' leaves be hinging,
The birdies dowie moaning,
    Shall a' be blythely singing,
    And every flower be springing;
Sae I'll rejoice the lee-lang day,
    When (by his mighty Warden)
My youth's return'd to fair Strathspey,
    And bonie Castle-Gordon.

BIRTHDAY ODE FOR 31ST DECEMBER, 1787

AFAR the illustrious Exile roams,
　　Whom kingdoms on this day should hail;
An inmate in the casual shed,
On transient pity's bounty fed,
　　Haunted by busy memory's bitter tale !
Beasts of the forest have their savage homes,
　　But he, who should imperial purple wear,
Owns not the lap of earth where rests his royal head !
　　His wretched refuge, dark despair,
While ravening wrongs and woes pursue,
And distant far the faithful few
　　Who would his sorrows share.

False flatterer, Hope, away !
　　Nor think to lure us as in days of yore :
We solemnise this sorrowing natal day,
　　To prove our loyal truth—we can no more,
And owning Heaven's mysterious sway,
　　Submissive, low, adore.
Ye honored, mighty Dead,
　　Who nobly perished in the glorious cause,
　　Your KING, your Country, and her laws,
From great DUNDEE, who smiling Victory led,
　　And fell a Martyr in her arms
　　(What breast of northern ice but warms ?)
　　To bold BALMERINO's undying name,
　　Whose soul of fire, lighted at Heaven's high flame,
Deserves the proudest wreath departed heroes claim :
　　Not unrevenged your fate shall lie,
　　　It only lags, the fatal hour,
　　Your blood shall, with incessant cry,
　　　Awake at last th' unsparing Power;
　　　As from the cliff, with thundering course,
　　　The snowy ruin smokes along
With doubling speed and gathering force,

Till deep it, crushing, whelms the cottage in the vale;
　　So Vengeance' arm, ensanguin'd, strong,
　　Shall with resistless might assail,
Usurping Brunswick's pride shall lay,
And STEWART's wrongs and yours, with tenfold weight,
　　repay.

PERDITION, baleful child of night!
Rise and revenge the injured right
　　Of STEWART's royal race:
Lead on the unmuzzled hounds of hell,
Till all the frighted echoes tell
　　The blood-notes of the chase!
Full on the quarry point their view,
Full on the base, usurping crew,
The tools of faction, and the nation's curse!
　　Hark how the cry grows on the wind;
　　They leave the lagging gale behind,
Their savage fury, pityless, they pour;
With murdering eyes already they devour;
See Brunswick spent, a wretched prey,
His life one poor despairing day,
Where each avenging hour still ushers in a worse!
　　Such havock, howling all abroad,
　　　Their utter ruin bring;
　　The base apostates to their GOD,
　　　Or rebels to their KING.

ON THE DEATH OF ROBERT DUNDAS, ESQ.
OF ARNISTON

LATE LORD PRESIDENT OF THE COURT OF SESSION

LONE on the bleaky hills the straying flocks
Shun the fierce storms among the sheltering rocks;
Down from the rivulets, red with dashing rains,
The gathering floods burst o'er the distant plains;
Beneath the blast the leafless forests groan;
The hollow caves return a sullen moan.

Ye hills, ye plains, ye forests, and ye caves,
Ye howling winds, and wintry swelling waves!
Unheard, unseen, by human ear or eye,
Sad to your sympathetic glooms I fly;
Where, to the whistling blast and water's roar,
Pale Scotia's recent wound I may deplore.

O heavy loss, thy country ill could bear!
A loss these evil days can ne'er repair!
Justice, the high vicegerent of her God,
Her doubtful balance eyed, and sway'd her rod:
Hearing the tidings of the fatal blow,
She sank, abandon'd to the wildest woe.

Wrongs, injuries, from many a darksome den,
Now, gay in hope, explore the paths of men:
See from his cavern grim Oppression rise,
And throw on Poverty his cruel eyes:
Keen on the helpless victim see him fly,
And stifle, dark, the feebly-bursting cry:
Mark ruffian Violence, distained with crimes,
Rousing elate in these degenerate times;
View unsuspecting Innocence a prey,
As guileful Fraud points out the erring way:
While subtile Litigation's pliant tongue
The life-blood equal sucks of Right and Wrong:
Hark, injur'd Want recounts th' unlisten'd tale,
And much-wrong'd Mis'ry pours th' unpitied wail!

Ye dark, waste hills, ye brown unsightly plains,
Congenial scenes, ye soothe my mournful strains:
Ye tempests, rage! ye turbid torrents, roll!
Ye suit the joyless tenor of my soul.
Life's social haunts and pleasures I resign;
Be nameless wilds and lonely wanderings mine,
To mourn the woes my country must endure—
That wound degenerate ages cannot cure.

SYLVANDER TO CLARINDA

When dear Clarinda, matchless fair,
   First struck Sylvander's raptur'd view,
He gaz'd, he listened, to despair,
   Alas! 'twas all he dared to do.

Love, from Clarinda's heavenly eyes,
   Transfixed his bosom thro' and thro';
But still in Friendship's guarded guise,
   For more the demon fear'd to do.

That heart, already more than lost,
   The imp beleaguer'd all *perdue ;*
For frowning Honor kept his post—
   To meet that frown he shrunk to do.

His pangs the Bard refused to own,
   Tho' half he wish'd Clarinda knew;
But Anguish wrung the unweeting groan—
   Who blames what frantic Pain must do?

That heart, where motley follies blend,
   Was sternly still to Honor true :
To prove Clarinda's fondest friend,
   Was what a lover sure might do.

The Muse his ready quill employed,
   Nor nearer bliss he could pursue;
This bliss Clarinda cold deny'd—
   'Send word by Charles how you do!'

The chill behest disarm'd his muse,
   Till passion, all impatient grew :
He wrote, and hinted for excuse,
   'Twas, 'cause 'he'd nothing else to do.'

But by those hopes I have above!
    And by those faults I dearly rue!
The deed, the boldest mark of love,
    For thee, that deed I dare to do!

O could the Fates but name the price
    Would bless me with your charms and you!
With frantic joy I'd pay it thrice,
    If human art and power could do!

Then take, Clarinda, friendship's hand
    (Friendship, at least, I may avow);
And lay no more your chill command,—
    I'll write, whatever I've to do.

SYLVANDER.

CLARINDA, MISTRESS OF MY SOUL

CLARINDA, mistress of my soul,
    The measur'd time is run!
The wretch beneath the dreary pole
    So marks his latest sun.

To what dark cave of frozen night
    Shall poor Sylvander hie;
Depriv'd of thee, his life and light,
    The sun of all his joy.

We part—but by these precious drops,
    That fill thy lovely eyes,
No other light shall guide my steps,
    Till thy bright beams arise!

She, the fair sun of all her sex,
    Has blest my glorious day;
And shall a glimmering planet fix
    My worship to its ray?

I'M O'ER YOUNG TO MARRY YET

Chorus.—I'm o'er young, I'm o'er young,
      I'm o'er young to marry yet;
      I'm o'er young, 'twad be a sin
        To tak me frae my mammy yet.

I AM my mammy's ae bairn,
    Wi' unco folk I weary, sir;
And lying in a strange bed,
    I'm fley'd it mak me eerie, sir.
      I'm o'er young, etc.

Hallowmass is come and gane,
    The nights are lang in winter, sir,
And you an' I in ae bed,
    In trowth, I dare na venture, sir.
      I'm o'er young, etc.

Fu' loud an' shill the frosty wind
    Blaws thro' the leafless timmer, sir;
But if ye come this gate again,
    I'll aulder be gin simmer, sir.
      I'm o'er young, etc.

TO THE WEAVER'S GIN YOU GO

My heart was ance as blythe and free
    As simmer days were lang;
But a bonie, westlin' weaver lad
    Has gart me change my sang.

Chorus.—To the weaver's gin you go, fair maids,
      To the weaver's gin you go;
      I rede you right, gang ne'er at night,
      To the weaver's gin you go.

My mither sent me to the town,
   To warp a plaiden wab;
But the weary, weary warpin' o't
   Has gart me sigh and sab.
         To the weaver's, etc.

A bonie, westlin' weaver lad
   Sat working at his loom;
He took my heart as wi' a net,
   In every knot and thrum.
         To the weaver's, etc.

I sat beside my warpin'-wheel,
   And ay I ca'd it roun';
But every shot and every knock,
   My heart it gae a stoun.
         To the weaver's, etc.

The moon was sinking in the west,
   Wi' visage pale and wan,
As my bonie, westlin' weaver lad
   Convoy'd me thro' the glen.
         To the weaver's, etc.

But what was said, or what was done,
   Shame fa' me gin I tell;
But oh! I fear the kintra soon
   Will ken as weel's mysel!
         To the weaver's, etc.

M'PHERSON'S FAREWELL

Tune—'M'Pherson's Rant.'

FAREWELL, ye dungeons dark and strong,
   The wretch's destinie!
M'Pherson's time will not be long
   On yonder gallows-tree.

Chorus.—Sae rantingly, sae wantonly,
    Sae dauntingly gaed he;
      He play'd a spring, and danc'd it round,
    Below the gallows-tree.

O what is death but parting breath?
    On many a bloody plain
I've dared his face, and in this place
    I scorn him yet again!
      Sae rantingly, etc.

Untie these bands from off my hands,
    And bring to me my sword;
And there's no a man in all Scotland,
    But I'll brave him at a word.
      Sae rantingly, etc.

I've liv'd a life of sturt and strife;
    I die by treacherie:
It burns my heart, I must depart,
    And not avengèd be.
      Sae rantingly, etc.

Now farewell light, thou sunshine bright,
    And all beneath the sky!
May coward shame distain his name,
    The wretch that dare not die!
      Sae rantingly, etc.

STAY, MY CHARMER

Gaelic Air—'The Black-haired Lad.'

STAY, my charmer, can you leave me?
Cruel, cruel, to deceive me;
Well you know how much you grieve me;
    Cruel charmer, can you go?
    Cruel charmer, can you go?

By my love so ill-requited,
By the faith you fondly plighted,
By the pangs of lovers slighted,
    Do not, do not leave me so !
    Do not, do not leave me so !

MY HOGGIE

WHAT will I do gin my Hoggie die ?
    My joy, my pride, my Hoggie !
My only beast, I had nae mae,
    And vow but I was vogie !
The lee-lang night we watch'd the fauld,
    Me and my faithfu' doggie;
We heard nocht but the roaring linn,
    Amang the braes sae scroggie.

But the houlet cry'd frae the castle wa',
    The blitter frae the boggie;
The tod reply'd upon the hill,
    I trembled for my Hoggie.
When day did daw, and cocks did craw,
    The morning it was foggie;
An unco tyke, lap o'er the dyke,
    And maist has kill'd my Hoggie !

THE CARES O' LOVE

HE

THE cares o' Love are sweeter far
    Than onie other pleasure;
And if sae dear its sorrows are,
    Enjoyment, what a treasure !

SHE

I fear to try, I dare na try
    A passion sae ensnaring;
For light's her heart and blythe's her sang
    That for nae man is caring.

RAVING WINDS AROUND HER BLOWING

Tune—'M'Grigor of Roro's Lament.'

RAVING winds around her blowing,
Yellow leaves the woodlands strowing,
By a river hoarsely roaring,
Isabella stray'd deploring—

'Farewell, hours that late did measure
Sunshine days of joy and pleasure;
Hail, thou gloomy night of sorrow,
Cheerless night that knows no morrow!

'O'er the past too fondly wandering,
On the hopeless future pondering;
Chilly grief my life-blood freezes,
Fell despair my fancy seizes.

'Life, thou soul of every blessing,
Load to misery most distressing,
Gladly how would I resign thee,
And to dark oblivion join thee!'

UP IN THE MORNING EARLY

CAULD blaws the wind frae east to west,
    The drift is driving sairly;
Sae loud and shill 's I hear the blast—
    I'm sure it's winter fairly.

Chorus.—Up in the morning's no for me,
　　　　Up in the morning early;
　　　When a' the hills are cover'd wi' snaw,
　　　　I'm sure it's winter fairly.

The birds sit chittering in the thorn,
　　A' day they fare but sparely;
And lang's the night frae e'en to morn—
　　I'm sure it's winter fairly.
　　　　Up in the morning's, etc

HOW LONG AND DREARY IS THE NIGHT

How long and dreary is the night,
　　When I am frae my dearie !
I sleepless lie frae e'en to morn,
　　Tho' I were ne'er so weary :
I sleepless lie frae e'en to morn,
　　Tho' I were ne'er sae weary !

When I think on the happy days
　　I spent wi' you, my dearie :
And now what lands between us lie,
　　How can I be but eerie ?
And now what lands between us lie,
　　Now can I be but eerie ?

How slow ye move, ye heavy hours,
　　As ye were wae and weary !
It was na sae—ye glinted by,
　　When I was wi' my dearie !
It was na sae—ye glinted by,
　　When I was wi' my dearie !

THE DUSTY MILLER

HEY, the dusty miller,
   And his dusty coat,
He will win a shilling,
   Or he spend a groat:
Dusty was the coat,
   Dusty was the colour,
Dusty was the kiss
   That I gat frae the Miller.

Hey, the dusty Miller,
   And his dusty sack:
Leeze me on the calling
   Fills the dusty peck,
Fills the dusty peck,
   Brings the dusty siller;
I wad gae my coatie
   For the dusty Miller.

DUNCAN DAVIDSON

THERE was a lass, they ca'd her Meg,
And she held o'er the moors to spin;
There was a lad that follow'd her,
   They ca'd him Duncan Davidson.
The moon was dreigh, and Meg was skeigh,
   Her favour Duncan could na win;
For wi' the rock she wad him knock,
   And ay she shook the temper-pin.

As o'er the moor they lightly foor,
   A burn was clear, a glen was green,
Upon the banks they eas'd their shanks,
   And ay she set the wheel between:

But Duncan swoor a haly aith,
　　That Meg should be a bride the morn;
Then Meg took up her spinnin'-graith,
　　And flang them a' out o'er the burn.

We will big a wee, wee house,
　　And we will live like king and queen;
Sae blythe and merry 's we will be,
　　When ye set by the wheel at e'en.
A man may drink, and no be drunk;
　　A man may fight and no be slain;
A man may kiss a bonie lass,
　　And ay be welcome back again !

JUMPIN' JOHN

Her daddie forbad, her minnie forbad,
　　Forbidden she wadna be :
She wadna trow't, the browst she brew'd
　　Wad taste sae bitterlie.

Chorus.—The lang lad they ca' Jumpin' John
　　　　Beguil'd the bonie lassie,
　　　The lang lad they ca' Jumpin' John
　　　　Beguil'd the bonie lassie.

A cow and a cauf, a yowe and a hauf,
　　And thretty gude shillin's and three;
A vera gude tocher, a cotter-man's dochter,
　　The lass wi' the bonie black e'e.
　　　　The lang lad, etc.

TALK OF HIM THAT'S FAR AWA'

Musing on the roaring ocean,
　　Which divides my love and me;
Wearying heav'n in warm devotion,
　　For his weal where'er he be.

Hope and Fear's alternate billow
Yielding late to Nature's law,
Whispering spirits round my pillow,
Talk of him that's far awa'.

Ye whom sorrow never wounded,
Ye who never shed a tear,
Care-untroubled, joy-surrounded,
Gaudy day to you is dear.

Gentle night, do thou befriend me,
Downy sleep, the curtain draw;
Spirits kind, again attend me,
Talk of him that's far awa'!

TO DAUNTON ME

THE blude red rose at Yule may blaw,
The simmer lilies bloom in snaw,
The frost may freeze the deepest sea;
But an auld man shall never daunton me.

Refrain.—To daunton me, to daunton me,
An auld man shall never daunton me.

To daunton me, and me sae young,
Wi' his fause heart and flatt'ring tongue,
That is the thing you shall never see,
For an auld man shall never daunton me,
To daunton me, etc.

For a' his meal and a' his maut,
For a' his fresh beef and his saut,
For a' his gold and white monie,
An auld man shall never daunton me.
To daunton me, etc.

His gear may buy him kye and yowes,
His gear may buy him glens and knowes;
But me he shall not buy nor fee,
For an auld man shall never daunton me.
    To daunton me, etc.

He hirples twa-fauld as he dow,
Wi' his teethless gab and his auld beld pow,
And the rain rains down frae his red blear'd e'e;
That auld man shall never daunton me.
    To daunton me, etc.

THE WINTER IT IS PAST

THE winter it is past, and the summer comes at last,
  And the small birds, they sing on ev'ry tree;
Now ev'ry thing is glad, while I am very sad,
  Since my true love is parted from me.

The rose upon the breer, by the waters running clear,
  May have charms for the linnet or the bee;
Their little loves are blest, and their little hearts at rest,
  But my true love is parted from me.

THE BONIE LAD THAT'S FAR AWA'

O HOW can I be blythe and glad,
  Or how can I gang brisk and braw,
When the bonie lad that I lo'e best
  Is o'er the hills and far awa'!

It's no the frosty winter wind,
  It's no the driving drift and snaw;
But ay the tear comes in my e'e,
  To think on him that's far awa'.

My father pat me frae his door,
  My friends thay hae disown'd me a';
But I hae ane will tak my part,
  The bonie lad that's far awa'.

A pair o' glooves he bought to me,
  And silken snoods he gae me twa;
And I will wear them for his sake,
  The bonie lad that's far awa'.

O weary Winter soon will pass,
  And Spring will cleed the birken shaw;
And my young babie will be born,
  And he'll be hame that's far awa'.

VERSES TO CLARINDA

SENT WITH A PAIR OF WINE-GLASSES

FAIR Empress of the poet's soul,
  And Queen of poetesses;
Clarinda, take this little boon,
  This humble pair of glasses:

And fill them up with generous juice,
  As generous as your mind;
And pledge them to the generous toast,
  'The whole of human kind!'

'To those who love us!' second fill;
  But not to those whom *we* love;
Lest we love those who love not us—
  A third—'To thee and me, love!'

THE CHEVALIER'S LAMENT

Air—'Captain O'Kean.'

THE small birds rejoice in the green leaves returning,
The murmuring streamlet winds clear thro' the vale,
The primroses blow in the dews of the morning,
And wild scatter'd cowslips bedeck the green dale :
But what can give pleasure, or what can seem fair,
When the lingering moments are numbered wi' care?
No birds sweetly singing, nor flow'rs gaily springing,
Can soothe the sad bosom of joyless despair.

The deed that I dar'd, could it merit their malice?
A king and a father to place on his throne !
His right are these hills, and his right are these valleys,
Where the wild beasts find shelter, tho' I can find none
But 'tis not my suff'rings thus wretched, forlorn;
My brave gallant friends, 'tis your ruin I mourn;
Your faith proved so loyal in hot-bloody trial—
Alas ! can I make it no better return !

EPISTLE TO HUGH PARKER

IN this strange land, this uncouth clime,
A land unknown to prose or rhyme;
Where words ne'er cros't the Muse's heckles,
Nor limpit in poetic shackles :
A land that Prose did never view it,
Except when drunk he stacher't thro' it;
Here, ambush'd by the chimla cheek,
Hid in an atmosphere of reek,
I hear a wheel thrum i' the neuk,
I hear it—for in vain I leuk.

The red peat gleams, a fiery kernel,
Enhuskèd by a fog infernal :
Here, for my wonted rhyming raptures,
I sit and count my sins by chapters;
For life and spunk like ither Christians,
I'm dwindled down to mere existence,
Wi' nae converse but Gallowa' bodies,
Wi' nae kenn'd face but 'Jenny Geddes,'
Jenny, my Pegasean pride !
Dowie she saunters down Nithside,
And ay a westlin' leuk she throws,
While tears hap o'er her auld brown nose !
Was it for this, wi' cannie care,
Thou bure the Bard through many a shire ?
At howes or hillocks never stumbled,
And late or early never grumbled ?—
O had I power like inclination,
I'd heeze thee up a constellation,
To canter with the Sagitarre,
Or loup the ecliptic like a bar;
Or turn the pole like any arrow;
Or, when auld Phœbus bids good-morrow,
Down the zodiac urge the race,
And cast dirt on his godship's face :
For I could lay my bread and kail
He'd ne'er cast saut upo' thy tail.—
Wi' a' this care and a' this grief,
And sma', sma' prospect of relief,
And nought but peat reek i' my head,
How can I write what ye can read ?—
Tarbolton, twenty-fourth o' June,
Ye'll find me in a better tune;
But till we meet and weet our whistle,
Tak this excuse for nae epistle.

                              ROBERT BURNS.

OF A' THE AIRTS THE WIND CAN BLAW

Tune—'Miss Admiral Gordon's Strathspey.'

OF a' the airts the wind can blaw,
  I dearly like the west,
For there the bonie lassie lives,
  The lassie I lo'e best :
There's wild-woods grow, and rivers row,
  And mony a hill between :
But day and night my fancy's flight
  Is ever wi' my Jean.

I see her in the dewy flowers,
  I see her sweet and fair :
I hear her in the tunefu' birds,
  I hear her charm the air :
There's not a bonie flower that springs,
  By fountain, shaw, or green;
There's not a bonie bird that sings
  But minds me o' my Jean.

I HAE A WIFE O' MY AIN

I HAE a wife o' my ain,
  I'll partake wi' naebody;
I'll take cuckold frae nane,
  I'll gie cuckold to naebody.

I hae a penny to spend,
  There—thanks to naebody !
I hae naething to lend,
  I'll borrow frae naebody.

I am naebody's lord,
    I'll be slave to naebody;
I hae a gude braid sword,
    I'll tak dunts frae naebody.

I'll be merry and free,
    I'll be sad for naebody;
Naebody cares for me,
    I care for naebody.

VERSES IN FRIAR'S CARSE HERMITAGE

Thou whom chance may hither lead,
Be thou clad in russet weed,
Be thou deckt in silken stole,
Grave these maxims on thy soul.

Life is but a day at most,
Sprung from night in darkness lost;
Hope not sunshine every hour,
Fear not clouds will always lour.

Happiness is but a name,
Make content and ease thy aim,
Ambition is a meteor-gleam;
Fame a restless, idle dream;

Peace, th' tend'rest flow'r of spring;
Pleasures, insects on the wing;
Those that sip the dew alone—
Make the butterflies thy own;
Those that would the bloom devour—
Crush the locusts, save the flower.

For the future be prepared,
Guard wherever thou can'st guard;
But thy utmost duly done,
Welcome what thou can'st not shun.

B.P   L

Follies past, give thou to air,
Make their *consequence* thy care:
Keep the name of Man in mind,
And dishonour not thy kind.
Reverence with lowly heart
Him, whose wondrous work thou art;
Keep His Goodness still in view,
Thy trust, and thy example, too.

Stranger, go! Heaven be thy guide!
Quod the Beadsman of Nidside.

TO ALEX. CUNNINGHAM, ESQ., WRITER, EDINBURGH

ELLISLAND, NITHSDALE, *July* 27, 1788.

My godlike friend—nay, do not stare,
    You think the phrase is odd-like;
But 'God is Love,' the saints declare,
    Then surely thou art god-like.

And is thy ardour still the same?
    And kindled still at ANNA?
Others may boast a partial flame,
    But thou art a volcano!

Ev'n Wedlock asks not love beyond
    Death's tie-dissolving portal;
But thou, omnipotently fond,
    May'st promise love immortal!

Thy wounds such healing powers defy,
    Such symptoms dire attend them,
That last great antihectic try—
    MARRIAGE perhaps may mend them.

Sweet Anna has an air—a grace,
　　Divine, magnetic, touching;
She talks, she charms—but who can trace
　　The process of bewitching?

ANNA, THY CHARMS

Anna, thy charms my bosom fire,
　　And waste my soul with care;
But ah! how bootless to admire,
　　When fated to despair!

Yet in thy presence, lovely Fair,
　　To hope may be forgiven;
For sure 'twere impious to despair
　　So much in sight of Heaven.

THE FÊTE CHAMPÊTRE

Tune—'Killicrankie.'

O wha will to Saint Stephen's House,
　　To do our errands there, man?
O wha will to Saint Stephen's House
　　O' th' merry lads of Ayr, man?
Or will we send a man o' law?
　　Or will we send a sodger?
Or him wha led o'er Scotland a'
　　The meikle Ursa-Major?

Come, will ye court a noble lord,
　　Or buy a score o' lairds, man?
For worth and honour pawn their word,
　　Their vote shall be Glencaird's, man.

Ane gies them coin, ane gies them wine,
    Anither gies them clatter;
Annbank, wha guessed the ladies' taste,
    He gies a Fête Champêtre.

When Love and Beauty heard the news,
    The gay green woods amang, man;
Where, gathering flowers, and busking bowers,
    They heard the blackbird's sang, man :
A vow, they seal'd it with a kiss,
    Sir Politics to fetter;
As theirs alone, the patent bliss,
    To hold a Fête Champêtre.

Then mounted Mirth on gleesome wing,
    O'er hill and dale she flew, man;
Ilk wimpling burn, ilk crystal spring,
    Ilk glen and shaw she knew, man :
She summon'd every social sprite,
    That sports by wood or water,
On th' bonie banks of Ayr to meet,
    And keep this Fête Champêtre.

Cauld Boreas, wi' his boisterous crew,
    Were bound to stakes like kye, man;
And Cynthia's car, o' silver fu',
    Clamb up the starry sky, man :
Reflected beams dwell in the streams,
    Or down the current shatter;
The western breeze steals thro' the trees,
    To view this Fête Champêtre.

How many a robe sae gaily floats !
    What sparkling jewels glance, man !
To Harmony's enchanting notes,
    As moves the mazy dance, man.

The echoing wood, the winding flood,
　　Like Paradise did glitter,
When Angels met, at Adam's yett,
　　To hold their Fête Champêtre.

When Politics came there, to mix
　　And make his ether-stane, man!
He circled round the magic ground,
　　But entrance found he nane, man:
He blush'd for shame, he quat his name,
　　Forswore it, every letter,
Wi' humble prayer to join and share
　　This festive Fête Chamêptre.

EPISTLE TO ROBERT GRAHAM, ESQ., OF
FINTRY

REQUESTING A FAVOUR

When Nature her great masterpiece design'd,
And fram'd her last, best work, the human mind,
Her eye intent on all the mazy plan,
She form'd of various parts the various Man.

Then first she calls the useful many forth;
Plain plodding Industry, and sober Worth:
Thence peasants, farmers, native sons of earth,
And merchandise' whole genus take their birth:
Each prudent cit a warm existence finds,
And all mechanics' many apron'd kinds.
Some other rarer sorts are wanted yet,
The lead and buoy are needful to the net:
The *caput mortuum* of gross desires
Makes a material for mere knights and squires;

The martial phosphorus is taught to flow,
She kneads the lumpish philosophic dough,
Then marks th' unyielding mass with grave designs,
Law, physic, politics, and deep divines;
Last, she sublimes th' Aurora of the poles,
The flashing elements of female souls.

The order'd system fair before her stood,
Nature, well pleas'd, pronounc'd it very good;
But ere she gave creating labour o'er,
Half-jest, she tried one curious labour more.
Some spumy, fiery, *ignis fatuus* matter,
Such as the slightest breath of air might scatter;
With arch-alacrity and conscious glee,
(Nature may have her whim as well as we,
Her Hogarth-art perhaps she meant to show it,)
She forms the thing and christens it—a Poet:
Creature, tho' oft the prey of care and sorrow,
When blest to-day, unmindful of to-morrow;
A being form'd t' amuse his graver friends,
Admir'd and prais'd—and there the homage ends;
A mortal quite unfit for Fortune's strife,
Yet oft the sport of all the ills of life;
Prone to enjoy each pleasure riches give,
Yet haply wanting wherewithal to live;
Longing to wipe each tear, to heal each groan,
Yet frequent all unheeded in his own.
But honest Nature is not quite a Turk,
She laugh'd at first, then felt for her poor work:
Pitying the propless climber of mankind,
She cast about a *standard tree* to find;
And, to support his helpless woodbine state,
Attach'd him to the generous, truly great:
A title, and the only one I claim,
To lay strong hold for help on bounteous Graham.

Pity the tuneful Muses' hapless train,
Weak, timid landsmen on life's stormy main !

Their hearts no selfish, stern, absorbent stuff,
That never gives—tho' humbly takes enough;
The little fate allows, they share as soon,
Unlike sage, proverb'd Wisdom's hard-wrung boon :
The world were blest did bliss on them depend,
Ah, that 'the friendly e'er should want a friend !'
Let Prudence number o'er each sturdy son,
Who life and wisdom at one race begun,
Who feel by reason and who give by rule,
(Instinct's a brute, and sentiment a fool !)
Who make poor 'will do' wait upon 'I should'—
We own they're prudent, but who feels they're good ?
Ye wise ones, hence ! ye hurt the social eye !
God's image rudely etch'd on base alloy !
But come ye who the godlike pleasure know,
Heaven's attribute distinguish'd—to bestow !
Whose arms of love would grasp the human race :
Come *thou* who giv'st with all a courtier's grace;
FRIEND OF MY LIFE, true patron of my rhymes !
Prop of my dearest hopes for future times.
Why shrinks my soul half blushing, half afraid,
Backward, abash'd to ask thy friendly aid ?
I know my need, I know thy giving hand,
I crave thy friendship at thy kind command ;
But there are such who court the tuneful Nine—
Heavens ! should the branded character be mine !
Whose *verse* in manhood's pride sublimely flows,
Yet vilest reptiles in their begging *prose*.
Mark, how their lofty independent spirit
Soars on the spurning wing of injur'd merit !
Seek you the proofs in private life to find ?
Pity the best of words should be but wind !
So, to heaven's gates the lark's shrill song ascends,
But grovelling on the earth the carol ends.
In all the clam'rous cry of starving want,
They dun Benevolence with shameless front;
Oblige them, patronise their tinsel lays—
They persecute you all your future days !

Ere my poor soul such deep damnation stain,
My horny fist assume the plough again,
The pie-bald jacket let me patch once more,
On eighteenpence a week I've liv'd before.
Tho', thanks to Heaven, I dare even that last shift,
I trust, meantime, my boon is in thy gift :
That, plac'd by thee upon the wish'd-for height,
Where, man and nature fairer in her sight,
My Muse may imp her wing for some sublimer flight.

THE DAY RETURNS

Tune—'Seventh of November.'

The day returns, my bosom burns,
  The blissful day we twa did meet :
Tho' winter wild in tempest toil'd,
  Ne'er summer-sun was half sae sweet.
Than a' the pride that loads the tide,
  And crosses o'er the sultry line ;
Than kingly robes, than crowns and globes,
  Heav'n gave me more—it made thee mine !

While day and night can bring delight,
  Or Nature aught of pleasure give ;
While joys above my mind can move,
  For thee, and thee alone, I live.
When that grim foe of life below
  Comes in between to make us part,
The iron hand that breaks our band,
  It breaks my bliss—it breaks my heart !

A MOTHER'S LAMENT

FOR THE DEATH OF HER SON

FATE gave the word, the arrow sped,
    And pierc'd my darling's heart;
And with him all the joys are fled
    Life can to me impart.

By cruel hands the sapling drops,
    In dust dishonor'd laid;
So fell the pride of all my hopes,
    My age's future shade.

The mother-linnet in the brake
    Bewails her ravish'd young;
So I, for my lost darling's sake,
    Lament the live-day long.

Death, oft I've fear'd thy fatal blow,
    Now, fond, I bare my breast;
O, do thou kindly lay me low
    With him I love, at rest !

O WERE I ON PARNASSUS HILL

O WERE I on Parnassus hill,
Or had o' Helicon my fill,
That I might catch poetic skill,
    To sing how dear I love thee !
But Nith maun be my Muse's well,
My Muse maun be thy bonie sel,
On Corsincon I'll glow'r and spell,
    And write how dear I love thee.

Then come, sweet Muse, inspire my lay!
For a' the lee-lang simmer's day
I couldna sing, I couldna say,
    How much, how dear, I love thee.
I see thee dancing o'er the green,
Thy waist sae jimp, thy limbs sae clean,
Thy tempting lips, thy roguish een—
    By Heav'n and Earth I love thee!

By night, by day, a-field, at hame,
The thoughts o' thee my breast inflame;
And ay I muse and sing thy name—
    I only live to love thee.
Tho' I were doom'd to wander on,
Beyond the sea, beyond the sun,
Till my last weary sand was run;
    Till then—and then I love thee!

THE FALL OF THE LEAF

THE lazy mist hangs from the brow of the hill,
Concealing the course of the dark winding rill;
How languid the scenes, late so sprightly, appear!
As Autumn to Winter resigns the pale year.

The forests are leafless, the meadows are brown,
And all the gay foppery of summer is flown:
Apart let me wander, apart let me muse,
How quick Time is flying, how keen Fate pursues!

How long I have liv'd—but how much liv'd in vain,
How little of life's scanty span may remain,
What aspects old Time in his progress has worn,
What ties cruel Fate in my bosom has torn.

How foolish, or worse, till our summit is gain'd !
And downward, how weaken'd, how darken'd, how
    pain'd !
Life is not worth having with all it can give—
For something beyond it poor man sure must live.

I REIGN IN JEANIE'S BOSOM

Louis, what reck I by thee,
    Or Geordie on his ocean ?
Dyvor, beggar louns to me,
    I reign in Jeanie's bosom !

Let her crown my love her law,
    And in her breast enthrone me,
Kings and nations—swith awa' !
    Reif randies, I disown ye !

IT IS NA, JEAN, THY BONIE FACE

It is na, Jean, thy bonie face
    Nor shape that I admire;
Altho' thy beauty and thy grace
    Might weel awauk desire.

Something, in ilka part o' thee,
    To praise, to love, I find,
But dear as is thy form to me,
    Still dearer is thy mind.

Nae mair ungenerous wish I hae,
    Nor stronger in my breast,
Than, if I canna mak thee sae,
    At least to see thee blest.

Content am I, if heaven shall give
    But happiness to thee;
And as wi' thee I'd wish to live,
    For thee I'd bear to die.

AULD LANG SYNE

SHOULD auld acquaintance be forgot,
    And never brought to mind?
Should auld acquaintance be forgot,
    And auld lang syne?

Chorus.—For auld lang syne, my dear,
    For auld lang syne,
    We'll tak a cup o' kindness yet,
    For auld lang syne.

And surely ye'll be your pint stowp!
    And surely I'll be mine!
And we'll tak a cup o' kindness yet,
    For auld lang syne.
        For auld, etc.

We twa hae run about the braes,
    And pou'd the gowans fine;
But we've wander'd mony a weary fitt,
    Sin' auld lang syne.
        For auld, etc.

We twa hae paidl'd in the burn,
    Frae morning sun till dine;
But seas between us braid hae roar'd
    Sin' auld lang syne.
        For auld, etc.

And there's a hand, my trusty fiere !
    And gies a hand o' thine !
And we'll tak a right gude-willie waught,
    For auld lang syne.
        For auld, etc.

THE SILVER TASSIE

Go, fetch to me a pint o' wine,
    And fill it in a silver tassie;
That I may drink before I go,
    A service to my bonie lassie.
The boat rocks at the pier o' Leith;
    Fu' loud the wind blaws frae the Ferry;
The ship rides by the Berwick-law,
    And I maun leave my bonie Mary.

The trumpets sound, the banners fly,
    The glittering spears are rankèd ready :
The shouts o' war are heard afar,
    The battle closes deep and bloody;
It' not the roar o' sea or shore,
    Wad mak me langer wish to tarry;
Nor shouts o' war that's heard afar—
    It's leaving thee, my bonie Mary !

TO A KISS

HUMID seal of soft affections,
    Tenderest pledge of future bliss,
Dearest tie of young connections,
    Love's first snowdrop, virgin kiss !

Speaking silence, dumb confession,
   Passion's birth, and infant's play,
Dove-like fondness, chaste concession,
   Glowing dawn of future day!

Sorrowing joy, Adieu's last action
   (Lingering lips must now disjoin),
What words can ever speak affection
   So thrilling and sincere as thine!

WRITTEN IN FRIARS CARSE HERMITAGE, ON NITHSIDE

LATER VERSION

THOU whom chance may hither lead,
Be thou clad in russet weed,
Be thou deckt in silken stole,
Grave these counsels on thy soul.

   Life is but a day at most,
Sprung from night,—in darkness lost;
Hope not sunshine ev'ry hour,
Fear not clouds will always lour.

   As Youth and Love, with sprightly dance,
Beneath thy morning star advance,
Pleasure with her siren air
May delude the thoughtless pair;
Let Prudence bless Enjoyment's cup,
Then raptur'd sip, and sip it up.

   As thy day grows warm and high,
Life's meridian flaming high,
Dost thou spurn the humble vale?
Life's proud summits wouldst thou scale?

Check thy climbing step, elate,
Evils lurk in felon wait :
Dangers, eagle-pinioned, bold,
Soar around each cliffy hold !
While cheerful Peace, with linnet song,
Chants the lowly dells among.

As the shades of ev'ning close,
Beck'ning thee to long repose;
As life itself becomes disease,
Seek the chimney-nook of ease :
There ruminate with sober thought,
On all thou'st seen, and heard, and wrought,
And teach the sportive younkers round,
Saws of experience, sage and sound :
Say, man's true, genuine estimate,
The grand criterion of his fate,
Is not, art thou high or low ?
Did thy fortune ebb or flow ?
Did many talents gild thy span ?
Or frugal Nature grudge thee one ?
Tell them, and press it on their mind,
As thou thyself must shortly find,
The smile or frown of awful Heav'n,
To Virtue or to Vice is giv'n,
Say, to be just, and kind, and wise—
There solid self-enjoyment lies;
That foolish, selfish, faithless ways
Lead to be wretched, vile, and base.

Thus resign'd, and quiet, creep
To the bed of lasting sleep—
Sleep, whence thou shalt ne'er awake,
Night, where dawn shall never break,
Till future life, future no more,
To light and joy the good restore,
To light and joy unknown before.
Stranger, go ! Heav'n be thy guide !
Quod the Beadsman of Nithside.

THE POET'S PROGRESS

A POEM IN EMBRYO

THOU, Nature, partial Nature, I arraign;
Of thy caprice maternal I complain.

The peopled fold thy kindly care have found,
The horned bull, tremendous, spurns the ground;
The lordly lion has enough and more,
The forest trembles at his very roar;
Thou giv'st the ass his hide, the snail his shell,
The puny wasp, victorious, guards his cell.
Thy minions, kings defend, controul, devour,
In all th' omnipotence of rule and power :
Foxes and statesmen subtile wiles ensure;
The cit and polecat stink, and are secure :
Toads with their poison, doctors with their drug,
The priest and hedgehog, in their robes, are snug
E'en silly women have defensive arts,
Their eyes, their tongues—and nameless other parts

But O thou cruel stepmother and hard,
To thy poor fenceless, naked child, the Bard !
A thing unteachable in worldly skill,
And half an idiot too, more helpless still :
No heels to bear him from the op'ning dun,
No claws to dig, his hated sight to shun :
No horns, but those by luckless Hymen worn,
And those, alas ! not Amalthea's horn :
No nerves olfact'ry, true to Mammon's foot,
Or grunting, grub sagacious, evil's root :
The silly sheep that wanders wild astray,
Is not more friendless, is not more a prey;
Vampyre-booksellers drain him to the heart,
And viper-critics cureless venom dart.

Critics! appall'd I venture on the name,
Those cut-throat bandits in the paths of fame,
Bloody dissectors, worse than ten Monroes,
He hacks to teach, they mangle to expose:
By blockhead's daring into madness stung,
His heart by wanton, causeless malice wrung,
His well-won bays—than life itself more dear—
By miscreants torn who ne'er one sprig must wear;
Foil'd, bleeding, tortur'd in th' unequal strife,
The hapless Poet flounces on thro' life,
Till, fled each hope that once his bosom fired,
And fled each Muse that glorious once inspir'd,
Low-sunk in squalid, unprotected age,
Dead even resentment for his injur'd page,
He heeds no more the ruthless critic's rage.

So by some hedge the generous steed deceas'd,
For half-starv'd, snarling curs a dainty feast;
By toil and famine worn to skin and bone,
Lies, senseless of each tugging bitch's son.

.   .   .   .   .

A little upright, pert, tart, tripping wight,
And still his precious self his dear delight;
Who loves his own smart shadow in the streets,
Better than e'er the fairest she he meets;
Much specious lore, but little understood,
(Veneering oft outshines the solid wood),
His solid sense, by inches you must tell,
But meet his cunning by the Scottish ell!
A man of fashion too, he made his tour,
Learn'd 'vive la bagatelle et vive l'amour';
So travell'd monkeys their grimace improve,
Polish their grin—nay, sigh for ladies' love!
His meddling vanity, a busy fiend,
Still making work his selfish craft must mend.

.   .   .   .   .
.   .   .   .   .

                             Crochallan came,
The old cock'd hat, the brown surtout—the same;
His grisly beard just bristling in its might—
'Twas four long nights and days from shaving-night;
His uncomb'd, hoary locks, wild-staring, thatch'd
A head, for thought profound and clear, unmatch'd;
Yet, tho' his caustic wit was biting-rude,
His heart was warm, benevolent and good,

    O Dulness, portion of the truly blest
Calm, shelter'd haven of eternal rest !
Thy sons ne'er madden in the fierce extremes
Of Fortune's polar frost, or torrid beams;
If mantling high she fills the golden cup,
With sober, selfish ease they sip it up;
Conscious the bounteous meed they well deserve,
They only wonder 'some folks' do not starve !
The grave, sage hern thus easy picks his frog,
And thinks the mallard a sad, worthless dog.
When disappointment snaps the thread of Hope,
When, thro' disastrous night, they darkling grope,
With deaf endurance sluggishly they bear,
And just conclude that 'fools are Fortune's care';
So, heavy, passive to the tempest's shocks,
Strong on the sign-post stands the stupid ox.

    Not so the idle Muses' mad-cap train,
Not such the workings of their moon-struck brain;
In equanimity they never dwell,
By turns in soaring heaven, or vaulted hell !

ELEGY ON THE YEAR 1788

For lords or kings I dinna mourn,
    E'en let them die—for that they're born :
But oh ! prodigious to reflec' !
    A *Towmont*, sirs, is gane to wreck !

O *Eighty-eight*, in thy sma' space,
What dire events hae taken place !
Of what enjoyments thou hast reft us !
In what a pickle thou hast left us !

The Spanish empire's tint a head,
And my auld teethless Bawtie's dead :
The tulyie's teugh 'tween Pitt and Fox,
And 'tween our Maggie's twa wee cocks;
The tane is game, a bluidy devil,
But to the hen-birds unco civil;
The tither's something dour o' treadin',
But better stuff ne'er claw'd a midden.

Ye ministers, come mount the poupit,
An' cry till ye be hoarse an' roupet,
For *Eighty-eight*, he wished you weel,
An' gaed ya a' baith gear and meal;
E'en mony a plack, and mony a peck,
Ye ken yoursels, for little feck !

Ye bonie lasses, dight your e'en,
For some o' you hae tint a frien';
In *Eighty-eight*, ye ken, was ta'en,
What ye'll ne'er hae to gie again.

Observe the very nowt an' sheep,
How dowff an' daviely they creep;
Nay, even the yirth itsel does cry,
For E'nburgh wells are grutten dry.

O *Eighty-nine*, thou's but a bairn,
An' no owre auld, I hope, to learn !
Thou beardless boy, I pray tak care,
Thou now has got thy Daddy's chair;
Nae handcuff'd, mizl'd, hap-shackl'd *Regent*,
But, like himsel, a full, free agent,
Be sure you follow out the plan
Nae waur than he did, honest man !
As muckle better as you can.

January 1, 1789.

THE HENPECKED HUSBAND

Curs'd be the man, the poorest wretch in life,
The crouching vassal to a tyrant wife !
Who has no will but by her high permission;
Who has not sixpence but in her possession;
Who must to her his dear friend's secrets tell,
Who dreads a curtain lecture worse than hell.
Were such the wife had fallen to my part,
I'd break her spirit or I'd break her heart;
I'd charm her with the magic of a switch,
I'd kiss her maids, and kick the perverse b——h.

VERSICLES ON SIGN-POSTS

He looked just as your sign-post Lions do,
With aspect fierce, and quite as harmless too.

———

So heavy, passive to the tempest's shocks,
Dull on the sign-post stands the stupid ox.

———

His face with smile eternal drest,
Just like the landlord to his guest,
High as they hang with creaking din,
To index out the Country Inn.

———

A head, pure, sinless quite of brain and soul,
The very image of a barber's Poll;
It shows a human face, and wears a wig,
And looks, when well preserv'd, amazing big.

ROBIN SHURE IN HAIRST

Chorus.—Robin shure in hairst,
  I shure wi' him;
  Fient a heuk had I,
   Yet I stack by him.

I GAED up to Dunse,
  To warp a wab o' plaiden,
At his daddie's yett,
  Wha met me but Robin!
   Robin shure, etc.

Was na Robin bauld,
  Tho' I was a cottar,
Play'd me sic a trick,
  An' me the Eller's dochter!
   Robin shure, etc.

Robin promis'd me
  A' my winter vittle;
Fient haet he had but three
  Guse-feathers and a whittle!
   Robin shure, etc.

ODE, SACRED TO THE MEMORY OF MRS OSWALD OF AUCHENCRUIVE

DWELLER in yon dungeon dark,
Hangman of creation! mark,
Who in widow-weeds appears,
Laden with unhonour'd years.
Noosing with care a bursting purse,
Baited with many a deadly curse!

STROPHE

View the wither'd Beldam's face;
   Can thy keen inspection trace
Aught of Humanity's sweet, melting grace?
   Note that eye, 'tis rheum o'erflows;
   Pity's flood *there* never rose,
   See these hands, ne'er stretch'd to save,
   Hands that took, but never gave:
   Keeper of Mammon's iron chest,
   Lo, there she goes, unpitied and unblest,
She goes, but not to realms of everlasting rest!

ANTISTROPHE

Plunderer of Armies! lift thine eyes
   (A while forbear, ye torturing fiends);
Seest thou whose step, unwilling, hither bends?
No fallen angel, hurl'd from upper skies;
   'Tis thy trusty quondam Mate,
   Doom'd to share thy fiery fate;
   She, tardy, hell-ward plies.

EPODE

And are they of no more avail,
Ten thousand glittering pounds a year?
   In other worlds can Mammon fail,
      Omnipotent as he is here?
O, bitter mockery of the pompous bier,
   While down the wretched Vital Part is driven!
The cave-lodg'd Beggar, with a conscience clear,
   Expires in rags, unknown, and goes to Heaven.

PEGASUS AT WANLOCKHEAD

With Pegasus upon a day,
   Apollo weary flying,
Through frosty hills the journey lay,
   On foot the way was plying.

Poor slipshod giddy Pegasus
    Was but a sorry walker;
To Vulcan then Apollo goes,
    To get a frosty caulker.

Obliging Vulcan fell to work,
    Threw by his coat and bonnet,
And did Sol's business in a crack;
    Sol paid him with a sonnet.

Ye Vulcan's sons of Wanlockhead,
    Pity my sad disaster;
My Pegasus is poorly shod,
    I'll pay you like my master.

To JOHN TAYLOR, Ramage's, 3 *o'clock.*

SAPPHO REDIVIVA—A FRAGMENT

By all I lov'd, neglected and forgot,
No friendly face e'er lights my squalid cot;
Shunn'd, hated, wrong'd, unpitied, unredrest,
The mock'd quotation of the scorner's jest !
In vain would Prudence, with decorous sneer,
Point out a censuring world, and bid me fear;
Above the world, on wings of Love, I rise—
I know its worst, and can that worst despise :
Let Prudence' direst bodements on me fall,
M . . . . . . y, rich reward, o'erpays them all !

Mild zephyrs waft thee to life's farthest shore,
Nor think of me and my distresses more,—
Falsehood accurst ! No ! still I beg a place,
Still near thy heart some little, little trace;
For that dear trace the world I would resign :
O let me live, and die, and think it mine !

'I burn, I burn, as when thro' ripen'd corn
By driving winds the crackling flames are borne;'
Now raving-wild, I curse that fatal night,
Then bless the hour that charm'd my guilty sight
In vain the laws their feeble force oppose,
Chain'd at Love's feet, they groan, his vanquish'd
    foes:

In vain Religion meets my shrinking eye,
I dare not combat, but I turn and fly:
Conscience in vain upbraids th' unhallow'd fire,
Love grasps her scorpions—stifled they expire!
Reason drops headlong from his sacred throne,
Your dear idea reigns, and reigns alone;
Each thought intoxicated homage yields,
And riots wanton in forbidden fields.
By all on high adoring mortals know!
By all the conscious villain fears below!
By your dear self!—the last great oath I swear,
Not life, nor soul, were ever half so dear!

SHE'S FAIR AND FAUSE

She's fair and fause that causes my smart,
    I lo'ed her meikle and lang;
She's broken her vow, she's broken my heart,
    And I may e'en gae hang.

A coof cam in wi' routh o' gear,
And I hae tint my dearest dear;
But woman is but warld's gear,
    Sae let the bonie lass gang.

Whae'er ye be that woman love,
    To this be never blind;
Nae ferlie 'tis tho' fickle she prove,
    A woman has't by kind.

O woman lovely, woman fair!
An angel form's faun to thy share,
'Twad been o'er meikle to gien thee mair—
  I mean an angel mind.

EPITAPH ON ROBERT MUIR

What man could esteem, or what woman could love,
  Was he who lies under this sod :
If such Thou refusest admission above,
  Then whom wilt Thou favour, Good God ?

LINES TO CAPTAIN RIDDELL

ON RETURNING A NEWSPAPER

Your News and Review, sir,
  I've read through and through, sir,
With little admiring or blaming;
  The Papers are barren
  Of home-news or foreign,
No murders or rapes worth the naming.

Our friends, the Reviewers,
  Those chippers and hewers,
Are judges of mortar and stone, sir;
  But of *meet* or *unmeet*,
  In a fabric complete,
I'll boldly pronounce they are none, sir.

My goose-quill too rude is
  To tell all your goodness
Bestow'd on your servant, the Poet;
  Would to God I had one
  Like a beam of the sun,
And then all the world, sir, should know it!

Ellisland, *Monday morning.*

TO JOHN M'MURDO, ESQ., OF DRUMLANRI

SENT WITH SOME OF THE AUTHOR'S POEMS

O COULD I give thee India's wealth,
    As I this trifle send;
Because thy joy in both would be
    To share them with a friend.

But golden sands did never grace
    The Heliconian stream;
Then take what gold could never buy—
    An honest bard's esteem.

RHYMING REPLY TO A NOTE FROM CAPTAIN RIDDELL

DEAR SIR, at ony time or tide,
I'd rather sit wi' you than ride,
    Though 'twere wi' royal Geordie :
And troth, your kindness, soon and late,
Aft gars me to mysel look blate—
    The Lord in Heav'n reward ye !
                                R. BURNS.
ELLISLAND.

TO MISS CRUICKSHANK

A VERY YOUNG LADY

WRITTEN ON THE BLANK LEAF OF A BOOK, PRESENTE
TO HER BY THE AUTHOR

BEAUTEOUS Rosebud, young and gay,
Blooming on thy early May,
Never mayst thou, lovely flower,
Chilly shrink in sleety shower !

Never Boreas' hoary path,
Never Eurus' pois'nous breath,
Never baleful stellar lights,
Taint thee with untimely blights !
Never, never reptile thief
Riot on thy virgin leaf !
Nor even Sol too fiercely view
Thy bosom blushing still with dew !

Mayst thou long, sweet crimson gem,
Richly deck thy native stem;
Till some ev'ning, sober, calm,
Dropping dews, and breathing balm,
While all around the woodland rings,
And ev'ry bird thy requiem sings;
Thou, amid the dirgeful sound,
Shed thy dying honours round,
And resign to parent Earth
The loveliest form she e'er gave birth.

BEWARE O' BONIE ANN

Ye gallants bright, I rede you right,
  Beware o' bonie Ann;
Her comely face sae fu' o' grace,
  Your heart she will trepan :
Her een sae bright, like stars by night,
  Her skin is like the swan;
Sae jimply lac'd, her genty waist,
  That sweetly ye might span.

Youth, Grace, and Love attendant move,
  And Pleasure leads the van :
In a' their charms, and conquering arms,
  They wait on bonie Ann.

The captive bands may chain the hands,
　　But love enslaves the man
Ye gallants braw, I rede you a',
　　Beware o' bonie Ann!

ODE ON THE DEPARTED REGENCY BILL

DAUGHTER of Chaos' doting years,
Nurse of ten thousand hopes and fears
Whether thy airy, unsubstantial shade
(The rights of sepulture now duly paid)
Spread abroad its hideous form
On the roaring civil storm,
Deafening din and warring rage
Factions wild with factions wage;
Or under-ground, deep-sunk, profound,
　　Among the demons of the earth,
With groans that make the mountain shake,
　　Thou mourn thy ill-starr'd, blighted birth;
Or in the uncreated void,
　　Where seeds of future being fight,
With lessen'd step thou wander wide,
　　To greet thy Mother—Ancient Night,
And as each jarring, monster-mass is past,
Fond recollect what once thou wast:
In manner due, beneath this sacred oak,
Hear, Spirit, hear! thy presence I invoke!
　　By a Monarch's heaven-struck fate,
　　By a disunited State,
　　By a generous Prince's wrongs,
　　By a Senate's strife of tongues,
　　By a Premier's sullen pride,
　　Louring on the changing tide;
　　By dread Thurlow's powers to awe—
　　Rhetoric, blasphemy and law;

By the turbulent ocean—
A Nation's commotion,
By the harlot-caresses
Of borough addresses,
By days few and evil
(Thy portion, poor devil !)
By Power, Wealth, and Show,
  (Ye gods by men adored,)
By nameless Poverty,
  (Their hell abhorred,)
By all they hope, by all they fear,
Hear ! and appear !

—Stare not on me, thou ghastly Power !
Nor, grim with chained defiance lour :
  No Babel-structure would *I* build
Where, order exil'd from his native sway,
Confusion may the REGENT-sceptre wield,
  While all would rule and none obey :
  Go, to the world of Man relate
  The story of thy sad, eventful fate;
  And call presumptuous Hope to hear
  And bid him check his blind career;
  And tell the sore-prest sons of Care,
    Never, never to despair !
  Paint Charles's speed on wings of fire,
  The object of his fond desire,
  Beyond his boldest hopes, at hand :
  Paint all the triumph of the Portland Band;
  Mark how they lift the joy-exulting voice,
  And how their num'rous creditors rejoice;
  But just as hopes to warm enjoyment rise,
  Cry CONVALESCENCE ! and the vision flies.

Then next pourtray a dark'ning twilight gloom,
  Eclipsing sad a gay, rejoicing morn,
While proud Ambition to th' untimely tomb
  By gnashing, grim, despairing fiends is borne :

Paint ruin, in the shape of high D[undas]
 Gaping with giddy terror o'er the brow;
In vain he struggles, the fates behind him press,
 And clam'rous hell yawns for her prey below;
How fallen *That*, whose pride late scaled the
 skies!
And *This*, like Lucifer, no more to rise!
Again pronounce the powerful word;
See Day, triumphant from the Night, restored.

Then know this truth, ye Sons of Men!
 (Thus ends thy moral tale),
Your darkest terrors may be vain,
 Your brightest hopes may fail.

EPISTLE TO JAMES TENNANT
OF GLENCONNER

AULD comrade dear, and brither sinner,
How's a' the folk about Glenconner?
How do you this blae eastlin' wind,
That's like to blaw a body blind?
For me, my faculties are frozen,
My dearest member nearly dozen'd.
I've sent you here, by Johnie Simson,
Twa sage philosophers to glimpse on;
Smith, wi' his sympathetic feeling,
An' Reid, to common sense appealing.
Philosophers have fought and wrangled,
An' meikle Greek an' Latin mangled,
Till wi' their logic-jargon tir'd,
And in the depth of science mir'd,
To common sense they now appeal,
What wives and wabsters see and feel.

But, hark ye, friend! I charge you strictly,
Peruse them, an' return them quickly:
For now I'm grown sae cursed douce
I pray and ponder butt the house;
My shins, my lane, I there sit roastin',
Perusing Bunyan, Brown an' Boston,
Till, by an' by, if I haud on,
I'll grunt a reàl gospel groan:
Already I begin to try it,
To cast my een up like a pyet,
When by the gun she tumbles o'er
Flutt'ring an' gasping in her gore:
Sae shortly you shall see me bright,
A burning an' a shining light.

My heart-warm love to guid auld Glen,
The ace an' wale of honest men:
When bending down wi' auld gray hairs
Beneath the load of years and cares,
May He who made him still support him,
An' views beyond the grave comfort him;
His worthy fam'ly far and near,
God bless them a' wi' grace and gear!

My auld schoolfellow, preacher Willie,
The manly tar, my mason-billie,
And Auchenbay, I wish him joy;
If he's a parent, lass or boy,
May he be *dad*, and Meg the *mither*,
Just five-and-forty years thegither!
And no forgetting wabster Charlie,
I'm tauld he offers very fairly.
An', Lord, remember singing Sannock,
Wi' hale breeks, saxpence, an' a bannock!
And next, my auld acquaintance, Nancy,
Since she is fitted to her fancy,
An' her kind stars hae airted till her
A guid chiel wi' a pickle siller.

My kindest, best respects, I sen' it,
To cousin Kate, an' sister Janet:
Tell them, frae me, wi' chiels be cautious,
For, faith, they'll aiblins fin' them fashious;
To grant a heart is fairly civil,
But to grant a maidenhead's the devil.
An' lastly, Jamie, for yoursel,
May guardian angels tak a spell,
An' steer you seven miles south o' hell:
But first, before you see heaven's glory,
May ye get mony a merry story,
Mony a laugh, and mony a drink,
And ay eneugh o' needfu' clink.

Now fare ye weel, an' joy be wi' you:
For my sake, this I beg it o' you,
Assist poor Simson a' ye can,
Ye'll fin' him just an honest man;
Sae I conclude, and quat my chanter,
Yours, saint or sinner,

Rob the Ranter.

A NEW PSALM FOR THE CHAPEL OF KILMARNOCK

ON THE THANKSGIVING-DAY FOR HIS MAJESTY'S RECOVERY

O SING a new song to the Lord,
  Make, all and every one,
A joyful noise, even for the king
  His restoration.

The sons of Belial in the land
  Did set their heads together;
Come, let us sweep them off, said they,
  Like an o'erflowing river.

They set their heads together, I say,
  They set their heads together;
On right, on left, on every hand,
  We saw none to deliver.

Thou madest strong two chosen ones,
  To quell the Wicked's pride;
That Young Man, great in Issachar,
  The burden-bearing tribe.

And him, among the Princes, chief
  In our Jerusalem,
The judge that's mighty in Thy law,
  The Man that fears Thy name.

Yet they, even they, with all their strength,
  Began to faint and fail;
Even as two howling, ravenous wolves
  To dogs do turn their tail.

Th' ungodly o'er the just prevail'd,
  For so Thou hadst appointed;
That Thou might'st greater glory give
  Unto Thine own anointed.

And now Thou hast restored our State,
  Pity our Kirk also;
For she by tribulations
  Is now brought very low.

Consume that high-place Patronage,
  From off Thy holy hill;
And in Thy fury burn the book—
  Even of that man M'Gill.

Now hear our prayer, accept our song,
  And fight Thy chosen's battle :
We seek but little, Lord, from Thee;
  Thou kens we get as little.

B.P.

M

SKETCH IN VERSE

INSCRIBED TO THE RIGHT HON. C. J. FOX

How Wisdom and Folly meet, mix, and unite,
How Virtue and Vice blend their black and their white,
How Genius, th' illustrious father of fiction,
Confounds rule and law, reconciles contradiction—
I sing: If these mortals, the critics, should bustle,
I care not, not I—let the critics go whistle.

But now for a Patron, whose name and whose glory
At once may illustrate and honor my story.

Thou first of our orators, first of our wits;
Yet whose parts and acquirements seem just lucky hits
With knowledge so vast, and with judgment so strong,
No man, with the half of 'em e'er could go wrong;
With passions so potent, and fancies so bright,
No man with the half of 'em e'er could go right;
A sorry, poor, misbegot son of the Muses,
For using thy name offers fifty excuses.

Good L—d, what is Man! for as simple he looks,
Do but try to develop his hooks and his crooks;
With his depths and his shallows, his good and his evil,
All in all, he's a problem must puzzle the devil.

On his one ruling passion Sir Pope hugely labours,
That, like th' old Hebrew walking-switch, eats up its
    neighbours:
Mankind are his show-box—a friend, would you know
    him?
Pull the string, Ruling Passion the picture will show
    him.
What pity, in rearing so beauteous a system,
One trifling particular, *Truth*, should have miss'd him

For, spite of his fine theoretic positions,
Mankind is a science defies definitions.

Some sort all our qualities each to its tribe,
And think human nature they truly describe;
Have you found this, or t'other? There's more in the
    wind;
As by one drunken fellow his comrades you'll find.
But such is the flaw, or the depth of the plan,
In the make of that wonderful creature called Man;
No two virtues, whatever relation they claim,
Nor even two different shades of the same.
Though like as was ever twin brother to brother,
Possessing the one shall imply you've the other.

But truce with abstraction, and truth with a Muse
Whose rhymes you'll perhaps, Sir, ne'er deign to
    peruse:
Will you leave your justings, your jars, and your
    quarrels,
Contending with Billy for proud-nodding laurels?
My much-honor'd Patron, believe your poor poet,
Your courage, much more than your prudence, you
    show it:
In vain with Squire Billy for laurels you struggle;
He'll have them by fair trade, if not, he will smuggle:
Not cabinets even of kings would conceal 'em,
He'd up the back-stairs, and by G—— he would
    steal 'em!
Then feats like Squire Billy's you ne'er can achieve 'em;
It is not, out-do him—the task is, out-thieve him!

THE WOUNDED HARE

INHUMAN man! curse on thy barb'rous art
    And blasted be thy murder-aiming eye;
    May never pity soothe thee with a sigh,
Nor never pleasure glad thy cruel heart!

Go live, poor wand'rer of the wood and field!
    The bitter little that of life remains:
    No more the thickening brakes and verdant plains
To thee a home, or food, or pastime yield.

Seek, mangled wretch, some place of wonted rest,
    No more of rest, but now thy dying bed!
    The sheltering rushes whistling o'er thy head,
The cold earth with thy bloody bosom prest.

Perhaps a mother's anguish adds its woe;
    The playful pair crowd fondly by thy side;
    Ah! helpless nurslings, who will now provide
That life a mother only can bestow!

Oft as by winding Nith I, musing, wait
    The sober eve, or hail the cheerful dawn,
    I'll miss thee sporting o'er the dewy lawn,
And curse the ruffian's arm, and mourn thy hapless
    fate.

DELIA—AN ODE

Fair the face of orient day,
    Fair the tints of op'ning rose;
But fairer still my Delia dawns,
    More lovely far her beauty shows.

Sweet the lark's wild warbled lay,
    Sweet the tinkling rill to hear;
But, Delia, more delightful still,
    Steal thine accents on mine ear.

The flower-enamour'd, busy bee
    The rosy banquet loves to sip;
Sweet the streamlet's limpid laps
    To the sun-brown'd Arab's lip.

But, Delia, on thy balmy lips
  Let me, no vagrant insect, rove;
O let me steal one liquid kiss,
  For, oh! my soul is parch'd with love.

THE GARD'NER WI' HIS PAIDLE

Tune—'The Gardener's March.'

WHEN rosy May comes in wi' flowers,
To deck her gay, green-spreading bowers,
Then busy, busy are his hours,
      The Gard'ner wi' his paidle.

The crystal waters gently fa',
The merry birds are lovers a',
The scented breezes round him blaw—
      The Gard'ner wi' his paidle.

When purple morning starts the hare
To steal upon her early fare;
Then thro' the dew he maun repair—
      The Gard'ner wi' his paidle.

When day, expiring in the west,
The curtain draws o' Nature's rest,
He flies to her arms he lo'es best,
      The Gard'ner wi' his paidle.

ON A BANK OF FLOWERS

ON a bank of flowers in a summer day,
  For summer lightly drest,
The youthful, blooming Nelly lay,
  With love and sleep opprest;

When Willie, wand'ring thro' the wood,
Who for her favour oft had sued;
    He gaz'd, he wish'd,
    He fear'd, he blush'd,
And trembled where he stood.

Her closèd eyes, like weapons sheath'd,
    Were seal'd in soft repose;
Her lips, still as she fragrant breath'd,
    It richer dyed the rose;
The springing lilies, sweetly prest,
Wild-wanton kiss'd her rival breast;
    He gaz'd, he wish'd,
    He fear'd, he blush'd,
His bosom ill at rest.

Her robes light-waving in the breeze,
    Her tender limbs embrace;
Her lovely form, her native ease,
    All harmony and grace;
Tumultuous tides his pulses roll,
A faltering, ardent kiss he stole;
    He gaz'd, he wish'd,
    He fear'd, he blush'd,
And sigh'd his very soul.

As flies the partridge from the brake,
    On fear-inspirèd wings,
So Nelly starting, half-awake,
    Away affrighted springs;
But Willie follow'd—as he should,
He overtook her in the wood;
    He vow'd, he pray'd,
    He found the maid
Forgiving all and good.

YOUNG JOCKIE WAS THE BLYTHEST LAD

YOUNG Jockie was the blythest lad,
　In a' our town or here awa';
Fu' blythe he whistled at the gaud,
　Fu' lightly danc'd he in the ha' :

He roos'd my een sae bonie blue,
　He roos'd my waist sae genty sma';
An' ay my heart cam to my mou',
　When ne'er a body heard or saw.

My Jockie toils upon the plain,
　Thro' wind and weet, thro' frost and snaw
And o'er the lea I leuk fu' fain,
　When Jockie's owsen hameward ca'.

An' ay the night comes round again,
　When in his arms he taks me a';
An' ay he vows he'll be my ain,
　As lang as he has breath to draw.

THE BANKS OF NITH

THE Thames flows proudly to the sea,
　Where royal cities stately stand;
But sweeter flows the Nith to me,
　Where Comyns ance had high command.
When shall I see that honor'd land,
　That winding stream I love so dear !
Must wayward Fortune's adverse hand
　For ever, ever keep me here ?

How lovely, Nith, thy fruitful vales,
    Where bounding hawthorns gayly bloom;
And sweetly spread thy sloping dales,
    Where lambkins wanton through the broom.
Tho' wandering now must be my doom,
    Far from thy bonie banks and braes,
May there my latest hours consume,
    Amang the friends of early days!

JAMIE, COME TRY ME

Chorus.—Jamie, come try me,
            Jamie, come try me,
        If thou would win my love,
            Jamie, come try me.

If thou should ask my love,
    Could I deny thee?
If thou would win my love,
    Jamie, come try me!
        Jamie, come try me, etc.

If thou should kiss me, love,
    Wha could espy thee?
If thou wad be my love,
    Jamie, come try me!
        Jamie, come try me, etc.

I LOVE MY LOVE IN SECRET

My Sandy gied to me a ring,
Was a' beset wi' diamonds fine;
But I gied him a far better thing,
I gied my heart in pledge o' his ring.

Chorus.—My Sandy O, my Sandy O,
   My bonie, bonie Sandy O;
   Tho' the love that I owe
   To thee I dare na show,
 Yet I love my love in secret, my Sandy O.

My Sandy brak a piece o' gowd,
While down his cheeks the saut tears row'd;
He took a hauf, and gied it to me,
And I'll keep it till the hour I die.
   My Sandy O, etc.

SWEET TIBBIE DUNBAR

O WILT thou go wi' me, sweet Tibbie Dunbar?
O wilt thou go wi' me, sweet Tibbie Dunbar?
Wilt thou ride on a horse, or be drawn in a car,
Or walk by my side, O sweet Tibbie Dunbar?

I care na thy daddie, his lands and his money,
I care na thy kin, sae high and sae lordly;
But sae that thou'lt hae me for better or waur,
And come in thy coatie, sweet Tibbie Dunbar.

THE CAPTAIN'S LADY

Chorus.—O mount and go, mount and make ye ready,
   O mount and go, and be the Captain's lady.

WHEN the drums do beat, and the cannons rattle,
Thou shalt sit in state, and see thy love in battle:
When the drums do beat, and the cannons rattle,
Thou shalt sit in state, and see thy love in battle,
   O mount and go, etc.

When the vanquish'd foe sues for peace and quiet,
To the shades we'll go, and in love enjoy it :
When the vanquish'd foe sues for peace and quiet,
To the shades we'll go, and in love enjoy it.
  O mount and go, etc.

JOHN ANDERSON, MY JO

JOHN ANDERSON, my jo, John,
  When we were first acquent;
Your locks were like the raven,
  Your bonie brow was brent;
But now your brow is beld, John,
  Your locks are like the snaw;
But blessings on your frosty pow,
  John Anderson, my jo.

John Anderson, my jo, John,
  We clamb the hill thegither;
And mony a cantie day, John,
  We've had wi' ane anither :
Now we maun totter down, John,
  And hand in hand we'll go,
And sleep thegither at the foot,
  John Anderson, my jo.

MY LOVE, SHE'S BUT A LASSIE YET

MY love, she's but a lassie yet,
  My love, she's but a lassie yet;
We'll let her stand a year or twa,
  She'll no be hauf sae saucy yet;
I rue the day I sought her, O !
I rue the day I sought her, O !
Wha gets her need na say he's woo'd,
  But he may say he has bought her, O.

Come, draw a drap o' the best o't yet;
Come, draw a drap o' the best o't yet
Gae seek for pleasure whar you will,
  But here I never miss'd it yet,
We're a' dry wi' drinkin' o't;
We're a' dry wi' drinkin' o't;
The minister kiss't the fiddler's wife;
  He could na preach for thinkin' o't.

TAM GLEN

My heart is a-breaking, dear Tittie
  Some counsel unto me come len',
To anger them a' is a pity,
  But what will I do wi' Tam Glen?

I'm thinking, wi' sic a braw fellow,
  In poortith I might mak a fen';
What care I in riches to wallow,
  If I manna marry Tam Glen?

There's Lowrie the Laird o' Dumeller—
  'Gude day to you'—brute! he comes ben:
He brags and he blaws o' his siller,
  But when will he dance like Tam Glen?

My minnie does constantly deave me,
  And bids me beware o' young men;
They flatter, she says, to deceive me,
  But wha can think sae o' Tam Glen?

My daddie says, gin I'll forsake him,
  He'd gie me gude hunder marks ten;
But, if it's ordain'd I maun take him,
  O wha will I get but Tam Glen?

Yestreen at the Valentine's dealing,
　　My heart to my mou' gied a sten;
For thrice I drew ane without failing,
　　And thrice it was written 'Tam Glen!'

The last Halloween I was waukin'
　　My droukit sark-sleeve, as ye ken,
His likeness came up the house staukin',
　　And the very gray breeks o' Tam Glen!

Come, counsel, dear Tittie, don't tarry;
　　I'll gie ye my bonie black hen,
Gif ye will advise me to marry
　　The lad I lo'e dearly, Tam Glen.

CARLE, AN THE KING COME

Chorus.—Carle, an the King come,
　　　　Carle, an the King come,
　　　Thou shalt dance and I will sing,
　　　　Carle, an the King come.

An somebody were come again,
Then somebody maun cross the main,
And every man shall hae his ain,
　　Carle, an the King come.
　　　　Carle, an the King come, etc.

I trow we swappet for the worse,
We gae the boot and better horse;
An' that we'll tell them at the cross,
　　Carle, an the King come.
　　　　Carle, an the King come, etc.

Coggie, an the King come,
Coggie, an the King come,
I'se be fou, an thou 'se be toom,
　　Coggie, an the King come.
　　　　Coggie, an the King come, etc.

THE LADDIE'S DEAR SEL

THERE's a youth in this city, it were a great pity
 That he from our lasses should wander awa';
For he's bonie and braw, weel-favor'd witha',
 An' his hair has a natural buckle an' a'.

His coat is the hue o' his bonnet sae blue,
 His fecket is white as the new-driven snaw;
His hose they are blae, and his shoon like the slae,
 And his clear siller buckles, they dazzle us a'.

For beauty and fortune the laddie's been courtin';
 Weel-featur'd, weel-tocher'd, weel-mounted an'
  braw;
But chiefly the siller that gars him gang till her,
 The penny's the jewel that beautifies a'.

There's Meg wi' the mailen that fain wad a haen him,
 And Susie, wha's daddie was laird o' the Ha';
There's lang-tocher'd Nancy maist fetters his fancy,
 But the laddie's dear sel, he lo'es dearest of a'.

WHISTLE O'ER THE LAVE O'T

FIRST when Maggie was my care,
Heav'n, I thought, was in her air,
Now we're married—spier nae mair,
 But whistle o'er the lave o't!

Meg was meek, and Meg was mild,
Sweet and harmless as a child—
Wiser men than me's beguil'd;
 Whistle o'er the lave o't!

How we live, my Meg and me,
How we love, and how we gree,
I care na by how few may see—
　　Whistle o'er the lave o't !

Wha I wish were maggot's meat,
Dish'd up in her winding-sheet,
I could write—but Meg may see't—
　　Whistle o'er the lave o't !

MY EPPIE ADAIR

Chorus.—An' O my Eppie, my jewel, my Eppie,
　　Wha wad na be happy wi' Eppie Adair ?

By love and by beauty, by law and by duty,
I swear to be true to my Eppie Adair !
By love and by beauty, by law and by duty,
I swear to be true to my Eppie Adair !
　　An' O my Eppie, etc.

A' pleasure exile me, dishonour defile me,
If e'er I beguile ye, my Eppie Adair !
A' pleasure exile me, dishonour defile me,
If e'er I beguile thee, my Eppie Adair !
　　An' O my Eppie, etc.

ON THE LATE CAPTAIN GROSE'S PEREGRIN-ATIONS THROUGH SCOTLAND

COLLECTING THE ANTIQUITIES OF THAT KINGDOM

HEAR, Land o' Cakes, and brither Scots,
Frae Maidenkirk to Johnie Groat's,
If there's a hole in a' your coats,
　　I rede you tent it :
A chield's amang you takin' notes,
　　And faith he'll prent it :

If in your bounds ye chance to light
Upon a fine, fat, fodgel wight,
O' stature short, but genius bright,
  That's he, mark weel;
And wow! he has an unco sleight
  O' cauk and keel.

By some auld, houlet-haunted biggin',
Or kirk deserted by its riggin',
It's ten to ane ye'll find him snug in
  Some eldritch part,
Wi' deils, they say, L—d save's! colleaguin'
  At some black art.

Ilk ghaist that haunts auld ha' or chaumer,
Ye gipsy-gang that deal in glamour,
And you, deep-read in hell's black grammar,
  Warlocks and witches;
Ye'll quake at his conjuring hammer,
  Ye midnight bitches.

It's tauld he was a sodger bred,
And ane wad rather fa'n than fled;
But now he's quat the spurtle-blade,
  And dog-skin wallet,
And taen the—Antiquarian trade,
  I think they call it.

He has a fouth o' auld nick-nackets:
Rusty airn caps and jinglin' jackets,
Wad haud the Lothians three in tackets,
  A towmont gude;
And parritch-pats and auld saut-backets,
  Before the Flood.

Of Eve's first fire he has a cinder;
Auld Tubalcain's fire-shool and fender;
That which distinguishèd the gender
  O' Balaam's ass:
A broomstick o' the witch of Endor,
  Weel shod wi' brass.

Forbye, he'll shape you aff fu' gleg
The cut of Adam's philibeg;
The knife that nicket Abel's craig
         He'll prove you fully,
It was a faulding jocteleg,
         Or lang-kail gullie.

But wad ye see him in his glee,
For meikle glee and fun has he,
Then set him down, and twa or three
         Gude fellows wi' him :
And *port*, O *port !* shine thou a wee,
         And then ye'll see him !

Now, by the pow'rs o' verse and prose !
Thou art a dainty chield, O Grose !—
Whae'er o' thee shall ill suppose,
         They sair misca' thee;
I'd take the rascal by the nose,
         Wad say, 'Shame fa' thee.'

EPIGRAM ON FRANCIS GROSE THE ANTIQUARY

THE Devil got notice that Grose was a-dying,
So whip ! at the summons, old Satan came flying;
But when he approach'd where poor Francis lay
    moaning,
And saw each bed-post with its burthen a-groaning,
Astonish'd, confounded, cries Satan—'By G——,
I'll want him ere take such a damnable load !'

THE KIRK'S ALARM

Tune—'Come rouse, Brother Sportsmen!'

ORTHODOX! orthodox, who believe in John Knox,
    Let me sound an alarm to your conscience:
A heretic blast has been blown in the West,
    That 'what is no sense must be nonsense,'
Orthodox! That 'what is no sense must be nonsense.

Doctor Mac! Doctor Mac, you should streek on a
    rack,
    To strike evil-doers wi' terror:
To join Faith and Sense, upon any pretence,
    Was heretic, damnable error,
Doctor Mac! 'Twas heretic, damnable error.

Town of Ayr! town of Ayr, it was rash, I declare,
    To meddle wi' mischief a-brewing,
Provost John is still deaf to the Church's relief,
    And Orator Bob is its ruin,
Town of Ayr! Yes, Orator Bob is its ruin.

D'rymple mild! D'rymple mild, tho' your heart's
    like a child's,
    And your life like the new-driven snaw,
Yet that winna save you, auld Satan must have you,
    For preaching that three's ane an' twa,
D'rymple mild! For preaching that three's ane an'
    twa.

Calvin's sons! Calvin's sons, seize your spiritual
    guns,
    Ammunition you never can need;
Your hearts are the stuff will be powder enough,
    And your skulls are a storehouse o' lead,
Calvin's sons! Your skulls are a storehouse o' lead.

Rumble John ! rumble John, mount the steps with
   a groan,
     Cry, 'The Book is with heresy cramm'd';
Then out wi' your ladle, deal brimstone like aidle,
     And roar ev'ry note of the D—'d,
Rumble John ! And roar ev'ry note of the D—'d.

Simper James ! simper James, leave your fair Killie
   dames,
     There's a holier chase in your view :
I'll lay on your head, that the pack you'll soon lead
     For puppies like you there's but few,
Simper James ! For puppies like you there's but
   few.

Singet Sawnie ! singet Sawnie, are ye huirdin' the
   penny,
     Unconscious what danger awaits ?
With a jump, yell, and howl, alarm ev'ry soul,
     For Hannibal's just at your gates,
Singet Sawnie ! For Hannibal's just at your gates

Poet Willie ! poet Willie, gie the Doctor a volley,
     Wi' your 'Liberty's Chain' and your wit;
O'er Pegasus' side ye ne'er laid a stride,
     Ye but smelt, man, the place where he sh—t,
Poet Willie ! Ye but smelt, man, the place where he
   sh—t.

Barr Steenie ! Barr Steenie, what mean ye ? what
   mean ye ?
     If ye meddle nae mair wi' the matter,
Ye may hae some pretence, man, to havins and
   sense, man,
     Wi' people that ken ye nae better,
Barr Steenie ! Wi' people that ken ye nae better.

Jamie Goose ! Jamie Goose, ye made but toom roose,
    In hunting the wicked Lieutenant;
But the Doctor's your mark, for the L—d's holy ark,
    He has cooper'd an' ca'd a wrang pin in't,
Jamie Goose ! He has cooper'd an' ca'd a wrang pin
    in't.

Davie Bluster ! Davie Bluster, for a saint if ye
    muster,
    The core is no nice o' recruits;
Yet to worth let's be just, royal blood ye might boast,
    If the Ass were the king o' the brutes,
Davie Bluster ! If the Ass were the king o' the
    Brutes.

Cessnock-side ! Cessnock-side, wi' your turkey-cock
    pride,
    Of manhood but sma' is your share :
Ye've the figure, 'tis true, ev'n your foes maun allow,
    And your friends dare na say ye hae mair,
Cessnock-side ! And your friends dare na say ye
    hae mair.

Muirland Jock ! muirland Jock, when the L—d
    makes a rock,
    To crush common-sense for her sins;
If ill-manners were wit, there's no mortal so fit
    To confound the poor Doctor at ance,
Muirland Jock ! To confound the poor Doctor at
    ance.

Andro Gowk ! Andro Gowk, ye may slander the
    Book,
    An' the Book nought the waur, let me tell ye;
Tho' ye're rich, an' look big, lay by hat an' wig,
    An' ye'll hae a calf's head o' sma' value,
Andro Gowk ! Ye'll hae a calf's head o' sma' value.

Daddy Auld! daddie Auld, there's a tod in the
    fauld,
  A tod meikle waur than the clerk;
Tho' ye do little skaith, ye'll be in at the death,
    For if ye canna bite, ye may bark,
Daddy Auld! Gif ye canna bite, ye may bark.

Holy Will! holy Will, there was wit in your skull
    When ye pilfer'd the alms o' the poor;
The timmer is scant when ye're taen for a saunt,
    Wha should swing in a rape for an hour,
Holy Will! Ye should swing in a rape for an hour

Poet Burns! poet Burns, wi' your priest-skelpin
    turns,
    Why desert ye your auld native shire?
Your muse is a gipsy, yet were she e'en tipsy,
    She could ca' us nae waur than we are,
Poet Burns! She could ca' us nae waur than we are

PRESENTATION STANZAS TO CORRESPONDENTS

Factor John! Factor John, whom the L—d made
    alone,
    And ne'er made anither, thy peer,
Thy poor servant, the Bard, in respectful regard,
    He presents thee this token sincere,
Factor John! He presents thee this token sincere.

Afton's Laird! Afton's Laird, when your pen can
    be spared,
    A copy of this I bequeath,
On the same sicker score as I mention'd before,
    To that trusty auld worthy, Clackleith,
Afton's Laird! To that trusty auld worthy, Clack-
    leith.

SONNET ON RECEIVING A FAVOUR
AUG. 10, 1789.

Addressed to ROBERT GRAHAM, Esq., of Fintry.

I CALL no Goddess to inspire my strains,
A fabled Muse may suit a bard that feigns:
Friend of my life! my ardent spirit burns,
And all the tribute of my heart returns,
For boons accorded, goodness ever new,
The gift still dearer, as the giver you.
Thou orb of day! thou other paler light!
And all ye many sparkling stars of night!
If aught that giver from my mind efface,
If I that giver's bounty e'er disgrace,
Then roll to me along your wand'ring spheres,
Only to number out a villain's years!
I lay my hand upon my swelling breast,
And grateful would, but cannot speak the rest.

ON BEING APPOINTED TO AN EXCISE DIVISION

SEARCHING auld wives' barrels,
　　Ochon, the day!
That clarty barm should stain my laurels;
　　But—what'll ye say?
These movin' things ca'd wives an' weans,
Wad move the very hearts o' stanes!

WILLIE BREW'D A PECK O' MAUT

O WILLIE brew'd a peck o' maut,
　　And Rob and Allan cam' to pree;
Three blyther hearts, that lee-lang night,
　　Ye wad na found in Christendie.

Chorus.—We are na fou, we're nae that fou,
  But just a drappie in our e'e;
  The cock may craw, the day may daw,
  And ay we'll taste the barley bree.

Here are we met, three merry boys,
  Three merry boys I trow are we;
And mony a night we've merry been,
  And mony mae we hope to be !
   We are na fou, etc.

It is the moon, I ken her horn,
  That's blinkin' in the lift sae hie;
She shines sae bright to wyle us hame,
  But, by my sooth, she'll wait a wee !
   We are na fou', etc.

Wha first shall rise to gang awa',
  A cuckold, coward loun is he !
Wha first beside his chair shall fa',
  He is the King amang us three.
   We are na fou, etc.

CA' THE YOWES TO THE KNOWES

Chorus.—Ca' the yowes to the knowes,
  Ca' them where the heather grows,
  Ca' them where the burnie rowes,
  My bonie dearie.

As I gaed down the water-side,
  There I met my shepherd lad :
He row'd me sweetly in his plaid,
  An' ca'd me his dearie.
   Ca' the yowes, etc.

Will ye gang down the water-side,
And see the waves sae sweetly glide
Beneath the hazels spreading wide,
    The moon it shines fu' clearly.
        Ca' the yowes, etc.

Ye sall get gowns and ribbons meet,
Cauf-leather shoon upon your feet,
And in my arms thou'lt lie and sleep,
    An' ay sall be my dearie.
        Ca' the yowes, etc.

If ye'll but stand to what ye've said,
I'se gang wi' thee, my shepherd lad,
And ye may row me in your plaid,
    And I sall be your dearie.
        Ca' the yowes, etc.

While waters wimple to the sea,
While day blinks in the lift sae hie,
Till clay-cauld death sall blin' my e'e,
    Ye sall be my dearie.
        Ca' the yowes, etc.

I GAED A WAEFU' GATE YESTREEN

I GAED a waefu' gate yestreen,
    A gate I fear I'll dearly rue;
I gat my death frae twa sweet een,
    Twa lovely een o' bonie blue.
'Twas not her golden ringlets bright,
    Her lips, like roses wat wi' dew,
Her heaving bosom, lily-white—
    It was her een sae bonie blue.

She talk'd, she smil'd, my heart she wyl'd;
    She charm'd my soul I wist na how;
And ay the stound, the deadly wound,
    Cam frae her een sae bonie blue.
But 'spare to speak, and spare to speed';
    She'll aiblins listen to my vow :
Should she refuse, I'll lay my dead
    To her twa een sae bonie blue.

HIGHLAND HARRY BACK AGAIN

My Harry was a gallant gay,
    Fu' stately strade he on the plain;
But now he's banish'd far away,
    I'll never see him back again.

Chorus.—O for him back again !
    O for him back again !
    I wad gie a' Knockhaspie's land
    For Highland Harry back again.

When a' the lave gae to their bed,
    I wander dowie up the glen;
I set me down and greet my fill,
    And ay I wish him back again.
      O for him, etc.

O were some villains hangit high,
    And ilka body had their ain !
Then I might see the joyfu' sight,
    My Highland Harry back again.
      O for him, etc.

WHEN FIRST I SAW

Tune—'Maggie Lauder.'

Chorus.—She's aye, aye sae blythe, sae gay,
   She's aye sae blythe and cheerie;
   She's aye sae bonie, blythe and gay,
   O gin I were her dearie!

WHEN first I saw fair Jeanie's face,
 I couldna tell what ailed me;
My heart went fluttering pit-a-pat,
 My een they almost failed me.
She's aye sae neat, sae trim, sae tight,
 All grace does round her hover,
Ae look deprived me o' my heart,
 And I became her lover.

Had I Dundas's whole estate,
 Or Hopetoun's wealth to shine in;
Did warlike laurels crown my brow,
 Or humbler bays entwining;
I'd lay these a' at Jeanie's feet,
 Could I but hope to move her,
And prouder than a belted knight,
 I'd be my Jeanie's lover.

But sair I fear some happier swain
 Has gained my Jeanie's favour;
If so, may every bliss be hers,
 Though I maun never have her.
But gang she east, or gang she west,
 'Twixt Forth and Tweed all over,
While men have eyes, or ears, or taste,
 She'll always find a lover.

THE BATTLE OF SHERRAMUIR

Tune—'The Cameron Rant.'

'O CAM ye here the fight to shun,
  Or herd the sheep wi' me, man ?
Or were ye at the Sherra-moor,
  Or did the battle see, man ?'
I saw the battle, sair and teugh,
And reekin'-red ran mony a sheugh;
My heart, for fear, gaed sough for sough,
To hear the thuds, and see the cluds
O' clans frae woods, in tartan duds,
  Wha glaum'd at kingdoms three, man.
        La, la, la, la, etc.

The red-coat lads wi' black cockauds,
  To meet them were na slaw, man;
They rush'd and push'd, and blude outgush'd,
  And mony a bouk did fa', man :
The great Argyle led on his files,
I wat they glanc'd for twenty miles;
They hough'd the clans like nine-pin kyles,
They hack'd and hash'd, while braidswords clash'd
And thro' they dash'd, and hew'd and smash'd,
  Till fey men died awa', man.
        La, la, la, la, etc.

But had ye seen the philibegs,
  And skyrin tartan trews, man;
When in the teeth they dar'd our Whigs,
  And covenant Trueblues, man :
In lines extended lang and large,
When baig'nets overpower'd the targe,
And thousands hasten'd to the charge;
Wi' Highland wrath they frae the sheath
Drew blades o' death, till, out o' breath,
  They fled like frighted dows, man !
        La, la, la, la, etc.

'O how deil, Tam, can that be true?
  The chase gaed frae the north, man;
I saw mysel, they did pursue
  The horseman back to Forth, man :
And at Dunblane, in my ain sight,
They took the brig wi' a' their might,
And straught to Stirling wing'd their flight :
But, cursed lot ! the gates were shut;
And mony a huntit poor red-coat,
  For fear amaist did swarf, man !'
      La, la, la, la, etc.

My sister Kate cam up the gate
  Wi' crowdie unto me, man;
She swoor she saw some rebels run
  To Perth and to Dundee, man;
Their left-hand general had nae skill;
The Angus lads had nae good will
That day their neibors' blude to spill;
For fear, by foes, that they should lose
Their cogs o' brose; they scar'd at blows
  And hameward fast did flee, man.
      La, la, la, la, etc.

They've lost some gallant gentlemen,
  Amang the Highland clans, man !
I fear my Lord Panmure is slain,
  Or in his en'mies' hands, man.
Now wad ye sing this double flight,
Some fell for wrang, and some for right;
But mony bade the world gude-night;
Say, pell and mell, wi' muskets' knell
How Tories fell, and Whigs to hell
  Flew off in frighted bands, man !
      La, la, la, la, etc.

KILLIECRANKIE

WHARE hae ye been sae braw, lad?
　　Whare hae ye been sae brankie, O?
Whare hae ye been sae braw, lad?
　　Cam ye by Killiecrankie, O?

Chorus.—An' ye had been whare I hae been,
　　　　Ye wad na been sae cantie, O;
　　　An' ye had seen what I hae seen,
　　　　I' the Braes o' Killiecrankie, O.

I faught at land, I faught at sea,
　　At hame I faught my Auntie, O;
But I met the devil an' Dundee,
　　On the Braes o' Killiecrankie, O.
　　　　An' ye had been, etc.

The bauld Pitcur fell in a furr,
　　An' Clavers gat a clankie, O;
Or I had fed an Athole gled,
　　On the Braes o' Killiecrankie, O.
　　　　An' ye had been, etc.

AWA', WHIGS, AWA'

Chorus.—Awa', Whigs, awa'!
　　　Awa', Whigs, awa'!
　　　Ye're but a pack o' traitor louns,
　　　Ye'll do nae gude at a'.

OUR thrissles flourish'd fresh and fair,
　　And bonie bloom'd our roses;
But Whigs cam like a frost in June,
　　An' wither'd a' our posies.
　　　Awa', Whigs, etc.

Our ancient crown's fa'en in the dust—
    Deil blin' them wi' the stoure o't !
An' write their names in his black beuk,
    Wha gae the Whigs the power o't !
        Awa', Whigs, etc.

Our sad decay in Church and State
    Surpasses my descriving :
The Whigs cam o'er us for a curse,
    An' we hae done wi' thriving.
        Awa', Whigs, etc.

Grim vengeance lang has taen a nap,
    But we may see him waukin' :
Gude help the day when Royal heads
    Are hunted like a maukin' !
        Awa', Whigs, etc.

A WAUKRIFE MINNIE

WHARE are you gaun, my bonie lass,
    Whare are you gaun, my hiney ?
She answered me right saucilie,
    An errand for my minnie.

O whare live ye, my bonie lass,
    O whare live ye, my hiney ?
By yon burnside, gin ye maun ken,
    In a wee house wi' my minnie.

But I foor up the glen at e'en,
    To see my bonie lassie;
And lang before the gray morn cam,
    She was na haut sae saucie.

O weary fa' the waukrife cock,
    And the foumart lay his crawin' !
He wauken'd the auld wife frae her sleep,
    A wee blink or the dawin'.

An angry wife I wat she raise,
    And o'er the bed she brocht her ;
And wi' a meikle hazle rung
    She made her a weel-pay'd dochter.

O fare thee weel, my bonie lass,
    O fare thee weel, my hiney !
Thou art a gay an' a bonie lass,
    But thou hast a waukrife minnie.

AY WAUKIN', O

Chorus.—Ay waukin', O,
    Waukin' still and weary ;
  Sleep I can get nane,
    For thinking on my dearie.

SUMMER's a pleasant time ;
    Flowers of ev'ry colour,
The water rins o'er the heugh,
    And I long for my true lover.

When I sleep I dream,
    When I wauk I'm eerie ;
Sleep I can get nane,
    For I'm thinking on my dearie.

Lanely night comes on,
    A' the lave are sleepin' ;
I think on my dear lad,
    And bleer my een wi' greetin'.

FAREWELL TO THE HIGHLANDS

FAREWELL to the Highlands, farewell to the north,
The birthplace of Valour, the country of Worth;
Wherever I wander, wherever I rove,
The hills of the Highlands for ever I love.

Chorus.—My heart's in the Highlands, my heart is
not here,
My heart's in the Highlands, a-chasing the
deer;
A-chasing the wild deer, and following the
roe,
My heart's in the Highlands wherever I go.

Farewell to the mountains, high-cover'd with snow,
Farewell to the straths and green valleys below;
Farewell to the forests and wild-hanging woods,
Farewell to the torrents and loud-pouring floods.
My heart's in the Highlands, etc.

THE WHISTLE—A BALLAD

I SING of a Whistle, a Whistle of Worth,
I sing of a Whistle, the pride of the North,
Was brought to the court of our good Scottish King,
And long with this Whistle all Scotland shall ring.

Old Loda,[1] still rueing the arm of Fingal,
The god of the bottle sends down from his hall—
'This Whistle's your challenge, to Scotland get o'er,
And drink them to hell, Sir ! or ne'er see me more !'

[1] See Ossian's 'Caric-thura.'—*R.B.*

Old poets have sung, and old chronicles tell,
What champions ventur'd, what champions fell:
The son of great Loda was conqueror still,
And blew on the Whistle their requiem shrill.

Till Robert, the lord of the Cairn and the Scaur,
Unmatch'd at the bottle, unconquer'd in war,
He drank his poor god-ship as deep as the sea;
No tide of the Baltic e'er drunker than he.

Thus Robert, victorious, the trophy has gain'd;
Which now in his house has for ages remain'd;
Till three noble chieftains, and all of his blood,
The jovial contest again have renew'd.

Three joyous good fellows, with hearts clear of flaw
Craigdarroch, so famous for wit, worth, and law;
And trusty Glenriddel, so skill'd in old coins;
And gallant Sir Robert, deep-read in old wines.

Craigdarroch began, with a tongue smooth as oil,
Desiring Glenriddel to yield up the spoil;
Or else he would muster the heads of the clan,
And once more, in claret, try which was the man.

'By the gods of the ancients!' Glenriddel replies,
'Before I surrender so glorious a prize,
I'll conjure the ghost of the great Rorie More,
And bumper his horn with him twenty times o'er.'

Sir Robert, a soldier, no speech would pretend,
But he ne'er turn'd his back on his foe, or his friend,
Said, 'Toss down the Whistle, the prize of the field,'
And, knee-deep in claret, he'd die ere he'd yield.

To the board of Glenriddel our heroes repair,
So noted for drowning of sorrow and care;
But, for wine and for welcome, not more known t
    fame,
Than the sense, wit, and taste of a sweet lovely dame

A Bard was selected to witness the fray,
And tell future ages the feats of the day;
A Bard who detested all sadness and spleen,
And wish'd that Parnassus a vineyard had been.

The dinner being over, the claret they ply,
And ev'ry new cork is a new spring of joy;
In the bands of old friendship and kindred so set,
And the bands grew the tighter the more they were
    wet.

Gay pleasure ran riot as bumpers ran o'er;
Bright Phœbus ne'er witness'd so joyous a core,
And vow'd that to leave them he was quite forlorn,
Till Cynthia hinted he'd see them next morn.

Six bottles apiece had well wore out the night,
When gallant Sir Robert, to finish the fight,
Turn'd o'er in one bumper a bottle of red,
And swore 'twas the way that their ancestor did.

Then worthy Glenriddel, so cautious and sage,
No longer the warfare ungodly would wage;
A high Ruling Elder to wallow in wine;
He left the foul business to folks less divine.

The gallant Sir Robert fought hard to the end;
But who can with Fate and quart bumpers contend ?
Though Fate said, a hero should perish in light;
So uprose bright Phœbus—and down fell the knight.

Next uprose our Bard, like a prophet in drink :—
'Craigdarroch, thou'lt soar when creation shall sink !
But if thou would flourish immortal in rhyme,
Come—one bottle more—and have at the sublime !

'Thy line, that have struggled for freedom with Bruce,
Shall heroes and patriots ever produce :
So thine be the laurel, and mine be the bay;
The field thou hast won, by yon bright god of day !'

B.P.   N

TO MARY IN HEAVEN

THOU ling'ring star, with less'ning ray,
    That lov'st to greet the early morn,
Again thou usher'st in the day
    My Mary from my soul was torn.
O Mary! dear departed shade!
    Where is thy place of blissful rest?
See'st thou thy lover lowly laid?
    Hear'st thou the groans that rend his breast?

That sacred hour can I forget?
    Can I forget the hallow'd grove,
Where, by the winding Ayr, we met,
    To live one day of parting love?
Eternity can not efface
    Those records dear of transports past,
Thy image at our last embrace,
    Ah! little thought we 'twas our last!

Ayr, gurgling, kiss'd his pebbled shore,
    O'erhung with wild-woods, thickening green
The fragrant birch and hawthorn hoar,
    'Twin'd amorous round the raptur'd scene:
The flowers sprang wanton to be prest,
    The birds sang love on every spray;
Till too, too soon, the glowing west,
    Proclaim'd the speed of wingèd day.

Still o'er these scenes my mem'ry wakes,
    And fondly broods with miser-care;
Time but th' impression stronger makes,
    As streams their channels deeper wear.
My Mary! dear departed shade!
    Where is thy place of blissful rest?
See'st thou thy lover lowly laid?
    Hear'st thou the groans that rend his breast?

EPISTLE TO DR BLACKLOCK

ELLISLAND, 21st Oct., 1789.

Wow, but your letter made me vauntie!
And are ye hale, and weel, and cantie?
I ken'd it still, your wee bit jauntie
   Wad bring ye to:
Lord send you ay as weel's I want ye!
   And then ye'll do.

The ill-thief blaw the Heron south!
And never drink be near his drouth!
He tauld mysel by word o' mouth,
   He'd tak my letter;
I lippen'd to the chiel in trouth,
   And bade nae better.

But aiblins, honest Master Heron
Had, at the time, some dainty fair one
To ware his theologic care on,
   And holy study;
And tired o' sauls to waste his lear on,
   E'en tried the body.

But what d'ye think, my trusty fier,
I'm turn'd a gauger—Peace be here!
Parnassian queans, I fear, I fear,
   Ye'll now disdain me!
And then my fifty pounds a year
   Will little gain me.

Ye glaiket, gleesome, dainty damies,
Wha, by Castalia's wimplin' streamies,
Lowp, sing, and lave your pretty limbies,
   Ye ken, ye ken,
That strang necessity supreme is
   'Mang sons o' men.

I hae a wife and twa wee laddies;
They maun hae brose and brats o' duddies :
Ye ken yoursels my heart right proud is—
      I need na vaunt—
But I'll sned besoms, thraw saugh woodies,
      Before they want.

Lord help me thro' this warld o' care !
I'm weary sick o't late and air !
Not but I hae a richer share
      Than mony ithers;
But why should ae man better fare,
      And a' men brithers ?

Come, Firm Resolve, take thou the van,
Thou stalk o' carl-hemp in man !
And let us mind, faint heart ne'er wan
      A lady fair :
Wha does the utmost that he can,
      Will whyles do mair.

But to conclude my silly rhyme
(I'm scant o' verse and scant o' time),
To make a happy fireside clime
      To weans and wife,
That's the true pathos and sublime
      Of human life.

My compliments to sister Beckie,
And eke the same to honest Lucky;
I wat she is a daintie chuckie,
      As e'er tread clay;
And gratefully, my gude auld cockie,
      I'm yours for ay.
               ROBERT BURNS.

ADDRESS TO THE TOOTHACHE

My curse upon your venom'd stang,
That shoots my tortur'd gums alang,
An' thro' my lug gies sic a twang,
   Wi' gnawing vengeance,
Tearing my nerves wi' bitter pang,
   Like racking engines!

When fevers burn, or agues freeze us,
Rheumatics gnaw, or colics squeeze us,
Our neibor's sympathy can ease us,
   Wi' pitying moan;
But thee—thou hell o' a' diseases—
   They mock our groan.

Adown my beard the slavers trickle,
I throw the wee stools o'er the mickle,
While round the fire the giglets keckle,
   To see me loup,
An', raving mad, I wish a heckle
   Were in their doup!

In a' the numerous human dools,
Ill-hairsts, daft bargains, cutty stools,
Or worthy frien's rak'd i' the mools,—
   Sad sight to see!
The tricks o' knaves, or fash o' fools,
   Thou bear'st the gree!

Where'er that place be priests ca' hell,
Where a' the tones o' misery yell,
An' rankèt plagues their numbers tell,
   In dreadfu' raw,
Thou, TOOTHACHE, surely bear'st the bell,
   Amang them a'!

O thou grim, mischief-making chiel,
That gars the notes o' discord squeel,
Till daft mankind aft dance a reel
    In gore, a shoe-thick,
Gie a' the faes o' SCOTLAND'S weal
    A towmond's toothache!

THE FIVE CARLINS

AN ELECTION BALLAD

Tune—'Chevy Chase.'

THERE was five Carlins in the South,
 They fell upon a scheme,
To send a lad to London town,
 To bring them tidings hame.

Nor only bring them tidings hame,
 But do their errands there,
And aiblins gowd and honor baith
 Might be that laddie's share.

There was Maggie by the banks o' Nith,
 A dame wi' pride eneugh;
And Marjory o' the mony Lochs,
 A Carlin auld and teugh.

And blinkin' Bess of Annandale,
 That dwelt near Solway-side;
And whisky Jean, that took her gill,
 In Galloway sae wide.

And black Joan, frae Crichton Peel,
 O' gipsy kith an' kin;
Five wighter Carlins were na found
 The South countrie within.

To send a lad to London town,
    They met upon a day;
And mony a knight, and mony a laird,
    This errand fain wad gae.

O mony a knight, and mony a laird,
    This errand fain wad gae;
But nae ane could their fancy please,
    O ne'er a ane but twae.

The first ane was a belted Knight,
    Bred of a Border band;
And he wad gae to London town,
    Might nae man him withstand.

And he wad do their errands weel,
    And meikle he wad say;
And ilka ane about the court
    Wad bid to him gude-day.

The neist cam in a Soger youth,
    Wha spak wi' modest grace,
And he wad gae to London town,
    If sae their pleasure was.

He wad na hecht them courtly gifts,
    Nor meikle speech pretend;
But he wad hecht an honest heart,
    Wad ne'er desert his friend.

Then, wham to chuse, and wham refuse,
    At strife thir Carlins fell;
For some had Gentlefolks to please,
    And some wad please themsel.

Then out spak mim-mou'd Meg o' Nith,
    And she spak up wi' pride,
And she wad send the Soger youth,
    Whatever might betide.

For the auld Gudeman o' London court
   She didna care a pin;
But she wad send the Soger youth,
   To greet his eldest son.

Then up sprang Bess o' Annandale,
   And a deadly aith she's taen,
That she wad vote the Border Knight,
   Though she should vote her lane.

For far-off fowls hae feathers fair,
   And fools o' change are fain :
But I hae tried the Border Knight,
   And I'll try him yet again.

Says Black Joan frae Crichton Peel,
   A Carlin stoor and grim,
The auld Gudeman, and the young Gudeman
   For me may sink or swim;

For fools will prate o' right or wrang,
   While knaves laugh them to scorn;
But the Soger's friends hae blawn the best,
   So he shall bear the horn.

Then whisky Jean spak owre her drink,
   Ye weel ken, kimmers a'.
The auld Gudeman o' London court,
   His back's been at the wa';

And mony a friend that kiss'd his caup
   Is now a fremit wight;
But it's ne'er be said o' whisky Jean,—
   We'll send the Border Knight.

Then slow raise Marjory o' the Lochs,
   And wrinkled was her brow,
Her ancient weed was russet gray,
   Her auld Scots bluid was true;

There's some great folk set light by me,
  I set as light by them;
But I will send to London town
  Wham I like best at hame.

Sae how their weighty plea may end,
  Nae mortal wight can tell;
God grant the King and ilka man
  May look weel to himsel.

ELECTION BALLAD FOR WESTERHA'

THE Laddies by the banks o' Nith
  Wad trust his Grace wi' a', Jamie;
But he'll sair them, as he sair'd the King—
  Turn tail and rin awa', Jamie.

Chorus.—Up and waur them a', Jamie,
      Up and waur them a';
    The Johnstones hae the guidin' o't,
      Ye turncoat Whigs awa'!

The day he stude his country's friend,
  Or gied her faes a claw, Jamie,
Or frae puir man a blessin' wan,
  That day the Duke ne'er saw, Jamie.
    Up and waur them, etc.

But wha is he, his country's boast?
  Like him there is na twa, Jamie;
There's no a callant tents the kye,
  But kens o' Westerha', Jamie.
    Up and waur them, etc.

To end the wark, here's Whistlebirk,
 Lang may his whistle blaw, Jamie;
And Maxwell true, o' sterling blue;
 And we'll be Johnstones a', Jamie.
  Up and waur them, etc.

PROLOGUE SPOKEN AT THE THEATRE O DUMFRIES

ON NEW YEAR'S DAY EVENING, 1790

No song nor dance I bring from yon great city,
That queens it o'er our taste—the more's the pity
Tho' by the bye, abroad why will you roam ?
Good sense and taste are natives here at home :
But not for panegyric I appear,
I come to wish you all a good New Year !
Old Father Time deputes me here before ye,
Not for to preach, but tell his simple story :
The sage grave Ancient cough'd, and bade me say
'You're one year older this important day,'
If *wiser* too—he hinted some suggestion,
But 'twould be rude, you know, to ask the question
And with a would-be-roguish leer and wink,
Said—'Sutherland, in one word, bid them THINK

Ye sprightly youths, quite flush with hope an
 spirit,
Who think to storm the world by dint of merit,
To you the dotard has a deal to say,
In his sly, dry, sententious, proverb way !
He bids you mind, amid your thoughtless rattle,
That the first blow is ever half the battle;
That tho' some by the skirt may try to snatch him
Yet by the forelock is the hold to catch him;

That whether doing, suffering, or forbearing,
You may do miracles by persevering.

Last, tho' not least in love, ye youthful fair,
Angelic forms, high Heaven's peculiar care !
To you old Bald-pate smoothes his wrinkled brow,
And humbly begs you'll mind the important—NOW !
To crown your happiness he asks your leave,
And offers, bliss to give and to receive.

For our sincere, tho' haply weak endeavours,
With grateful pride we own your many favours;
And howsoe'er our tongues may ill reveal it,
Believe our glowing bosoms truly feel it.

NEW YEAR'S DAY [1790]

TO MRS DUNLOP

THIS day, Time winds th' exhausted chain;
To run the twelvemonths' length again :
I see the old, bald-pated fellow,
With ardent eyes, complexion sallow,
Adjust the unimpair'd machine,
To wheel the equal, dull routine.

The absent lover, minor heir,
In vain assail him with their prayer;
Deaf as my friend, he sees them press,
Nor makes the hour one moment less.
Will you (the Major's with the hounds,
The happy tenants share his rounds;
Coila's fair Rachel's care to-day,
And blooming Keith's engaged with Gray)

From housewife cares a minute borrow
(That grandchild's cap will do to-morrow),
And join with me a-moralising;
This day's propitious to be wise in.

First, what did yesternight deliver?
'Another year has gone for ever.'
And what is this day's strong suggestion?
'The passing moment's all we rest on!'
Rest on—for what? what do we here?
Or why regard the passing year?
Will Time, amus'd with proverb'd lore,
Add to our date one minute more?
A few days may—a few years must—
Repose us in the silent dust.
Then, is it wise to damp our bliss?
Yes—all such reasonings are amiss!
The voice of Nature loudly cries,
And many a message from the skies,
That something in us never dies:
That on this frail, uncertain state,
Hang matters of eternal weight:
That future life in worlds unknown
Must take its hue from this alone;
Whether—as heavenly glory bright,
Or dark as Misery's woeful night.

Since then, my honour'd first of friends,
On this poor being all depends;
Let us th' important *now* employ,
And live as those who never die.
Tho' you, with days and honour crown'd,
Witness that filial circle round
(A sight life's sorrows to repulse,
A sight pale Envy to convulse),
Others now claim your chief regard;
Yourself, you wait your bright reward.

PROLOGUE FOR MR SUTHERLAND

ON HIS BENEFIT NIGHT AT THE THEATRE, DUMFRIES

WHAT needs this din about the town o' Lon'on,
How this new play an' that new sang is comin'?
Why is outlandish stuff sae meikle courted?
Does nonsense mend, like brandy, when imported?
Is there nae poet, burning keen for fame,
Will try to gie us sangs and plays at hame?
For Comedy abroad he need na toil,
A fool and knave are plants of every soil;
Nor need he hunt as far as Rome or Greece,
To gather matter for a serious piece;
There's themes enow in Caledonian story,
Would show the Tragic Muse in a' her glory.

Is there no daring Bard will rise and tell
How glorious Wallace stood, how—hapless fell?
Where are the Muses fled that could produce
A drama worthy o' the name o' Bruce?
How here, even here, he first unsheath'd the sword
'Gainst mighty England and her guilty lord;
And after mony a bloody, deathless doing,
Wrench'd his dear country from the jaws of Ruin!
O for a Shakespeare or an Otway scene,
To draw the lovely, hapless Scottish Queen!
Vain all th' omnipotence of female charms
'Gainst headlong, ruthless, mad Rebellion's arms:
She fell, but fell with spirit truly Roman,
To glut that direst foe—a vengeful woman;
A woman (tho' the phrase may seem uncivil),
As able and as wicked as the Devil!
One Douglas lives in Home's immortal page,
But Douglasses were heroes every age:
And tho' your fathers, prodigal of life,
A Douglas followed to the martial strife,

Perhaps, if bowls row right, and Right succeeds,
Ye yet may follow where a Douglas leads!

As ye hae generous done, if a' the land
Would take the Muses' servants by the hand;
Not only hear, but patronise, befriend them,
And where ye justly can commend, commend them;
And aiblins when they winna stand the test,
Wink hard, and say 'The folks hae done their best!'
Would a' the land do this, then I'll be caution,
Ye'll soon hae poets o' the Scottish nation
Will gar Fame blaw until her trumpet crack,
And warsle Time, an' lay him on his back!

For us and for our Stage, should ony spier,
'Whase aught thae chiels maks a' this bustle here?'
My best leg foremost, I'll set up my brow—
We have the honour to belong to you!
We're your ain bairns, e'en guide us as ye like,
But like good mithers, shore before ye strike;
And gratefu' still, I trust ye'll ever find us,
For gen'rous patronage, and meikle kindness
We've got frae a' professions, sorts and ranks:
God help us! we're but poor—ye'se get but thanks.

LINES TO A GENTLEMAN

WHO HAD SENT THE POET A NEWSPAPER, AND OFFERED TO CONTINUE IT FREE OF EXPENSE

KIND Sir, I've read your paper through,
And faith, to me, 'twas really new!
How guessed ye, Sir, what maist I wanted?
This mony a day I've grain'd and gaunted,

To ken what French mischief was brewin';
Or what the drumlie Dutch were doin';
That vile doup-skelper, Emperor Joseph,
If Venus yet had got his nose off;
Or how the collieshangie works
Atween the Russians and the Turks,
Or if the Swede, before he halt,
Would play anither Charles the Twalt;
If Denmark, any body spak o't;
Or Poland, wha had now the tack o't :
How cut-throat Prussian blades were hingin';
How libbet Italy was singin';
If Spaniard, Portuguese, or Swiss,
Were sayin' or takin' aught amiss;
Or how our merry lads at hame,
In Britain's court kept up the game;
How royal George, the Lord leuk o'er him !
Was managing St Stephen's quorum;
If sleekit Chatham Will was livin',
Or glaikit Charlie got his nieve in;
How daddie Burke the plea was cookin',
If Warren Hastings' neck was yeukin';
How cesses, stents, and fees were rax'd,
Or if bare a—— yet were tax'd;
The news o' princes, dukes, and earls,
Pimps, sharpers, bawds, and opera-girls;
If that daft buckie, Geordie Wales,
Was threshin' still at hizzie's tails;
Or if he was grown oughtlins douser,
And no a perfect kintra cooser :
A' this and mair I never heard of;
And, but for you, I might despair'd of.
So, gratefu', back your news I send you,
And pray a' gude things may attend you !

ELLISLAND, *Monday Morning*, 1790.

ELEGY ON WILLIE NICOL'S MARE

PEG NICHOLSON was a good bay mare,
    As ever trod on iron;
But now she's floating down the Nith,
    And past the mouth o' Cairn :

Peg Nicholson was a good bay mare,
    An' rode thro' thick an' thin;
But now she's floating down the Nith,
    And wanting even the skin.

Peg Nicholson was a good bay mare,
    And ance she bore a priest;
But now she's floating down the Nith,
    For Solway fish a feast.

Peg Nicholson was a good bay mare,
    An' the priest he rode her sair;
And much oppress'd, and bruis'd she was,
    As priest-rid cattle are.

THE GOWDEN LOCKS OF ANNA

YESTREEN I had a pint o' wine,
    A place where body saw na;
Yestreen lay on this breast o' mine
    The gowden locks of Anna.

The hungry Jew in wilderness,
    Rejoicing o'er his manna,
Was naething to my hiney bliss
    Upon the lips of Anna.

Ye monarchs, take the East and West,
　　Frae Indus to Savannah;
Gie me, within my straining grasp,
　　The melting form of Anna:

There I'll despise Imperial charms,
　　An Empress or Sultana,
While dying raptures, in her arms,
　　I give and take wi' Anna!

Awa', thou flaunting God of Day!
　　Awa', thou pale Diana!
Ilk Star, gae hide thy twinkling ray,
　　When I'm to meet my Anna!

Come, in thy raven plumage, Night
　　(Sun, Moon, and Stars, withdrawn a');
And bring an angel-pen to write
　　My transports with my Anna!

POSTSCRIPT

The Kirk an' State may join an' tell,
　　To do sic things I mauna:
The Kirk an' State may gae to h—l,
　　And I'll gae to my Anna.

She is the sunshine o' my e'e,
　　To live but her I canna;
Had I on earth but wishes three,
　　The first should be my Anna.

I MURDER HATE

I MURDER hate by flood or field,
　　Tho' glory's name may screen us;
In wars at home I'll spend my blood—
　　Life-giving wars of Venus.

The deities that I adore
　　Are social Peace and Plenty;
I'm better pleas'd to make one more,
　　Than be the death of twenty.

I would not die like Socrates,
　　For all the fuss of Plato;
Nor would I with Leonidas,
　　Nor yet would I with Cato:
The zealots of the Church and State
　　Shall ne'er my mortal foes be;
But let me have bold Zimri's fate,
　　Within the arms of Cozbi!

GUDEWIFE, COUNT THE LAWIN'

GANE is the day, and mirk's the night,
But we'll ne'er stray for faute o' light;
Gude ale and brandy's stars and moon,
And blude-red wine's the rysin' sun.

Chorus.—Then, gudewife, count the lawin',
　　　　The lawin', the lawin',
　　　　Then, gudewife, count the lawin',
　　　　And bring a coggie mair.

There's wealth and ease for gentlemen,
And simple folk maun fecht and fen';
But here we're a' in ae accord,
For ilka man that's drunk's a lord.
　　　　Then, gudewife, etc.

My coggie is a haly pool
That heals the wounds o' care and dool:
And Pleasure is a wanton trout,
An' ye drink it a', ye'll find him out.
　　　　Then, gudewife, etc.

ELECTION BALLAD

AT CLOSE OF THE CONTEST FOR REPRESENTING THE DUMFRIES BURGHS, 1790

Addressed to R. GRAHAM, Esq., of Fintry.

FINTRY, my stay in worldly strife,
Friend o' my Muse, friend o' my life,
   Are ye as idle's I am?
Come then, wi' uncouth kintra fleg,
O'er Pegasus I'll fling my leg,
   And ye shall see me try him.

But where shall I go rin a ride,
That I may splatter nane beside?
   I wad na be uncivil:
In manhood's various paths and ways
There's ay some doytin body strays,
   And *I* ride like the devil.

Thus I break aff wi' a' my birr,
An' down yon dark, deep alley spur,
   Where Theologics daunder:
Alas! curst wi' eternal fogs,
And damn'd in everlasting bogs,
   As sure's the creed I'll blunder!

I'll stain a band, or jaup a gown,
Or rin my reckless, guilty crown
   Against the haly door:
Sair do I rue my luckless fate,
When, as the Muse an' Deil wad hae't,
   I rade that road before.

Suppose I take a spurt, and mix
Amang the wilds o' Politics—
   Elector and elected,

Where dogs at Court (sad sons of bitches !)
Septennially a madness touches,
      Till all the land's infected.

All hail ! Drumlanrig's haughty Grace,
Discarded remnant of a race
      Once godlike—great in story;
Thy forbears' virtues all contrasted,
The very name of Douglas blasted,
      Thine that inverted glory !

Hate, envy, oft the Douglas bore,
But thou hast superadded more,
      And sunk them in contempt;
Follies and crimes have stain'd the name,
But, Queensberry, thine the virgin claim,
      From aught that's good exempt.

I'll sing the zeal Drumlanrig bears,
Who left the all-important cares
      Of princes, and their darlings :
And, bent on winning borough towns,
Came shaking hands wi' wabster-loons,
      And kissing barefit carlins.

Combustion thro' our boroughs rode,
Whistling his roaring pack abroad
      Of mad unmuzzled lions;
As Queensberry blue and bluff unfurl'd,
And Westerha' and Hopetoun hurl'd,
      To every Whig defiance.

But cautious Queensberry left the war,
Th' unmanner'd dust might soil his star,
      Besides, he hated *bleeding*;
But left behind him heroes bright,
Heroes in Cæsarean fight,
      Or Ciceronian pleading.

O for a throat like huge Mons-Meg,
To muster o'er each ardent Whig
        Beneath Drumlanrig's banners;
Heroes and heroines commix,
All in the field of politics,
        To win immortal honors.

M'Murdo and his lovely spouse
(Th' enamour'd laurels kiss her brows!)
        Led on the Loves and Graces:
She won each gaping burgess' heart,
While he, sub rosa, played his part
        Among their wives and lasses.

Craigdarroch led a light-arm'd core,
Tropes, metaphors, and figures pour,
        Like Hecla streaming thunder:
Glenriddel, skill'd in rusty coins,
Blew up each Tory's dark designs,
        And bared the treason under.

In either wing two champions fought;
Redoubted Staig, who set at nought
        The wildest savage Tory;
And Welsh, who ne'er yet flinch'd his ground,
High-wav'd his magnum-bonum round
        With Cyclopean fury.

Miller brought up the artillery ranks,
The many-pounders of the Banks,
        Resistless desolation!
While Maxwelton, that baron bold,
'Mid Lawson's port entrench'd his hold,
        And threaten'd worse damnation.

To these what Tory hosts oppos'd,
With these what Tory warriors clos'd,
        Surpasses my descriving:

Squadrons, extended long and large,
With furious speed rush to the charge,
          Like furious devils driving.

What verse can sing, what prose narrate,
The butcher deeds of bloody fate,
          Amid this mighty tulyie !
Grim Horror girn'd, pale Terror roar'd,
As Murder at his thrapple shor'd,
          And Hell mix'd in the brulyie.

As Highland craigs by thunder cleft,
When lightnings fire the stormy lift,
          Hurl down with crashing **rattle;**
As flames among a hundred woods,
As headlong foam a hundred floods,
          Such is the rage of Battle.

The stubborn Tories dare to die;
As soon the rooted oaks would fly
          Before th' approaching fellers :
The Whigs come on like Ocean's roar,
When all his wintry billows pour
          Against the Buchan Bullers.

Lo, from the shades of Death's deep night,
Departed Whigs enjoy the fight,
          And think on former daring :
The muffled murtherer of Charles
The Magna Charter flag unfurls,
          All deadly gules its bearing.

Nor wanting ghosts of Tory fame;
Bold Scrimgeour follows gallant Graham;
          Auld Covenanters shiver—
Forgive ! forgive ! much-wrong'd Montrose !
Now Death and Hell engulph thy foes,
          Thou liv'st on high for ever.

Still o'er the field the combat burns,
The Tories, Whigs, give way by turns;
            But Fate the word has spoken :
For woman's wit and strength o' man,
Alas ! can do but what they can;
            The Tory ranks are broken.

O that my een were flowing burns !
My voice, a lioness that mourns
            Her darling cubs' undoing !
That I might greet, that I might cry,
While Tories fall, while Tories fly,
            And furious Whigs pursuing !

What Whig but melts for good Sir James,
Dear to his country, by the names,
            Friend, Patron, Benefactor !
Not Pulteney's wealth can Pulteney save;
And Hopeton falls, the generous, brave;
            And Stewart, bold as Hector.

Thou, Pitt, shalt rue this overthrow,
And Thurlow growl a curse of woe,
            And Melville melt in wailing :
Now Fox and Sheridan rejoice,
And Burke shall sing, O Prince, arise !
            Thy power is all prevailing !

For your poor friend, the Bard, afar
He only hears and sees the war,
            A cool spectator purely !
So, when the storm the forest rends,
The robin in the hedge descends,
            And sober chirps securely.

Now, for my friends' and brethren's sakes,
And for my dear'-lov'd Land o' Cakes,
            I pray with holy fire :
Lord, send a rough-shod troop o' Hell
O'er a' wad Scotland buy or sell,
            To grind them in the mire !

ELEGY ON CAPTAIN MATTHEW HENDERSON

A GENTLEMAN WHO HELD THE PATENT FOR HIS HONOURS
IMMEDIATELY FROM ALMIGHTY GOD

Should the poor be flattered.—SHAKESPEARE.

O DEATH! thou tyrant fell and bloody!
The meikle devil wi' a woodie
Haurl thee hame to his black smiddie,
  O'er hurcheon hides,
And like stock-fish come o'er his studdie
  Wi' thy auld sides!

He's gane, he's gane! he's frae us torn,
The ae best fellow e'er was born!
Thee, Matthew, Nature's sel shall mourn,
  By wood and wild,
Where, haply, Pity strays forlorn,
  Frae man exil'd.

Ye hills, near neibours o' the starns,
That proudly cock your cresting cairns!
Ye cliffs, the haunts of sailing earns,
  Where Echo slumbers!
Come, join ye, Nature's sturdiest bairns,
  My wailing numbers!

Mourn, ilka grove the cushat kens!
Ye haz'ly shaws and briery dens!
Ye burnies, wimplin' down your glens,
  Wi' toddlin' din,
Or foaming, strang, wi' hasty stens,
  Frae lin to lin.

Mourn, little harebells o'er the lea;
Ye stately foxgloves, fair to see;
Ye woodbines hanging bonilie,
  In scented bow'rs;
Ye roses on your thorny tree,
  The first o' flow'rs.

At dawn, when ev'ry grassy blade
Droops with a diamond at his head,
At ev'n, when beans their fragrance shed,
    I' th' rustling gale,
Ye maukins, whiddin' thro' the glade,
      Come join my wail.

Mourn, ye wee songsters o' the wood;
Ye grouse that crap the heather bud;
Ye curlews, calling thro' a clud;
    Ye whistling plover;
And mourn, ye whirring paitrick brood;
      He's gane for ever !

Mourn, sooty coots, and speckled teals;
Ye fisher herons, watching eels;
Ye duck and drake, wi' airy wheels
    Circling the lake;
Ye bitterns, till the quagmire reels,
      Rair for his sake.

Mourn, clam'ring craiks at close o' day,
'Mang fields o' flow'ring clover gay;
And when ye wing your annual way
    Frae our cauld shore,
Tell thae far warlds wha lies in clay,
      Wham we deplore.

Ye houlets, frae your ivy bow'r
In some auld tree, or eldritch tow'r,
What time the moon, wi' silent glow,
    Sets up her horn,
Wail thro' the dreary midnight hour,
      Till waukrife morn !

O rivers, forests, hills, and plains !
Oft have ye heard my canty strains :
But now, what else for me remains
    But tales of woe;
And frae my een the drapping rains
      Maun ever flow.

Mourn, Spring, thou darling of the year !
Ilk cowslip cup shall kep a tear :
Thou, Simmer, while each corny spear
  Shoots up its head,
Thy gay, green, flow'ry tresses shear,
  For him that's dead !

Thou, Autumn, wi' thy yellow hair,
In grief thy sallow mantle tear !
Thou, Winter, hurling thro' the air
  The roaring blast,
Wide o'er the naked world declare
  The worth we've lost !

Mourn him, thou Sun, great source of light !
Mourn, Empress of the silent night !
And you, ye twinkling starnies bright,
  My Matthew mourn !
For through your orbs he's taen his flight,
  Ne'er to return.

O Henderson ! the man ! the brother !
And art thou gone, and gone for ever !
And hast thou crost that unknown river,
  Life's dreary bound !
Like thee, where shall I find another,
  The world around ?

Go to your sculptur'd tombs, ye great,
In a' the tinsel trash o' state !
But by thy honest turf I'll wait,
  Thou man of worth !
And weep the ae best fellow's fate
  E'er lay in earth.

THE EPITAPH

Stop, passenger ! my story's brief,
 And truth I shall relate, man;
I tell nae common tale o' grief,
 For Matthew was a great man.

If thou uncommon merit hast,
  Yet spurn'd at Fortune's door, man;
A look of pity hither cast,
  For Matthew was a poor man.

If thou a noble sodger art,
  That passest by this grave, man;
There moulders here a gallant heart,
  For Matthew was a brave man.

If thou on men, their works and ways,
  Canst throw uncommon light, man;
Here lies wha weel had won thy praise,
  For Matthew was a bright man.

If thou, at Friendship's sacred ca',
  Wad life itself resign, man;
Thy sympathetic tear maun fa',
  For Matthew was a kind man.

If thou art staunch, without a stain,
  Like the unchanging blue, man;
This was a kinsman o' thy ain,
  For Matthew was a true man.

If thou hast wit, and fun, and fire,
  And ne'er guid wine did fear, man;
This was thy billie, dam, and sire,
  For Matthew was a queer man.

If ony whiggish, whingin' sot,
  To blame poor Matthew dare, man;
May dool and sorrow be his lot,
  For Matthew was a rare man.

But now his radiant course is run,
  For Matthew's was a bright one!
His soul was like the glorious sun,
  A matchless, Heav'nly light, man.

VERSES ON CAPTAIN GROSE

WRITTEN ON AN ENVELOPE, ENCLOSING A LETTER TO HIM

KEN ye ought o' Captain Grose ?—Igo and ago,
If he's among his friends or foes ?—Iram, coram, dago,
Is he to Abra'm's bosom gane ?—Igo and ago,
Or haudin Sarah by the wame ?—Iram, coram, dago.

Is he south or is he north ?—Igo and ago,
Or drownèd in the river Forth ?—Iram, coram, dago,
Is he slain by Hielan' bodies ?—Igo and ago,
And eaten like a wether haggis ?—Iram, coram, dago.

Where'er he be, the Lord be near him !—Igo and ago,
As for the deil, he daur na steer him,—Iram, coram,
　　dago,
But please transmit th' enclosèd letter,—Igo and ago,
Which will oblige your humble debtor,—Iram, coram,
　　dago.

So may ye hae auld stanes in store,—Igo and ago,
The very stanes that Adam bore,—Iram, coram, dago,
So may ye get in glad possession,—Igo and ago,
The coins o' Satan's coronation !—Iram, coram, dago.

TAM O' SHANTER

A TALE

Of Brownyis and of Bogillis full is this Buke.
　　　　　　　　　　　　　　　　GAWIN DOUGLAS.

WHEN chapman billies leave the street,
And drouthy neibors, neibors meet;
As market days are wearing late,
An' folk begin to tak the gate;

While we sit bowsing at the nappy,
An' getting fou and unco happy,
We think na on the lang Scots miles,
The mosses, waters, slaps, and styles,
That lie between us and our hame,
Where sits our sulky, sullen dame,
Gathering her brows like gathering storm,
Nursing her wrath to keep it warm.

This truth fand honest TAM O' SHANTER,
As he frae Ayr ae night did canter:
(Auld Ayr, whom ne'er a town surpasses,
For honest men and bonie lasses).

O Tam! hadst thou but been sae wise,
As taen thy ain wife Kate's advice!
She tauld thee weel thou was a skellum,
A bletherin', blusterin', drunken blellum;
That frae November till October,
Ae market-day thou was na sober;
That ilka melder wi' the miller,
Thou sat as lang as thou had siller;
That ev'ry naig was ca'd a shoe on
The smith and thee gat roarin' fou on;
That at the L—d's house, ev'n on Sunday,
Thou drank wi' Kirkton Jean till Monday.
She prophesied that, late or soon,
Thou wad be found, deep drown'd in Doon,
Or catch'd wi' warlocks in the mirk,
By Alloway's auld haunted kirk.

Ah, gentle dames! it gars me greet,
To think how mony counsels sweet,
How mony lengthen'd sage advices,
The husband frae the wife despises!

But to our tale:—Ae market night,
Tam had got planted unco right,

Fast by an ingle, bleezing finely,
Wi' reaming swats, that drank divinely;
And at his elbow, Souter Johnie,
His ancient, trusty, drouthy cronie:
Tam lo'ed him like a very brither;
They had been fou for weeks thegither.
The night drave on wi' sangs an' clatter;
And ay the ale was growing better:
The Landlady and Tam grew gracious,
Wi' secret favours, sweet and precious:
The Souter tauld his queerest stories;
The Landlord's laugh was ready chorus:
The storm without might rair and rustle,
Tam did na mind the storm a whistle.

Care, mad to see a man sae happy,
E'en drown'd himsel amang the nappy.
As bees flee hame wi' lades o' treasure,
The minutes wing'd their way wi' pleasure:
Kings may be blest, but Tam was glorious,
O'er a' the ills o' life victorious!

But pleasures are like poppies spread,
You seize the flow'r, its bloom is shed;
Or like the snowfall in the river,
A moment white—then melts for ever;
Or like the borealis race,
That flit ere you can point their place;
Or like the rainbow's lovely form
Evanishing amid the storm.
Nae man can tether Time nor Tide,
The hour approaches Tam maun ride—
That hour, o' night's black arch the key-stane,
That dreary hour Tam mounts his beast in;
And sic a night he taks the road in,
As ne'er poor sinner was abroad in.

The wind blew as 'twad blawn its last;
The rattling showers rose on the blast;

The speedy gleams the darkness swallow'd;
Loud, deep, and lang the thunder bellow'd;
That night, a child might understand,
The deil had business on his hand.

Weel mounted on his gray mare, Meg,
A better never lifted leg,
Tam skelpit on thro' dub and mire,
Despising wind, and rain, and fire;
Whiles holding fast his gude blue bonnet,
Whiles crooning o'er an auld Scots sonnet,
Whiles glow'ring round wi' prudent cares,
Lest bogles catch him unawares;
Kirk-Alloway was drawing nigh,
Where ghaists and houlets nightly cry.

By this time he was 'cross the ford,
Where in the snaw the chapman smoor'd;
And past the birks and meikle stane,
Where drunken Charlie brak 's neck-bane;
And thro' the whins, and by the cairn,
Where hunters fand the murder'd bairn;
And near the thorn, aboon the well,
Where Mungo's mither hang'd hersel.
Before him Doon pours all his floods,
The doubling storm roars thro' the woods,
The lightnings flash frae pole to pole,
Near and more near the thunders roll,
When, glimmering thro' the groaning trees,
Kirk-Alloway seem'd in a bleeze,
Thro' ilka bore the beams were glancing,
And loud resounded mirth and dancing.

Inspiring, bold John Barleycorn!
What dangers thou canst make us scorn!
Wi' tippenny, we fear nae evil;
Wi' usquabae, we'll face the devil!
The swats sae ream'd in Tammie's noddle,
Fair play, he car'd na deils a boddle,

But Maggie stood, right sair astonish'd,
Till, by the heel and hand admonish'd,
She ventur'd forward on the light;
And, wow! Tam saw an unco sight!

Warlocks and witches in a dance:
Nae cotillion, brent new frae France,
But hornpipes, jigs, strathspeys, and reels,
Put life and mettle in their heels.
A winnock-bunker in the east,
There sat auld Nick, in shape o' beast;
A towzie tyke, black, grim, and large,
To gie them music was his charge:
He screw'd the pipes, and gart them skirl,
Till roof and rafters a' did dirl.—
Coffins stood round, like open presses,
That shaw'd the dead in their last dresses;
And (by some devilish cantraip sleight)
Each in its cauld hand held a light,
By which heroic Tam was able
To note upon the haly table,
A murderer's banes, in gibbet-airns;
Twa span-lang, wee unchristen'd bairns;
A thief, new-cutted frae a rape,
Wi' his last gasp his gab did gape;
Five tomahawks, wi' blude red-rusted;
Five scymitars, wi' murder crusted;
A garter, which a babe had strangled;
A knife, a father's throat had mangled,
Whom his ain son of life bereft,
The gray hairs yet stack to the heft;
Wi' mair of horrible and awfu',
Which even to name wad be unlawfu.

As Tammie glowr'd, amaz'd, and curious,
The mirth and fun grew fast and furious;
The piper loud and louder blew,
The dancers quick and quicker flew,

They reel'd, they set, they cross'd, they cleekit,
Till ilka carlin swat and reekit,
And coost her duddies on the wark,
And linket at it in her sark !

Now Tam, O Tam ! had they been queans,
A' plump and strapping in their teens !
Their sarks, instead o' creeshie flannen,
Been snaw-white seventeen hunder linen !—
Thir breeks o' mine, my only pair,
That ance were plush, o' guid blue hair,
I wad hae gien them off my hurdies,
For ae blink o' the bonie burdies !
But wither'd beldams, auld and droll,
Rigwoodie hags wad spean a foal,
Louping an' flinging on a crummock,
I wonder did na turn thy stomach.

But Tam kent what was what fu' brawlie :
There was ae winsome wench and waulie,
That night enlisted in the core,
Lang after kenn'd on Carrick shore
(For mony a beast to dead she shot,
And perish'd mony a bonie boat,
And shook baith meikle corn and bear,
And held the country-side in fear) ;
Her cutty sark', o' Paisley harn,
That while a lassie she had worn,
In longitude tho' sorely scanty,
It was her best, and she was vauntie.
Ah ! little kent thy reverend grannie,
That sark she coft for her wee Nannie,
Wi' two pund Scots ('twas a' her riches),
Wad ever grace'd a dance o' witches !

But here my Muse her wing maun cour,
Sic flights are far beyond her power ;
To sing how Nannie lap and flang
(A souple jade she was and strang),

B.P.   O

And how Tam stood, like ane bewitch'd,
And thought his very een enrich'd;
Even Satan glowr'd, and fidg'd fu' fain,
And hotch'd and blew wi' might and main:
Till first ae caper, syne anither,
Tam tint his reason a' thegither,
And roars out, 'Weel done, Cutty-sark!'
And in an instant all was dark:
And scarcely had he Maggie rallied,
When out the hellish legion sallied.

As bees bizz out wi' angry fyke,
When plundering herds assail their byke;
As open pussie's mortal foes,
When, pop! she starts before their nose;
As eager runs the market-crowd,
When 'Catch the thief!' resounds aloud;
So Maggie runs, the witches follow,
Wi' mony an eldritch skriech and hollow.

Ah, Tam! ah, Tam! thou'll get thy fairin'!
In hell they'll roast thee like a herrin'!
In vain thy Kate awaits thy comin'!
Kate soon will be a woefu' woman!
Now, do thy speedy utmost, Meg,
And win the key-stane o' the brig;
There, at them thou thy tail may toss,
A running stream they dare na cross.
But ere the key-stane she could make,
The fient a tail she had to shake!
For Nannie, far before the rest,
Hard upon noble Maggie prest,
And flew at Tam wi' furious ettle;
But little wist she Maggie's mettle!
Ae spring brought off her master hale,
But left behind her ain grey tail:
The carlin caught her by the rump,
And left poor Maggie scarce a stump.

Now, wha this tale o' truth shall read,
Each man, and mother's son, take heed:
Whene'er to drink you are inclin'd,
Or Cutty-sarks rin in your mind,
Think! ye may buy the joys o'er dear,
Remember Tam o' Shanter's mare.

ON THE BIRTH OF A POSTHUMOUS CHILD

BORN IN PECULIAR CIRCUMSTANCES OF FAMILY DISTRESS

SWEET flow'ret, pledge o' meikle love,
    And ward o' mony a prayer,
What heart o' stane wad thou na move,
    Sae helpless, sweet, and fair.

November hirples o'er the lea,
    Chill, on thy lovely form:
And gane, alas! the shelt'ring tree,
    Should shield thee frae the storm.

May He who gives the rain to pour,
    And wings the blast to blaw,
Protect thee frae the driving show'r,
    The bitter frost and snaw.

May He, the friend o' Woe and Want,
    Who heals life's various stounds,
Protect and guard the mother plant,
    And heal her cruel wounds.

But late she flourish'd, rooted fast,
    Fair on the summer morn,
Now, feebly bends she, in the blast,
    Unshelter'd and forlorn.

Blest be thy bloom, thou lovely gem,
  Unscath'd by ruffian hand !
And from thee many a parent stem
  Arise to deck our land !

ELEGY ON THE LATE MISS BURNET OF
MONBODDO

LIFE ne'er exulted in so rich a prize,
As Burnet, lovely from her native skies;
Nor envious death so triumph'd in a blow,
As that which laid th' accomplish'd Burnet low.

Thy form and mind, sweet maid, can I forget ?
In richest ore the brightest jewel set !
In thee, high Heaven above was truest shown,
As by His noblest work the Godhead best is known.

In vain ye flaunt in summer's pride, ye groves;
  Thou crystal streamlet with thy flowery shore,
Ye woodland choir that chaunt your idle loves,
  Ye cease to charm—Eliza is no more.

Ye heathy wastes, immix'd with reedy ferns;
  Ye mossy streams, with sedge and rushes stor'd;
Ye rugged cliffs, o'erhanging dreary glens,
  To you I fly—ye with my soul accord.

Princes, whose cumb'rous pride was all their worth,
  Shall venal lays their pompous exit hail,
And thou, sweet excellence ! forsake our earth,
  And not a Muse with honest grief bewail ?

We saw thee shine in youth and beauty's pride,
  And Virtue's light, that beams beyond the spheres;
But, like the sun eclips'd at morning tide,
  Thou left us, darkling in a world of tears.

The parent's heart that nestled fond in thee,
  That heart how sunk, a prey to grief and care;
So deckt the woodbine sweet yon aged tree;
  So, from it ravish'd, leaves it bleak and bare.

LAMENT OF MARY, QUEEN OF SCOTS

ON THE APPROACH OF SPRING

Now Nature hangs her mantle green
  On every blooming tree,
And spreads her sheets o' daisies white
  Out o'er the grassy lea:
Now Phœbus cheers the crystal streams,
  And glads the azure skies;
But nought can glad the weary wight
  That fast in durance lies.

Now laverocks wake the merry morn
  Aloft on dewy wing;
The merle, in his noontide bow'r,
  Makes woodland echoes ring;
The mavis wild, wi' mony a note,
  Sings drowsy day to rest:
In love and freedom they rejoice,
  Wi' care nor thrall opprest.

Now blooms the lily by the bank,
  The primrose down the brae;
The hawthorn's budding in the glen,
  And milk-white is the slae:
The meanest hind in fair Scotland
  May rove thae sweets amang;
But I, the Queen of a' Scotland,
  Maun lie in prison strang.

I was the Queen o' bonie France,
    Where happy I hae been;
Fu' lightly rase I in the morn,
    As blythe lay down at e'en :
And I'm the sov'reign of Scotland,
    And mony a traitor there;
Yet here I lie in foreign bands,
    And never-ending care.

But as for thee, thou false woman,
    My sister and my fae,
Grim Vengeance yet shall whet a sword
    That thro' thy soul shall gae :
The weeping blood in woman's breast
    Was never known to thee;
Nor th' balm that drops on wounds of woe
    Frae woman's pitying e'e.

My son ! my son ! may kinder stars
    Upon thy fortune shine;
And may those pleasures gild thy reign,
    That ne'er wad blink on mine !
God keep thee frae thy mother's faes,
    Or turn their hearts to thee :
And where thou meet'st thy mother's friends,
    Remember him for me !

O ! soon, to me, may Summer suns
    Nae mair light up the morn !
Nae mair to me the Autumn winds
    Wave o'er the yellow corn !
And, in the narrow house of death,
    Let Winter round me rave;
And the next flow'rs that deck the Spring,
    Bloom on my peaceful grave !

HERE'LL NEVER BE PEACE TILL JAMIE COMES HAME

By yon Castle wa', at the close of the day,
I heard a man sing, tho' his head it was gray;
And as he was singing, the tears doon came,—
There'll never be peace till Jamie comes hame.

The Church is in ruins, the State is in jars,
Delusions, oppressions, and murderous wars,
We dare na weel say't, but we ken wha's to blame,—
There'll never be peace till Jamie comes hame.

My seven braw sons for Jamie drew sword,
But now I greet round their green beds in the yerd;
It brak the sweet heart o' my faithfu' auld dame.
There'll never be peace till Jamie comes hame.

Now life is a burden that bows me down,
Sin' I tint my bairns, and he tint his crown;
But till my last moments my words are the same—
There'll never be peace till Jamie comes hame.

OUT OVER THE FORTH

Out over the Forth, I look to the north;
    But what is the north and its Highlands to me?
The south nor the east gie ease to my breast,
    The far foreign land, or the wide rolling sea.

But I look to the west when I gae to rest,
    That happy my dreams and my slumbers may
        be;
For far in the west lives he I lo'e best,
    The man that is dear to my babie and me.

THE BANKS O' DOON

FIRST VERSION

SWEET are the banks—the banks o' Doon,
    The spreading flowers are fair,
And everything is blythe and glad,
    But I am fu' o' care.
Thou'll break my heart, thou bonie bird,
    That sings upon the bough;
Thou minds me o' the happy days
    When my fause Luve was true :
Thou'll break my heart, thou bonie bird,
    That sings beside thy mate;
For sae I sat, and sae I sang,
    And wist na o' my fate.

Aft hae I rov'd by bonie Doon,
    To see the woodbine twine;
And ilka bird sang o' its Luve,
    And sae did I o' mine :
Wi' lightsome heart I pu'd a rose,
    Upon its thorny tree;
But my fause Luver staw my rose,
    And left the thorn wi' me :
Wi' lightsome heart I pu'd a rose,
    Upon a morn in June;
And sae I flourished on the morn,
    And sae was pu'd or' noon !

THE BANKS O' DOON

SECOND VERSION

YE flowery banks o' bonie Doon,
    How can ye blume sae fair ?
How can ye chant, ye little birds,
    And I sae fu' o' care ?

Thou'll break my heart, thou bonie bird,
    That sings upon the bough;
Thou minds me o' the happy days
    When my fause Luve was true.
Thou'll break my heart, thou bonie bird,
    That sings beside thy mate;
For sae I sat, and sae I sang,
    And wist na o' my fate.

Aft hae I rov'd by bonie Doon,
    To see the woodbine twine;
And ilka bird sang o' its Luve,
    And sae did I o' mine :
Wi' lightsome heart I pu'd a rose,
    Upon a morn in June;
How like that rose my blooming morn,
    Sae darkly set ere noon !
Wi' lightsome heart I pu'd a rose,
    Upon its thorny tree;
But my fause Luver staw my rose,
    And left the thorn wi' me.

THE BANKS O' DOON

THIRD VERSION

YE banks and braes o' bonie Doon,
    How can ye bloom sae fresh and fair ?
How can ye chant, ye little birds,
    And I sae weary fu' o' care ?
Thou'll break my heart, thou warbling bird,
    That wantons thro' the flowering thorn :
Thou minds me o' departed joys,
    Departed never to return.

Aft hae I rov'd by bonie Doon,
    To see the rose and woodbine twine;
And ilka bird sang o' its Luve,
    And fondly sae did I o' mine;

Wi' lightsome heart I pu'd a rose,
    Fu' sweet upon its thorny tree!
And my fause Luver staw my rose,
    But ah! he left the thorn wi' me.

LAMENT FOR JAMES, EARL OF GLENCAIRN

The wind blew hollow frae the hills,
    By fits the sun's departing beam
Look'd on the fading yellow woods,
    That wav'd o'er Lugar's winding stream:
Beneath a craigy steep, a Bard,
    Laden with years and meikle pain,
In loud lament bewail'd his lord,
    Whom Death had all untimely taen.

He lean'd him to an ancient aik,
    Whose trunk was mould'ring down with years
His locks were bleachèd white with time,
    His hoary cheek was wet wi' tears:
And as he touch'd his trembling harp,
    And as he tun'd his doleful sang,
The winds, lamenting thro' their caves,
    To Echo bore the notes alang.

'Ye scatter'd birds that faintly sing,
    The reliques o' the vernal queire!
Ye woods that shed on a' the winds
    The honors o' the agèd year!
A few short months, and, glad and gay,
    Again ye'll charm the ear and e'e;
But nocht in all revolving time
    Can gladness bring again to me.

'I am a bending, agèd tree,
    That long has stood the wind and rain;
But now has come a cruel blast,
    And my last hold of earth is gane;
Nae leaf o' mine shall greet the spring,
    Nae simmer sun exalt my bloom;
But I maun lie before the storm,
    And others plant them in my room.

'I've seen sae mony changefu' years,
    On earth I am a stranger grown:
I wander in the ways of men,
    Alike unknowing, and unknown:
Unheard, unpitied, unreliev'd,
    I bear alane my lade o' care,
For silent, low, on beds of dust,
    Lie a' that would my sorrows share.

'And last (the sum of a' my griefs!)
    My noble master lies in clay;
The flow'r amang our barons bold,
    His country's pride, his country's stay:
In weary being now I pine,
    For a' the life of life is dead,
And hope has left my aged ken,
    On forward wing for ever fled.

'Awake thy last sad voice, my harp!
    The voice of woe and wild despair!
Awake, resound thy latest lay,
    Then sleep in silence evermair!
And thou, my last, best, only friend,
    That fillest an untimely tomb,
Accept this tribute from the Bard
    Thou brought from Fortune's mirkest gloom.

'In Poverty's low barren vale,
    Thick mists obscure, involv'd me round;
Though oft I turn'd the wistful eye,
    Nae ray of fame was to be found:

Thou found'st me, like the morning sun
    That melts the fogs in limpid air,
The friendless Bard and rustic song
    Became alike thy fostering care.

'O ! why has worth so short a date,
    While villains ripen gray with time !
Must thou, the noble, gen'rous, great,
    Fall in bold manhood's hardy prime !
Why did I live to see that day—
    A day to me so full of woe ?
O ! had I met the mortal shaft
    That laid my benefactor low !

'The bridegroom may forget the bride
    Was made his wedded wife yestreen;
The monarch may forget the crown
    That on his head an hour has been;
The mother may forget the child
    That smiles sae sweetly on her knee;
But I'll remember thee, Glencairn,
    And a' that thou hast done for me !'

LINES TO SIR JOHN WHITEFOORD, BART

SENT WITH THE FOREGOING POEM

THOU, who thy honor as thy God rever'st,
Who, save thy mind's reproach, nought earthly
    fear'st,
To thee this votive offering I impart,
The tearful tribute of a broken heart.
The *Friend* thou valued'st, I, the *Patron* lov'd;
His worth, his honor, all the world approved :
We'll mourn till we too go as he has gone,
And tread the shadowy path to that dark world
    unknown.

CRAIGIEBURN WOOD

SWEET closes the ev'ning on Craigieburn Wood,
  And blythely awaukens the morrow;
But the pride o' the spring on the Craigieburn
      Wood
  Can yield me nought but sorrow.

Chorus.—Beyond thee, dearie, beyond thee, dearie,
      And O to be lying beyond thee !
    O sweetly, soundly, weel may he sleep
      That's laid in the bed beyond thee !

I see the spreading leaves and flowers,
  I hear the wild birds singing;
But pleasure they hae nane for me,
  While care my heart is wringing.
      Beyond thee, etc.

I canna tell, I maunna tell,
  I daur na for your anger;
But secret love will break my heart,
  If I conceal it langer.
      Beyond thee, etc.

I see thee gracefu', straight and tall,
  I see thee sweet and bonie;
But oh, what will my torment be,
  If thou refuse thy Johnie !
      Beyond thee, etc.

To see thee in another's arms,
  In love to lie and languish,
'Twad be my dead, that will be seen,
  My heart wad burst wi' anguish.
      Beyond thee, etc.

But Jeanie, say thou wilt be mine,
　　Say thou lo'es nane before me;
And a' my days o' life to come
　　I'll gratefully adore thee.
　　　　Beyond thee, etc.

THE BONIE WEE THING

Chorus.—Bonie wee thing, cannie wee thing,
　　　　Lovely wee thing, wert thou mine,
　　I wad wear thee in my bosom,
　　　　Lest my jewel it should tine.

WISHFULLY I look and languish
　　In that bonie face o' thine,
And my heart it stounds wi' anguish,
　　Lest my wee thing be na mine.
　　　　Bonie wee thing, etc.

Wit and Grace, and Love, and Beauty,
　　In ae constellation shine;
To adore thee is my duty,
　　Goddess o' this soul o' mine!
　　　　Bonie wee thing, etc.

EPIGRAM ON MISS DAVIES

ON BEING ASKED WHY SHE HAD BEEN FORMED SO
　　LITTLE, AND MRS A—— SO BIG

ASK why God made the gem so small?
And why so huge the granite?—
Because God meant mankind should set
　　That higher value on it.

THE CHARMS OF LOVELY DAVIES

O how shall I, unskilfu', try
    The poet's occupation ?
The tunefu' powers, in happy hours,
    That whisper inspiration;
Even they maun dare an effort mair
    Than aught they ever gave us,
Ere they rehearse, in equal verse,
    The charms o' lovely Davies.

Each eye, it cheers when she appears,
    Like Phœbus in the morning.
When past the shower, and every flower
    The garden is adorning;
As the wretch looks o'er Siberia's shore,
    When winter-bound the wave is;
Sae droops our heart, when we maun part
    Frae charming, lovely Davies.

Her smile's a gift frae 'boon the lift,
    That maks us mair than princes;
A sceptred hand, a king's command,
    Is in her darting glances;
The man in arms 'gainst female charms,
    Even he her willing slave is,
He hugs his chain, and owns the reign
    Of conquering, lovely Davies.

My Muse ! to dream of such a theme,
    Thy feeble powers surrender :
The eagle's gaze alone surveys
    The sun's meridian splendor.
I wad in vain essay the strain,
    The deed too daring brave is;
I'll drap the lyre, and mute admire
    The charms o' lovely Davies.

WHAT CAN A YOUNG LASSIE DO WI' AN AULD MAN?

WHAT can a young lassie, what shall a young lassie,
    What can a young lassie do wi' an auld man?
Bad luck on the penny that tempted my minnie
    To sell her puir Jenny for siller an' lan'!
Bad luck on the penny that tempted my minnie
    To sell her puir Jenny for siller an' lan'!

He's always compleenin' frae mornin' to e'enin',
    He hoasts and he hirples the weary day lang;
He's doylt and he's dozin', his blude it is frozen,—
    O dreary's the night wi' a crazy auld man!
He's doylt and he's dozin', his blude it is frozen,
    O dreary's the night wi' a crazy auld man.

He hums and he hankers, he frets and he cankers,
    I never can please him, do a' that I can;
He's peevish an' jealous o' a' the young fellows,—
    O dool on the day I met wi' an auld man!
He's peevish an' jealous o' a' the young fellows,
    O dool on the day I met wi' an auld man.

My auld auntie Katie upon me taks pity,
    I'll do my endeavour to follow her plan;
I'll cross him an' wrack him, until I heartbreak him,
    And then his auld brass 'ill buy me a new pan!
I'll cross him an' wrack him, until I heartbreak him,
    And then his auld brass 'ill buy me a new pan.

THE POSIE

O LUVE will venture in where it daur na weel be seen,
O luve will venture in where wisdom ance hath been;
But I will doun yon river rove, amang the wood sae
    green,
    And a' to pu' a Posie to my ain dear May.

The primrose I will pu', the firstling o' the year,
And I will pu' the pink, the emblem o' my dear;
For she's the pink o' womankind, and blooms without
    a peer,
  And a' to be a Posie to my ain dear May.

I'll pu' the budding rose, when Phœbus peeps in
    view,
For it's like a baumy kiss o' her sweet, bonie mou';
The hyacinth's for constancy wi' its unchanging blue,
  And a' to be a Posie to my ain dear May.

The lily it is pure, and the lily it is fair,
And in her lovely bosom I'll place the lily there;
The daisy's for simplicity and unaffected air,
  And a' to be a Posie to my ain dear May.

The hawthorn I will pu', wi' its locks o' siller gray,
Where, like an aged man, it stands at break o' day;
But the songster's nest within the bush I winna tak
    away,
  And a' to be a Posie to my ain dear May.

The woodbine I will pu', when the e'ening star is
    near,
And the diamond draps o' dew shall be her een sae
    clear;
The violet's for modesty, which weel she fa's to wear,
  And a' to be a Posie to my ain dear May.

I'll tie the Posie round wi' the silken band o' luve,
And I'll place it in her breast, and I'll swear by a'
    above,
That to my latest draught o' life the band shall ne'er
    remove,
  And this will be a Posie to my ain dear May.

ON GLENRIDDELL'S FOX BREAKING HIS CHAIN

A FRAGMENT, 1791

THOU, Liberty, thou art my theme;
Not such as idle poets dream,
Who trick thee up a heathen goddess
That a fantastic cap and rod has;
Such stale conceits are poor and silly;
I paint thee out, a Highland filly,
A sturdy, stubborn, handsome dapple,
As sleek's a mouse, as round's an apple,
That when thou pleasest can do wonders;
But when thy luckless rider blunders,
Or if thy fancy should demur there,
Wilt break thy neck ere thou go further.

These things premised, I sing—a Fox
Was caught among his native rocks,
And to a dirty kennel chained,
How he his liberty regained.

Glenriddell! a Whig without a stain,
A Whig in principle and grain,
Couldst thou enslave a free-born creature,
A native denizen of Nature?
How couldst thou, with a heart so good
(A better ne'er was sluiced with blood),
Nail a poor devil to a tree,
That ne'er did harm to thine or thee?

The staunchest Whig Glenriddel was,
Quite frantic in his country's cause;
And oft was Reynard's prison passing,
And with his brother-Whigs canvassing
The Rights of Men, the Powers of Women,
With all the dignity of Freemen.

    Sir Reynard daily heard debates
Of Princes', Kings', and Nations' fates,
With many rueful, bloody stories
Of Tyrants, Jacobites, and Tories:
From liberty how angels fell,
That now are galley-slaves in hell;
How Nimrod first the trade began
Of binding Slavery's chains on Man;

How fell Semiramis—G—d d—mn her!
Did first, with sacrilegious hammer
(And ills till then were trivial matters),
For Man dethron'd forge hen-peck fetters,
How Xerxes, that abandoned Tory,
Thought cutting throats was reaping glory,
Until the stubborn Whigs of Sparta
Taught him great Nature's Magna Charta;
How mighty Rome her fiat hurl'd
Resistless o'er a bowing world,
And, kinder than they did desire,
Polish'd mankind with sword and fire;
With much, too tedious to relate,
Of ancient and of modern date,
But ending still, how Billy Pitt
(Unlucky boy!) with wicked wit,
Has gagg'd old Britain, drain'd her coffer,
As butchers bind and bleed a heifer.

    Thus wily Reynard, by degrees,
In kennel listening at his ease,
Suck'd in a mighty stock of knowledge,
As much as some folks at a College;
Knew Britain's rights and constitution,
Her aggrandisement, diminution,
How fortune wrought us good from evil;
Let no man, then, despise the Devil,
As who should say, 'I ne'er can need him',
Since we to scoundrels owe our freedom.

   .   .   .   .   .

CALEDONIA—A BALLAD

Tune—'Caledonian Hunt's Delight' of Mr Gow.

THERE was once a time, but old Time was then young
   That brave Caledonia, the chief of her line,
From some of your northern deities sprung,
   (Who knows not that brave Caledonia's divine?)
From Tweed to the Orcades was her domain,
   To hunt, or to pasture, or do what she would:
Her heav'nly relations there fixèd her reign,
   And pledg'd her their godheads to warrant it good.

A lambkin in peace, but a lion in war,
   The pride of her kindred, the heroine grew:
Her grandsire, old Odin, triumphantly swore,—
   'Whoe'er shall provoke thee, th' encounter shall rue
With tillage or pasture at times she would sport,;
   To feed her fair flocks by her green rustling corn
But chiefly the woods were her fav'rite resort,
   Her darling amusement, the hounds and the horn.

Long quiet she reigned; till thitherward steers
   A flight of bold eagles from Adria's strand:
Repeated, successive, for many long years,
   They darken'd the air, and they plunder'd the land
Their pounces were murder, and terror their cry,
   They'd conquer'd and ruin'd a world beside;
She took to her hills, and her arrows let fly,
   The daring invaders, they fled or they died.

The Cameleon-Savage disturb'd her repose,
   With tumult, disquiet, rebellion, and strife;
Provok'd beyond bearing, at last she arose,
   And robb'd him at once of his hopes and his life:
The Anglian lion, the terror of France,
   Oft prowling, ensanguin'd the Tweed's silver flood
But, taught by the bright Caledonian lance,
   He learnèd to fear in his own native wood.

The fell Harpy-raven took wing from the north,
    The scourge of the seas, and the dread of the shore;
The wild Scandinavian boar issued forth
    To wanton in carnage and wallow in gore :
O'er countries and kingdoms their fury prevail'd,
    No arts could appease them, no arms could repel;
But brave Caledonia in vain they assail'd,
    As Largs well can witness, and Loncartie tell.

Thus bold, independent, unconquer'd, and free,
    Her bright course of glory for ever shall run :
For brave Caledonia immortal must be;
    I'll prove it from Euclid as clear as the sun :
Rectangle-triangle, the figure we'll chuse :
    The upright is Chance, and old Time is the base;
But brave Caledonia's the hypothenuse;
    Then, ergo, she'll match them, and match them
        always.

POEM ON PASTORAL POETRY

HAIL, Poesie ! thou Nymph reserv'd !
In chase o' thee, what crowds hae swerv'd
Frae common sense, or sunk enerv'd
        'Mang heaps o' clavers :
And och ! o'er aft thy joes hae starv'd,
        'Mid a' thy favors !

Say, lassie, why thy train amang,
While loud the trump's heroic clang,
And sock or buskin skelp alang
        To death or marriage;
Scarce ane has tried the shepherd-sang
        But wi' miscarriage ?

In Homer's craft Jock Milton thrives;
Æschylus' pen Will Shakespeare drives;
Wee Pope, the knurlin, till him rives
      Horatian fame;
In thy sweet sang, Barbauld, survives
      Even Sappho's flame.

But thee, Theocritus, wha matches?
They're no herd's ballats, Maro's catches;
Squire Pope but busks his skinklin' patches
      O' heathen tatters:
I pass by hunders, nameless wretches,
      That ape their betters.

In this braw age o' wit and lear,
Will nane the Shepherd's whistle mair
Blaw sweetly in its native air,
      And rural grace;
And, wi' the far-famed Grecian, share
      A rival place?

Yes! there is ane; a Scottish callan'!
There's ane; come forrit, honest Allan!
Thou need na jouk behint the hallan,
      A chiel sae clever;
The teeth o' time may gnaw Tantallan,
      But thou's for ever.

Thou paints auld Nature to the nines,
In thy sweet Caledonian lines;
Nae gowden stream thro' myrtles twines,
      Where Philomel,
While nightly breezes sweep the vines,
      Her griefs will tell!

In gowany glens thy burnie strays,
Where bonie lasses bleach their claes,
Or trots by hazelly shaws and braes,
      Wi' hawthorns gray,
Where blackbirds join the shepherd's lays,
      At close o' day.

Thy rural loves are Nature's sel ;
Nae bombast spates o' nonsense swell;
Nae snap conceits, but that sweet spell
    O' witchin' love,
That charm that can the strongest quell,
    The sternest move.

VERSES ON THE DESTRUCTION OF THE WOODS NEAR DRUMLANRIG

As on the banks of winding Nith,
    Ae smiling simmer morn I stray'd,
And traced its bonie holms and haughs,
    Where linties sang and lammies play'd,
I sat me down upon a craig,
    And drank my fill o' fancy's dream
When from the eddying deep below,
    Up rose the genius of the stream.

Dark, like the frowning rock, his brow,
    And troubled, like his wintry wave,
And deep, as sughs the boding wind
    Amang his caves, the sigh he gave—
'And come ye here, my son,' he cried,
    'To wander in my birken shade ?
To muse some favourite Scottish theme,
    Or sing some favourite Scottish maid ?

'There was a time, it's nae lang syne,
    Ye might hae seen me in my pride,
When a' my banks sae bravely saw
    Their woody pictures in my tide;
When hanging beech and spreading elm
    Shaded my stream sae clear and cool :
And stately oaks their twisted arms
    Threw broad and dark across the pool;

'When, glinting thro' the trees appear'd
    The wee white cot aboon the mill,
And peacefu' rose its ingle reek,
    That, slowly curling, clamb the hill.
But now the cot is bare and cauld
    Its leafy bield for ever gane,
And scarce a stinted birk is left
    To shiver in the blast its lane.'

'Alas! quoth I, 'what ruefu' chance
    Has twin'd ye o' your stately trees?
Has laid your rocky bosom bare—
    Has stripped the cleeding aff your braes?
Was it the bitter eastern blast,
    That scatters blight in early spring?
Or was 't the wil'fire scorch'd their boughs,
    Or canker-worm wi' secret sting?'

'Nae eastlin' blast,' the sprite replied;
    'It blaws na here sae fierce and fell,
And on my dry and halesome banks
    Nae canker-worms get leave to dwell:
Man! cruel man! the genius sighed—
    As through the cliffs he sank him down—
'The worm that gnaw'd my bonie trees,
    That reptile wears a Ducal crown.'

THE GALLANT WEAVER

WHERE Cart rins rowin' to the sea,
By mony a flower and spreading tree,
There lives a lad, the lad for me,
    He is a gallant Weaver.
O I had wooers aught or nine,
They gied me rings and ribbons fine;
And I was fear'd my heart wad tine,
    And I gied it to the Weaver.

My daddie sign'd my tocher-band,
To gie the lad that has the land,
But to my heart I'll add my hand,
   And give it to the Weaver.
While birds rejoice in leafy bowers,
While bees delight in opening flowers,
While corn grows green in summer showers,
   I'll love my gallant Weaver.

EPIGRAM AT BROWNHILL INN

AT Brownhill we always get dainty good cheer,
And plenty of bacon each day in the year;
We've a' thing that's nice, and mostly in season,
But why always Bacon—come tell me the reason?

YOU'RE WELCOME, WILLIE STEWART

Chorus.—You're welcome, Willie Stewart,
     You're welcome, Willie Stewart,
      There's ne'er a flower that blooms in May,
      That's half sae welcome's thou art!

COME, bumpers high, express your joy,
   The bowl we maun renew it,
The tappet hen, gae bring her ben,
   To welcome Willie Stewart.
      You're welcome, Willie Stewart, etc.

May foes be strang, and friends be slack,
   Ilk action, may he rue it,
May woman on him turn her back
   That wrangs thee, Willie Stewart!
      You're welcome, Willie Stewart, etc.

LOVELY POLLY STEWART

Chorus.—O lovely Polly Stewart,
　　　　O charming Polly Stewart,
　　　　There's ne'er a flower that blooms in Ma
　　　　That's half so fair as thou art !

THE flower it blaws, it fades, it fa's,
　　And art can ne'er renew it;
But worth and truth, eternal youth
　　Will gie to Polly Stewart.
　　　　O lovely Polly Stewart, etc.

May he whase arms shall fauld thy charms
　　Possess a leal and true heart !
To him be given to ken the heaven
　　He grasps in Polly Stewart !
　　　　O lovely Polly Stewart, etc.

DAMON AND SYLVIA

Tune—'The Tither Morn.'

YON wandering rill that marks the hill,
　　And glances o'er the brae, Sir,
Slides by a bower, where mony a flower
　　Sheds fragrance on the day, Sir;
There Damon lay with Sylvia gay,
　　To love they thought no crime, Sir;
The wild birds sang, the echoes rang,
　　While Damon's heart beat time, Sir.

COCK UP YOUR BEAVER

WHEN first my brave Johnie lad came to the town,
He had a blue bonnet that wanted the crown;
But now he has gotten a hat and a feather,
Hey, brave Johnie lad, cock up your beaver!

Cock up your beaver, and cock it fu' sprush,
We'll over the border and gie them a brush;
There's somebody there we'll teach better behaviour,
Hey, brave Johnie lad, cock up your beaver!

MY EPPIE MACNAB

O SAW ye my dearie, my Eppie Macnab?
O saw ye my dearie, my Eppie Macnab?
   She's down in the yard, she's kissin' the laird,
She winna come hame to her ain Jock Rab.

O come thy ways to me, my Eppie Macnab;
O come thy ways to me, my Eppie Macnab;
   Whate'er thou hast dune, be it late, be it sune,
Thou's welcome again to thy ain Jock Rab.

What says she, my dearie, my Eppie Macnab?
What says she, my dearie, my Eppie Macnab?
   She let's thee to wit that she has thee forgot,
And forever disowns thee, her ain Jock Rab.

O had I ne'er seen thee, my Eppie Macnab!
O had I ne'er seen thee, my Eppie Macnab!
   As light as the air, and as fause as thou's fair,
Thou's broken the heart o' thy ain Jock Rab.

ALTHO' HE HAS LEFT ME

ALTHO' he has left me for greed o' the siller,
    I dinna envy him the gains he can win;
I rather wad bear a' the lade o' my sorrow,
    Than ever hae acted sae faithless to him.

MY TOCHER'S THE JEWEL

O MEIKLE thinks my luve o' my beauty,
    And meikle thinks my luve o' my kin;
But little thinks my luve I ken brawlie
    My tocher's the jewel has charms for him.
It's a' for the apple he'll nourish the tree,
    It's a' for the hiney he'll cherish the bee,
My laddie's sae meikle in luve wi' the siller,
    He canna hae luve to spare for me.

Your proffer o' luve's an airle-penny,
    My tocher's the bargain ye wad buy;
But an ye be crafty, I am cunnin',
    Sae ye wi' anither your fortune may try.
Ye're like to the timmer o' yon rotten wood,
    Ye're like to the bark o' yon rotten tree,
Ye'll slip frae me like a knotless thread,
    And ye'll crack your credit wi' mair nor me.

O FOR ANE AN' TWENTY, TAM

Chorus.—An' O for ane an' twenty, Tam !
            And hey, sweet ane an' twenty, Tam !
        I'll learn my kin a rattlin' sang,
            An' I saw ane an' twenty, Tam.

THEY snool me sair, and haud me doon,
  An' gar me look like bluntie, Tam;
But three short years will soon wheel roon',
  An' then comes ane an' twenty, Tam.
     An' O for, etc.

A glieb o' lan', a claut o' gear,
  Was left me· by my Auntie, Tam;
At kith or kin I need na spier,
  An I saw ane an' twenty, Tam.
     An' O for, etc.

They'll hae me wed a wealthy coof,
  Tho' I mysel hae plenty, Tam;
But hear'st thou, laddie! there's my loof,
  I'm thine at ane an' twenty, Tam.
     An' O for, etc.

THOU FAIR ELIZA

TURN again, thou fair Eliza!
  Ae kind blink before we part;
Rue on thy despairing lover,
  Canst thou break his faithfu' heart?
Turn again, thou fair Eliza!
  If to love thy heart denies,
Oh, in pity hide the sentence
  Under friendship's kind disguise!

Thee, sweet maid, hae I offended?
  My offence is loving thee;
Canst thou wreck his peace for ever,
  Wha for thine would gladly die?

While the life beats in my bosom,
   Thou shalt mix in ilka throe :
Turn again, thou lovely maiden,
   Ae sweet smile on me bestow.

Not the bee upon the blossom,
   In the pride o' sinny noon;
Not the little sporting fairy,
   All beneath the simmer moon;
Not the Minstrel, in the moment
   Fancy lightens in his e'e,
Kens the pleasure, feels the rapture,
   That thy presence gies to me.

MY BONIE BELL

THE smiling Spring comes in rejoicing,
   And surly Winter grimly flies;
Now crystal clear are the falling waters,
   And bonie blue are the sunny skies.
Fresh o'er the mountains breaks forth the
     morning,
   The ev'ning gilds the ocean's swell;
All creatures joy in the sun's returning,
   And I rejoice in my Bonie Bell.

The flowery Spring leads sunny Summer,
   The yellow Autumn presses near;
Then in his turn comes gloomy Winter,
   Till smiling Spring again appear :
Thus seasons dancing, life advancing,
   Old Time and Nature their changes tell;
But never ranging, still unchanging,
   I adore my Bonie Bell.

SWEET AFTON

I charge you, O ye daughters of Jerusalem, that ye stir
ot, nor awake my love—my dove, my undefiled! The
owers appear on the earth, the time of the singing of the
irds is come, and the voice of the turtle is heard in our land.

Flow gently, sweet Afton! among thy green braes,
Flow gently, I'll sing thee a song in thy praise;
My Mary's asleep by thy murmuring stream,
Flow gently, sweet Afton, disturb not her dream.

Thou stock-dove whose echo resounds thro' the glen,
Ye wild whistling blackbirds, in yon thorny den,
Thou green-crested lapwing thy screaming forbear,
I charge you, disturb not my slumbering Fair.

How lofty, sweet Afton, thy neighbouring hills,
Far mark'd with the courses of clear, winding rills;
There daily I wander as noon rises high,
My flocks and my Mary's sweet cot in my eye.

How pleasant thy banks and green valleys below,
Where, wild in the woodlands, the primroses blow;
There oft, as mild Ev'ning weeps over the lea,
The sweet-scented birk shades my Mary and me.

Thy crystal stream, Afton, how lovely it glides,
And winds by the cot where my Mary resides;
How wanton thy waters her snowy feet lave,
As, gathering sweet flowerets, she stems thy clear
    wave.

Flow gently, sweet Afton, among thy green braes,
Flow gently, sweet river, the theme of my lays;
My Mary's asleep by thy murmuring stream,
Flow gently, sweet Afton, disturb not her dream.

ADDRESS TO THE SHADE OF THOMSON

ON CROWNING HIS BUST AT EDNAM, ROXBURGHSHIRE WITH A WREATH OF BAYS

WHILE virgin Spring by Eden's flood,
   Unfolds her tender mantle green,
Or pranks the sod in frolic mood,
   Or tunes Eolian strains between.

While Summer, with a matron grace,
   Retreats to Dryburgh's cooling shade,
Yet oft, delighted, stops to trace
   The progress of the spikey blade.

While Autumn, benefactor kind,
   By Tweed erects his aged head,
And sees, with self-approving mind,
   Each creature on his bounty fed.

While maniac Winter rages o'er
   The hills whence classic Yarrow flows,
Rousing the turbid torrent's roar,
   Or sweeping, wild, a waste of snows.

So long, sweet Poet of the year!
   Shall bloom that wreath thou well hast won
While Scotia, with exulting tear,
   Proclaims that THOMSON is her son.

NITHSDALE'S WELCOME HAME

THE noble Maxwells and their powers
   Are coming o'er the border,
And they'll gae big Terreagles' towers,
   And set them a' in order

And they declare Terreagles fair,
    For their abode they choose it;
There's no a heart in a' the land
    But's lighter at the news o't.

Tho' stars in skies may disappear,
    And angry tempests gather;
The happy hour may soon be near
    That brings us pleasant weather:
The weary night o' care and grief
    May hae a joyfu' morrow;
So dawning day has brought relief,
    Fareweel our night o' sorrow.

FRAE THE FRIENDS AND LAND I LOVE

FRAE the friends and land I love,
    Driv'n by Fortune's felly spite;
Frae my best belov'd I rove,
    Never mair to taste delight:
Never mair maun hope to find
    Ease frae toil, relief frae care;
When Remembrance wracks the mind,
    Pleasures but unveil despair.

Brightest climes shall mirk appear,
    Desert ilka blooming shore,
Till the Fates, nae mair severe,
    Friendship, love, and peace restore.
Till Revenge, wi' laurel'd head,
    Bring our banished hame again;
And ilk loyal, bonie lad
    Cross the seas, and win his ain.

SUCH A PARCEL OF ROGUES IN A NATIO.

FAREWEEL to a' our Scottish fame,
    Fareweel our ancient glory;
Fareweel ev'n to the Scottish name,
    Sae fam'd in martial story.
Now Sark rins over Solway sands,
    An' Tweed rins to the ocean,
To mark where England's province stands—
    Such a parcel of rogues in a nation !

What force or guile could not subdue,
    Thro' many warlike ages,
Is wrought now by a coward few,
    For hireling traitor's wages.
The English steel we could disdain,
    Secure in valour's station;
But English gold has been our bane—
    Such a parcel of rogues in a nation !

O would, ere I had seen the day
    That Treason thus could sell us,
My auld grey head had lien in clay,
    Wi' Bruce and loyal Wallace !
But pith and power, till my last hour,
    I'll mak this declaration;
We're bought and sold for English gold—
    Such a parcel of rogues in a nation !

YE JACOBITES BY NAME

YE Jacobites by name, give an ear, give an ear,
Ye Jacobites by name, give an ear,
    Ye Jacobites by name,
    Your fautes I will proclaim,
Your doctrines I maun blame, you shall hear.

What is Right, and What is Wrang, by the law,
    by the law ?
What is Right, and what is Wrang, by the law ?
  What is Right, and what is Wrang ?
  A short sword, and a lang,
A weak arm and a strang, for to draw.

What makes heroic strife, famed afar, famed afar ?
What makes heroic strife, famed afar ?
  What makes heroic strife ?
  To whet th' assassin's knife,
Or hunt a Parent's life, wi' bluidy war ?

Then let your schemes alone, in the state, in the
    state,
Then let your schemes alone, in the state.
  Then let your schemes alone,
  Adore the rising sun,
And leave a man undone, to his fate.

I HAE BEEN AT CROOKIEDEN

I HAE been at Crookieden,
  My bonie laddie, Highland laddie,
Viewing Willie and his men,
  My bonie laddie, Highland laddie.
There our foes that burnt and slew,
  My bonie laddie, Highland laddie,
There, at last, they gat their due,
  My bonie laddie, Highland laddie.

Satan sits in his black neuk,
  My bonie laddie, Highland laddie,
Breaking sticks to roast the Duke,
  My bonie laddie, Highland laddie.

The bloody monster gae a yell,
  My bonie laddie, Highland laddie,
And loud the laugh gied round a' hell,
  My bonie laddie, Highland laddie.

KENMURE'S ON AND AWA', WILLIE

O KENMURE's on and awa', Willie,
  O Kenmure's on and awa';
An' Kenmure's lord's the bravest lord
  That ever Galloway saw.
Success to Kenmure's band, Willie!
  Success to Kenmure's band!
There's no a heart that fears a Whig,
  That rides by Kenmure's hand.

Here's Kenmure's health in wine, Willie!
  Here's Kenmure's health in wine!
There's ne'er a coward o' Kenmure's blude,
  Nor yet o' Gordon's line.
O Kenmure's lads are men, Willie,
  O Kenmure's lads are men;
Their hearts and swords are metal true,
  And that their foes shall ken.

They'll live or die wi' fame, Willie,
  They'll live or die wi' fame;
But sune, wi' sounding victorie,
  May Kenmure's lord come hame!
Here's him that's far awa', Willie!
  Here's him that's far awa'!
And here's the flower that I lo'e best,
  The rose that's like the snaw.

EPISTLE TO JOHN MAXWELL, ESQ., OF TERRAUGHTY

ON HIS SEVENTY-FIRST BIRTHDAY

HEALTH to the Maxwell's veteran Chief!
Health, ay unsour'd by care or grief:
Inspir'd, I turn'd Fate's sibyl leaf,
      This natal morn,
I see thy life is stuff o' prief,
      Scarce quite half-worn.

This day thou metes threescore eleven,
And I can tell that bounteous Heaven,
(The second-sight, ye ken, is given
      To ilka Poet)
On thee a tack o' seven times seven
      Will yet bestow it.

If envious buckies view wi' sorrow
Thy lengthen'd days on this blest morrow,
May Desolation's lang-teeth'd harrow,
      Nine miles an hour,
Rake them, like Sodom and Gomorrah,
      In brunstane stoure.

But for thy friends, and they are mony,
Baith honest men, and lasses bonie,
May couthie Fortune, kind and cannie,
      In social glee,
Wi' mornings blythe, and e'enings funny,
      Bless them and thee!

Fareweel, auld birkie! Lord be near ye,
And then the deil, he daurna steer ye:
Your friends ay love, your faes ay fear ye;
      For me, shame fa' me,
If neist my heart I dinna wear ye,
      While BURNS they ca' me.

SECOND EPISTLE TO ROBERT GRAHAM, ESQ OF FINTRY

OCTOBER 5, 1791

LATE crippl'd of an arm, and now a leg,
About to beg a pass for leave to beg;
Dull, listless, teas'd, dejected, and deprest
(Nature is adverse to a cripple's rest);
Will generous Graham list to his Poet's wail?
(It soothes poor Misery, hearkening to her tale)
And hear him curse the light he first survey'd,
And doubly curse the luckless rhyming trade?

Thou, Nature! partial Nature, I arraign;
Of thy caprice maternal I complain:
The lion and the bull thy care have found,
One shakes the forests, and one spurns the groun
Thou giv'st the ass his hide, the snail his shell;
Th' envenom'd wasp, victorious, guards his cell
Thy minions kings defend, control, devour,
In all th' omnipotence of rule and power;
Foxes and statesmen subtile wiles ensure;
The cit and pole cat stink, and are secure;
Toads with their poison, doctors with their dru
The priest and hedgehog in their robes, are snu
Ev'n silly woman has her warlike arts,
Her tongue and eyes—her dreaded spear and dar

But oh! thou bitter step-mother and hard,
To thy poor, fenceless, naked child—the Bard
A thing unteachable in world's skill,
And half an idiot too, more helpless still:
No heels to bear him from the op'ning dun;
No claws to dig, his hated sight to shun;
No horns, but those by luckless Hymen worn,
And those, alas! not, Amalthea's horn:

No nerves olfact'ry, Mammon's trusty cur,
Clad in rich Dulness' comfortable fur;
In naked feeling, and in aching pride,
He bears th' unbroken blast from ev'ry side :
Vampyre booksellers drain him to the heart,
And scorpion critics cureless venom dart :

Critics—appall'd, I venture on the name;
Those cut-throat bandits in the paths of fame :
Bloody dissectors, worse than ten Monroes;
He hacks to teach, they mangle to expose :

His heart by causeless wanton malice wrung,
By blockheads' daring into madness stung;
His well-won bays, than life itself more dear,
By miscreants torn, who ne'er one sprig must wear;
Foil'd. bleeding, tortur'd in th' unequal strife,
The hapless Poet flounders on thro' life :
Till, fled each hope that once his bosom fir'd,
And fled each muse that glorious once inspir'd,
Low sunk in squalid, unprotected age,
Dead even resentment for his injur'd page,
He heeds or feels no more the ruthless critic's rage !
So, by some hedge, the gen'rous steed deceas'd,
For half-starv'd snarling curs a dainty feast;
By toil and famine worn to skin and bone,
Lies, senseless of each tugging bitch's son.

O Dulness ! portion of the truly blest !
Calm shelter'd haven of eternal rest !
Thy sons ne'er madden in the fierce extremes
Of Fortune's polar frost, or torrid beams.
If mantling high she fills the golden cup,
With sober selfish ease they sip it up;
Conscious the bounteous meed they well deserve,
They only wonder 'some folks' do not starve.
The grave sage hern thus easy picks his frog,
And thinks the mallard a sad worthless dog.

When disappointment snaps the clue of hope,
And thro' disastrous night they darkling grope,
With deaf endurance sluggishly they bear,
And just conclude 'that fools are fortune's care
So, heavy, passive to the tempest's shocks,
Strong on the sign-post stands the stupid ox.

Not so the idle Muses' mad-cap train,
Not such the workings of their moon-struck brai
In equanimity they never dwell.
By turns in soaring heav'n, or vaulted hell.

I dread thee, Fate, relentless and severe,
With all a poet's, husband's, father's fear !
Already one strong hold of hope is lost—
Glencairn, the truly noble, lies in dust
(Fled, like the sun eclips'd as noon appears,
And left us darkling in a world of tears);
O ! hear my ardent, grateful, selfish pray'r !
Fintry, my other stay, long bless and spare !
Thro' a long life his hopes and wishes drown,
And bright in cloudless skies his sun go down
May bliss domestic smooth his private path;
Give energy to life; and soothe his latest brea
With many a filial tear circling the bed of deat

THE SONG OF DEATH

Scene.—A Field of Battle—Time of the day, evenin
The wounded and dying of the victorious army are suppo
to join in the following song.

FAREWELL, thou fair day, thou green earth and
skies,
Now gay with the broad setting sun;
Farewell, loves and friendships, ye dear tender ties
Our race of existence is run !

hou Grim King of Terrors; thou Life's gloomy foe!
  Go, frighten the coward and slave;
o, teach them to tremble, fell tyrant! but know
  No terrors hast thou to the brave!

hou strik'st the dull peasant—he sinks in the dark,
  Nor saves e'en the wreck of a name;
hou strik'st the young hero—a glorious mark·
  He falls in the blaze of his fame!
a the field of proud honour—our swords in our hands,
  Our king and our country to save;
/hile victory shines on Life's last ebbing sands,—
  O who would not die with the brave?

POEM ON SENSIBILITY

SENSIBILITY, how charming,
  Dearest Nancy, thou canst tell;
But distress, with horrors arming,
  Thou alas! hast known too well!

Fairest flower, behold the lily
  Blooming in the sunny ray;
Let the blast sweep o'er the valley,
  See it prostrate in the clay.

Hear the woodlark charm the forest,
  Telling o'er his little joys;
But alas! a prey the surest
  To each pirate of the skies.

Dearly bought the hidden treasure
  Finer feelings can bestow:
Chords that vibrate sweetest pleasure,
  Thrill the deepest notes of woe.

VERSICLES

THE TOADEATER

Of lordly acquaintance you boast,
    And the Dukes that you dined with yestreen
Why, an insect's an insect at most,
    Tho' it crawl on the curl of a Queen!

IN THE KIRK OF LAMINGTON

As cauld a wind as ever blew,
A caulder kirk, and in't but few:
A caulder Preacher never spak—
Ye'se a' be het or I come back.

THE KEEKIN' GLASS

How daur ye ca' me 'Howlet-face'?
    Ye blear-e'ed, withered spectre!
Ye only spied the keekin'-glass,
    An' there ye saw your picture.

A GRACE BEFORE DINNER—EXTEMPORE

O Thou who kindly dost provide
    For every creature's want!
We bless Thee, God of Nature wide,
    For all Thy goodness lent:

And if it please Thee, heavenly Guide,
    May never worse be sent;
But, whether granted or denied,
    Lord, bless us with content.   Amen!

A GRACE AFTER DINNER—EXTEMPORE

O THOU, in whom we live and move—
    Who made the sea and shore;
Thy goodness constantly we prove,
    And, grateful, would adore:

And, if it please Thee, Power above!
    Still grant us, with such store,
The friend we trust, the fair we love—
    And we desire no more.   Amen!

THE DEAREST O' THE QUORUM

O MAY, thy morn was ne'er sae sweet
    As the mirk night o' December!
For sparkling was the rosy wine,
    And private was the chamber:
And dear was she I dare na name,
    But I will ay remember:
And dear was she I dare na name,
    But I will ay remember.

And here's to them that, like oursel,
    Can push about the jorum!
And here's to them that wish us weel,
    May a' that's gude watch o'er 'em!
And here's to them, we dare na tell,
    The dearest o' the quorum!
And here's to them, we dare na tell,
    The dearest o' the quorum.

PARTING SONG TO CLARINDA

Ae fond kiss, and then we sever;
Ae fareweel, and then for ever!
Deep in heart-wrung tears I'll pledge thee,
Warring sighs and groans I'll wage thee,
Who shall say that Fortune grieves him,
While the star of hope she leaves him?
Me, nae cheerful twinkle lights me;
Dark despair around benights me.

I'll ne'er blame my partial fancy,
Naething could resist my Nancy:
But to see her was to love her;
Love but her, and love for ever.
Had we never lov'd sae kindly,
Had we never lov'd sae blindly,
Never met—or never parted,
We had ne'er been broken-hearted.

Fare-thee-weel, thou first and fairest!
Fare-thee-weel, thou best and dearest!
Thine be ilka joy and treasure,
Peace, Enjoyment, Love, and Pleasure!
Ae fond kiss, and then we sever!
Ae fareweel, alas, for ever!
Deep in heart-wrung tears I'll pledge thee,
Warring sighs and groans I'll wage thee.

BEHOLD THE HOUR, THE BOAT, ARRIVI

Behold the hour, the boat, arrive!
  My dearest Nancy, O fareweel!
Severed frae thee, can I survive,
  Frae thee whom I hae lov'd sae weel?

Endless and deep shall be my grief;
  Nae ray of comfort shall I see,
But this most precious, dear belief,
  That thou wilt still remember me !

Alang the solitary shore
  Where flitting sea-fowl round me cry,
Across the rolling, dashing roar,
  I'll westward turn my wishful eye.

'Happy thou Indian grove,' I'll say,
  'Where now my Nancy's path shall be !
While thro' your sweets she holds her way,
  O tell me, does she muse on me ?'

THOU GLOOMY DECEMBER

ANCE mair I hail thee, thou gloomy December !
  Ance mair I hail thee wi' sorrow and care;
Sad was the parting thou makes me remember
  Parting wi' Nancy, oh, ne'er to meet mair !

Fond lovers' parting is sweet, painful pleasure,
  Hope beaming mild on the soft parting hour;
But the dire feeling, O farewell for ever !
  Anguish unmingled, and agony pure !

Wild as the winter now tearing the forest,
  Till the last leaf o' the summer is flown,
Such is the tempest has shaken my bosom,
  Till my last hope and last comfort is gone.

Still as I hail thee, thou gloomy December,
  Still shall I hail thee wi' sorrow and care;
For sad was the parting thou makes me remember,
  Parting wi' Nancy, oh, ne'er to meet mair.

MY NATIVE LAND SAE FAR AWA'

O SAD and heavy, should I part,
    But for her sake sae far awa';
Unknowing what my way may thwart,
    My native land sae far awa'.

Thou that of a' things Maker art,
    That formed this Fair sae far awa',
Gie body strength, then I'll ne'er start,
    At this my way sae far awa'.

How true is love to pure desert!
    Like mine for her sae far awa';
And nocht shall heal my bosom's smart,
    While, oh, she is sae far awa'!

Nane other love, nane other dart,
    I feel but hers sae far awa';
But fairer never touch'd a heart
    Than hers, the Fair, sae far awa'.

DOWN THE BURN, DAVIE

As down the burn they took their way,
    And thro' the flowery dale,
His cheek to hers he aft did lay,
    And love was ay the tale:
With 'Mary, when shall we return,
    Sic pleasures to renew?'
Quoth Mary—'Love, I like the burn,
    And ay shall follow you.'

LINES ON FERGUSSON, THE POET

ILL-FATED genius ! Heaven-taught Fergusson,
  What heart that feels and will not yield a tear,
To think Life's sun did set e'er well begun
  To shed its influence on thy bright career.

O why should truest Worth and Genius pine
  Beneath the iron grasp of Want and Woe,
While titled knaves and idiot-Greatness shine
  In all the splendour Fortune can bestow ?

I DO CONFESS THOU ART SAE FAIR

I DO confess thou art sae fair,
  I wad been o'er the lugs in luve,
Had I na found the slightest prayer
  That lips could speak thy heart could muve :

I do confess thee sweet, but find
  Thou art so thriftless o' thy sweets,
Thy favours are the silly wind
  That kisses ilka thing it meets.

See yonder rosebud, rich in dew,
  Amang its native briers sae coy;
How sune it tines its scent and hue,
  When pu'd and worn a common toy;

Sic fate ere lang shall thee betide,
  Tho' thou may gaily bloom awhile;
And sune thou shalt be thrown aside,
  Like ony common weed and vile.

THE WEARY PUND O' TOW

Chorus.—The weary pund, the weary pund,
  The weary pund o' tow;
   I think my wife will end her life,
    Before she spin her tow.

I BOUGHT my wife a stane o' lint,
  As gude as e'er did grow,
And a' that she has made o' that
  Is ae puir pund o' tow.
    The weary pund, etc.

There sat a bottle in a bole,
  Ayont the ingle low;
And aye she took the tither souk,
  To drouk the stourie tow.
    The weary pund, etc.

Quoth I, for shame, ye dirty dame,
  Gae spin your tap o' tow!
She took the rock, and wi' a knock,
  She brake it o'er my pow.
    The weary pund, etc.

At last her feet—I sang to see't!
  Gaed foremost o'er the knowe,
And or I wad anither jad,
  I'll wallop in a tow.
    The weary pund, etc.

WHEN SHE CAM BEN SHE BOBBET

O WHEN she cam ben she bobbet fu' low,
O when she cam ben she bobbet fu' low,
And when she cam ben, she kiss'd Cockpen,
And syne she deny'd she did it ava.

And was na Cockpen right saucy witha' ?
And was na Cockpen right saucy witha' ?
In leaving the daughter o' a lord,
And kissin' a collier lassie an' a' !

O never look doon, my lassie, at a',
O never look down, my lassie, at a',
Thy lips are as sweet, and thy figure complete,
As the finest dame in castle or ha'.

Tho' thou hast nae silk, and holland sae sma',
Tho' thou hast nae silk, and holland sae sma',
Thy coat and thy sark are thy ain handywark,
And lady Jean was never sae braw.

SCROGGAM, MY DEARIE

THERE was a wife wonn'd in Cockpen,
    Scroggam;
She brew'd gude ale for gentlemen;
    Sing auld Cowl, lay ye down by me,
      Scroggam, my dearie, ruffum.

The gudewife's dochter fell in a fever,
    Scroggam;
The priest o' the parish he fell in anither;
    Sing auld Cowl, lay ye down by me,
      Scroggam, my dearie, ruffum.

They laid them side by side thegither,
    Scroggam;
That the heat o' the taen might cool the tither;
    Sing auld Cowl, lay ye down by me,
      Scroggam, my dearie, ruffum.

MY COLLIER LADDIE

WHARE live ye, my bonie lass?
  And tell me what they ca' ye;
My name, she says, is mistress Jean,
  And I follow the Collier laddie.
            My name, she says, etc.

See you not yon hills and dales
  The sun shines on sae brawlie;
They a' are mine, and they shall be thine,
  Gin ye'll leave your Collier laddie.
            They a' are mine, etc.

Ye shall gang in gay attire,
  Weel buskit up sae gaudy;
And ane to wait on every hand,
  Gin ye'll leave your Collier laddie.
            And ane to wait, etc.

Tho' ye had a' the sun shines on,
  And the earth conceals sae lowly,
I wad turn my back on you and it a',
  And embrace my Collier laddie.
            I wad turn my back, etc.

I can win my five pennies in a day,
  An' spend it at night fu' brawlie;
And make my bed in the collier's neuk,
  And lie down wi' my Collier laddie.
            And make my bed, etc.

Loove for loove is the bargain for me,
  Tho' the wee cot-house should haud me;
And the warld before me to win my bread,
  And fair fa' my Collier laddie!
            And the warld before me,
                    etc.

SIC A WIFE AS WILLIE HAD

WILLIE WASTLE dwalt on Tweed,
  ·The spot they ca'd it Linkumdoddie.
Willie was a wabster gude,
    Could stown a clue wi' ony body :
He had a wife was dour and din,
    O Tinkler Maidgie was her mither;
Sic a wife as Willie had,
    I wad na gie a button for her.

She has an e'e, she has but ane,
    The cat has twa the very colour;
Five rusty teeth, forbye a stump,
    A clapper tongue wad deave a miller;
A whiskin beard about her mou',
    Her nose and chin they threaten ither;
Sic a wife as Willie had,
    I wad na gie a button for her.

She's bow-hough'd, she's hen-shin'd,
    Ae limpin' leg a hand-breed shorter;
She's twisted right, she's twisted left,
    To balance fair in ilka quarter :
She has a hump upon her breast,
    The twin o' that upon her shouther;
Sic a wife as Willie had,
    I wad na gie a button for her.

Auld baudrons by the ingle sits
    An' wi' her loof her face a-washin';
But Willie's wife is nae sae trig,
    She dights her grunzie wi' a hushion :
Her walie nieves like midden-creels,
    Her face wad fyle the Logan Water;
Sic a wife as Willie had,
    I wad na gie a button for her.

LADY MARY ANN

O LADY MARY ANN looks o'er the Castle wa',
She saw three bonie boys playing at the ba',
The youngest he was the flower amang them a',
    My bonie laddie's young, but he's growin' yet

O father, O father, an' ye think it fit,
We'll send him a year to the college yet,
We'll sew a green ribbon round about his hat,
    And that will let them ken he's to marry yet.

Lady Mary Ann was a flower in the dew,
Sweet was its smell and bonie was its hue,
And the langer it blossom'd the sweeter it grew,
    For the lily in the bud will be bonier yet.

Young Charlie Cochran was the sprout of an aik,
Bonie and bloomin' and straught was its make,
The sun took delight to shine for its sake,
    And it will be the brag o' the forest yet.

The simmer is gane when the leaves they were green
And the days are awa' that we hae seen,
But far better days I trust will come again;
    For my bonie laddie's young, but he's growin'
        yet.

KELLY BURN BRAES

THERE leevit a carl in Kelly Burn Braes,
    Hey, and the rue grows bonie wi' thyme;
And he had a wife was the plague o' his days,
    And the thyme it is wither'd, and rue is in prime.

Ae day as the carl gaed up the lang glen,
   Hey, and the rue grows bonie wi' thyme;
He met wi' the Deil, wha said, 'How do you fen?'
   And the thyme it is wither'd, and rue is in prime.

'I've got a bad wife, sir, that's a' my complaint,
   Hey, and the rue grows bonie wi' thyme;
For, saving your presence, to her ye're a saint,
   And the thyme it is wither'd, and rue is in prime.'

'It's neither your stot nor your staig I shall crave,
   Hey, and the rue grows bonie wi' thyme;
But gie me your wife, man, for her I must have,
   And the thyme it is wither'd, and rue is in prime.'

'O welcome most kindly!' the blythe carl said,
   Hey, and the rue grows bonie wi' thyme;
'But if ye can match her ye're waur than ye're ca'd,
   And the thyme it is wither'd, and rue is in prime.'

The Devil has got the auld wife on his back,
   Hey, and the rue grows bonie wi' thyme;
And like a poor pedlar he's carried his pack,
   And the thyme it is wither'd, and rue is in prime.

He's carried her hame to his ain hallan door,
   Hey, and the rue grows bonie wi' thyme;
Syne bade her gae in for a b—, and a w—,
   And the thyme it is wither'd, and rue is in prime.

Then straight he makes fifty, the pick o' his band,
   Hey, and the rue grows bonie wi' thyme;
Turn out on her guard in the clap o' a hand,
   And the thyme it is wither'd, and rue is in prime

The carlin gaed thro' them like ony wud bear,
   Hey, and the rue grows bonie wi' thyme;
Whae'er she gat hands on cam ne'er her nae mair,
   And the thyme it is wither'd, and rue is in prime.

A reekit wee deevil looks over the wa',
  Hey, and the rue grows bonie wi' thyme;
'O help, maister, help, or she'll ruin us a'!'
  And the thyme it is wither'd, and rue is in prime.

The Devil he swore by the edge o' his knife,
  Hey, and the rue grows bonie wi' thyme;
He pitied the man that was tied to a wife,
  And the thyme it is wither'd, and rue is in prime.

The Devil he swore by the kirk and the bell,
  Hey, and the rue grows bonie wi' thyme;
He was not in wedlock, thank Heav'n, but in hell,
  And the thyme it is wither'd, and rue is in prime.

Then Satan has travell'd again wi' his pack,
  Hey, and the rue grows bonie wi' thyme;
And to her auld husband he's carried her back,
  And the thyme it is wither'd, and rue is in prime.

'I hae been a Deevil the feck o' my life,
  Hey, and the rue grows bonie wi' thyme;
But ne'er was in hell till I met wi' a wife,
  And the thyme it is wither'd, and rue is in prime.

THE SLAVE'S LAMENT

It was in sweet Senegal that my foes did me enthral,
  For the lands of Virginia, ginia O:
Torn from that lovely shore, and must never see it
    more;
  And alas! I am weary, weary O:
Torn from that lovely shore, and must never see it
    more;
  And alas! I am weary, weary O.

All on that charming coast is no bitter snow and frost,
 Like the lands of Virginia, ginia O :
There streams for ever flow, and flowers for ever blow,
 And alas ! I am weary, weary O :
There streams for ever flow, and flowers for ever blow,
 And alas ! I am weary, weary O.

The burden I must bear, while the cruel scourge I fear,
 In the lands of Virginia, ginia O;
And I think on friends most dear, with the bitter,
  bitter tear,
 And alas ! I am weary, weary O :
And I think on friends most dear, with the bitter,
  bitter tear,
 And alas ! I am weary, weary O.

O CAN YE LABOUR LEA ?

Chorus.—O can ye labour lea, young man,
  O can ye labour lea ?
  It fee nor bountith shall us twine
  Gin ye can labour lea.

I FEE'D a man at Michaelmas,
 Wi' airle pennies three;
But a' the faut I had to him,
 He could na labour lea.
  O can ye labour lea, etc.

O clappin's gude in Febarwar,
 An' kissin's sweet in May;
But my delight's the ploughman lad,
 That weel can labour lea.
  O can ye labour lea, etc.

O kissin' is the key o' luve,
And clappin' is the lock;
An' makin' o's the best thing yet,
That e'er a young thing gat.
O can ye labour lea, etc.

THE DEUK'S DANG O'ER MY DADDIE

THE bairns gat out wi' an unco shout,
The deuk's dang o'er my daddie, O !
The fien-ma-care, quo' the feirrie auld wife,
He was but a paidlin' body, O !
He paidles out, and he paidles in,
An' he paidles late and early, O !
This seven lang years I hae lien by his side,
An' he is but a fusionless carlie, O.

O haud your tongue, my feirrie auld wife,
O haud your tongue, now Nansie, O :
I've seen the day, and sae hae ye,
Ye wad na hae been sae donsie, O.
I've seen the day ye butter'd my brose,
And cuddl'd me late and early, O;
But downa-do's come o'er me now,
And och, I find it sairly, O !

THE DEIL'S AWA' WI' TH' EXCISEMAN

THE deil cam fiddlin' thro' the town,
And danc'd awa' wi' the Exciseman,
And ilka wife cries, 'Auld Mahoun,
I wish you luck o' the prize, man.'

Chorus.—The deil's awa', the deil's awa',
  The deil's awa' wi' th' Exciseman,
  He's danc'd awa', he's danc'd awa',
  He's danc'd awa' wi' th' Exciseman.

We'll mak our maut, and we'll brew our drink,
 We'll laugh, sing, and rejoice, man,
And mony braw thanks to the meikle black deil,
 That danc'd awa' wi' th' Exciseman.
    The deil's awa', etc.

There's threesome reels, there's foursome reels,
 There's hornpipes and strathspeys, man,
But the ae best dance e'er cam to the land
 Was the deil's awa' wi' th' Exciseman.
    The deil's awa', etc.

THE COUNTRY LASS

In simmer, when the hay was mawn,
 And corn wav'd green in ilka field,
While claver blooms white o'er the lea
 And roses blaw in ilka bield !
Blythe Bessie in the milking shiel,
 Says—I'll be wed, come o't what will :
Out spake a dame in wrinkled eild—
 O' gude advisement comes nae ill.

It's ye hae wooers mony ane,
 And lassie, ye're but young, ye ken ;
Then wait a wee, and cannie wale
 A routhie butt, a routhie ben ;
There's Johnie o' the Buskie-glen,
 Fu' is his barn, fu' is his byre ;
Tak this frae me, my bonie hen,
 It's plenty beets the luver's fire.

For Johnie o' the Buskie-glen,
    I dinna care a single flie;
He lo'es sae weel his craps and kye,
    He has nae luve to spare for me;
But blythe the blink o' Robie's e'e,
    And weel I wat he lo'es me dear ;
Ae blink o' him I wad na gie
    For Buskie-glen and a' his gear.

O thoughtless lassie, life's a faught;
    The canniest gate, the strife is sair;
But ay fu'-han't is fechtin' best,
    A hungry care's an unco care :
But some will spend and some will spare,
    An' wilfu' folk maun hae their will;
Syne as ye brew, my maiden fair,
    Keep mind that ye maun drink the yill.

O gear will buy me rigs o' land,
    And gear will buy me sheep and kye;
But the tender heart o' leesome luve,
    The gowd and siller canna buy;
We may be poor—Robie and I—
    Light is the burden luve lays on;
Content and luve brings peace and joy—
    What mair hae Queens upon a throne ?

BESSY AND HER SPINNIN'-WHEEL

O LEEZE me on my spinnin'-wheel,
And leeze me on my rock and reel;
Frae tap to tae that cleeds me bien,
And haps me biel and warm at e'en,
I'll set me down and sing and spin,
While laigh descends the simmer sun,
Blest wi' content, and milk and meal,
O leeze me on my spinnin'-wheel.

On ilka hand the burnies trot,
And meet below my theekit cot;
The scented birk and hawthorn white,
Across the pool their arms unite,
Alike to screen the birdie's nest,
And little fishes' caller rest;
The sun blinks kindly in the biel,
Where blythe I turn my spinnin'-wheel.

On lofty aiks the cushats wail,
And Echo cons the doolfu' tale;
The lintwhites in the hazel braes,
Delighted, rival ither's lays;
The craik amang the claver hay,
The paitrick whirrin' o'er the ley,
The swallow jinkin' round my shiel,
Amuse me at my spinnin'-wheel.

Wi' sma' to sell and less to buy,
Aboon distress, below envy,
O wha wad leave this humble state,
For a' the pride of a' the great?
Amid their flaring, idle toys,
Amid their cumbrous, dinsome joys,
Can they the peace and pleasure feel
Of Bessy at her spinnin'-wheel?

FRAGMENT OF SONG

No cold approach, no altered mien,
  Just what would make suspicion start;
No pause the dire extremes between,
  He made me blest—and broke my heart.

LOVE FOR LOVE

ITHERS seek they ken na what,
Features, carriage, and a' that;
Gie me loove in her I court,
Loove to loove maks a' the sport.

Let loove sparkle in her e'e;
Let her lo'e nae man but me;
That's the tocher gude I prize,
There the luver's treasure lies.

FRAGMENT ON MARIA

How gracefully Maria leads the dance !
She's life itself : I never saw a foot
So nimble and so elegant. It speaks,
And the sweet whispering Poetry it makes
Shames the musician.

Adriano, or, The first of June.

SAW YE BONIE LESLEY

O SAW ye bonie Lesley,
    As she gaed o'er the Border ?
She's gane, like Alexander,
    To spread her conquests farther.

To see her is to love her,
    And love but her for ever;
For Nature made her what she is,
    And never made anither !

Thou art a queen, fair Lesley,
   Thy subjects, we before thee;
Thou art divine, fair Lesley,
   The hearts o' men adore thee.

The deil he could na scaith thee,
   Or aught that wad belang thee;
He'd look into thy bonie face,
   And say—'I canna wrang thee!'

The Powers aboon will tent thee,
   Misfortune sha'na steer thee;
Thou'rt like themsel sae lovely,
   That ill they'll ne'er let near thee.

Return again, fair Lesley,
   Return to Caledonie!
That we may brag we hae a lass
   There's nane again sae bonie.

THE LEA-RIG

WHEN o'er the hill the e'ening star
   Tells bughtin' time is near, my jo,
And owsen frae the furrow'd field
   Return sae dowf and weary O;
Down by the burn, where birken buds
   Wi' dew are hangin' clear, my jo,
I'll meet thee on the lea-rig,
   My ain kind Dearie O.

At midnight hour, in mirkest glen,
   I'd rove, and ne'er be eerie O,
If thro' that glen I gaed to thee,
   My ain kind Dearie O;

Altho' the night were ne'er sae wild,
    And I were ne'er sae weary O,
I'll meet thee on the lea-rig,
    My ain kind Dearie O.

The hunter lo'es the morning sun,
    To rouse the mountain deer, my jo;
At noon the fisher takes the glen
    Adown the burn to steer, my jo:
Gie me the hour o' gloamin' gray,
    It maks my heart sae cheery O,
To meet thee on the lea-rig,
    My ain kind Dearie O.

MY WIFE'S A WINSOME WEE THING

Air—'My Wife's a Wanton Wee Thing.'

Chorus.—She is a winsome wee thing,
        She is a handsome wee thing,
        She is a lo'esome wee thing,
        This dear wee wife o' mine.

I never saw a fairer,
I never lo'ed a dearer,
And neist my heart I'll wear her,
    For fear my jewel tine.
        She is a winsome, etc.

The warld's wrack we share o't;
The warstle and the care o't;
Wi' her I'll blythely bear it,
    And think my lot divine.
        She is a winsome, etc.

HIGHLAND MARY

Tune—'Katherine Ogie.'

YE banks and braes and streams around
  The castle o' Montgomery!
Green be your woods, and fair your flowers,
  Your waters never drumlie:
There Simmer first unfauld her robes,
  And there the langest tarry;
For there I took the last Fareweel
  O' my sweet Highland Mary.

How sweetly bloom'd the gay, green birk,
  How rich the hawthorn's blossom,
As underneath their fragrant shade,
  I clasp'd her to my bosom!
The golden Hours on angel wings,
  Flew o'er me and my Dearie;
For dear to me, as light and life,
  Was my sweet Highland Mary.

Wi' mony a vow, and lock'd embrace,
  Our parting was fu' tender;
And, pledging aft to meet again,
  We tore oursels asunder;
But oh! fell Death's untimely frost,
  That nipt my Flower sae early!
Now green's the sod, and cauld's the clay
  That wraps my Highland Mary!

O pale, pale now, those rosy lips,
  I aft hae kiss'd sae fondly!
And clos'd for ay, the sparkling glance
  That dwelt on me sae kindly!
And mouldering now in silent dust,
  That heart that lo'ed me dearly!
But still within my bosom's core
  Shall live my Highland Mary.

THE RIGHTS OF WOMAN

AN OCCASIONAL ADDRESS
SPOKEN BY MISS FONTENELLE ON HER BENEFIT
NIGHT, NOVEMBER 26, 1792

WHILE Europe's eye is fix'd on mighty things,
The fate of empires and the fall of kings;
While quacks of State must each produce his plan,
And even children lisp the Rights of Man;
Amid this mighty fuss just let me mention,
The Rights of Women merit some attention.

First, in the sexes' intermix'd connection,
One sacred Right of Women is *protection*.
The tender flower that lifts its head, elate,
Helpless, must fall before the blasts of fate,
Sunk on the earth, defac'd its lovely form,
Unless your shelter ward th' impending storm.

Our second Right—but needless here is caution,
To keep that right inviolate's the fashion;
Each man of sense has it so full before him,
He'd die before he'd wrong it—'tis *decorum*.
There was, indeed, in far less polish'd days,
A time, when rough rude man had naughty ways;
Would swagger, swear, get drunk, kick up a riot,
Nay even thus invade a lady's quiet.
Now, thank our stars ! these Gothic times are fled;
Now, well-bred men—and you are all well bred—
Most justly think (and we are much the gainers)
Such conduct neither spirit, wit, nor manners.
For Right the third, our last, our best, our dearest,
That right to fluttering female hearts the nearest;
Which even the Rights of Kings, in low prostration
Most humbly own—'tis dear, dear *admiration* !

In that blest sphere alone we live and move;
There taste that life of life—immortal love.
Smiles, glances, sighs, tears, fits, flirtations, airs;
'Gainst such an host what flinty savage dares,
When awful Beauty joins with all her charms—
Who is so rash as rise in rebel arms ?
But truce with kings, and truce with constitutions,
With bloody armaments and revolutions;
Let Majesty your first attention summon,
Ah! ça ira! THE MAJESTY OF WOMAN !

ON SEEING MISS FONTENELLE IN A
FAVOURITE CHARACTER

SWEET naïveté of feature,
    Simple, wild, enchanting elf,
Not to thee, but thanks to Nature,
    Thou art acting but thyself.

Wert thou awkward, stiff, affected,
    Spurning Nature, torturing art;
Loves and Graces all rejected,
    Then indeed thou'dst act a part.

EXTEMPORE ON SOME COMMEMORATIONS
OF THOMSON

DOST thou not rise, indignant shade,
    And smile wi' spurning scorn,
When they wha wad hae starved thy life,
    Thy senseless turf adorn ?

B.P.   9

Helpless, alane, thou clamb the brae,
  Wi' meikle honest toil,
And claught th' unfading garland there—
  Thy sair-won, rightful spoil.

And wear it there! and call aloud
  This axiom undoubted—
Would thou hae Nobles' patronage?
  First learn to live without it!

To whom hae much, more shall be given,
  Is every Great man's faith;
But he, the helpless, needful wretch,
  Shall lose the mite he hath.

AULD ROB MORRIS

THERE'S Auld Rob Morris that wons in yon glen,
He's the King o' gude fellows, and wale o' auld me.
He has gowd in his coffers, he has owsen and kin
And ae bonie lass, his dautie and mine.

She's fresh as the morning, the fairest in May;
She's sweet as the ev'ning amang the new hay;
As blythe and as artless as the lambs on the lea,
And dear to my heart as the light to my e'e.

But oh! she's an Heiress, auld Robin's a laird,
And my daddie has nought but a cot-house and yard
A wooer like me maunna hope to come speed,
The wounds I must hide that will soon be my dea

The day comes to me, but delight brings me nane
The night comes to me, but my rest it is gane;
I wander my lane like a night-troubled ghaist,
And I sigh as my heart it wad burst in my breast

O had she but been of a lower degree,
I then might hae hop'd she wad smil'd upon me !
O how past descriving had then been my bliss,
As now my distraction nae words can express.

WEARY FA' YOU, DUNCAN GRAY

Tune—'Duncan Gray.'

WEARY fa' you, Duncan Gray !
 Ha, ha, the girdin o't !
Wae gae by you, Duncan Gray !
 Ha, ha, the girdin o't !
When a' the lave gae to their play,
Then I maun sit the lee-lang day,
And jeeg the cradle wi' my tae,
 And a' for the girdin o't.

Bonie was the Lammas moon,
 Ha, ha, the girdin o't !
Glow'rin' a' the hills aboon,
 Ha, ha, the girdin o't !
The girdin brak, the beast cam doun,
I tint my curch and baith my shoon,
And, Duncan, ye're an unco loon—
 Wae on the girdin o't !

But, Duncan, gin ye'll keep your aith,
 Ha, ha, the girdin o't !
I'se bless you wi' my hindmost breath,
 Ha, ha, the girdin o't !
Duncan, gin ye'll keep your aith,
The beast again can bear us baith,
And Auld Mess John will mend the skaith,
 And clout the bad girdin o't.

DUNCAN GRAY

DUNCAN GRAY cam here to woo,
 Ha, ha, the wooing o't,
On blythe Yule-night when we were fou,
 Ha, ha, the wooing o't,
Maggie coost her head fu' high,
Look'd asklent and unco skeigh,
Gart poor Duncan stand abeigh;
 Ha, ha, the wooing o't.

Duncan fleech'd and Duncan pray'd;
 Ha, ha, the wooing o't,
Meg was deaf as Ailsa Craig,
 Ha, ha, the wooing o't :
Duncan sigh'd baith out and in,
Grat his e'en baith blear't an' blin',
Spak o' lowpin' o'er a linn;
 Ha, ha, the wooing o't.

Time and Chance are but a tide,
 Ha, ha, the wooing o't,
Slighted love is sair to bide,
 Ha, ha, the wooing o't :
Shall I like a fool, quoth he,
For a haughty hizzie die ?
She may gae to—France for me !
 Ha, ha, the wooing o't.

How it comes let doctors tell,
 Ha, ha, the wooing o't;
Meg grew sick, as he grew hale,
 Ha, ha, the wooing o't.
Something in her bosom wrings,
For relief a sigh she brings :
And oh ! her een they spak sic things !
 Ha, ha, the wooing o't.

Duncan was a lad o' grace,
　　Ha, ha, the wooing o't;
Maggie's was a piteous case,
　　Ha, ha, the wooing o't;
Duncan could na be her death,
Swelling Pity smoor'd his wrath;
Now they're crouse and canty baith,
　　Ha, ha, the wooing o't.

HERE'S A HEALTH TO THEM THAT'S AWA'

HERE's a health to them that's awa',
Here's a health to them that's awa';
And wha winna wish gude luck to our cause,
May never gude luck be their fa'!
It's gude to be merry and wise,
It's gude to be honest and true;
It's gude to support Caledonia's cause,
And bide by the buff and the blue.

Here's a health to them that's awa',
Here's a health to them that's awa',
Here's a health to Charlie the chief o' the clan,
Altho' that his band be but sma'!
May Liberty meet wi' success!
May Prudence protect her frae evil!
May tyrants and tyranny tine i' the mist,
And wander their way to the devil!

Here's a health to them that's awa',
Here's a health to them that's awa';
Here's a health to Tammie, the Norlan' laddie,
That lives at the lug o' the law!
Here's freedom to them that wad read,
Here's freedom to them that wad write,
There's nane ever fear'd that the truth should be
　　heard,
But they whom the truth would indite.

Here's a health to them that's awa',
An' here's to them that's awa'!
Here's to Maitland and Wycombe, let wha does
    na like 'em
Be built in a hole in the wa',
Here's timmer that's red at the heart,
Here's fruit that is sound at the core;
And may he that wad turn the buff and blue coat
Be turn'd to the back o' the door.

Here's a health to them that's awa',
Here's a health to them that's awa';
Here's chieftain M'Leod, a chieftain worth gowd,
Tho' bred amang mountains o' snaw,
Here's friends on baith sides o' the firth,
And friends on baith sides o' the Tweed;
And wha wad betray old Albion's right,
May they never eat of her bread!

A TIPPLING BALLAD

ON THE DUKE OF BRUNSWICK'S BREAKING UP HIS
CAMP, AND THE DEFEAT OF THE AUSTRIANS, BY
DUMOURIER, NOV., 1792

WHEN Princes and Prelates,
    And hot-headed zealots,
A' Europe had set in a low, a low,
    The poor man lies down,
    Nor envies a crown,
And comforts himself as he dow, as he dow,
And comforts himself as he dow.

The black-headed eagle,
 As keen as a beagle,
He hunted o'er height, and o'er howe, o'er howe,
 In the braes o' Gemappe,
 He fell in a trap,
E'en let him come out as he dow, dow, dow,
E'en let him come out as he dow.

 . . . . . .

 But truce with commotions,
 And new-fangled notions,
A bumper, I trust, you'll allow;
 Here's George our good king,
 And Charlotte his queen,
And lang may they ring as they dow, dow, dow,
And lang may they ring as they dow.

WRITTEN ON A WINDOW-PANE

A.D. 1793

IN Politics if thou wouldst mix,
 And mean thy fortunes be;
Bear this in mind, be deaf and blind,
 Let great folk hear and see.

POORTITH CAULD AND RESTLESS LOVE

Tune—'Cauld Kail in Aberdeen.'

O POORTITH cauld, and restless love,
 Ye wrack my peace between ye;
Yet poortith a' I could forgive,
 An' 'twere na for my Jeanie.

Chorus.—O why should Fate sic pleasure have,
 Life's dearest bands untwining ?
 Or why sae sweet a flower as love
  Depend on Fortune's shining ?

The warld's wealth, when I think on,
 Its pride and a' the lave o't;
O fie on silly coward man,
 That he should be the slave o't !
  O why, etc.

Her een, sae bonie blue, betray
 How she repays my passion;
But prudence is her o'erword ay,
 She talks o' rank and fashion.
  O why, etc.

O wha can prudence think upon,
 And sic a lassie by him ?
O wha can prudence think upon,
 And sae in love as I am ?
  O why, etc.

How blest the simple cotter's fate !
 He woo's his artless dearie;
The silly bogles, wealth and state,
 Can never make him eerie.
  O why, etc.

BRAW LADS O' GALLA WATER

BRAW, braw lads on Yarrow braes,
 They rove amang the blooming heather;
But Yarrow braes, nor Ettrick shaws
 Can match the lads o' Galla Water.

But there is ane, a secret ane,
  Aboon them a' I lo'e him better;
And I'll be his, and he'll be mine,
  The bonie lad o' Galla Water.

Altho' his daddie was nae laird,
  And tho' I hae na meikle tocher,
Yet rich in kindest, truest love,
  We'll tent our flocks by Galla Water.

It ne'er was wealth, it ne'er was wealth,
  That coft contentment, peace, or pleasure:
The bands and bliss o' mutual love,
  O that's the chiefest warld's treasure.

SONNET WRITTEN ON THE AUTHOR'S BIRTHDAY

ON HEARING A THRUSH SING IN HIS MORNING WALK

Sing on, sweet thrush, upon the leafless bough,
  Sing on, sweet bird, I listen to thy strain,
  See agèd Winter, 'mid his surly reign,
At thy blythe carol, clears his furrowed brow.

So in lone Poverty's dominion drear,
  Sits meek Content with light, unanxious heart;
  Welcomes the rapid moments, bids them part,
Nor asks if they bring ought to hope or fear.

I thank thee, Author of this opening day!
  Thou whose bright sun now gilds yon orient skies!
  Riches denied, Thy boon was purer joys—
What wealth could never give nor take away!

Yet come, thou child of poverty and care,
The mite high Heaven bestow'd, that mite with thee
  I'll share.

LORD GREGORY

O MIRK, mirk is this midnight hour,
　And loud the tempest's roar;
A waefu' wanderer seeks thy tower,
　Lord Gregory, ope thy door.
An exile frae her father's ha',
　And a' for sake o' thee;
At least some pity on me shaw,
　If love it may na be.

Lord Gregory, mind'st thou not the grove
　By bonie Irwine side,
Where first I own'd that virgin love
　I lang, lang had denied.
How aften didst thou pledge and vow,
　Thou wad for ay be mine !
And my fond heart, itsel sae true,
　It ne'er mistrusted thine.

Hard is thy heart, Lord Gregory,
　And flinty is thy breast :
Thou bolt of Heaven that flashest by,
　O, wilt thou bring me rest !
Ye mustering thunders from above,
　Your willing victims see;
But spare and pardon my fause Love,
　His wrangs to Heaven and me.

WANDERING WILLIE

FIRST VERSION

HERE awa', there awa', wandering Willie,
　Now tired with wandering, haud awa' hame;
Come to my bosom, my ae only dearie,
　And tell me thou bring'st me my Willie the same.

Loud blew the cauld winter winds at our parting;
　　It was na the blast brought the tear in my e'e :
Now welcome the Simmer, and welcome my Willie,
　　The Simmer to Nature, my Willie to me.

Ye hurricanes rest in the cave o' your slumbers,
　　O how your wild horrors a lover alarms !
Awaken, ye breezes, row gently, ye billows,
　　And waft my dear laddie ance mair to my arms.
But if he's forgotten his faithfullest Nannie,
　　O still flow between us, thou wide roaring main;
May I never see it, may I never trow it,
　　But, dying, believe that my Willie's my ain !

WANDERING WILLIE

REVISED VERSION

HERE awa', there awa', wandering Willie,
　　Here awa', there awa', haud awa' hame;
Come to my bosom, my ain only dearie,
　　Tell me thou bring'st me my Willie the same.
Winter winds blew loud and cauld at our parting,
　　Fears for my Willie brought tears to my e'e,
Welcome now Simmer, and welcome my Willie,
　　The Simmer to Nature, my Willie to me.

Rest, ye wild storms, in the cave of your slumbers,
　　How your dread howling a lover alarms !
Wauken, ye breezes, row gently, ye billows,
　　And waft my dear laddie ance mair to my arms.
But oh, if he's faithless, and mind na his Nannie,
　　Flow still between us, thou wide roaring main !
May I never see it, may I never trow it,
　　But, dying, believe that my Willie's my ain.

OPEN THE DOOR TO ME, OH

Oh, open the door, some pity to show,
　Oh, open the door to me, oh,
Tho' thou hast been false, I'll ever prove true,
　Oh, open the door to me, oh.

Cauld is the blast upon my pale cheek,
　But caulder thy love for me, oh:
The frost that freezes the life at my heart,
　Is nought to my pains frae thee, oh.

The wan Moon is setting behind the white wave,
　And Time is setting with me, oh:
False friends, false love, farewell! for mair
　I'll ne'er trouble them, nor thee, oh.

She has open'd the door, she has open'd it wide,
　She sees the pale corse on the plain, oh:
'My true love!' she cried, and sank down by his
　　side,
　Never to rise again, oh.

LOVELY YOUNG JESSIE

True hearted was he, the sad swain o' the Yarrow,
　And fair are the maids on the banks of the Ayr;
But by the sweet side o' the Nith's winding river,
　Are lovers as faithful, and maidens as fair:
To equal young Jessie seek Scotland all over;
　To equal young Jessie you seek it in vain,
Grace, beauty, and elegance fetter her lover,
　And maidenly modesty fixes the chain.

Fresh is the rose in the gay, dewy morning,
　And sweet is the lily at evening close;
But in the fair presence o' lovely young Jessie,
　Unseen is the lily, unheeded the rose.

Love sits in her smile, a wizard ensnaring;
  Enthron'd in her een he delivers his law:
And still to her charms SHE alone is a stranger;
  Her modest demeanour's the jewel of a'.

MEG O' THE MILL

O KEN ye what Meg o' the Mill has gotten,
An' ken ye what Meg o' the Mill has gotten?
She's gotten a coof wi' a claute o' siller,
And broken the heart o' the barley Miller.

The Miller was strappin', the Miller was ruddy;
A heart like a lord, and a hue like a lady;
The laird was a widdifu' bleerit knurl;
She's left the gude fellow, and taen the churl.

The Miller he hecht her a heart leal and loving,
The laird did address her wi' matter mair moving,
A fine pacing-horse wi' a clear chainèd bridle,
A whip by her side, and a bonie side-saddle.

O wae on the siller, it is sae prevailin',
And wae on the love that is fixed on a mailen!
A tocher's nae word in a true lover's parl,
But gie me my love, and a fig for the warl!

MEG O' THE MILL

ANOTHER VERSION

O KEN ye what Meg o' the Mill has gotten,
An' ken ye what Meg o' the Mill has gotten?
A braw new naig wi' the tail o' a rattan,
And that's what Meg o' the Mill has gotten.

O ken ye what Meg o' the Mill lo'es dearly,
An' ken ye what Meg o' the Mill lo'es dearly?
A dram o' gude strunt in a morning early,
And that's what Meg o' the Mill lo'es dearly.

O ken ye how Meg o' the Mill was married,
An' ken ye how Meg o' the Mill was married?
The priest he was oxter'd, the clark he was carried
And that's how Meg o' the Mill was married.

O ken ye how Meg o' the Mill was bedded,
An' ken ye how Meg o' the Mill was bedded?
The groom gat sae fu', he fell awald beside it,
And that's how Meg o' the Mill was bedded.

THE SOLDIER'S RETURN

Air—'The Mill, Mill, O.'

WHEN wild war's deadly blast was blawn,
    And gentle peace returning,
Wi' mony a sweet babe fatherless,
    And mony a widow mourning;
I left the lines and tented field,
    Where lang I'd been a lodger,
My humble knapsack a' my wealth,
    A poor but honest sodger.

A leal, light heart was in my breast,
    My hand unstain'd wi' plunder;
And for fair Scotia, hame again,
    I cheery on did wander:
I thought upon the banks o' Coil,
    I thought upon my Nancy,
I thought upon the witching smile
    That caught my youthful fancy.

At length I reach'd the bonie glen,
   Where early life I sported;
I pass'd the mill and trysting thorn,
   Where Nancy aft I courted :
Wha spied I but my ain dear maid,
   Down by her mother's dwelling !
And turn'd me round to hide the flood
   That in my een was swelling.

Wi' alter'd voice, quoth I, Sweet lass,
   Sweet as yon hawthorn's blossom,
O ! happy, happy may he be,
   That's dearest to thy bosom :
My purse is light, I've far to gang,
   And fain would be thy lodger;
I've served my king and country lang—
   Take pity on a sodger.

Sae wistfully she gaz'd on me,
   And lovelier was than ever;
Quo' she, A sodger ance I lo'ed,
   Forget him shall I never :
Our humble cot, and hamely fare,
   Ye freely shall partake it;
That gallant badge—the dear cockade,
   Ye're welcome for the sake o't.

She gaz'd—she redden'd like a rose—
   Syne pale like ony lily;
She sank within my arms, and cried,
   Art thou my ain dear Willie ?
By Him who made yon sun and sky !
   By whom true love's regarded,
I am the man; and thus may still
   True lovers be rewarded !

The wars are o'er, and I'm come hame,
   And find thee still true-hearted;
Tho' poor in gear, we're rich in love,
   And mair we'se ne'er be parted.

Quo' she, My grandsire left me gowd,
　　A mailen plenish'd fairly;
And come, my faithfu' sodger lad,
　　Thou'rt welcome to it dearly!

For gold the merchant ploughs the main,
　　The farmer ploughs the manor;
But glory is the sodger's prize,
　　The sodger's wealth is honour:
The brave poor sodger ne'er despise,
　　Nor count him as a stranger;
Remember he's his country's stay,
　　In day and hour of danger.

ON COMMISSARY GOLDIE'S BRAINS

LORD, to account who dares Thee call,
　　Or e'er dispute Thy pleasure?
Else why, within so thick a wall,
　　Enclose so poor a treasure?

LINES INSCRIBED IN A LADY'S POCKET ALMANAC

GRANT me, indulgent Heaven, that I may live,
To see the miscreants feel the pains they give;
Deal Freedom's sacred treasures free as air,
Till Slave and Despot be but things that were.

THANKSGIVING FOR A NATIONAL VICTORY

YE hypocrites! are these your pranks?
To murder men, and give God thanks!
Desist, for shame!—proceed no further,
God won't accept your thanks for MURTHER!

LINES ON THE COMMEMORATION OF RODNEY'S VICTORY

INSTEAD of a song, boys, I'll give you a toast;
Here's to the memory of those we have lost !
That we *lost*, did I say ?—nay, by Heav'n, that we
 found ;
For their fame it will last while the world goes round.
The next in succession I'll give you 's THE KING !
Whoe'er would betray him, on high may he swing !
And here's the grand fabric, the free CONSTITUTION,
As built on the base of our great Revolution !
And longer with Politics not to be cramm'd,
Be ANARCHY curs'd, and be TYRANNY damn'd !
And who would to LIBERTY e'er prove disloyal,
May his son be a hangman—and himself his first
 trial !

KIRK AND STATE EXCISEMEN

YE men of wit and wealth, why all this sneering
'Gainst poor Excisemen ? Give the cause a hearing :
What are your Landlord's rent-rolls ?—taxing ledgers !
What Premiers ?—what ev'n Monarchs ?—mighty
 Gaugers !
Nay, what are Priests ? (those seeming godly wise-men),
What are they, pray, but Spiritual Excisemen !

THE RAPTURES OF FOLLY

THOU graybeard, old Wisdom ! may boast of thy
 treasures;
 Give me with old Folly to live;
I grant thee thy calm-blooded, time-settled pleasures,
 But Folly has raptures to give.

YE TRUE LOYAL NATIVES

YE true 'Loyal Natives' attend to my song;
In uproar and riot rejoice the night long!
From Envy and Hatred your core is exempt,
But where is your shield from the darts of Contempt?

EXTEMPORE REPLY TO AN INVITATION

THE King's most humble servant, I
　　Can scarcely spare a minute;
But I'll be wi' you by an' by;
　　Or else the Deil's be in it.

GRACE AFTER MEAT

L—D, we thank, and Thee adore,
　　For temporal gifts we little merit;
At present we will ask no more—
　　Let *William Hislop* give the spirit.

GRACE BEFORE AND AFTER MEAT

O LORD, when hunger pinches sore,
　　Do Thou stand us in stead,
And send us, from Thy bounteous store,
　　A tup or wether head! Amen.

O Lord, since we have feasted thus,
　　Which we so little merit,
Let Meg now take away the flesh,
　　And Jock bring in the spirit! Amen.

IMPROMPTU ON GENERAL DUMOURIER'S DESERTION FROM THE FRENCH REPUBLICAN ARMY

You're welcome to Despots, Dumourier;
You're welcome to Despots, Dumourier :
    How does Dampiere do ?
    Aye, and Bournonville too ?
Why did they not come along with **you,**
    Dumourier ?

I will fight France with you, Dumourier;
I will fight France with you, Dumourier;
    I will fight France with you,
    I will take my chance with you,
By my soul, I'll dance with you, Dumourier.

Then let us fight about, Dumourier;
Then let us fight about, Dumourier;
    Then let us fight about,
    Till Freedom's spark be out,
Then we'll be d—d, no doubt, Dumourier.

THE LAST TIME I CAME O'ER THE MOOR

The last time I came o'er the moor,
    And left Maria's dwelling,
What throes, what tortures passing **cure,**
    Were in my bosom swelling :
Condemn'd to drag a hopeless chain,
    And yet in secret languish;
To feel a fire in every vein,
    Yet dare not speak my anguish.

The wretch of love unseen, unknown,
   I fain my crime would cover:
The bursting sigh, th' unweeting groan,
   Betray the guilty lover.
I know my doom must be despair,
   Thou wilt nor canst relieve me;
But oh, Maria, hear my prayer,
   For Pity's sake, forgive me!

The music of thy tongue I heard,
   Nor wist while it enslav'd me;
I saw thine eyes, yet nothing fear'd,
   Till fear no more had sav'd me:
The unwary sailor thus, aghast,
   The wheeling torrent viewing,
'Mid circling horrors yields at last
   To overwhelming ruin.

BLYTHE HAE I BEEN ON YON HILL

BLYTHE hae I been on yon hill,
   As the lambs before me;
Careless ilka thought and free,
   As the breeze flew o'er me;
Now nae langer sport and play,
   Mirth or sang can please me;
LESLEY is sae fair and coy,
   Care and anguish seize me.

Heavy, heavy is the task,
   Hopeless love declaring;
Trembling, I dow nocht but glow'r,
   Sighing, dumb despairing!
If she winna ease the thraws
   In my bosom swelling,
Underneath the grass-green sod,
   Soon maun be my dwelling.

LOGAN BRAES

O LOGAN, sweetly didst thou glide,
That day I was my Willie's bride,
And years sin syne hae o'er us run,
Like Logan to the simmer sun:
But now thy flowery banks appear
Like drumlie Winter, dark and drear,
While my dear lad maun face his faes,
Far, far frae me and Logan braes.

Again the merry month of May
Has made our hills and valleys gay;
The birds rejoice in leafy bowers,
The bees hum round the breathing flowers;
Blythe Morning lifts his rosy eye,
And Evening's tears are tears o' joy:
My soul, delightless, a' surveys,
While Willie's far frae Logan braes.

Within yon milk-white hawthorn bush,
Amang her nestlings sits the thrush;
Her faithfu' mate will share her toil,
Or wi' his song her cares beguile;
But I wi' my sweet nurslings here,
Nae mate to help, nae mate to cheer,
Pass widow'd nights and joyless days,
While Willie's far frae Logan braes.

O wae be to you, Men o' State,
That brethren rouse in deadly hate!
As ye make mony a fond heart mourn,
Sae may it on your heads return!
How can your flinty hearts enjoy
The widow's tear, the orphan's cry?
But soon may peace bring happy days,
And Willie hame to Logan braes!

O WERE MY LOVE YON LILAC FAIR

Air—'Hughie Graham.'

O WERE my love yon Lilac fair,
　　Wi' purple blossoms to the Spring,
And I, a bird to shelter there,
　　When wearied on my little wing!
How I wad mourn when it was torn
　　By Autumn wild, and Winter rude!
But I wad sing on wanton wing,
　　When youthfu' May its bloom renew'd.

O gin my love were yon red rose,
　　That grows upon the castle wa';
And I mysel a drap o' dew,
　　Into her bonie breast to fa'!
O there, beyond expression blest,
　　I'd feast on beauty a' the night;
Seal'd on her silk-saft faulds to rest,
　　Till fley'd awa' by Phœbus' light!

BONIE JEAN

THERE was a lass, and she was fair,
　　At kirk and market to be seen;
When a' our fairest maids were met,
　　The fairest maid was bonie Jean.

And ay she wrought her mammie's wark,
　　And ay she sang sae merrilie;
The blythest bird upon the bush
　　Had ne'er a lighter heart than she.

But hawks will rob the tender joys
    That bless the little lintwhite's nest;
And frost will blight the fairest flowers,
    And love will break the soundest rest.

Young Robie was the brawest lad,
    The flower and pride of a' the glen;
And he had owsen, sheep, and kye,
    And wanton naigies nine or ten.

He gaed wi' Jeanie to the tryste,
    He danc'd wi' Jeanie on the down;
And, lang ere witless Jeanie wist,
    Her heart was tint, her peace was stown!

As in the bosom of the stream,
    The moonbeam dwells at dewy e'en;
So trembling, pure, was tender love
    Within the breast of bonie Jean.

And now she works her mammie's wark,
    And ay she sighs wi' care and pain;
Ye wist na what her ail might be,
    Or what wad make her weel again.

But did na Jeanie's heart loup light,
    And did na joy blink in her e'e;
As Robie tauld a tale of love:
    Ae e'enin' on the lily lea?

The sun was sinking in the west,
    The birds sang sweet in ilka grove;
His cheek to hers he fondly laid,
    And whisper'd thus his tale o' love:

'O Jeanie fair, I lo'e thee dear;
    O canst thou think to fancy me,
Or wilt thou leave thy mammie's cot,
    And learn to tent the farms wi' me?

'At barn or byre thou shalt na drudge,
  Or naething else to trouble thee;
But stray amang the heather-bells,
  And tent the waving corn wi' me.'

Now what could artless Jeanie do?
  She had na will to say him na:
At length she blush'd a sweet consent,
  And love was ay between them twa.

LINES ON JOHN M'MURDO, ESQ.

BLEST be M'Murdo to his latest day!
No envious cloud o'ercast his evening ray;
No wrinkle, furrow'd by the hand of care,
Nor ever sorrow add one silver hair!
O may no son the father's honour stain,
Nor ever daughter give the mother pain!

EPITAPH ON A LAPDOG

IN wood and wild, ye warbling throng,
  Your heavy loss deplore;
Now, half extinct your powers of song,
  Sweet 'Echo' is no more.

Ye jarring, screeching things around,
  Scream your discordant joys;
Now, half your din of tuneless sound
  With 'Echo' silent lies.

EPIGRAMS AGAINST THE EARL OF GALLOWAY

WHAT dost thou in that mansion fair?
　　Flit, Galloway, and find
Some narrow, dirty, dungeon cave,
　　The picture of thy mind.

No Stewart art thou, Galloway,
　　The Stewarts all are brave;
Besides, the Stewarts were but fools,
　　Not one of them a knave.

Bright ran thy line, O Galloway,
　　Thro' many a far-famed sire!
So ran the far-famed Roman way,
　　And ended in a mire.

Spare me thy vengeance, Galloway!
　　In quiet let me live:
I ask no kindness at thy hand,
　　For thou hast none to give.

EPIGRAM ON THE LAIRD OF LAGGAN

WHEN Morine, deceas'd, to the Devil went down,
'Twas nothing would serve him but Satan's own crown;
'Thy fool's head,' quoth Satan, 'that crown shall wear
　　never,
I grant thou'rt as wicked, but not quite so clever.'

PHILLIS THE FAIR

WHILE larks, with little wing, fann'd the pure air,
Tasting the breathing Spring, forth I did fare:
    Gay the sun's golden eye
    Peep'd o'er the mountains high;
Such thy morn! did I cry, Phillis the fair.

In each bird's careless song, glad I did share;
While yon wild-flow'rs among, chance led me there
    Sweet to the op'ning day,
    Rosebuds bent the dewy spray;
Such thy bloom! did I say, Phillis the fair.

Down in the shady walk, doves cooing were;
Mark'd I the cruel hawk caught in a snare:
    So kind may fortune be,
    Such make his destiny,
He who would injure thee, Phillis the fair.

HAD I A CAVE

Tune—'Robin Adair.'

HAD I a cave on some wild distant shore,
Where the winds howl to the wave's dashing roar
    There would I weep my woes,
    There seek my lost repose,
    Till grief my eyes should close,
      Ne'er to wake more!

Falsest of womankind, canst thou declare
All thy fond, plighted vows fleeting as air!
    To thy new lover hie,
    Laugh o'er thy perjury;
    Then in thy bosom try
      What peace is there!

BY ALLAN STREAM

By Allan stream I chanc'd to rove,
  While Phœbus sank beyond Benledi;
The winds were whispering through the grove,
  The yellow corn was waving ready :
I listen'd to a lover's sang,
  An' thought on youthfu' pleasures mony;
And ay the wild-wood echoes rang—
  'O, dearly do I lo'e thee, Annie !

'O happy be the woodbine bower,
  Nae nightly bogle make it eerie;
Nor ever sorrow stain the hour,
  The place and time I met my dearie !
Her head upon my throbbing breast,
  She, sinking, said, "I'm thine for ever !"
While mony a kiss the seal imprest—
  The sacred vow we ne'er should sever.'

The haunt o' Spring's the primrose-brae,
  The Summer joys the flocks to follow;
How cheery thro' her short'ning day,
  Is Autumn in her weeds o' yellow;
But can they melt the glowing heart,
  Or chain the soul in speechless pleasure ?
Or thro' each nerve the rapture dart,
  Like meeting her, our bosom's treasure ?

WHISTLE AND I'LL COME TO YE, MY LAD

Chorus.—O whistle an' I'll come to ye, my lad,
    O whistle an' I'll come to ye, my lad,
    Tho' father an' mither an' a' should gae
      mad,
    O whistle an' I'll come to ye, my lad.

But warily tent when ye come to court me,
  And come nae unless the back-yett be a-jee;
Syne up the back style, and let naebody see,
  And come as ye were na comin' to me,
  And come as ye were na comin' to me,
    O whistle an' I'll come, etc.

At kirk, or at market, whene'er ye meet me,
  Gang by me as tho' that ye car'd na a flie;
But steal me a blink o' your bonie black e'e,
  Yet look as ye were na lookin' to me,
  Yet look as ye were na lookin' to me,
    O whistle an' I'll come, etc.

Ay vow and protest that ye care na for me,
  And whyles ye may lightly my beauty a-wee;
But court na anither tho' jokin' ye be,
  For fear that she wyle your fancy frae me,
  For fear that she wyle your fancy frae me.
    O whistle an' I'll come, etc.

PHILLIS THE QUEEN O' THE FAIR

Adown winding Nith I did wander,
  To mark the sweet flowers as they spring;
Adown winding Nith I did wander,
  Of Phillis to muse and to sing.

Chorus.—Awa' wi' your Belles and your Beauties,
      They never wi' her can compare,
    Whaever has met wi' my Phillis,
      Has met wi' the queen o' the Fair.

The Daisy amus'd my fond fancy,
  So artless, so simple, so wild;
Thou emblem, said I, o' my Phillis—
  For she is Simplicity's child.
    Awa' wi' your Belles, etc.

The Rosebud's the blush o' my charmer,
    Her sweet balmy lip when 'tis prest :
How fair and how pure is the Lily !
    But fairer and purer her breast.
          Awa' wi' your Belles, etc.

Yon knot of gay flowers in the arbour,
    They ne'er wi' my Phillis can vie :
Her breath is the breath of the woodbine,
    Its dew-drop o' diamond her eye.
          Awa' wi' your Belles, etc.

Her voice is the song o' the morning,
    That wakes thro' the green-spreading grove
When Phœbus peeps over the mountains,
    On music, and pleasure, and love.
          Awa' wi' your Belles, etc.

But, Beauty, how frail and how fleeting !
    The bloom of a fine summer's day;
While worth in the mind o' my Phillis,
    Will flourish without a decay.
          Awa' wi' your Belles, etc.

COME, LET ME TAKE THEE TO MY BREAST

Come, let me take thee to my breast,
    And pledge we ne'er shall sunder;
And I shall spurn, as vilest dust,
    The world's wealth and grandeur :
And do I hear my Jeanie own
    That equal transports move her ?
I ask for dearest life alone,
    That I may live to love her.

Thus, in my arms, wi' a' her charms,
    I clasp my countless treasure;
I'll seek nae mair o' Heav'n to share,
    Than sic a moment's pleasure:
And by thy een sae bonie blue,
    I swear I'm thine for ever!
And on thy lips I seal my vow,
    And break it shall I never.

DAINTY DAVIE

Now rosy May comes in wi' flowers,
To deck her gay, green-spreading bowers;
And now comes in the happy hours,
    To wander wi' my Davie.

Chorus.—Meet me on the warlock knowe,
        Dainty Davie, dainty Davie;
        There I'll spend the day wi' you,
        My ain dear, dainty Davie.

The crystal waters round us fa',
The merry birds are lovers a',
The scented breezes round us blaw,
    A-wandering wi' my Davie.
        Meet me on, etc.

As purple morning starts the hare,
To steal upon her early fare,
Then thro' the dews I will repair,
    To meet my faithfu' Davie.
        Meet me on, etc.

When day, expiring in the west,
The curtain draws o' Nature's rest,
I flee to his arms I loe the best,
    And that's my ain dear Davie.
        Meet me on, etc.

ROBERT BRUCE'S MARCH TO BANNOCKBURN

Scots, wha hae wi' WALLACE bled,
Scots, wham Bruce has aften led,
Welcome to your gory bed,
   Or to Victorie!
Now's the day and now's the hour;
See the front o' battle lour;
See approach proud EDWARD's power—
   Chains and Slaverie!

Wha will be a traitor knave?
Wha can fill a coward's grave?
Wha sae base as be a slave?
   Let him turn and flee!
Wha for Scotland's King and Law,
Freedom's sword will strongly draw,
FREE-MAN stand, or FREE-MAN fa',
   Let him follow me!

By Oppression's woes and pains!
By your Sons in servile chains!
We will drain our dearest veins,
   But they *shall* be free!
Lay the proud Usurpers low!
Tyrants fall in every foe!
LIBERTY's in every blow!
   Let us Do—or Die!

BEHOLD THE HOUR, THE BOAT ARRIVE

VERSION SECOND

Behold the hour, the boat arrive;
 Thou goest, the darling of my heart;
Sever'd from thee, can I survive,
 But Fate has will'd and we must part.

I'll often greet the surging swell,
　Yon distant Isle will often hail:
'E'en here I took the last farewell;
　There, latest mark'd her vanish'd sail.'

Along the solitary shore,
　While flitting sea-fowl round me cry
Across the rolling, dashing roar,
　I'll westward turn my wistful eye:
'Happy, thou Indian grove,' I'll say,
　'Where now my Nancy's path may be!
While thro' thy sweets she loves to stray,
　O tell me, does she muse on me!'

THOU HAST LEFT ME EVER, JAMIE

Tune—'Fee him, father, fee him.'

THOU hast left me ever, Jamie,
　Thou hast left me ever:
Thou hast left me ever, Jamie,
　Thou hast left me ever:
Aften hast thou vow'd that Death
　Only should us sever;
Now thou'st left thy lass for ay—
　I maun see thee never, Jamie,
　I'll see thee never.

Thou hast me forsaken, Jamie,
　Thou hast me forsaken;
Thou hast me forsaken, Jamie,
　Thou hast me forsaken;
Thou canst love another jo,
　While my heart is breaking;
Soon my weary een I'll close,
　Never mair to waken, Jamie,
　Never mair to waken!

WHERE ARE THE JOYS I HAE MET?

Tune—'Saw ye my father.'

WHERE are the joys I hae met in the morning,
    That danc'd to the lark's early sang?
Where is the peace that awaited my wand'ring,
    At e'ening the wild-woods amang?

Nae mair a-winding the course o' yon river,
    And marking sweet flow'rets sae fair,
Nae mair I trace the light footsteps o' Pleasure,
    But Sorrow and sad-sighing Care.

Is it that Summer's forsaken our valleys,
    And grim, surly Winter is near?
No, no, the bees humming round the gay roses
    Proclaim it the pride o' the year.

Fain wad I hide what I fear to discover,
    Yet lang, lang, too well hae I known;
A' that has caused the wreck in my bosom,
    Is Jenny, fair Jenny alone.

Time cannot aid me, my griefs are immortal,
    Not Hope dare a comfort bestow:
Come, then, enamour'd and fond of my anguish,
    Enjoyment I'll seek in my woe.

DELUDED SWAIN, THE PLEASURE

Tune—'The Collier's Dochter.'

DELUDED swain, the pleasure
    The fickl Fair can give thee,
Is but a fairy treasure,
    Thy hopes will soon deceive thee:

B.P.   R

The billows on the ocean,
  The breezes idly roaming,
The cloud's uncertain motion,
  They are but types of Woman.

O art thou not asham'd
  To doat upon a feature?
If Man thou wouldst be nam'd
  Despise the silly creature.
Go, find an honest fellow,
  Good claret set before thee,
Hold on till thou art mellow,
  And then to bed in glory!

THINE AM I, MY FAITHFUL FAIR

Tune—'The Quaker's Wife.'

THINE am I, my faithful Fair,
  Thine, my lovely Nancy;
Ev'ry pulse along my veins,
  Ev'ry roving fancy.
To thy bosom lay my heart,
  There to throb and languish;
Tho' despair had wrung its core,
  That would heal its anguish.

Take away those rosy lips,
  Rich with balmy treasure;
Turn away thine eyes of love,
  Lest I die with pleasure!
What is life when wanting Love?
  Night without a morning:
Love's the cloudless summer sun,
  Nature gay adorning.

ON MRS RIDDELL'S BIRTHDAY,

NOVEMBER 4, 1793

OLD WINTER, with his frosty beard,
Thus once to Jove his prayer preferred:
'What have I done of all the' year,
To bear this hated doom severe?
My cheerless suns no pleasure know;
Night's horrid car drags dreary slow;
My dismal months no joys are crowning,
But spleeny English hanging, drowning.

'Now Jove, for once be mighty civil,
To counterbalance all this evil;
Give me, and I've no more to say,
Give me Maria's natal day!
That brilliant gift shall so enrich me,
Spring, Summer, Autumn, cannot match me.'
''Tis done!' says Jove; so ends my story,
And Winter once rejoiced in glory.

MY SPOUSE NANCY

Tune—'My Jo Janet.'

'HUSBAND, husband, cease your strife,
  Nor longer idly rave, Sir;
Tho' I am **your** wedded wife,
  Yet I am not your slave, Sir.'
'One of two must still obey,
  Nancy, Nancy;
Is it Man or Woman, say,
  My spouse Nancy?'

'If 'tis still the lordly word,
    Service and obedience;
I'll desert my sov'reign lord,
    And so, good-bye, allegiance!'
'Sad will I be, so bereft,
    Nancy, Nancy;
Yet I'll try to make a shift,
    My spouse Nancy.'

'My poor heart, then break it must,
    My last hour I'm near it:
When you lay me in the dust,
    Think how you will bear it.'
'I will hope and trust in Heaven,
    Nancy, Nancy;
Strength to bear it will be given,
    My spouse Nancy.'

'Well, Sir, from the silent dead,
    Still I'll try to daunt you;
Ever round your midnight bed
    Horrid sprites shall haunt you!'
'I'll wed another like my dear
    Nancy, Nancy;
Then all hell will fly for fear,
    My spouse Nancy.'

ADDRESS

SPOKEN BY MISS FONTENELLE ON HER BENEFIT NIGH
DECEMBER 4, 1793, AT THE THEATRE, DUMFRIES

STILL anxious to secure your partial favour,
And not less anxious, sure, this night than ever,
A Prologue, Epilogue, or some such matter,
'Twould vamp my bill, said I, if nothing better;

So sought a poet, roosted near the skies,
Told him, I came to feast my curious eyes;
Said, nothing like his works was ever printed;
And last, my prologue-business slily hinted.
'Ma'am, let me tell you,' quoth my man of rhymes,
'I know your bent—these are no laughing times:
Can you—but, Miss, I own I have my fears—
Dissolve in pause, and sentimental tears;
With laden sighs, and solemn-rounded sentence,
Rouse from his sluggish slumbers, fell Repentance;
Paint Vengeance as he takes his horrid stand,
Waving on high the desolating brand,
Calling the storms to bear him o'er a guilty land?'

I could no more—askance the creature eyeing,
D'ye think, said I, this face was made for crying?
I'll laugh, that's poz—nay more, the world shall know it;
And so, your servant! gloomy Master Poet!
Firm as my creed, Sirs, 'tis my fix'd belief,
That Misery's another word for Grief:
I also think—so may I be a bride!
That so much laughter, so much life enjoy'd.

Thou man of crazy care and ceaseless sigh,
Still under bleak Misfortune's blasting eye;
Doom'd to that sorest task of man alive—
To make three guineas do the work of five:
Laugh in Misfortune's face—the beldam witch!
Say, you'll be merry, tho' you can't be rich.

Thou other man of care, the wretch in love,
Who long with jiltish arts and airs hast strove;
Who, as the boughs all temptingly project,
Measur'st in desperate thought—a rope—thy neck—
Or, where the beetling cliff o'erhangs the deep,
Peerest to meditate the healing leap:

Wouldst thou be cur'd, thou silly, moping elf?
Laugh at her follies—laugh e'en at thyself:
Learn to despise those frowns now so terrific,
And love a kinder—that's your grand specific.

To sum up all, be merry, I advise;
And as we're merry, may we still be wise.

COMPLIMENTARY EPIGRAM ON
MARIA RIDDELL

'PRAISE Woman still,' his lordship roars,
    'Deserv'd or not, no matter!'
But thee, whom all my soul adores,
    Ev'n Flattery cannot flatter:
MARIA, all my thought and dream,
    Inspires my vocal shell;
The more I praise my lovely theme,
    The more the truth I tell.

REMORSEFUL APOLOGY

THE friend whom, wiled from Wisdom's way,
    The fumes of wine infuriate send,
(Not moony madness more astray)
    Who but deplores that hapless friend?

Mine was th' insensate frenzied part,
    Ah! why should I such scenes outlive?
Scenes so abhorrent to my heart!—
    'Tis thine to pity and forgive.

WILT THOU BE MY DEARIE?

Tune—'The Sutor's Dochter.'

WILT thou be my Dearie?
When sorrow wrings thy gentle heart,
  O wilt thou let me cheer thee!
By the treasure of my soul,
  That's the love I bear thee:
I swear and vow that only thou
  Shall ever be my Dearie!
Only thou, I swear and vow,
  Shall ever be my Dearie!

Lassie, say thou lo'es me;
Or, if thou wilt na be my ain,
  O say na thou'lt refuse me!
If it winna, canna be,
  Thou for thine may choose me,
Let me, lassie, quickly die,
  Still trusting that thou lo'es me!
Lassie, let me quickly die,
  Still trusting that thou lo'es me!

A FIDDLER IN THE NORTH

Tune—'The King o' France he rade a race.'

AMANG the trees, where humming bees,
  At buds and flowers were hinging, O,
Auld Caledon drew out her drone,
  And to her pipe was singing, O:
'Twas Pibroch, Sang, Strathspeys and Reels,
  She dirl'd them aff fu' clearly, O;
When there cam a yell o' foreign squeels,
  That dang her tapsalteerie, O.

Their capon craws an' queer ' ha, ha's,'
  They made our lugs grow eerie, O ;
The hungry bike did scrape and fyke,
  Till we were wae and weary O :
But a royal ghaist, wha ance was cas'd,
  A prisoner, aughteen year awa',
He fir'd a Fiddler in the North,
  That dang them tapsalteerie, O.

AS I STOOD BY YON ROOFLESS TOWER

As I stood by yon roofless tower,
  Where the wa'flow'r scents the dewy air,
Where the howlet mourns in her ivy bower,
  And tells the midnight moon her care.

Chorus.—A lassie all alone, was making her moan,
      Lamenting our lads beyond the sea ;
    In the bluidy wars they fa', and ou
      honor's gane an' a',
    And broken-hearted we maun die.

The winds were laid, the air was still,
  The stars they shot along the sky ;
The tod was howling on the hill,
  And the distant-echoing glens reply.
      A lassie all alone, etc.

The burn, adown its hazelly path,
  Was rushing by the ruin'd wa',
Hasting to join the sweeping Nith,
  Whase roarings seemed to rise and fa'.
      A lassie all alone, etc.

The cauld blae North was streaming forth
   Her lights, wi' hissing, eerie din,
Athort the lift they start and shift,
    Like Fortune's favors, tint as win'.
       A lassie all alone, etc.

Now, looking over frith and fauld,
   Her horn the pale-faced Cynthia rear'd,
When lo ! in form of Minstrel auld,
    A stern and stalwart ghaist appear'd.
       A lassie all alone, etc.

And frae his harp sic strains did flow,
   Might rous'd the slumbering Dead to hear;
But oh, it was a tale of woe,
    As ever met a Briton's ear !
       A lassie all alone, etc.

He sang wi' joy his former day,
   He, weeping, wail'd his latter times;
But what he said—it was nae play,
    I winna ventur't in my rhymes.
       A lassie all alone, etc.

A VISION

As I stood by yon roofless tower,
   Where the wa'flower scents the dewy air,
Where the howlet mourns in her ivy bower,
    And tells the midnight moon her care.

The winds were laid, the air was still,
   The stars they shot alang the sky;
The fox was howling on the hill,
    And the distant echoing glens reply.

The stream, adown its hazely path,
  Was rushing by the ruin'd wa's,
To join yon river on the Strath,
  Whase distant roaring swells and fa's.

The cauld blae North was streaming forth
  Her lights, wi' hissing, eerie din;
Athwart the lift they start and shift,
  Like Fortune's favors, tint as win.

By heedless chance I turn'd my eyes,
  And, by the moonbeam, shook to see
A stern and stalwart ghaist arise,
  Attir'd as Minstrels wont to be.

Had I statue been o' stane,
  His daring look had daunted me;
And on his bonnet grav'd was plain,
  The sacred posy—'LIBERTIE !'

And frae his harp sic strains did flow,
  Might rous'd the slumb'ring Dead to hear
But oh, it was a tale of woe,
  As ever met a Briton's ear !

He sang wi' joy his former day,
  He, weeping, wailed his latter times;
But what he said—it was nae play,
  I winna ventur't in my rhymes.

MY LUVE IS LIKE A RED, RED ROSE

My Luve is like a red, red rose,
  That's newly sprung in June :
My Luve is like the melodie,
  That's sweetly play'd in tune.

As fair art thou, my bonie lass,
  So deep in luve am I;
And I will luve thee still, my Dear,
  Till a' the seas gang dry.

Till a' the seas gang dry, my Dear,
  And the rocks melt wi' the sun;
And I will luve thee still, my Dear,
  While the sands o' life shall run.

And fare-thee-weel, my only Luve!
  And fare-thee-weel, a while!
And I will come again, my Luve,
  Tho' 'twere ten thousand mile!

YOUNG JAMIE

Young Jamie, pride of a' the plain,
Sae gallant and sae gay a swain,
Thro' a' our lasses he did rove,
And reign'd resistless King of Love.

But now, wi' sighs and starting tears,
He strays amang the woods and breers;
Or in the glens and rocky caves,
His sad complaining dowie raves :—

'I wha sae late did range and rove,
And chang'd with every moon my love,
I little thought the time was near,
Repentance I should buy sae dear.

'The slighted maids my torments see,
And laugh at a' the pangs I dree;
While she, my cruel, scornful Fair,
Forbids me e'er to see her mair.'

THE FLOWERY BANKS OF CREE

HERE is the glen, and here the bower
    All underneath the birchen shade;
The village-bell has told the hour,
    O what can stay my lovely maid?

'Tis not Maria's whispering call;
    'Tis but the balmy-breathing gale,
Mixt with some warbler's dying fall,
    The dewy star of eve to hail.

It is Maria's voice I hear;
    So calls the woodlark in the grove,
His little, faithful mate to cheer;
    At once 'tis music—and 'tis love.

And art thou come! and art thou true!
    O welcome dear to love and me!
And let us all our vows renew,
    Along the flowery banks of Cree.

MONODY

ON A LADY FAMED FOR HER CAPRICE

How cold is that bosom which folly once fired,
    How pale is that cheek where the rouge lately
        glisten'd;
How silent that tongue which the echoes oft tired
    How dull is that ear which to flatt'ry so listen'd!

If sorrow and anguish *their* exit await,
    From friendship and dearest affection remov'd;
How doubly severer, Maria, thy fate,
    Thou diedst unwept, as thou livedst unlov'd.

Loves, Graces, and Virtues, I call not on you;
  So shy, grave, and distant, ye shed not a tear:
But come, all ye offspring of Folly so true,
  And flowers let us cull for Maria's cold bier.

We'll search the garden for each silly flower,
  We'll roam thro' the forest for each idle weed;
But chiefly the nettle, so typical, shower,
  For none e'er approach'd her but rued the rash
    deed.

We'll sculpture the marble, we'll measure the lay;
  Here Vanity strums on her idiot lyre;
There keen Indignation shall dart on his prey,
  Which spurning Contempt shall redeem from his
    ire.

THE EPITAPH

Here lies, now a prey to insulting neglect,
  What once was a butterfly, gay in life's beam;
Want only of wisdom denied her respect,
  Want only of goodness denied her esteem.

PINNED TO MRS WALTER RIDDELL'S CARRIAGE

If you rattle along like your Mistress's tongue,
  Your speed will outrival the dart;
But a fly for your load, you'll break down on the road,
  If your stuff be as rotten's her heart.

EPITAPH FOR MR WALTER RIDDELL

Sic a reptile was Wat, sic a miscreant slave,
That the worms ev'n d—d him when laid in his grave;
In his flesh there's a famine,' a starved reptile cries,
And his heart is rank poison!' another replies.

EPISTLE FROM ESOPUS TO MARIA

From those drear solitudes and frowsy cells,
Where Infamy with sad Repentance dwells;
Where turnkeys make the jealous portal fast,
And deal from iron hands the spare repast,
Where truant 'prentices, yet young in sin,
Blush at the curious stranger peeping in;
Where strumpets, relics of the drunken roar,
Resolve to drink, nay half—to whore no more;
Where tiny thieves not destin'd yet to swing,
Beat hemp for others, riper for the string :
From these dire scenes my wretched lines I date,
To tell Maria her Esopus' fate.

'Alas ! I feel I am no actor here !'
'Tis real hangmen real scourges bear !
Prepare, Maria, for a horrid tale
Will turn thy very rouge to deadly pale;
Will make thy hair, tho' erst from gipsy poll'd,
By barber woven, and by barber sold,
Though twisted smooth with Harry's nicest care
Like hoary bristles to erect and stare.

The hero of the mimic scene, no more
I start in Hamlet, in Othello roar;
Or, haughty Chieftain, 'mid the din of arms,
In Highland bonnet, woo Malvina's charms;
While sans-culottes stoop up the mountain high,
And steal from me Maria's prying eye.
Blest Highland bonnet ! once my proudest dress,
Now prouder still, Maria's temples press;
I see her wave thy towering plumes afar,
And call each coxcomb to the wordy war :
I see her face the first of Ireland's sons,
And even out-Irish his Hibernian bronze;

The crafty Colonel leaves the tartan'd lines,
For other wars, where he a hero shines :
The hopeful youth, in Scottish senate bred,
Who owns a Bushby's heart without the head,
Comes 'mid a string of coxcombs, to display
That *veni, vidi, vici,* is his way :
The shrinking Bard adown the alley skulks,
And dreads a meeting worse than Woolwich hulks;
Though there, his heresies in Church and State
Might well award him Muir and Palmer's fate :
Still she undaunted reels and rattles on,
And dares the public like a noontide sun.
What scandal called Maria's jaunty stagger
The ricket reeling of a crooked swagger ?
Whose spleen (e'en worse than Burns's venom, when
He dips in gall unmix'd his eager pen,
And pours his vengeance in the burning line)—
Who christen'd thus Maria's lyre-divine
The idiot strum of Vanity bemus'd,
And even th' abuse of Poesy abus'd ?—
Who called her verse a Parish Workhouse, made
For motley foundling Fancies, stolen or strayed ?

A Workhouse ! ah, that sound awakes my woes,
And pillows on the thorn my rack'd repose !
In durance vile here must I wake and weep,
And all my frowsy couch in sorrow steep;
That straw where many a rogue has lain of yore,
And vermin'd gipsies litter'd heretofore.

Why, Lonsdale, thus thy wrath on vagrants pour ?
Must earth no rascal save thyself endure ?
Must thou alone in guilt immortal swell,
And make a vast monopoly of hell ?
Thou know'st the Virtues cannot hate thee worse;
The Vices also, must they club their curse ?
Or must no tiny sin to others fall,
Because thy guilt's supreme enough for all ?

Maria, send me to thy griefs and cares;
In all of thee sure thy Esopus shares.
As thou at all mankind the flag unfurls,
Who on my fair one Satire's vengeance hurls?
Who calls thee pert, affected, vain coquette,
A wit in folly, and a fool in wit?
Who says that fool alone is not thy due,
And quotes thy treacheries to prove it true?

Our force united on thy foes we'll turn,
And dare the war with all of woman born:
For who can write and speak as thou and I?
My periods that decyphering defy,
And thy still matchless tongue that conquers all reply!

EPITAPH ON A NOTED COXCOMB

CAPTAIN WM. RODDICK, OF CORBISTON

Light lay the earth on Billy's breast,
  His chicken heart so tender;
But build a castle on his head,
  His *scull* will prop it under.

ON CAPTAIN LASCELLES

When Lascelles thought fit from this world to depart,
Some friends warmly thought of embalming his heart;
A bystander whispers—'Pray don't make so much o't,
The subject is poison, no reptile will touch it.'

ON WM. GRAHAM, ESQ., OF MOSSKNOWE

'Stop, thief!' dame Nature called to Death,
  As Willy drew his latest breath;
How shall I make a fool again?
  My choicest model thou hast taen.

N JOHN BUSHBY, ESQ., TINWALD DOWNS

HERE lies John Bushby—*honest man*,
Cheat him, Devil—if you can!

SONNET ON THE DEATH OF ROBERT RIDDELL,

OF GLENRIDDELL AND FRIARS' CARSE

o more, ye warblers of the wood! no more;
 Nor pour your descant grating on my soul;
 Thou young-eyed Spring! gay in thy verdant stole,
ore welcome were to me grim Winter's wildest roar.

ow can ye charm, ye flowers, with all your dyes?
 Ye blow upon the sod that wraps my friend!
 How can I to the tuneful strain attend?
hat strain flows round the untimely tomb where
  Riddell lies.

es, pour, ye warblers! pour the notes of woe,
 And soothe the Virtues weeping o'er his bier:
 The man of worth—and hath not left his peer!
 in his 'narrow house,' for ever darkly low.

hee, Spring! again with joy shall others greet;
e, memory of my loss will only meet.

THE LOVELY LASS O' INVERNESS

THE lovely lass o' Inverness,
 Nae joy nor pleasure can she see;
For, e'en to morn she cries, 'alas!'
 And ay the saut tear blin's her e'e.

'Drumossie moor, Drumossie day—
    A waefu' day it was to me !
For there I lost my father dear,
    My father dear, and brethren three.

'Their winding-sheet the bluidy clay,
    Their graves are growin' green to see;
And by them lies the dearest lad
    That ever blest a woman's e'e !

'Now wae to thee, thou cruel lord,
    A bluidy man I trow thou be;
For mony a heart thou hast made sair,
    That ne'er did wrang to thine or thee !'

CHARLIE, HE'S MY DARLING

'TWAS on a Monday morning,
    Right early in the year,
That Charlie came to our town,
    The young Chevalier.

Chorus.—An' Charlie, he's my darling,
    My darling, my darling,
Charlie, he's my darling,
    The young Chevalier.

As he was walking up the street,
    The city for to view,
O there he spied a bonie lass
    The window looking through.
        An' Charlie, etc.

Sae light's he jumpèd up the stair,
    And tirl'd at the pin;
And wha sae ready as hersel
    To let the laddie in ?
        An' Charlie, etc.

He set his Jenny on his knee,
    All in his Highland dress;
For brawly well he ken'd the way
    To please a bonie lass.
            An' Charlie, etc.

It's up yon heathery mountain,
    An' down yon scroggie glen,
We daur na gang a milking,
    For Charlie and his men.
            An' Charlie, etc.

BANNOCKS O' BEAR MEAL

Chorus.—Bannocks o' bear meal,
            Bannocks o' barley,
        Here's to the Highlandman's
            Bannocks o' barley !

WHA, in a brulyie, will
    First cry 'A parley' ?
Never the lads wi' the
    Bannocks o' barley.
            Bannocks o' bear meal, etc.

Wha, in his wae days,
    Were loyal to Charlie ?
Wha but the lads wi' the
    Bannocks o' barley !
            Bannocks o' bear meal, etc.

THE HIGHLAND BALOU

HEE balou, my sweet wee Donald,
Picture o' the great Clanronald;
Brawlie kens our wanton Chief
Wha gat my young Highland thief.

Leeze me on thy bonie craigie,
An thou live, thou'll steal a naigie,
Travel the country thro' and thro',
And bring hame a Carlisle cow.

Thro' the Lawlands, o'er the Border,
Weel, my babie, may thou furder !
Harry the louns o' the laigh Countrie,
Syne to the Highlands hame to me.

THE HIGHLAND WIDOW'S LAMENT

OH I am come to the low Countrie,
 Ochon, Ochon, Ochrie !
Without a penny in my purse,
 To buy a meal to me.

It was na sae in the Highland hills,
 Ochon, Ochon, Ochrie !
Nae woman in the Country wide,
 Sae happy was as me.

For then I had a score o' kye,
 Ochon, Ochon, Ochrie !
Feeding on yon hill sae high,
 And giving milk to me.

And there I had three score o' yowes,
 Ochon, Ochon, Ochrie !
Skipping on yon bonie knowes,
 And casting woo to me.

I was the happiest of a' the Clan,
 Sair, sair may I repine;
For Donald was the brawest man,
 And Donald he was mine.

Till Charlie Stewart cam at last,
    Sae far to set us free;
My Donald's arm was wanted then,
    For Scotland and for me.

Their waefu' fate what need I tell,
    Right to the wrang did yield;
My Donald and his country fell,
    Upon Culloden field.

Ochon ! O Donald, oh !
    Ochon, Ochon, Ochrie !
Nae woman in the warld wide,
    Sae wretched now as me.

IT WAS A' FOR OUR RIGHTFU' KING

It was a' for our rightfu' King
    We left fair Scotland's strand;
It was a' for our rightfu' King
    We e'er saw Irish land, my dear,
    We e'er saw Irish land.

Now a' is done that men can do,
    And a' is done in vain;
My Love and Native Land fareweel,
    For I maun cross the main, my dear,
    For I maun cross the main.

He turn'd him right and round about,
    Upon the Irish shore;
And gae his bridle reins a shake,
    With adieu for evermore, my dear,
    And adieu for evermore.

The soger frae the war returns,
    The sailor frae the main;
But I hae parted frae my Love,
    Never to meet again, my dear,
    Never to meet again.

When day is gane, and night is come,
    And a' folk bound to sleep;
I think on him that's far awa',
    The lee-lang night and weep, my dear,
    The lee-lang night and weep.

ODE FOR GENERAL WASHINGTON'S BIRTHDAY

No Spartan tube, no Attic shell,
    No lyre Æolian I awake;
'Tis Liberty's bold note I swell,
    Thy harp, Columbia, let me take!
See gathering thousands, while I sing,
    A broken chain exulting bring,
        And dash it in a tyrant's face,
And dare him to his very beard,
And tell him he no more is feared—
    No more the despot of Columbia's race!
A tyrant's proudest insults brav'd,
They shout—a People freed! They hail an Empire
        saved.

Where is man's godlike form?
    Where is that brow erect and bold—
    That eye that can unmov'd behold
The wildest rage, the loudest storm
That e'er created fury dared to raise?
Avaunt! thou caitiff, servile, base,
That tremblest at a despot's nod,
Yet, crouching under the iron rod,
    Canst laud the hand that struck th' insulting blow!

Art thou of man's Imperial line?
Dost boast that countenance divine?
  Each skulking feature answers, No!
But come, ye sons of Liberty,
Columbia's offspring, brave as free,
In danger's hour still flaming in the van,
Ye know, and dare maintain, the Royalty of Man!

Alfred! on thy starry throne,
  Surrounded by the tuneful choir,
  The bards that erst have struck the patriot lyre,
  And rous'd the freeborn Briton's soul of fire,
No more thy England own!
Dare injured nations form the great design,
  To make detested tyrant's bleed?
  Thy England execrates the glorious deed!
  Beneath her hostile banners waving,
  Every pang of honour braving,
England in thunder calls, 'The tyrant's cause is mine!'
That hour accurst how did the fiends rejoice,
And hell, thro' all her confines, raise the exulting voice,
That hour which saw the generous English name
Linkt with such damned deeds of everlasting shame!

Thee, Caledonia! thy wild heaths among,
Fam'd for the martial deed, the heaven-taught song,
  To thee I turn with swimming eyes;
Where is that soul of Freedom fled?
Immingled with the mighty dead,
  Beneath that hallow'd turf where Wallace lies!
Hear it not, WALLACE! in thy bed of death.
  Ye babbling winds! in silence weep,
  Disturb not ye the hero's sleep,
Nor give the coward secret breath!
Is this the ancient Caledonian form,
Firm as the rock, resistless as the storm?

Show me that eye which shot immortal hate,
  Blasting the despot's proudest bearing;
Show me that arm which, nerv'd with thundering fate,
  Crush'd Usurpation's boldest daring !—
Dark-quench'd as yonder sinking star,
No more that glance lightens afar;
That palsied arm no more whirls on the waste of war.

TO MISS GRAHAM OF FINTRY

WITH A COPY OF THOMSON'S 'SCOTTISH AIRS'

HERE, where the Scottish Muse immortal lives,
  In sacred strains and tuneful numbers joined,
Accept the gift; though humble he who gives,
  Rich is the tribute of the grateful mind.

So may no ruffled feeling in thy breast,
  Discordant, jar thy bosom-chords among;
But Peace attune thy gentle soul to rest,
  Or Love ecstatic wake his seraph song.

Or Pity's notes, in luxury of tears,
  As modest Want the tale of woe reveals;
While conscious Virtue all the strains endears,
  And heaven-born Piety her sanction seals.

ON THE SEAS AND FAR AWAY

Tune—'Over the hills and far away.

How can my poor heart be glad,
When absent from my sailor lad?
How can I the thought forego—
He's on the seas to meet the foe?

Let me wander, let me rove,
Still my heart is with my love;
Nightly dreams, and thoughts by day,
Are with him that's far away.

Chorus.—On the seas and far away,
On stormy seas and far away;
Nightly dreams and thoughts by day,
Are ay with him that's far away.

When in summer noon I faint,
As weary flocks around me pant,
Haply in this scorching sun,
My sailor's thund'ring at his gun;
Bullets, spare my only joy !
Bullets, spare my darling boy !
Fate, do with me what you may,
Spare but him that's far away.
On the seas and far away,
On stormy seas and far away
Fate, do with me what you may,
Spare but him that's far away.

At the starless, midnight hour
When Winter rules with boundless power;
As the storms the forests tear,
And thunders rend the howling air,
Listening to the doubling roar,
Surging on the rocky shore,
All I can—I weep and pray
For his weal that's far away.
On the seas and far away,
On stormy seas and far away;
All I can—I weep and pray,
For his weal that's far away.

Peace, thy olive wand extend,
And bid wild War his ravage end,
Man with brother Man to meet,
And as a brother kindly greet;

Then may Heav'n with prosperous gales,
Fill my sailor's welcome sails;
To my arms their charge convey,
My dear lad that's far away.
On the seas and far away,
On stormy seas and far away;
To my arms their charge convey,
My dear lad that's far away.

CA' THE YOWES TO THE KNOWES

SECOND VERSION

Chorus.—Ca' the yowes to the knowes,
Ca' them where the heather grows,
Ca' them where the burnie rowes,
My bonie Dearie.

HARK, the mavis' e'ening sang,
Sounding Clouden's woods amang;
Then a-faulding let us gang,
My bonie Dearie.
Ca' the yowes, etc.

We'll gae down by Clouden side,
Thro' the hazels spreading wide,
O'er the waves that sweetly glide,
To the moon sae clearly.
Ca' the yowes, etc.

Yonder Clouden's silent towers,
Where, at moonshine's midnight hours,
O'er the dewy bending flowers,
Fairies dance sae cheery.
Ca' the yowes, etc.

Ghaist nor bogle shalt thou fear,
Thou'rt to Love and Heav'n sae dear,
Nocht of ill may come thee near;
   My bonie Dearie.
      Ca' the yowes, etc.

Fair and lovely as thou art,
Thou hast stown my very heart;
I can die—but canna part,
   My bonie Dearie.
      Ca' the yowes, etc.

SHE SAYS SHE LO'ES ME BEST OF A'

Tune—'Oonagh's Waterfall.'

SAE flaxen were her ringlets,
   Her eyebrows of a darker hue,
Bewitchingly o'er-arching
   Twa laughing een o' lovely blue;
Her smiling, sae wyling,
   Wad make a wretch forget his woe;
What pleasure, what treasure,
   Unto these rosy lips to grow !
Such was my Chloris' bonie face,
   When first that bonie face I saw
And ay my Chloris' dearest charm—
   She says she lo'es me best of a'.

Like harmony her motion,
   Her pretty ankle is a spy
Betraying fair proportion,
   Wad make a saint forget the sky :
Sae warming, sae charming,
   Her faultless form and gracefu' air;
Ilk feature—auld Nature
   Declar'd that she could do nae mair :

Hers are the willing chains o' love,
　By conquering Beauty's sovereign law;
And still my Chloris' dearest charm—
　She says she lo'es me best o' a'.

Let others love the city,
　And gaudy show, at sunny noon;
Gie me the lonely valley,
　The dewy eve, and rising moon,
Fair beaming, and streaming,
　Her silver light the boughs amang;
While falling, recalling,
　The amorous thrush concludes his sang:
Then, dearest Chloris, wilt thou rove,
　By wimpling burn and leafy shaw,
And hear my vows o' truth and love,
　And say thou lo'es me best of a'.

TO DR. MAXWELL

ON MISS JESSIE STAIG'S RECOVERY

MAXWELL, if here you merit crave,
　That merit I deny;
You save fair Jessie from the grave!—
　An angel could not die!

TO THE BEAUTIFUL MISS ELIZA J——N

ON HER PRINCIPLES OF LIBERTY AND EQUALITY

How, Liberty! girl, can it be by thee nam'd?
Equality too! hussey, art not asham'd?
Free and equal indeed, while mankind thou enchainest,
And over their hearts a proud Despot so reignest.

ON CHLORIS

REQUESTING ME TO GIVE HER A SPRIG OF BLOSSOMED THORN

FROM the white-blossom'd sloe my dear Chloris
  requested
A sprig, her fair breast to adorn :
No, by Heavens ! I exclaim'd, let me perish if ever
I plant in that bosom a thorn !

ON SEEING MRS KEMBLE IN YARICO

KEMBLE, thou cur'st my unbelief
  Of Moses and his rod;
At Yarico's sweet note of grief
  The rock with tears had flow'd.

EPIGRAM ON A COUNTRY LAIRD

NOT QUITE SO WISE AS SOLOMON

BLESS Jesus Christ, O Cardoness,
  With grateful, lifted eyes,
Who taught that not the soul alone,
  But *body* too shall rise;
For had He said 'The soul alone
  From death I will deliver,'
Alas, alas ! O Cardoness,
  Then hadst thou lain for ever.

ON BEING SHOWN A BEAUTIFUL
COUNTRY SEAT

BELONGING TO THE SAME LAIRD

WE grant they're thine, those beauties all,
    So lovely in our eye;
Keep them, thou eunuch, Cardoness,
    For others to enjoy!

ON HEARING IT ASSERTED FALSEHOOD

IS EXPRESSED IN THE REV. DR BABINGTON'S VERY LOOKS

THAT there is a falsehood in his looks,
    I must and will deny:
They tell their master is a knave,
    And sure they do not lie.

ON A SUICIDE

EARTH'D up, here lies an imp o' hell,
    Planted by Satan's dibble;
Poor silly wretch, he's damned himsel,
    To save the Lord the trouble.

ON A SWEARING COXCOMB

HERE cursing, swearing Burton lies,
A buck, a beau, or 'Dem my eyes!'
Who in his life did little good,
And his last words were, 'Dem my blood!'

ON AN INNKEEPER NICKNAMED 'THE MARQUIS'

HERE lies a mock Marquis, whose titles were
    shamm'd,
If ever he rise, it will be to be damn'd.

ON ANDREW TURNER

IN se'enteen hunder'n forty-nine,
The deil gat stuff to make a swine,
    An' coost it in a corner;
But wilily he chang'd his plan,
An' shap'd it something like a man,
    An' ca'd it Andrew Turner.

PRETTY PEG

As I gaed up by yon gate-end,
    When day was waxin' weary,
Wha did I meet come down the street,
    But pretty Peg, my dearie !

Her air sae sweet, an' shape complete,
    Wi nae proportion wanting,
The Queen of Love did never move
    Wi' motion mair enchanting.

Wi' linkèd hands, we took the sands,
    Adown yon winding river;
Oh, that sweet hour and shady bower,
    Forget it shall I never !

ESTEEM FOR CHLORIS

Ah, Chloris, since it may not be,
  That thou of love wilt hear;
If from the lover thou maun flee,
  Yet let the *friend* be dear.

Altho' I love my Chloris mair
  Than ever tongue could tell;
My passion I will ne'er declare—
  I'll say, I wish thee well.

Tho' a' my daily care thou art,
  And a' my nightly dream,
I'll hide the struggle in my heart,
  And say it is esteem.

SAW YOU MY DEAR, MY PHILLY

Tune—'When he cam ben she bobbet.'

O saw ye my Dear, my Philly?
O saw ye my Dear, my Philly?
She's down i' the grove, she's wi' a new Love,
  She winna come hame to her Willy.

What says she my Dear, my Philly?
What says she my Dear, my Philly?
She lets thee to wit she has thee forgot,
  And for ever disowns thee, her Willy.

O had I ne'er seen thee, my Philly!
O had I ne'er seen thee, my Philly!
As light as the air, and fause as thou's fair,
  Thou's broken the heart o' thy Willy.

HOW LANG AND DREARY IS THE NIGHT

Tune—'Cauld Kail in Aberdeen.'

How lang and dreary is the night
When I am frae my Dearie;
I restless lie frae e'en to morn
Tho' I were ne'er sae weary.

Chorus.—For oh, her lanely nights are lang!
And oh, her dreams are eerie;
And oh, her widow'd heart is sair,
That's absent frae her Dearie!

When I think on the lightsome days
I spent wi' thee, my Dearie;
And now what seas between us roar,
How can I be but eerie?
For oh, etc.

How slow ye move, ye heavy hours;
The joyless day how dreary:
It was na sae—ye glinted by,
When I was wi' my Dearie!
For oh, etc.

INCONSTANCY IN LOVE

Tune—'Duncan Gray.'

Let not Woman e'er complain
Of inconstancy in love;
Let not Woman e'er complain
Fickle Man is apt to rove:
Look abroad thro' Nature's range,
Nature's mighty Law is change,
Ladies, would it not seem strange
Man should then a monster prove?

B.P.   S

> Mark the winds, and mark the skies,
>   Ocean's ebb, and ocean's flow,
> Sun and moon but set to rise,
>   Round and round the seasons go.
> Why then ask of silly Man
> To oppose great Nature's plan?
> We'll be constant while we can—
>   You can be no more, you know.

THE LOVER'S MORNING SALUTE TO HIS MISTRESS

Tune—'Deil tak the wars.'

SLEEP'ST thou, or wak'st thou, fairest creature?
  Rosy morn now lifts his eye,
Numbering ilka bud which Nature
  Waters wi' the tears o' joy.
    Now, to the streaming fountain,
    Or up the heathy mountain,
The hart, hind, and roe, freely, wildly-wanton stray;
    In twining hazel bowers,
    Its lay the linnet pours,
    The laverock to the sky
    Ascends, wi' sangs o' joy,
While the sun and thou arise to bless the day.

Phœbus gilding the brow of morning,
  Banishes ilka darksome shade,
Nature, gladdening and adorning;
  Such to me my lovely maid.
    When frae my Chloris parted,
    Sad, cheerless, broken-hearted,
The night's gloomy shades, cloudy, dark, o'ercast
    my sky:

But when she charms my sight,
In pride of Beauty's light—
When thro' my very heart
Her burning glories dart;
'Tis then—'tis then I wake to life and joy!

THE WINTER OF LIFE

But lately seen in gladsome green,
   The woods rejoic'd the day,
Thro' gentle showers, the laughing flowers
   In double pride were gay:
But now our joys are fled
   On winter blasts awa';
Yet maiden May, in rich array,
   Again shall bring them a'.

But my white pow, nae kindly thowe
   Shall melt the snaws of Age;
My trunk of eild, but buss or bield,
   Sinks in Time's wintry rage.
Oh, Age has weary days,
   And nights o' sleepless pain:
Thou golden time o' Youthfu' prime,
   Why comes thou not again!

BEHOLD, MY LOVE, HOW GREEN THE GROVES

Tune—'My lodging is on the cold ground.'

Behold, my love, how green the groves,
   The primrose banks how fair;
The balmy gales awake the flowers,
   And wave thy flowing hair.

The lav'rock shuns the palace gay,
　And o'er the cottage sings :
For Nature smiles as sweet, I ween,
　To Shepherds as to Kings.

Let minstrels sweep the skilfu' strings,
　In lordly lighted ha' :
The Shepherd stops his simple reed,
　Blythe in the birken shaw.

The Princely revel may survey
　Our rustic dance wi' scorn;
But are their hearts as light as ours,
　Beneath the milk-white thorn ?

The shepherd, in the flowery glen;
　In shepherd's phrase, will woo :
The courtier tells a finer tale,
　But is his heart as true ?

These wild-wood flowers I've pu'd, to deck
　That spotless breast o' thine :
The courtier's gems may witness love,
　But, 'tis na love like mine.

THE CHARMING MONTH OF MAY

SONG, ALTERED FROM AN OLD ENGLISH ONE

It was the charming month of May,
When all the flow'rs were fresh and gay,
One morning, by the break of day,
　The youthful, charming Chloe—
From peaceful slumber she arose,
Girt on her mantle and her hose,
And o'er the flow'ry mead she goes—
　The youthful, charming Chloe.

Chorus.—Lovely was she by the dawn,
              Youthful Chloe, charming Chloe,
          Tripping o'er the pearly lawn,
              The youthful, charming Chloe.

The feather'd people you might see
Perch'd all around on every tree,
In notes of sweetest melody
    They hail the charming Chloe;
Till, painting gay the eastern skies,
The glorious sun began to rise,
Outrivall'd by the radiant eyes
    Of youthful, charming Chloe.
        Lovely was she, etc.

LASSIE WI' THE LINT-WHITE LOCKS

Tune—'Rothiermurchie's Rant.'

Chorus.—Lassie wi' the lint-white locks,
              Bonie lassie, artless lassie,
          Wilt thou wi' me tent the flocks,
              Wilt thou be my Dearie, O ?

Now Nature cleeds the flowery lea,
And a' is young and sweet like thee,
O wilt thou share its joys wi' me,
    And say thou'lt be my Dearie, O.
        Lassie wi' the, etc.

The primrose bank, the wimpling burn,
The cuckoo on the milk-white thorn,
The wanton lambs at early morn,
    Shall welcome thee, my Dearie, O.
        Lassie wi' the, etc.

And when the welcome summer shower
Has cheer'd ilk drooping little flower,
We'll to the breathing woodbine-bower,
 At sultry noon, my Dearie, O.
  Lassie wi' the, etc.

When Cynthia lights, wi' silver ray,
The weary shearer's hameward way,
Thro' yellow waving fields we'll stray,
 And talk o' love, my Dearie, O.
  Lassie wi' the, etc.

And when the howling wintry blast
Disturbs my lassie's midnight rest,
Enclaspèd to my faithfu' breast,
 I'll comfort thee, my Dearie, O.
  Lassie wi' the, etc.

PHILLY AND WILLY

Tune—'The Sow's tail to Geordie.'

He. O Philly, happy be that day,
  When roving thro' the gather'd hay,
  My youthfu' heart was stown away,
   And by thy charms, my Philly.
She. O Willy, ay I bless the grove
  Where first I own'd my maiden love,
  Whilst thou did pledge the Powers above,
   To be my ain dear Willy.
Both. For a' the joys that gowd can gie,
  I dinna care a single flie;

The $\begin{Bmatrix} \text{lad} \\ \text{lass} \end{Bmatrix}$ I love's the $\begin{Bmatrix} \text{lad} \\ \text{lass} \end{Bmatrix}$ for me,

 And that's my ain dear $\begin{Bmatrix} \text{Willy.} \\ \text{Philly.} \end{Bmatrix}$

He. As songsters of the early year
 Are ilka day mair sweet to hear,
 So ilka day to me mair dear
  And charming is my Philly.

She. As on the brier the budding rose
 Still richer breathes and fairer blows,
 So in my tender bosom grows
  The love I bear my Willy.
 Both. For a' the joys, etc.

He. The milder sun and bluer sky
 That crown my harvest cares wi' joy,
 Were ne'er sae welcome to my eye
  As is the sight o' Philly.

She. The little swallow's wanton wing,
 Tho' wafting o'er the flowery Spring,
 Did ne'er to me sic tidings bring,
  As meeting o' my Willy.
 Both. For a' the joys, etc.

He. The bee that thro' the sunny hour
 Sips nectar in the op'ning flower,
 Compar'd wi' my delight is poor,
  Upon the lips o' Philly.

She. The woodbine in the dewy weet,
 When ev'ning shades in silence meet,
 Is nocht sae fragrant or sae sweet
  As is a kiss o' Willy.
 Both. For a' the joys, etc.

He. Let fortune's wheel at random rin,
 And fools may tyne, and knaves may win,
 My thoughts are a' bound up in ane,
  And that's my ain dear Philly.

She. What's a' the joys that gowd can gie?
 I dinna care a single flie;
 The lad I love's the lad for me,
  And that's my ain dear Willy.
 Both. For a' the joys, etc.

CONTENTED WI' LITTLE AND CANTIE WI' MAIR

CONTENTED wi' little, and cantie wi' mair,
Whene'er I forgather wi' Sorrow and Care,
I gie them a skelp as they're creepin' alang,
Wi' a cog o' gude swats and an auld Scottish sang.
                    Chorus.—Contented wi' little, etc.

I whyles claw the elbow o' troublesome thought;
But Man is a soger, and Life is a faught;
My mirth and gude humour are coin in my pouch,
And my Freedom's my Lairdship nae monarch dare
    touch.
                            Contented wi' little, etc.

A towmond o' trouble, should that be my fa',
A night o' gude fellowship sowthers it a':
When at the blythe end o' our journey at last,
Wha the deil ever thinks o' the road he has past?
                        Contented wi' little, etc.

Blind chance, let her snapper and stoyte on her way;
Be't to me, be't frae me, e'en let the jade gae:
Come Ease, or come Travail, come Pleasure or Pain,
My warst word is: 'Welcome, and welcome again!'
                            Contented wi' little, etc.

FAREWELL, THOU STREAM

Air—'Nansie's to the greenwood gane.'

FAREWELL, thou stream that winding flows
    Around Eliza's dwelling;
O mem'ry! spare the cruel throes
    Within my bosom swelling.

Condemn'd to drag a hopeless chain,
   And yet in secret languish;
To feel a fire in every vein,
   Nor dare disclose my anguish.

Love's veriest wretch, unseen, unknown,
   I fain my griefs would cover;
The bursting sigh, th' unweeting groan,
   Betray the hapless lover.
I know thou doom'st me to despair,
   Nor wilt, nor canst relieve me;
But, O Eliza, hear one prayer—
   For pity's sake forgive me!

The music of thy voice I heard,
   Nor wist while it enslav'd me!
I saw thine eyes, yet nothing fear'd,
   Till fears no more had sav'd me:
Th' unwary sailor thus, aghast,
   The wheeling torrent viewing,
'Mid circling horrors sinks at last,
   In overwhelming ruin.

ANST THOU LEAVE ME THUS, MY KATIE?

Tune—'Roy's Wife.'

Chorus.—Canst thou leave me thus, my Katie?
      Canst thou leave me thus, my Katie?
   Well thou know'st my aching heart,
      And canst thou leave me thus, for pity?

Is this thy plighted, fond regard,
　　Thus cruelly to part, my Katie?
Is this thy faithful swain's reward—
　　An aching, broken heart, my Katie?
　　　　　　　　Canst thou leave me, etc.

Farewell! and ne'er such sorrows tear
　　That fickle heart of thine, my Katie!
Thou mayst find those will love thee dear,
　　But not a love like mine, my Katie.
　　　　　　　　Canst thou leave me, etc.

MY NANIE'S AWA'

Tune—'There'll never be peace till Jamie comes hame.'

Now in her green mantle blythe Nature arrays,
And listens the lambkins that bleat o'er the braes,
While birds warble welcome in ilka green shaw,
But to me it's delightless—my Nanie's awa'.

The snawdrap and primrose our woodlands adorn,
And violets bathe in the weet o' the morn;
They pain my sad bosom, sae sweetly they blaw,
They mind me o' Nanie—and Nanie's awa'.

Thou lav'rock that springs frae the dews of the lawn
The shepherd to warn o' the gray-breaking dawn,
And thou mellow mavis that hails the night-fa'.
Give over for pity—my Nanie's awa'.

Come Autumn, sae pensive, in yellow and gray,
And sooth me wi' tidings o' Nature's decay:
The dark, dreary Winter, and wild-driving snaw
Alane can delight me—now Nanie's awa'.

THE TEAR-DROP

WAE is my heart, and the tear's in my e'e;
Lang, lang has Joy been a stranger to me:
Forsaken and friendless, my burden I hear,
And the sweet voice o' Pity ne'er sounds in my ear.

Love, thou hast pleasures, and deep hae I lov'd;
Love, thou hast sorrows, and sair hae I prov'd;
But this bruisèd heart that now bleeds in my breast,
I can feel by its throbbings, will soon be at rest.

Oh, if I were—where happy I hae been—
Down by yon stream, and yon bonie castle-green;
For there he is wand'ring and musing on me,
Wha wad soon dry the tear-drop that clings to my
    e'e.

FOR THE SAKE O' SOMEBODY

My heart is sair—I dare na tell,
    My heart is sair for Somebody;
I could wake a winter night
    For the sake o' Somebody.
        O-hon! for Somebody!
        O-hey! for Somebody!
I could range the world around,
    For the sake o' Somebody.

Ye Powers that smile on virtuous love,
    O, sweetly smile on Somebody!
Frae ilka danger keep him free,
    And send me safe my Somebody!
        O-hon! for Somebody!
        O-hey! for Somebody!
I wad do—what wad I not?
    For the sake o' Somebody.

A MAN'S A MAN FOR A' THAT

Tune—'For a' that.'

Is there for honest Poverty
    That hings his head, an' a' that;
The coward slave—we pass him by,
    We dare be poor for a' that!
For a' that, an' a' that,
    Our toils obscure an' a' that,
The rank is but the guinea's stamp,
    The Man's the gowd for a' that.

What though on hamely fare we dine,
    Wear hoddin gray, an' a' that;
Gie fools their silks, and knaves their wine,
    A Man's a Man for a' that:
For a' that, an' a' that,
    Their tinsel show, an' a' that;
The honest man, tho' e'er sae poor,
    Is king o' men for a' that.

Ye see yon birkie ca'd 'a lord,'
    Wha struts, an' stares, an' a' that;
Tho' hundreds worship at his word,
    He's but a coof for a' that:
For a' that, an' a' that,
    His ribband, star, an' a' that;
The man o' independent mind
    He looks an' laughs at a' that.

A prince can mak a belted knight,
    A marquis, duke, an' a' that;
But an honest man's aboon his might,
    Gude faith, he mauna fa' that!
For a' that, an' a' that,
    Their dignities, an' a' that;
The pith o' sense, an' pride o' worth,
    Are higher rank than a' that.

Then let us pray that come it may
    (As come it will for a' that),
That Sense and Worth o'er a' the earth,
    Shall bear the gree, an' a' that.
For a' that, an' a' that,
    It's comin' yet for a' that,
That Man to Man, the world o'er,
    Shall brothers be for a' that.

CRAIGIEBURN WOOD

SECOND VERSION

SWEET fa's the eve on Craigieburn,
    And blythe awakes the morrow;
But a' the pride o' Spring's return
    Can yield me nocht but sorrow.

I see the flowers and spreading trees,
    I hear the wild birds singing;
But what a weary wight can please,
    And Care his bosom wringing!

Fain, fain would I my griefs impart,
    Yet dare na for your anger;
But secret love will break my heart,
    If I conceal it langer.

If thou refuse to pity me,
    If thou shalt love another,
When yon green leaves fade frae the tree,
    Around my grave they'll wither.

THE SOLEMN LEAGUE AND COVENANT

THE Solemn League and Covenant
  Now brings a smile, now brings a tear;
But sacred Freedom, too, was theirs:
  If thou'rt a slave, indulge thy sneer.

TO JOHN SYME OF RYEDALE

WITH A PRESENT OF A DOZEN OF PORTER

O HAD the malt thy strength of mind,
  Or hops the flavour of thy wit,
'Twere drink for first of human kind,
  A gift that ev'n for Syme were fit.

JERUSALEM TAVERN, DUMFRIES.

INSCRIPTION ON A GOBLET

THERE's Death in the cup, so beware!
  Nay more—there is danger in touching;
But who can avoid the fell snare,
  The man and his wine's so bewitching!

APOLOGY FOR DECLINING AN INVITATION
TO DINE

No more of your guests, be they titled or not,
  And cookery the first in the nation;
Who is proof to thy personal converse and wit,
  Is proof to all other temptation.

EPITAPH FOR MR GABRIEL RICHARDSON

HERE Brewer Gabriel's fire's extinct,
    And empty all his barrels:
He's blest—if, as he brew'd, he drink,
    In upright, honest morals.

EPIGRAM ON MR JAMES GRACIE

GRACIE, thou art a man of worth,
    O be thou Dean for ever!
May he be d—d to hell henceforth,
    Who fauts thy weight or measure!

INSCRIPTION AT FRIARS' CARSE
HERMITAGE

TO THE MEMORY OF ROBERT RIDDELL

To RIDDELL, much lamented man,
    This ivied cot was dear;
Wand'rer, dost value matchless worth?
    This ivied cot revere.

BONIE PEG-A-RAMSAY

CAULD is the e'enin' blast
    O' Boreas o'er the pool,
An' dawin' it is dreary,
    When birks are bare at Yule.

Cauld blaws the e'enin' blast,
When bitter bites the frost,
And, in the mirk and dreary drift,
The hills and glens are lost :

Ne'er sae murky blew the night,
That drifted o'er the hill,
But bonie Peg-a-Ramsay
Gat grist to her mill.

OVER SEA, OVER SHORE

THERE was a bonie lass, and a bonie, bonie lass,
And she lo'ed her bonie laddie dear;
Till War's loud alarms tore her laddie frae her arms
Wi' mony a sigh, and a tear.
Over sea, over shore, where the canons loudly roar
He still was a stranger to fear;
And nocht could him quail, or his bosom assail,
But the bonie lass he lo'ed sae dear.

WEE WILLIE GRAY

WEE Willie Gray, and his leather wallet,
Peel a willow wand to be him boots and jacket;
The rose upon the breer will be him trews an' doublet
The rose upon the breer will be him trews an' doublet

Wee Willie Gray, and his leather wallet,
Twice a lily-flower will be him sark and cravat;
Feathers of a flee wad feather up his bonnet,
Feathers of a flee wad feather up his bonnet.

AY MY WIFE SHE DANG ME

Chorus.—O ay my wife she dang me,
   An' aft my wife she bang'd me,
  If ye gie a woman a' her will,
   Gude faith! she'll soon o'er-gang ye.

On peace an' rest my mind was bent,
 And, fool I was! I married;
But never honest man's intent
 Sae cursedly miscarried.
   O ay my wife, etc.

Some sairie comfort at the last,
 When a' thir days are done, man,
My 'pains o' hell' on earth is past,
 I'm sure o' bliss aboon, man.
   O ay my wife, etc.

GUDE ALE KEEPS THE HEART ABOON

Chorus.—O gude ale comes, and gude ale goes;
   Gude ale gars me sell my hose,
  Sell my hose, and pawn my shoon—
   Gude ale keeps my heart aboon!

I had sax owsen in a pleugh,
 And they drew a' weel eneugh:
I sell'd them a' just ane by ane—
 Gude ale keeps the heart aboon!
   O gude ale comes, etc.

Gude ale hauds me bare and busy,
Gars me moop wi' the servant hizzie,
Stand i' the stool when I hae dune—
 Gude ale keeps the heart aboon!
   O gude ale comes, etc.

STEER HER UP AN' HAUD HER GAUN

O STEER her up, an' haud her gaun,
  Her mither's at the mill, jo;
An' gin she winna tak a man,
  E'en let her tak her will, jo.
First shore her wi' a gentle kiss,
  And ca' anither gill, jo;
An' gin she tak the thing amiss,
  E'en let her flyte her fill, joe.

O steer her up, an' be na blate,
  An gin she tak it ill, jo,
Then leave the lassie till her fate,
  And time nae langer spill, jo :
Ne'er break your heart for ae rebute,
  But think upon it still, jo :
That gin the lassie winna do't,
  Ye'll find anither will, jo.

THE LASS O' ECCLEFECHAN

Tune—'Jack o Latin.'

GAT ye me, O gat ye me,
  O gat ye me wi' naething ?
Rock and reel, and spinning wheel,
  A mickle quarter basin :
Bye attour, my Gutcher has
  A heich house and a laich ane,
A' forbye my bonie sel,
  The toss o' Ecclefechan.

O haud your tongue now, Lucky Lang,
   O haud your tongue and jauner;
I held the gate till you I met,
   Syne I began to wander :
I tint my whistle and my sang,
   I tint my peace and pleasure;
But your green graff, now, Lucky Lang,
   Wad airt me to my treasure.

O LET ME IN THIS AE NIGHT

O LASSIE, are ye sleepin' yet,
   Or are ye waukin, I wad wit ?
For Love has bound me hand an' fit,
   And I would fain be in, jo.

Chorus.—O let me in this ae night,
     This ae, ae, ae night;
     O let me in this ae night,
     I'll no come back again, jo !

O hear'st thou not the wind an' weet ?
Nae star blinks thro' the driving sleet;
Tak pity on my weary feet,
   And shield me frae the rain, jo.
     O let me in, etc.

The bitter blast that round me blaws,
Unheeded howls, unheeded fa's;
The cauldness o' thy heart's the cause
   Of a' my care and pine, jo.
     O let me in, etc.

HER ANSWER

O tell na me o' wind and rain,
Upbraid na me wi' cauld disdain,
Gae back the gate ye cam again,
   I winna let ye in, jo.

Chorus.—I tell you now this ae night,
   This ae, ae, ae night;
  And ance for a' this ae night,
   I winna let ye in, jo.

The snellest blast, at mirkest hours,
That round the pathless wand'rer pours,
Is nocht to what poor she endures,
  That's trusted faithless man, jo.
   I tell you now, etc.

The sweetest flower that deck'd the mead,
Now trodden like the vilest weed—
Let simple maid the lesson read,
  The weird may be her ain, jo.
   I tell you now, etc.

The bird that charm'd his summer day,
Is now the cruel Fowler's prey;
Let witless, trusting Woman say
  How aft her fate's the same, jo !
   I tell you now, etc.

I'LL AY CA' IN BY YON TOWN

Air—'I'll gang nae mair to yon town.'

Chorus.—I'll ay ca' in by yon town,
   And by yon garden-green again;
  I'll ay ca' in by yon town,
   And see my bonie Jean again.

THERE's nane shall ken, there's nane can guess
 What brings me back the gate again,
But she, my fairest, faithfu' lass,
 And stow'nlins we sall meet again.
   I'll ay ca' in, etc.

She'll wander by the aiken tree,
　When trystin' time draws near again;
And when her lovely form I see,
　O haith! she's doubly dear again.
　　　　I'll ay ca' in, etc.

WAT YE WHA'S IN YON TOWN?

Air—'I'll gang nae mair to yon town.'

Chorus—O wat ye wha's in yon town,
　　　　Ye see the e'enin' sun upon?
　　　　The dearest maid's in yon town,
　　　　That e'enin' sun is shining on.

Now haply down yon gay green shaw,
　She wanders by yon spreading tree;
How blest ye flowers that round her blaw,
　Ye catch the glances o' her e'e!
　　　　O wat ye wha's, etc.

How blest ye birds that round her sing,
　And welcome in the blooming year;
And doubly welcome be the Spring,
　The season to my Jeanie dear.
　　　　O wat ye wha's, etc.

The sun blinks blythe in yon town,
　Among the broomy braes sae green;
But my delight in yon town,
　And dearest pleasure, is my Jean.
　　　　O wat ye wha's, etc.

Without my Fair, not a' the charms
　O' Paradise could yield me joy;
But give me Jeanie in my arms,
　And welcome Lapland's dreary sky!
　　　　O wat ye wha's, etc.

My cave wad be a lover's bower,
　Tho' raging Winter rent the air;
And she a lovely little flower,
　That I wad tent and shelter there.
　　　　　O wat ye wha's, etc.

O sweet is she in yon town,
　The sinkin' Sun's gane down upon;
A fairer than's in yon town,
　His setting beam ne'er shone upon.
　　　　　O wat ye wha's, etc.

If angry Fate is sworn my foe,
　And suff'ring I am doom'd to bear;
I careless quit aught else below,
　But spare, O spare me Jeanie dear.
　　　　　O wat ye wha's, etc.

For while life's dearest blood is warm,
　Ae thought frae her shall ne'er depart,
And she, as fairest is her form,
　She has the truest, kindest heart.
　　　　　O wat ye wha's, etc.

BALLADS ON MR HERON'S ELECTION, 1795

BALLAD FIRST

WHOM will you send to London town,
　To Parliament and a' that?
Or wha in a' the country round
　The best deserves to fa' that?
　　For a' that, and a' that,
　　Thro' Galloway and a' that,
　Where is the Laird or belted Knight
　　That best deserves to fa' that?

Wha sees Kerroughtree's open yett
  (And wha is't never saw that?)
Wha ever wi' Kerroughtree met,
  And has a doubt of a' that?
    For a' that, and a' that,
      Here's Heron yet for a' that!
    The independent patriot,
      The honest man, and a' that.

Tho' wit and worth, in either sex,
  Saint Mary's Isle can shaw that,
Wi' Dukes and Lords let Selkirk mix,
  And weel does Selkirk fa' that.
    For a' that, and a' that,
      Here's Heron yet for a' that!
    The independent commoner
      Shall be the man for a' that.

But why should we to Nobles jouk,
  And is't against the law, that?
For why, a Lord may be a gowk,
  Wi' ribband, star, and a' that.
    For a' that, and a' that,
      Here's Heron yet for a' that!
    A Lord may be a lousy loon,
      Wi' ribband, star and a' that.

A beardless boy comes o'er the hills,
  Wi' uncle's purse and a' that;
But we'll hae ane frae 'mang oursels,
  A man we ken, and a' that.
    For a' that, and a' that,
      Here's Heron yet for a' that!
    For we're not to be bought and sold,
      Like naigs, and nowte, and a' that.

Then let us drink—The Stewartry,
  Kerroughtree's laird, and a' that,
Our representative to be,
  For weel he's worthy a' that.

For a' that, and a' that,
 Here's Heron yet for a' that!
A House of Commons such as he,
 They wad be blest that saw that.

BALLAD SECOND—ELECTION DAY

Tune—'Fy, let us a' to the Bridal.'

Fy, let us a' to Kirkcudbright,
 For there will be bickerin' there;
For Murray's *light horse* are to muster,
 And O how the heroes will swear!
And there will be *Murray*, Commander,
 And Gordon, the battle to win;
Like brothers they'll stand by each other,
 Sae knit in alliance and kin.

And there will be black-nebbit *Johnie*,
 The tongue o' the trump to them a';
An he get na Hell for his haddin',
 The Deil gets nae justice ava;
And there will be *Kempleton's* birkie,
 A boy no sae black at the bane;
But as to his fine *Nabob* fortune,
 We'll e'en let the subject alane.

And there will be Wigton's new Sheriff;
 Dame Justice fu' brawly has sped,
She's gotten the heart of a *Bushby*,
 But, Lord! what's become o' the head?
And there will be *Cardoness*, Esquire,
 Sae mighty in *Cardoness*' eyes;
A wight that will weather damnation,
 The Devil the prey will despise.

And there will be *Douglasses* doughty,
   New christening towns far and near;
Abjuring their democrat doings,
   By kissin' the —— o' a Peer :
And there will be folk frae *Saint Mary's*,
   A *house* o' great merit and note;
The deil ane but honors them highly—
   The deil ane will gie them his vote !

And there will be *Kenmure* sae gen'rous,
   Whose honor is proof to the storm,
To save them from stark reprobation,
   He lent them his name in the Firm.
And there will be lads o' the gospel,
   Muirhead, wha's as *gude* as he's *true* ;
And there will be Buittle's *Apostle*,
   Wha's mair o' the black than the blue.

And there will be *Logan M'Dowall*,
   Sculdudd'ry an' he will be there,
And also the *Wild Scot o' Galloway*,
   Sogering, gunpowder *Blair*.
But we winna mention Redcastle,
   The *body*, e'en let him escape !
He'd venture the gallows for siller,
   An' 'twere na the cost o' the rape.

But where is the Doggerbank hero
   That made 'Hogan Mogan' to skulk ?
Poor *Keith's* gane to h—ll to be fuel,
   The auld rotten wreck of a hulk.
And where is our King's Lord Lieutenant,
   Sae fam'd for his *gratefu'* return ?
The birkie is gettin' his questions
   To say in Saint Stephen's the morn.

But mark ye ! there's trusty *Kerroughtree*,
   Whose honor was ever his law;
If the Virtues were pack'd in a parcel,
   His worth might be sample for a';

And strang an' respectfu's his backing,
    The maist o' the lairds wi' him stand;
Nae gipsy-like nominal barons,
    Wha's property's paper—not land.

And there, frae the Niddisdale borders,
    The *Maxwells* will gather in droves,
Teugh *Jockie*, staunch *Geordie*, an' *Wellwood*,
    That griens for the fishes and loaves,
And there will be *Heron*, the Major,
    Wha'll ne'er be forgot in the *Greys;*
Our flatt'ry we'll keep for some other,
    HIM, only it's justice to praise.

And there will be maiden *Kilkerran*,
    And also *Barskimming's* gude Knight,
And there will be roarin' *Birtwhistle*,
    Yet luckily roars i' the right.
And there'll be Stamp Office *Johnie*
    (Tak tent how ye purchase a dram!)
And there will be gay *Cassencarry*,
    And there'll be gleg Colonel *Tam*.

And there'll be wealthy young *Richard*,
    Dame Fortune should hing by the neck,
For prodigal, thriftless bestowing—
    His merit had won him respect.
And there will be rich brother *Nabobs*
    (Tho' *Nabobs*, yet men not the worst),
And there will be *Collieston's* whiskers,
    And *Quintin*—a lad o' the first.

Then hey! the *chaste* Interest o' Broughton,
    And hey! for the blessin's 'twill bring;
It may send *Balmaghie* to the Commons,
    In Sodom 'twould make him a king;
And hey! for the sanctified Murray,
    Our land wha wi' chapels has stor'd;
He foundered his horse among harlots,
    But gied the auld naig to the Lord.

BALLAD THIRD

JOHN BUSHBY'S LAMENTATION

Tune—'Babes in the Wood.'

'TWAS in the seventeen hunder year
O' grace, and ninety-five,
That year I was the wae'est man
Of ony man alive.

In March the three-an'-twentieth morn,
The sun raise clear an' bright;
But oh! I was a waefu' man,
Ere to-fa' o' the night.

Yerl Galloway lang did rule this land,
Wi' *equal* right and fame,
And thereto was his kinsmen join'd,
The Murray's noble name.

Yerl Galloway's man o' men was I,
And chief o' Broughton's host;
So twa blind beggars, on a string,
The faithfu' tyke will trust.

But now Yerl Galloway's sceptre's broke,
And Broughton's wi' the slain,
And I my ancient craft may try,
Sin' honesty is gane.

'Twas by the banks o' bonie Dee,
Beside Kirkcudbright's towers,
The Stewart and the Murray there,
Did muster a' their powers.

Then Murray on the auld gray yaud,
 Wi' *winged spurs* did ride,
That auld grey yaud a' Nidsdale rade,
 He staw upon Nidside.

An' there had na been the Yerl himsel,
 O there had been nae play;
But Garlies was to London gane,
 And say the kye might stray.

And there was Balmaghie, I ween,
 In front rank he wad shine;
But Balmaghie had better been
 Drinkin' Madeira wine.

And frae Glenkens cam to our aid
 A chief o' doughty deed;
In case that worth should wanted be,
 O' Kenmure we had need.

And by our banners march'd Muirhead,
 And Buittle was na slack;
Whase haly priesthood nane could stain,
 For wha could dye the black?

And there was grave squire Cardoness,
 Look'd on till a' was done;
Sae in the tower o' Cardoness
 A howlet sits at noon.

And there led I the Bushby clan,
 My gamesome billie, Will,
And my son Maitland, wise as brave,
 My footsteps follow'd still.

The Douglas and the Heron's name
 We set nought to their score;
The Douglas and the Heron's name,
 Had felt our weight before.

But Douglasses o' weight had we,
　　The pair o' lusty lairds,
For building cot-houses sae fam'd,
　　And christenin' kail-yards.

And then Redcastle drew his sword,
　　That ne'er was stain'd wi' gore,
Save on a wand'rer, lame and blind,
　　To drive him frae his door.

And last cam creepin' Collieston,
　　Was mair in fear than wraith;
Ae knave was constant in his mind—
　　To keep that knave frae scaith.

INSCRIPTION FOR AN ALTAR OF INDEPENDENCE

AT KERROUGHTREE, THE SEAT OF MR HERON

THOU of an independent mind,
With soul resolv'd, with soul resign'd;
Prepar'd Power's proudest frown to brave,
Who wilt not be, nor have a slave;
Virtue alone who dost revere,
Thy own reproach alone dost fear—
Approach this shrine, and worship here.

THE CARDIN' O'T, THE SPINNIN' O'T

I COFT a stane o' haslock woo,
　　To mak a wab to Johnie o't;
For Johnie is my only jo,
　　I lo'e him best of onie yet.

Chorus.—The cardin' o't, the spinnin' o't,
      The warpin' o't, the winnin' o't;
    When ilka ell cost me a groat,
      The tailor staw the lynin' o't.

For tho' his locks be lyart gray,
    And tho' his brow be beld aboon;
Yet I hae seen him on a day
    The pride of a' the parishen.
      The cardin' o't, etc.

THE COOPER O' CUDDY

Tune—'Bab at the bowster.'

Chorus.—We'll hide the Cooper behint the door,
    Behint the door, behint the door,
    We'll hide the Cooper behint the door,
      And cover him under a mawn, O.

The Cooper o' Cuddy came here awa',
He ca'd the girrs out o'er us a';
An' our gudewife has gotten a ca',
    That's anger'd the silly gudeman, O.
      We'll hide the Cooper, etc.

He sought them out, he sought them in,
    Wi' deil hae her! an' deil hae him!
But the body he was sae doited and blin',
    He wist na where he was gaun, O.
      We'll hide the Cooper, etc.

They cooper'd at e'en, they cooper'd at morn,
Till our gudeman has gotten the scorn;
On ilka brow she's planted a horn,
    And swears that there they sall stan', O.
      We'll hide the Cooper, etc.

THE LASS THAT MADE THE BED TO ME

When Januar' wind was blawin' cauld,
 As to the north I took my way,
The mirksome night did me enfauld,
 I knew na whare to lodge till day:
By my gude luck a maid I met,
 Just in the middle o' my care,
And kindly she did me invite
 To walk into a chamber fair.

I bow'd fu' low unto this maid,
 And thank'd her for her courtesie;
I bow'd fu' low unto this maid,
 An' bade her make a bed to me;
She made the bed baith large and wide,
 Wi' twa white hands she spread it doun;
She put the cup to her rosy lips,
 And drank—'Young man, now sleep ye soun'.'

Chorus.—The bonie lass made the bed to me,
   The braw lass made the bed to me,
  I'll ne'er forget, till the day I die,
   The lass that made the bed to me.

She snatch'd the candle in her hand,
 And frae my chamber went wi' speed;
But I call'd her quickly back again,
 To lay some mair below my head:
A cod she laid below my head,
 And served me with due respect,
And, to salute her wi' a kiss,
 I put my arms about her neck.

'Haud aff your hands, young man!' she said,
 'And dinna sae uncivil be;
Gif ye hae ony luve for me,
 O wrang na my virginitie.'

Her hair was like the links o' gowd,
    Her teeth were like the ivorie,
Her cheeks like lilies dipt in wine,
    The lass that made the bed to me:

Her bosom was the driven snaw,
    Twa drifted heaps sae fair to see;
Her limbs the polish'd marble stane,
    The lass that made the bed to me.
I kiss'd her o'er and o'er again,
    And ay she wist na what to say:
I laid her 'tween me and the wa';
    The lassie thocht na lang till day.

Upon the morrow, when we raise,
    I thank'd her for her courtesie;
But ay she blush'd and ay she sigh'd,
    And said, 'Alas, ye've ruined me.'
I clasp'd her waist, and kiss'd her syne,
    While the tear stood twinkling in her e'e;
I said, 'My lassie, dinna cry,
    For ye ay shall make the bed to me.'

She took her mither's holland sheets,
    An' made them a' in sarks to me;
Blythe and merry may she be,
    The lass that made the bed to me.
The bonie lass made the bed to me,
    The braw lass made the bed to me,
I'll ne'er forget till the day I die,
    The lass that made the bed to me.

HAD I THE WYTE?

HAD I the wyte, had I the wyte,
    Had I the wyte? she bade me,
She watch'd me by the hie-gate side,
    And up the loan she shaw'd me.

And when I wadna venture in,
    A coward loon she ca'd me :
Had Kirk an' State been in the gate,
    I'd lighted when she bade me.

Sae craftilie she took me ben,
    And bade me mak nae clatter;
'For our ramgunshoch, glum gudeman,
    Is o'er ayont the water.'
Whae'er shall say I wanted grace
    When I did kiss and dawte her,
Let him be planted in my place,
    Syne say I was the fautor.

Could I for shame, could I for shame,
    Could I for shame refus'd her ?
And wadna manhood been to blame,
    Had I unkindly used her ?
He claw'd her wi' the ripplin'-kame,
    And blae and bluidy bruis'd her;
When sic a husband was frae hame,
    What wife but wad excus'd her !

I dighted aye her e'en sae blue,
    An' bann'd the cruel randy,
And weel I wat, her willin' mou'
    Was sweet as sugar-candie.
At gloamin'-shot, it was, I wot,
    I lighted—on the Monday;
But I cam thro' the Tyseday's dew,
    To wanton Willie's brandy.

DOES HAUGHTY GAUL INVASION THREAT?

Tune—'Push about the Jorum.'

DOES haughty Gaul invasion threat ?
    Then let the louns beware, Sir;
There's WOODEN WALLS upon our seas,
    And VOLUNTEERS on shore, Sir :

B.P.

T

The *Nith* shall run to *Corsincon*,
  And *Criffel* sink in *Solway*,
Ere we permit a Foreign Foe
  On British ground to rally!
We'll ne'er permit a Foreign Foe
  On British ground to rally!

O let us not, like snarling curs,
  In wrangling be divided,
Till, slap! come in an *unco loun*,
  And wi' a rung decide it!
Be Britain still to Britain true,
  Amang ourselves united;
For never but by *British hands*
  Maun *British wrangs* be righted!
No! never but by *British hands*
  Shall *British wrangs* be righted!

The *Kettle* o' the Kirk and State,
  Perhaps a *clout* may fail in't;
But deil a *foreign* tinkler loun
  Shall ever ca' a nail in't.
Our FATHER'S BLUDE the *Kettle* bought,
  And wha wad dare to spoil it;
By Heav'ns! the sacrilegious dog
  Shall fuel be to boil it!
By Heav'ns! the sacrilegious dog
  Shall fuel be to boil it!

The wretch that would a *tyrant* own,
  And the wretch, his true-born brother,
Who would set the *Mob* aboon the *Throne*.
  May they be damn'd together!
Who will not sing 'God save the King'
  Shall hang as high's the steeple;
But while we sing 'God save the King,'
  We'll ne'er forget THE PEOPLE!
But while we sing 'God save the King,'
  We'll ne'er forget THE PEOPLE!

ADDRESS TO THE WOODLARK

Tune—'Loch Erroch Side.'

O STAY, sweet warbling woodlark, stay,
Nor quit for me the trembling spray,
A hapless lover courts thy lay,
      Thy soothing, fond complaining.
Again, again that tender part,
That I may catch thy melting art;
For surely that wad touch her heart
      Wha kills me wi' disdaining.

Say, was thy little mate unkind,
And heard thee as the careless wind?
Oh, nocht but love and sorrow join'd,
      Sic notes o' woe could wauken!
Thou tells o' never-ending care;
O' speechless grief, and dark despair:
For pity's sake, sweet bird, nae mair!
      Or my poor heart is broken.

ON CHLORIS BEING ILL

Tune—'Ay wauken, O.'

Chorus.—Long, long the night,
            Heavy comes the morrow,
         While my soul's delight
            Is on her bed of sorrow.

   CAN I cease to care,
      Can I cease to languish,
   While my darling Fair
      Is on the couch of anguish?
         Long, long, etc.

Ev'ry hope is fled,
  Ev'ry fear is terror;
Slumber ev'n I dread,
  Ev'ry dream is horror,
        Long, long, etc.

Hear me, Powers Divine!
  Oh, in pity, hear me!
Take aught else of mine,
  But my Chloris spare me!
        Long, long, etc.

HOW CRUEL ARE THE PARENTS

ALTERED FROM AN OLD ENGLISH SONG

Tune—'John Anderson, my jo.'

How cruel are the parents
  Who riches only prize,
And to the wealthy booby
  Poor Woman sacrifice!
Meanwhile, the hapless Daughter
  Has but a choice of strife;
To shun a tyrant Father's hate—
  Become a wretched Wife.

The ravening hawk pursuing,
  The trembling dove thus flies,
To shun impelling ruin,
  Awhile her pinions tries;
Till, of escape despairing,
  No shelter or retreat,
She trusts the ruthless Falconer,
  And drops beneath his feet.

YONDER POMP OF COSTLY FASHION

Tune—'Deil tak the wars.'

MARK yonder pomp of costly fashion
   Round the wealthy, titled bride :
But when compar'd with real passion,
   Poor is all that princely pride.
         Mark yonder, etc.

What are the showy treasures,
   What are the noisy pleasures,
The gay, gaudy glare of vanity and art ?
   The polish'd jewel's blaze
   May draw the wond'ring gaze;
   And courtly grandeur bright
   The fancy may delight,
But never, never can come near the heart.

But did you see my dearest Chloris,
   In simplicity's array,
Lovely as yonder sweet opening flower is,
   Shrinking from the gaze of day.
         But did you see, etc.

O then, the heart alarming,
   And all resistless charming,
In Love's delightful fetters she chains the willing
      soul !
   Ambition would disown
   The world's imperial crown,
   Ev'n Avarice would deny,
   His worshipp'd deity,
And feel thro' every vein Love's raptures roll.

T2

'TWAS NA HER BONIE BLUE E'E

Tune—'Laddie, lie near me.'

'TWAS na her bonie blue e'e was my ruin,
Fair tho' she be, that was ne'er my undoin';
'Twas the dear smile when nae body did mind us,
'Twas the bewitching, sweet, stoun glance o' kindnes
'Twas the bewitching, sweet, stoun glance o' kindnes

Sair do I fear that to hope is denied me,
Sair do I fear that despair maun abide me,
But tho' fell fortune should fate us to sever,
Queen shall she be in my bosom for ever :
Queen shall she be in my bosom for ever.

Chloris, I'm thine wi' a passion sincerest,
And thou hast plighted me love o' the dearest !
And thou'rt the angel that never can alter,
Sooner the sun in his motion would falter :
Sooner the sun in his motion would falter.

THEIR GROVES O' SWEET MYRTLE

Tune—'Humours of Glen.'

THEIR groves o' sweet myrtle let Foreign Lands reckо
　Where bright beaming summers exalt the perfume
Far dearer to me yon lone glen o' green breckan,
　Wi' the burn stealing under the lang, yellow broo
Far dearer to me are yon humble broom bowers,
　Where the blue-bell and gowan lurk, lowly, unsee
For there, lightly tripping, among the wild flowers,
　A-list'ning the linnet, aft wanders my Jean.

Tho' rich is the breeze in their gay, sunny valleys,
　And cauld Caledonia's blast on the wave;

heir sweet-scented woodlands that skirt the proud
    palace,
What are they ?—the haunt of the Tyrant and Slave.
he Slave's spicy forests, and gold-bubbling fountains,
    The brave Caledonian views with disdain;
e wanders as free as the winds of his mountains,
    Save Love's willing fetters—the chains o' his Jean.

ORLORN, MY LOVE, NO COMFORT NEAR

Air—'Let me in this ae night.'

FORLORN, my Love, no comfort near,
    Far, far from thee, I wander here :
    Far, far from thee, the fate severe,
        At which I most repine, Love.

Chorus.—O wert thou, Love, but near me !
        But near, near, near me !
        How kindly thou wouldst cheer me,
           And mingle sighs with mine, Love.

Around me scowls the wintry sky,
Blasting each bud of hope and joy;
And shelter, shade, nor home have I;
    Save in these arms of thine, Love.
        O wert thou, etc.

Cold, alter'd Friendship's cruel part,
To poison Fortune's ruthless dart—
Let me not break thy faithful heart
    And say that fate is mine, Love.
        O wert thou, etc.

But, dreary tho' the moments fleet,
O let me think we yet shall meet;
That only ray of solace sweet
    Can on thy Chloris shine, Love !
        O wert thou, etc.

WHY, WHY TELL THE LOVER

Tune—'Caledonian Hunt's delight.'

WHY, why tell the lover
 Bliss he never must enjoy?
Why, why undeceive him,
 And give all his hopes the lie?
O why, while fancy, raptur'd, slumbers,
 'Chloris, Chloris,' all the theme,
Why, why wouldst thou, cruel,
 Wake thy lover from his dream.

THE BRAW WOOER

Tune—'The Lothian Lassie.'

LAST May a braw wooer cam doun the lang glen,
 And sair wi' his love he did deave me;
I said there was naething I hated like men—
 The deuce gae wi'm, to believe me, believe me;
 The deuce gae wi'm to believe me.

He spake o' the darts in my bonie black een,
 And vow'd for my love he was diein',
I said he might die when he liket—for Jean—
 The Lord forgie me for liein', for liein';
 The Lord forgie me for liein'!

A weel-stocket mailen, himsel for the laird,
 And marriage aff-hand, were his proffers;
I never loot on that I kenn'd it, or car'd,
 But thought I might hae waur offers, waur offers;
 But thought I might hae waur offers.

But what wad ye think?—in a fortnight or less—
  The deil tak his taste to gae near her!
He up the *Gate-slack* to my black cousin, Bess—
  Guess ye how, the jad! I could bear her, could
    bear her;
  Guess ye how, the jad! I could bear her.

But a' the neist week, as I petted wi' care,
  I gaed to the tryst o' Dalgarnock;
And wha but my fine fickle wooer was there,
  I glowr'd as I'd seen a warlock, a warlock,
  I glowr'd as I'd seen a warlock.

But owre my left shouther I gae him a blink,
  Lest neibours might say I was saucy;
My wooer he caper'd as he'd been in drink,
  And vow'd I was his dear lassie, dear lassie,
  And vow'd I was his dear lassie.

I spier'd for my cousin fu' couthy and sweet,
  Gin she had recover'd her hearin',
And how her new shoon fit her auld shachl't feet,
  But heavens! how he fell a swearin', a swearin',
  But heavens! how he fell a swearin'.

He begged, for gudesake, I wad be his wife,
  Or else I wad kill him wi' sorrow;
So e'en to preserve the poor body in life,
  I think I maun wed him to-morrow, to-morrow;
  I think I maun wed him to-morrow.

THIS IS NO MY AIN LASSIE

Tune—'This is no my house.'

Chorus.—This is no my ain lassie,
          Fair tho' the lassie be;
          Weel ken I my ain lassie,
          Kind love is in her e'e.

I SEE a form, I see a face,
Ye weel may wi' the fairest place;
It wants, to me, the witching grace,
    The kind love that's in her e'e.
        This is no my ain, etc.

She's bonie, blooming, straight, and tall,
And lang has had my heart in thrall;
And ay it charms my very saul,
    The kind love that's in her e'e.
        This is no my ain, etc.

A thief sae pawkie is my Jean,
To steal a blink, by a' unseen;
But gleg as light are lover's een,
    When kind love is in the e'e.
        This is no my ain, etc.

It may escape the courtly sparks,
It may escape the learned clerks;
But weel the watching lover marks
    The kind love that's in her e'e.
        This is no my ain, etc.

O BONIE WAS YON ROSY BRIER

O BONIE was yon rosy brier,
    That blooms sae far frae haunt o' man;
And bonie she, and ah, how dear!
    It shaded frae the e'enin' sun.

Yon rosebuds in the morning dew,
    How pure, amang the leaves sae green;
But purer was the lover's vow
    They witness'd in their shade yestreen.

All in its rude and prickly bower,
    That crimson rose, how sweet and fair;
But love is far a sweeter flower,
    Amid life's thorny path o' care.

The pathless wild, and wimpling burn,
    Wi' Chloris in my arms, be mine;
And I the warld, nor wish, nor scorn,
    Its joys and griefs alike resign.

NOW SPRING HAS CLAD THE GROVE IN GREEN

INSCRIBED TO ALEXANDER CUNNINGHAM

Now Spring has clad the grove in green,
    And strew'd the lea wi' flowers;
The furrow'd, waving corn is seen
    Rejoice in fostering showers.
While ilka thing in nature join
    Their sorrows to forego,
O why thus all alone are mine
    The weary steps o' woe!

The trout in yonder wimplin' burn
    That glides—a silver dart,
And, safe beneath the shady thorn
    Defies the angler's art;
My life was ance that careless stream,
    That wanton trout was I;
But Love, wi' unrelenting beam,
    Has scorch'd my fountains dry.

That little floweret's peaceful lot,
    In yonder cliff that grows,
Which, save the linnet's flight, I wot,
    Nae ruder visit knows,

Was mine, till Love has o'er me past,
    And blighted a' my bloom;
And now, beneath the withering blast,
    My youth and joy consume.

The waken'd lav'rock warbling springs,
    And climbs the early sky,
Winnowing blythe his dewy wings
    In morning's rosy eye;
As little reck'd I sorrow's power,
    Until the flowery snare
O' witching Love, in luckless hour,
    Made me the thrall o' care.

O had my fate been Greenland snows,
    Or Afric's burning zone,
Wi' man and nature leagu'd my foes,
    So Peggy ne'er I'd known !
The wretch whose doom is 'hope nae mair,'
    What tongue his woes can tell;
Within whase bosom, save Despair,
    Nae kinder spirits dwell.

O THAT'S THE LASSIE O' MY HEART

Tune—'Morag.'

O WAT ye wha that lo'es me,
    And has my heart a-keeping ?
O sweet is she that lo'es me,
    As dews o' summer weeping,
    In tears the rosebuds steeping !

Chorus.—O that's the lassie o' my heart,
        My lassie, ever dearer;
    O she's the queen o' womankind,
        And ne'er a ane to peer her.

If thou shalt meet a lassie,
  In grace and beauty charming,
That e'en thy chosen lassie,
  Erewhile thy breast sae warming,
  Had ne'er sic power alarming;
    O that's the lassie, etc.

If thou hadst heard her talking
  (And thy attention's plighted),
That ilka body talking,
  But her, by thee is slighted,
  And thou art all-delighted;
    O that's the lassie, etc.

If thou hast met this Fair One,
  When frae her thou hast parted,
If every other Fair One
  But her, thou hast deserted,
  And thou art broken-hearted;
O that's the lassie o' my heart,
  My lassie, ever dearer;
O that's the queen o' womanhood,
  And ne'er a ane to peer her.

INSCRIPTION

WRITTEN ON THE BLANK LEAF OF A COPY OF THE LAST
EDITION OF MY POEMS, PRESENTED TO THE LADY
WHOM, IN SO MANY FICTITIOUS REVERIES OF
PASSION, BUT WITH THE MOST ARDENT SENTI-
MENTS OF REAL FRIENDSHIP, I HAVE SO OFTEN
SUNG UNDER THE NAME OF 'CHLORIS'

'Tis Friendship's pledge, my young, fair Friend,
  Nor thou the gift refuse,
Nor with unwilling ear attend
  The moralising Muse.

Since thou, in all thy youth and charms,
    Must bid the world adieu
(A world 'gainst Peace in constant arms)
    To join the friendly few.

Since thy gay morn of life o'ercast,
    Chill came the tempest's lour
(And ne'er Misfortune's eastern blast
    Did nip a fairer flower).

Since life's gay scenes must charm no more,
    Still much is left behind,
Still nobler wealth hast thou in store—
    The comforts of the mind !

Thine is the self-approving glow
    Of conscious Honor's part;
And (dearest gift of Heaven below)
    Thine Friendship's truest heart.

The joys refin'd of sense and taste,
    With every Muse to rove :
And doubly were the Poet blest,
    These joys could he improve.

                R. B.

LEEZIE LINDSAY

WILL ye go to the Hielands, Leezie Lindsay,
    Will ye go to the Hielands wi' me ?
Will ye go to the Hielands, Leezie Lindsay,
    My pride and my darling to be ?

THE WREN'S NEST

THE Robin to the Wren's nest
    Cam keekin' in, cam keekin' in;
O weel's me on your auld pow,
    Wad ye be in, wad ye be in ?

Thou's ne'er get leave to lie without,
 And I within, and I within,
Sae lang's I hae an auld clout
 To rowe ye in, to rowe ye in.

COMIN' THRO' THE RYE

Chorus.—O Jenny's a' weet, poor body,
 Jenny's seldom dry;
  She draigl't a' her petticoatie,
  Comin' thro' the rye.

Comin' thro' the rye, poor body,
 Comin' thro' the rye,
She draigl't a' her petticoatie,
 Comin' thro' the rye.

Gin a body meet a body
 Comin' thro' the rye,
Gin a body kiss a body,
 Need a body cry?

Gin a body meet a body
 Comin' thro' the glen,
Gin a body kiss a body,
 Need the warld ken?

Chorus.—O Jenny's a' weet, poor body,
 Jenny's seldom dry;
  She draigl't a' her petticoatie,
  Comin' thro' the rye.

NEWS, LASSES, NEWS

There's news, lasses, news,
 Gude news I've to tell!
There's a boatfu' o' lads
 Come to our town to sell.

Chorus.—The wean wants a cradle,
   And the cradle wants a cod :
  I'll no gang to my bed,
   Until I get a nod.

Father, quo' she, Mither, quo' she,
  Do what you can,
I'll no gang to my bed,
  Until I get a man.
     The wean, etc.

I hae as gude a craft rig
  As made o' yird and stane;
And waly fa' the ley-crap,
  For I maun till'd again.
     The wean, etc.

CROWDIE EVER MAIR

O THAT I had ne'er been married,
  I wad never had nae care,
Now I've gotten wife an' weans,
  An' they cry 'Crowdie' ever mair.

Chorus.—Ance crowdie, twice crowdie,
   Three times crowdie in a day;
  Gin ye 'crowdie' ony mair,
   Ye'll crowdie a' my meal away.

Waefu' Want and Hunger fley me,
  Glowrin' by the hallan en';
Sair I fecht them at the door,
  But ay I'm eerie they come ben.
    Ance crowdie, etc.

MALLY'S MEEK, MALLY'S SWEET

Chorus.—Mally's meek, Mally's sweet,
      Mally's modest and discreet;
    Mally's rare, Mally's fair,
      Mally's every way complete.

As I was walking up the street,
    A barefit maid I chanc'd to meet;
But O the road was very hard
    For that fair maiden's tender feet.
      Mally's meek, etc.

It were mair meet that those fine feet
    Were weel laced up in silken shoon;
An' 'twere more fit that she should sit
    Within yon chariot gilt aboon.
      Mally's meek, etc.

Her yellow hair, beyond compare,
    Comes trinklin' down her swan-like neck,
And her two eyes, like stars in skies,
    Would keep a sinking ship frae wreck.
      Mally's meek, etc.

JOCKEY'S TAEN THE PARTING KISS

Air—'Bonie lass tak a man.'

JOCKEY's taen the parting kiss,
    O'er the mountain he is gane,
And with him is a' my bliss,
    Nought but griefs with me remain.
Spare my Love, ye winds that blaw,
    Plashy sleets and beating rain!
Spare my Love, thou feath'ry snaw,
    Drifting o'er the frozen plain!

When the shades of evening creep
    O'er the day's fair, gladsome e'e,
Sound and safely may he sleep,
    Sweetly blythe his waukening be.
He will think on her he loves,
    Fondly he'll repeat her name;
For where'er he distant roves,
    Jockey's heart is still the same.

VERSES TO COLLECTOR MITCHELL

FRIEND of the Poet, tried and leal,
Wha, wanting thee, might beg or steal;
Alake, alake, the meikle deil
        Wi' a' his witches
Are at it, skelpin', jig and reel,
        In my poor pouches!

I modestly fu' fain wad hint it,
That *One-pound-one*, I sairly want it;
If wi' the hizzie down ye sent it,
        It would be kind;
And while my heart wi' life-blood dunted,
        I'd bear't in mind.

So may the Auld year gang out moanin'
To see the New come laden, groanin',
Wi' double plenty o'er the loanin',
        To thee and thine;
Domestic peace and comforts crownin'
        The hale design.

POSTSCRIPT

Ye've heard this while how I've been licket,
And by fell Death was nearly nicket;

Grim loon ! he got me by the fecket,
    And sair me sheuk;
But by gude luck I lap a wicket,
    And turn'd a neuk.

But by that health, I've got a share o't,
And by that life, I'm promis'd mair o't,
My hale and weel, I'll take a care o't,
    A tentier way;
Then farewell folly, hide and hair o't,
    For ance and ay !

THE DEAN OF FACULTY

A NEW BALLAD

Tune—'The Dragon of Wantry.'

DIRE was the hate at old Harlaw,
    That Scot to Scot did carry;
And dire the discord Langside saw
    For beauteous, hapless Mary :
But Scot to Scot ne'er met so hot,
    Or were more in fury seen, Sir,
Than 'twixt Hal and Bob for the famous job,
    Who should be the Faculty's Dean, Sir.

This Hal for genius, wit and lore,
    Among the first was number'd;
But pious Bob, 'mid learning's store,
    Commandment the tenth remember'd :
Yet simple Bob the victory got,
    And wan his heart's desire,
Which shows that Heaven can boil the pot,
    Tho' the Deil piss in the fire.

Squire Hal, besides, had in this case
Pretensions rather brassy;
For talents, to deserve a place,
Are qualifications saucy.
So their worships of the Faculty,
Quite sick of merit's rudeness,
Chose one who should owe it all, d'ye see,
To their gratis grace and goodness.

As once on Pisgah purg'd was the sight
Of a son of Circumcision,
So may be, on this Pisgah height,
Bob's purblind mental vision—
Nay, Bobby's *mouth* may be open'd yet,
Till for eloquence you hail him,
And swear that he has the angel met
That met the ass of Balaam.

In your heretic sins may you live and die,
Ye heretic Eight-and-Thirty!
But accept, ye sublime Majority,
My congratulations hearty.
With your honors, as with a certain king,
In your servants this is striking,
The more incapacity they bring,
The more they're to your liking.

EPISTLE TO COLONEL DE PEYSTER

My honor'd Colonel, deep I feel
Your interest in the Poet's weal;
Ah! now sma' heart hae I to speel
    The steep Parnassus,
Surrounded thus by bolus pill,
    And potion glasses.

O what a canty warld were it,
Would pain and care and sickness spare;
And Fortune favour worth and merit
    As they deserve;
And ay rowth o' roast-beef and claret,
      Syne, wha wad starve?

Dame Life, tho' fiction out may trick her,
And in paste gems and frippery deck her;
Oh! flickering, feeble, and unsicker
    I've found her still,
Ay wavering like the willow-wicker,
      'Tween good and ill.

Then that curst carmagnole, auld Satan,
Watches like baudrons by a ratton
Our sinfu' saul to get a claut on,
    Wi' felon ire;
Syne, whip! his tail ye'll ne'er cast saut on,
      He's aff like fire.

Ah Nick! ah Nick! it is na fair.
First showing us the tempting ware,
Bright wines, and bonie lasses rare,
    To put us daft;
Syne weave, unseen, thy spider snare
      O' hell's damned waft.

Poor Man, the flie, aft bizzes by,
And aft, as chance he comes thee nigh,
Thy damn'd auld elbow yeuks wi' joy
    And hellish pleasure;
Already in thy fancy's eye,
      Thy sicker treasure.

Soon, heels o'er gowdie, in he gangs,
And, like a sheep-head on a tangs,
Thy girning laugh enjoys his pangs,
    And murdering wrestle,
As, dangling in the wind, he hangs
      A gibbet's tassle.

But lest you think I am uncivil,
To plague you with this draunting drivel,
Abjuring a' intentions evil,
    I quat my pen,
The Lord preserve us frae the devil!
    Amen! Amen!

A LASS WI' A TOCHER

Tune—'Ballinamona Ora.'

Awa' wi' your witchcraft o' Beauty's alarms,
The slender bit Beauty you grasp in your arms,
O, gie me the lass that has acres o' charms,
O, gie me the lass wi' the weel-stockit farms.

Chorus.—Then hey, for a lass wi' a tocher,
    Then hey, for a lass wi' a tocher;
    Then hey, for a lass wi' a tocher;
        The nice yellow guineas for me.

Your Beauty's a flower, in the morning that blows,
And withers the faster, the faster it grows:
But the rapturous charm o' the bonie green knowes,
Ilk spring they're new deckit wi' bonie white yowes.
        Then hey, for a lass, etc.

And e'en when this Beauty your bosom hath blest,
The brightest o' Beauty may cloy when possess'd;
But the sweet, yellow darlings wi' Geordie impress'd,
The langer ye hae them, the mair they're carest.
        Then hey, for a lass, etc.

HERON ELECTION BALLAD, NO. IV

THE TROGGER

Tune—'Buy Broom Besoms.'

WHA will buy my troggin, fine election ware,
Broken trade o' Broughton, a' in high repair?
   Chorus.—Buy braw troggin frae the banks o' Dee;
       Wha wants troggin let him come to me.

There's a noble Earl's fame and high renown,
For an auld sang—it's thought the gudes were
    stown—
       Buy braw troggin, etc.

Here's the worth o' Broughton in a needle's e'e;
Here's a reputation tint by Balmaghie.
     Buy braw troggin, etc.

Here's its stuff and lining, Cardoness's head,
Fine for a soger, a' the wale o' lead.
     Buy braw troggin, etc.

Here a little wadset, Buittle's scrap o' truth,
Pawn'd in a gin-shop, quenching holy drouth.
     Buy braw troggin, etc.

Here's an honest conscience might a prince adorn;
Frae the downs o' Tinwald, so was never worn.
     Buy braw troggin, etc.

Here's armorial bearings frae the manse o' Urr;
The crest, a sour crab-apple, rotten at the core.
     Buy braw troggin, etc.

Here is Satan's picture, like a bizzard gled,
Pouncing poor Redcastle, sprawling like a taed.
      Buy braw troggin, etc.

Here's the font where Douglas stane and mortar names;
Lately used at Caily christening Murray's crimes.
      Buy braw troggin, etc.

Here's the worth and wisdom Collieston can boast;
By a thievish midge they had been nearly lost.
      Buy braw troggin, etc.

Here is Murray's fragments o' the Ten Commands;
Gifted by black Jock to get them aff his hands.
      Buy braw troggin, etc.

Saw ye e'er sic troggin ? if to buy ye're slack,
Hornie's turnin' chapman—he'll buy a' the pack.
      Buy braw troggin, etc.

EPITAPH ON THE AUTHOR

HE who of Rankine sang, lies stiff and dead,
And a green grassy hillock hides his head;
Alas ! alas ! a devilish change indeed !

VERSICLES TO JESSIE LEWARS

THE TOAST

FILL me with the rosy wine,
Call a toast, a toast divine;
Give the Poet's darling flame,
Lovely Jessie be her name;
Then thou mayest freely boast,
Thou hast given a peerless toast.

THE MENAGERIE

Talk not to me of savages
　From Afric's burning sun;
No savage e'er could rend my heart
　As, Jessie, thou hast done:
But Jessie's lovely hand in mine,
　A mutual faith to plight,
Not even to view the heavenly choir
　Would be so blest a sight.

JESSIE'S ILLNESS

Say, sages, what's the charm on earth
　Can turn Death's dart aside!
It is not purity and worth,
　Else Jessie had not died.

ON HER RECOVERY

But rarely seen since Nature's birth,
　The natives of the sky;
Yet still one seraph's left on earth,
　For Jessie did not die.

LAY THY LOOF IN MINE, LASS

Chorus.—O lay thy loof in mine, lass,
　　In mine, lass, in mine, lass;
　　And swear on thy white hand, lass,
　　That thou wilt be my ain.

A SLAVE to Love's unbounded sway,
He aft has wrought me meikle wae;
But now he is my deadly fae,
    Unless thou be my ain.
            O lay thy loof, etc.

There's mony a lass has broke my rest,
That for a blink I hae lo'ed best;
But thou art Queen within my breast,
    For ever to remain.
            O lay thy loof, etc.

A HEALTH TO ANE I LOE DEAR

Chorus.—Here's a health to ane I loe dear,
        Here's a health to ane I loe dear;
    Thou art sweet as the smile when fond lovers
        meet,
        And soft as their parting tear—Jessie.

ALTHO' thou maun never be mine,
    Altho' even hope is denied;
'Tis sweeter for thee despairing,
    Than aught in the world beside—Jessie.
        Here's a health, etc.

I mourn thro' the gay, gaudy day,
    As hopeless I muse on thy charms;
But welcome the dream o' sweet slumber,
    For then I am lockt in thine arms—Jessie.
        Here's a health, etc.

I guess by the dear angel smile,
    I guess by the love-rolling e'e;
But why urge the tender confession,
    'Gainst Fortune's fell, cruel decree—Jessie.
        Here's a health, etc.

O WERT THOU IN THE CAULD BLAST

O WERT thou in the cauld blast,
  On yonder lea, on yonder lea,
My plaidie to the angry airt,
  I'd shelter thee, I'd shelter thee;
Or did Misfortune's bitter storms
  Around thee blaw, around thee blaw,
Thy bield should be my bosom,
  To share it a', to share it a'.

Or were I in the wildest waste,
  Sae black and bare, sae black and bare,
The desert were a Paradise,
  If thou wert there, if thou wert there;
Or were I Monarch o' the globe,
  Wi' thee to reign, wi' thee to reign,
The brightest jewel in my crown
  Wad be my Queen, wad be my Queen.

INSCRIPTION TO MISS JESSIE LEWARS

ON A COPY OF THE 'SCOTS MUSICAL MUSEUM,' IN FOUR
VOLUMES, PRESENTED TO HER BY BURNS

THINE be the volumes, Jessie fair,
And with them take the Poet's prayer,
That Fate may, in her fairest page,
With ev'ry kindliest, best presage
Of future bliss, enroll thy name :
With native worth and spotless fame,
And wakeful caution, still aware
Of ill—but chief, Man's felon snare;
All blameless joys on earth we find,
And all the treasures of the mind—
These be thy guardian and reward;
So prays thy faithful friend, the Bard.

DUMFRIES, *June* 26, 1796.

FAIREST MAID ON DEVON BANKS

Tune—'Rothiermurchie.'

Chorus.—Fairest maid on Devon banks,
   Crystal Devon, winding Devon,
   Wilt thou lay that frown aside,
    And smile as thou wert wont to do?

FULL well thou know'st I love thee dear
Could thou to malice lend an ear?
O did not Love exclaim, 'Forbear,
 Nor use a faithful lover so.'
  Fairest maid, etc.

Then come, thou fairest of the fair,
Those wonted smiles, O let me share;
And by thy beauteous self I swear,
 No love but thine my heart shall know.
  Fairest maid, etc.

GLOSSARY

A', all.

Aback, behind; away; aloof.

'O would they stay aback frae courts !'

Abeigh or *Abiegh*, at a shy distance.

'Gar't puir Duncan stand abeigh.'

Aboon or *Abune*, above.

Abread, abroad; in breadth.

Abreed, in breadth.

Acquent, acquainted.

'When we were first acquent.'

A'day, all day.

Adle or *Aidle*, foul water; liquid manure.

Ado, to do. *Muckle ado*, much excitement.

Advisement, advice.

'O guid advisement comes nae ill.'

Ae, one.

'O let me in this ae night.'

Aff, off.

Aff-hand, at once; without hesitation.

Aff-loof, off-hand; extemporaneously.

A-fiel', a-field; in the field.

Afore, before.

Aft, often.

Aften, often.

Agee or *Ajee*, to one side; half open.

Come na unless the back-yett be ajee.'

Agley, aslant; off the straight

'The best laid schemes o' mice and men,

Gang aft agley.'

Ahin, behind.

Ahint, behind.

Aiblins, perhaps; maybe.

Aik, oak.

Aiken, oaken.

Ain, own.

Air or *Ear'*, early.

Airle, to handsel.

Airles, handsel; earnest-money.

'And name the airles and the fee.'

Airle-penny, fee-penny.

Airn, iron.

Airt, direction; to direct.

'Of a' the airts the win' can blaw.

Airted, directed.

Aith, oath.

Aits, oats.

Aiver, an old horse.

'And a ragged cowt's been known To mak' a noble aiver.'

Aizle, a hot cinder; a red ember.

Ajee, to one side.

'His bonnet he, a thocht ajee, Look'd sprush.'

Alake, alas.

Alane, alone.

Amaist, almost.

Amang, among.

An, if. See *Gif* and *Gin*.

An', and.

Ance, once.

Ane, one.

Aneath, beneath.

Anent, concerning; opposite.

Anes, ones.

Anither, another.

An's, and is.

' An's thankru' for them yet.'

Aqua-fontis, spring water.

Aqua-vitæ, whisky.

Aqueesh, between.

Artfu', artful.

Ase, ashes.

Asklent, aslant; obliquely.

' Looked asklent and unco skeigh.'

Aspar, aspread; with legs apart.

Asteer, astir.

A'thegether, altogether.

Athort, athwart.

Atweel, in truth; certainly.

Atweel na, by no means.

Atween or *Atweesh*, between.

Aucht or *Aught*, eight; to own.

Aughteen, eighteen.

Aughtlins, anything; in the least; in any degree.

The hizzies, if they're aughtlins faws'nt.'

Auld, old.

Auld-farran' or *Auld-farrant*, sagacious; prudent; cunning.

Auld lang syne, long, long ago.

Auld Reekie, Edinburgh.

Auld shoon, old shoes.

Auld warld, old world; antique.

Aumous, alms; a gift to a beggar.

Aumous-dish, a dish to receive alms.

While she held up her greedy gab, Just like an aumous dish.'

Ava, at all; of all.

' I've aften wonder'd . . . What way puir bodies liv'd ava.'

'An' lows'd his ill-tongu'd wicked scaul—
　　　Was warst ava.'

Awa', away.

Awauk, awake.

Awauken, to waken.

Awe, owe; to owe.

Awee, a little; *Bide awee*, wait a minute.

' Hear me, Auld Hangie, for awee.'

Awfu', awful.

Awn, the beard of barley, o oats.

Awnie, bearded.

' An' sets up their awnie horn.'

Ay, yes; always.

Aye, always.

Ayont, beyond.

' The wee short hours ayont the twal

Ba', ball; a ball.

Bab at the bowster, a dance.

Babie-clouts or *Baby-clouts* child's first clothes.

' Oh wha my babie-clouts will buy

Backet, bucket or box fo removing ashes.

Backet, backed; as *howe backet*, hollow-backed.

Backlins - comin, comin back; returning.

Back-yett, gate at the back.

' Come na unless the back-yett l ajee.'

Bade, endured; did stay.

Baggie, the belly.

' Hae, there's a ripp to thy au baggie.'

Baig'nets, bayonets.

Bailie, the Scotch equivaler of an alderman.

Bainie, with large bone muscular.

Bairin', laying bare.

Bairn, a child.

Bairn-time, time of issue.

' The bonie bairn-time Heaven ha lent.'

Baith, both.

Bakes, biscuits.

Baiveridge, handsel drink; beverage.

Ballats or Ballants, ballads.

Bamboozle, to mystify; confuse.

Ban, to swear, or curse.

Ban, a band.

Bandster, a binder of sheaves.

Bane, bone.

Bang, to drive; to beat. *Wi' unco bang*, with extraordinary effort.

Bannet, bonnet.

Bannock, a round flat cake.

Bardie, diminutive of *bard*.

'Accept a bardie's gratefu' thanks.'

Barefit, barefooted.

Barket, barked.

Barkin', barking.

Barley-bree or Barley-broo, juice of barley; whisky.

'But ay we'll taste the barley-bree.'

Barm, yeast.

Barmy, yeasty; frothy; quick-tempered.

'My barmie-noddle's workin' prime.'

Barn-yard, stack-yard.

Batch, a company; a gang.

'And there, a batch o' wabster lads, Blackguarding frae Kilmarnock.'

Batts, the botts; a colic.

Baudrons, a cat.

Bauk or Bawk, a cross-beam; a narrow path dividing lands.

Bauk-en', beam-end.

Baukie-bird, the bat.

'Wavering like the baukie-bird.'

Bauks, rafters.

Bauld, bold.

Baumy, balmy.

Baws'nt, having a white stripe down the face, as in horses.

'His honest, sonsie, baws'nt face.'

Bawtie, pet name for a dog.

Be or Bee, to let be; as *let abee*, leave alone.

Be't, be it.

Bear or Bere, barley.

Bearded-bear, bearded barley.

Beast, cattle; sometimes vermin.

Beastie, diminutive of *beast*.

Beck, to curtsey. *Beck an' boo*, to curtsey and bow.

Beet, to fan; to feed; to warm.

'It heats me, it beets me,
And sets me a' on flame.'

Befa', befall.

Behadden, beholden.

Behin, Behint, behind.

Belang, belong.

Beld, bald.

Bellum, assault; attack.

Bellyfu', bellyful.

Bellys, bellows.

Belyve, by-and-by.

'Belyve the elder bairns cam drapping in.'

Ben, in. *Ben-end*, inner end; the parlour.

Benmost, innermost.

'Frightened rattans backward look,
And seek the benmost bore.'

Benorth, north of.

Bent, coarse grass; the bare open field.

Bent, stretched.

'Are bent like drums.'

Besouth, south of.

Bethanket, bethanked; full of gratitude.

'Then auld guidman, maist like to rive,
Bethanket hums.'

Beuk, a book.

Bicker, a wooden dish; a short rapid race.

'Leeward whiles, against my will,
I took a bicker.'

Bickerin', hurrying; sometimes quarrelling.

Bid, to ask; to offer.

Bide, to stay; abide.

Biel' or *Bield*, shelter; habitation.

Bien, prosperous; comfortable.

'That live sae bien and snug.'

Big, to build.

Bigget, built.

Biggin, a building; a house.

'The auld clay biggin.'

Bike or *Byke*, a wild bee's nest.

Bill, a bull.

Billie, fellow; comrade.

Billies, male companions; lively young fellows.

Bing, a heap; as *corn-bing*, a heap of grain.

Birdie, diminutive of *bird*.

Birk, the birch.

Birken, birchen.

'To wander in the birken shaw.'

Birkie, a plucky little fellow.

Birks, collection of birch trees.

Birr, vigour; forceful flow.

Birrin,' whirring, like partridges when they rise.

'Rejoice, ye birrin paitricks a'.'

Birsies, bristles.

Birth, berth.

Bit, place; nick of time; sometimes small, as

'Bonie bit lassie.'

Bitch-fou', very drunk.

Bizz, bustle; to buzz.

Bizzard, the buzzard.

Bizzie, busy.

Black-bonnet, the elder.

'A greedy glower black-bonnet throws.'

Blae, blue; livid.

Blastet or *Blastit*, blasted; worthless.

Blastie, a shrivelled wicked dwarf.

Blate, bashful; sheepish.

Blather, a bladder; a windy fellow.

Blatherie, idle talk; flattery.

Blaud, to slap or bang.

Blauding, pelting; banging.

'To shun the bitter blauding shower.'

Blaw, to boast; to blow.

Blawn, blown.

Blear't or *Blearit*, bedimmed with weeping.

'Grat his een baith blear't an' blin'.'

Bleer, to blear.

Bleeze, blaze; flame.

Bleezin', blazing; flaming.

Blellum, a babbler; loud-voiced nonsense.

'A bletherin,' blusterin', drunken blellum.'

Blether, to talk idly.

Bleth'rin', talking idly.

Blin', blind.

Blink, a moment; a glance; a smile.

'I gat a paper in a blink.'
'Ae blink o' the bonie burdies.'
'A blink o' your bonie black e'e'

Blinkers, female oglers.

Blinkin', glancing; smiling roguishly.

Blin't, blinded.

Blirt and blearie, bleared by excess of weeping.

Blithe or *Blythe*, cheerful; happy.

Blitter or *Blutter*, the mire snipe.

Blue-gowns, licensed beggars, who annually, on the king's birthday, were presented with a blue gown, or cloak, with a badge.

Bluid or *Blude*, blood.

Bluidy, bloody.

Blume, bloom.

Blunty, a stupid person.

Blype, a large shred.

' Till skin in blypes cam haurlin'.

Bobbit, bobbed ; becked ; danced.

Bock, to vomit.

Bocket, gushed ; vomited.

Boddle, a small coin, value two pennies Scots.

Bodkin, a pointed instrument for making holes in cloth.

' Your bodkin's bauld.'

Boggie, marshy ; a small morass.

Bogle, a hobgoblin.

Bole, a hole in the wall.

' The bole ayont the ingle-lowe.'

Bonie or *Bonnie*, beautiful ; sweet-looking.

Boord, board.

Boord-en', board end ; head of the table.

Boortree, the shrub-elder.

' Rustlin' through the boortrees comin'.'

Boost, behoved ; must needs.

Boot, To boot, payment to the bargain.

Bore, a small hole.

' Thro' ilka bore the beams were glancin'.'

Botch, an angry tumour.

Bother, annoyance ; to tease.

Bouk, bulk ; body.

Bow-hough'd, bandy-legged.

Bow-kail, cabbage.

Bow't, bent ; crooked.

Brachens or *Brackens*, ferns.

Brae, the slope of a small hill.

' Ye banks and braes o' bonie Doon.'

Braid, broad.

Braid-cloth, broadcloth.

Braid Scots, broad Scotch.

Braik, a set of harrows.

'An' pownies reek in plow or braik.'

Braindge, to plunge rashly forward.

Braindg't, plunged.

' Thou never braindg't and fetched and flisket.'

Brak, broke ; did break.

Brankie, spruce ; well attired.

Branks, a bridle with wooden curbs.

Brany, brandy.

Brash, a brief illness ; water-brash.

Brats, small pieces ; rags ; children.

' Wi' sowpes o' kail and brats o' claes.'

Brattle, a short, rapid race.

Braw, gallant ; handsome ; finely dressed.

Brawly or *Brawlies*, very well ; finely.

' Tam kent what was what fu' brawly.'

Brawny, of brawn and muscle ; strong.

Braws, fine clothes.

Braxies, sheep suffering from, or that have died of, the disease called braxy.

Braxy, the flesh of sheep that have been killed because of disease.

Breastet or *Briestit*, sprang up with forward motion.

Breastie or *Briestie*, diminutive of *breast*.

Brecham or *Brechan*, a horse collar.

Bree, juice ; liquid.

Breeks, breeches.

Breer or *Briar*, briar.

Brent, polished.

Brent-bright, brightly polished.

Brent-new, brand new.

Brief, writ; writing.
Brig, bridge.
Brisket, the breast.
Brither, brother.
Brock, a badger.

'They gang as saucy by puir folk,
As I wad by a stinking brock.'

Brogue, a trick.
Broo, brow; also meaning soup, liquid, juice.
Broose, a race at country weddings.

'At brooses thou had ne'er a fallow
For pith and speed.'

Brose, a dish of oatmeal and hot water, seasoned with salt.
Browst, a brewing of ale.
Browster-wives, ale-wives.
Brugh, a burgh; a lunar halo.
Brulzie, a broil; a quarrel.
Brunstane, brimstone.
Brunt, burnt.
Buchan-bullers, a wild part of the sea on the rocky coast of Buchan, commonly called 'The Bullers of Buchan.'
Budgets, tinkers' bags of tools.
Buff, to bang.
Bught, sheep-fold.
Bughtin', folding the sheep.
Bughtin'-time, the time for gathering the sheep into the fold for the night.

'Bughtin'-time is near, my Jo.'

Buirdly, stout made; broad built.
Bum, the buttocks; to hum.
Bum-bees, humble bees.
Bum-clock, the humming beetle.
Bummin', making a humming noise.

Aft yont the dyke she's heard thee bummin,'

Bummle, to drone; a blunderer.
Bunker, a seat; generally a seat in the window.

'A winnock bunker in the east,
There sat Auld Nick in shape o' beast.'

Burdies, birdies. *Bonnie burdies*, beautiful maidens.
Bure, did bear.
Burn or *Burnie*, a rivulet.
Burnewin (burn the wind), the blacksmith.
Burr-thistle, the spear thistle, or thistle of Scotland.
Busk, to dress neatly.
Buskit, dressed with taste.
Buss, a bush.
But, without; void of.
But and ben, kitchen and parlour.

'Now but and ben the change-house fills.'

By, past; beside.
By attour, aside and at a distance.
By himsel, beside himself; distracted.
Byke, a wild bee's nest.
By-past, past.
Byre, a cow-house.

Ca' ,call; to drive.
Ca'd or *Ca't*, called; driven, also calved.

'When new-ca'd kye rowte at the stake.'

Cadger, a hawker.
Cadie or *Caddie*, a message-runner; a fellow.
Caff, chaff.
Caird, a tinker; a sturdy beggar; also to heckle.
Cairn, a loose heap of stones.
Calf-ward, an enclosure for calves.

'His braw calf-ward where gowan grew.'

Calimanco, thick cotton cloth.

Callan or *Callant*, a boy.

Caller or *Cauler*, fresh and cool.

'The caller air.' 'The cauler spring.'

Callet, follower of a camp; a trull.

Cam, came.

Canker't or *Cankrie*, crabbed; ill-natured.

Canna, cannot.

Cannie, gentle;

Cannilie, gently; quietly.

Cantie or *Canty* cheerful; lively.

Cantraip or *Cantrip*, a spell; a charm.

'By some devilish cantraip slight,
Each in its cauld hand held a light.

Cap'rin', capering.

Cap-stane, cope-stone; key-stone.

Care-na-by, regardless; do not care.

Cark, anxiety.

Carl or *Carle*, an old man.

Carl-hemp, the male stalk of hemp.

Carlie, diminutive of *carl*.

Carlin, a stout old woman.

Cartes, cards.

Castock, the core or pith of the cabbage-stalk.

Caudron, cauldron.

'To fry them in his caudrons.'

Cauf, calf.

Cauk, chalk. *Cauk and keel*, chalk and red clay.

Cauld, cold.

Caup, a cup; a quaich.

Causey, the causeway.

Causey-cleaner, a scavenger.

Cavie, a hen-coop.

Chamer or *Chaumer*, chamber.

Change-house, tavern.

Chanter, the tune-pipe in a set of bagpipes.

Chap, a fellow.

Chapman, a pedlar.

Chapman billies, pedlar fellows.

Chaup, a knock; a blow.

'Comes on like Death at every chaup.'

Cheek for chow, cheek by jowl; side by side.

Cheep, chirp.

Chiel or *Child*, a young fellow.

'Buirdly chiels and clever hizzies.'

Chimla, chimney; the fire-place.

Chimla-lug, the fireside.

Chitterin', shivering with cold.

Chows, chews.

Christendie, Christendom.

Chuckie, a hen.

Chuffie, fat-faced.

Clachan, a small village; a hamlet.

Claes, clothes.

Claith, cloth.

Claithing, clothing.

Clamb, did climb.

Clankie, a noisome stroke.

Clap, a stroke. *Clap hands*, to strike hands.

Clapper, the clapper of a mill.

Clark, a clerk.

Clarkit, clerked; wrote.

Clarty, dirty; nasty.

Clash, idle talk; common gossip.

Clatter, sharp sounds rapidly repeated; common country talk.

Claught, caught.

Claut, to scrape. *A claut*, a handful.

Clavers, gossip. *Clavers and havers*, nonsensical talk.

Claw, to scratch.

Cleckin', a brood.

Cleed, to clothe.

Cleeding, clothing.

Cleek, to hook; a hook.

Cleekit, linked together.

Clegs, gad-flies.

Clink, a sharp stroke; money; rhyme.

Clinkin', with sudden, easy motion.

Clinkum-bell, the church bell-ringer.

'Now clinkum-bell wi' rattlin' tow
Begins to jow and croon.'

Clips, shears.

Clishmaclaver, idle conversation.

Clockin'-hen, brood-hen.

Clockin'-time, hatching-time.

Cloot, the hoof.

Clootie, Satan.

'Auld Hornie, Satan, Nick or Clootie.'

Clour, bump or swelling after a blow.

Clouts, ragged clothes. *To clout*, to patch.

Clud, a cloud.

Clue, a ball of yarn or twine.

Clunk, a hollow sound.

Coatie, diminutive of *coat*.

Coaxing, enticing.

Coble, a small fishing boat.

Cock, to Cock up, to set up.

Cockernony, a lock of hair tied up on a girl's head; a cap.

Cockie, diminutive of *cock*. *Cantie cockie*, cheerful old man.

Cod, a pillow.

Coft, bought.

Cog, a wooden dish.

Coggie, diminutive of *cog*.

Coila or *Kyle*, a district in Ayrshire.

Collie, the common farm-dog.

Collie-shangie, a quarrel among men; suggesting a dog-fight.

Comin', coming.

Comman's, commandments.

Cood, cud; to chew the cud.

Coof or *Cuif*, a blockhead; a ninny.

Cookit, appeared and disappeared by rapid turns.

Cooser, a stallion.

Coost, did cast.

Coot, the ankle. *To cool his coots*, to cool his ankles.

Cootie, a wooden kitchen dish.

Corbies, carrion crows; ravens.

Core, corps; company.

Corn, oats; grain of oats.

Corn-bing, a heap of the grain of oats.

Corn-mou, corn heap.

Corn't, fed with oats.

Corse, corpse.

Cou'dna or *Couldna*, could not.

Coup, to heel over.

Coup the cran, to give premature birth.

Couthie, kind; loving.

Cowe, to crop. *Cowe the nettle*, crop the nettle.

Cowe, to scare. *Cowe the caddie*, scare the fellow.

Cowp, to heel over; to tumble.

Cowp, to barter. *Horse-cowper*, a dealer in horses.

Cowpit, tumbled; bartered.

Cow'rin', cowering.

Cowte, a colt.

Cozie or *Cozy*, snug and warm.

Crack, a chat. *Ca' the crack*, keep up the talk.

Crack, a flaw.

Crackie, full of talk.

Crackin', conversing.

Crackit, conversed; also *Crackit*, meaning of unsound mind.

Cracks, stories.

Craft, a croft.

Craig, a high rock; the neck.

'The knife that nicket Abel's craig.'

Craigie, diminutive of craig.

Craik, the corncrake, or landrail.

Craiks, cries.

Crambo-clink or Crambo-jingle, ready rhyming.

Crankous, fretful; captious.

Cranreuch, hoar-frost.

'In hoary cranreuch drest.'

Crap, a crop; did creep.

Craw, a crow; to crow.

Creel, a basket.

Creep, to crawl.

Creepie-stool, low stool.

Creeshie, greasy.

Crocks, old ewes.

O wha will tent the waifs and crocks?'

Cronie, friend; gossip.

Croon, a hollow, sustained moan; a crown.

'The deil or else some outler quey,
Gat up and gae a croon.'

Croon'd, hummed; crowned.

Croose, proud; cocksure.

Crowdie, oatmeal and cold water, or milk.

Crowdie-time, meal-time.

Crummie, a horned cow.

Crummie's nicks, marks on cow's horns indicating age.

Crummock, a staff with a crooked head.

Cuddle, to clasp fondly.

Cuddled, fondled.

Cuif. See Coof.

Curch, a 'kerchief worn on the head.

Her house sae bien, her curch sae clean.'

Curchie, a curtsey.

Curmurring, murmuring.

Curpan, the rump; the crupper.

Cushat, wood-pigeon.

Cutty, short.

'Her cutty sark o' Paisley harn,
That while a lassie she had worn.'

Cutty-stool, stool of repentance.

Dad or Daddie, father.

Daes't, dazed; stupefied.

'I've seen me daes't upon a time.'

Daffin, merriment.

Daft, merry; giddy; foolish.

Daimen, rare; now and then.

Daimen-icker, an occasional ear of corn.

'A daimen-icker in a thrave's a sma' request.'

Dainty, plump and thriving; good-humoured.

Dam, pent-up water.

Dander, to wander.

Dang, drove.

Danton, daunton; subdue.

Dappl't, dappled.

Darg, a measure of work.

Darklins, in the dark.

Daud or Dawd, a large piece of bread; to thrash.

Daudin' showers, rains urged by wind.

Daur, dare. Daur't, dared.

Daurna, dare not

Daut or Dawt, to fondle.

'I fatherly will kiss and daut thee.'

Davie or Davoc, diminutive of David.

Daw, dawn.

'The cock may craw, the day may daw.'

Dawds, large portions.

Dawin', the dawning of the day.

Dead-sweer, very loathe; averse.

Dearie, diminutive of dear: sweetheart.

Deave, to deafen.

Deil haet, devil a whit.

　'Deil haet ails them.'

Deil-ma-care, reckless; it matters not.

Deleerit, delirious.

Delve, to dig.

Delvin', digging.

Dern'd, hid.

Descrive, to describe; to perceive.

Deuks, ducks.

　The deuk's dang o'er my daddie.'

Devel, a stunning blow.

Diddle, to jog a tune.

Dight, to winnow corn; to wipe.

Din, noise; sallow.

'He had a wife was dour and din.'

Ding, to excel; to surpass; to push.

Dink, neat; trim.

Dinna, do not

Dirl, vibration from a stroke.

Diz'n or *Dizzen*, a dozen.

Dochter, daughter.

Doited, stupid; bewildered.

Donsie, neat and trim.

Doo, dove. *My doo*, my love.

Doodle, to dandle.

Dook, to duck.

Dool, sorrow.

Dorty, saucy; pettish.

Douce, sober; prudent; wise.

Doukit, ducked.

Doup, bottom.

Doup-skelper, bottom-smacker.

That vile doup-skelper, Emperor Joseph.'

Dour, obstinate.

Dour and din, stubborn and sallow.

Dow, can. *The best he dow*, the best he can.

Dowff, pithless.

'Her dowff excuses put me daft.'

Dowie, sad; lonesome.

Dowilie, mournfully.

Downa, cannot; not able.

'They downa bide the stink o powther.'

Doxy or *Doxie*, a mistress.

'His doxy lay within his arms.'

Doylt or *Doylte*, stupefied crazed.

Dozen't, benumbed.

Drab, a young female beggar

Draigl't, draggled; dirty and wet.

'She's draigl't a' her petticoatie.'

Drap, a drop.

Drappie, diminutive of *drap Taste the drappie*, taste the drink.

Drappin', dropping.

Drauntin', drawling.

Drauntin' drivel, tedious small talk.

'To plague you wi' their drauntin' drivel.'

Dree, to suffer; endure.

Dreep, to ooze; to drop.

Dreigh, tedious; long about it.

Dress, to chastise.

Dribble, drizzle; slaver.

Driddle, the motion of a poor fiddler; to totter.

Drift, snow moved by the wind; intention.

Droddum, the breech; the end.

'Wad dress your droddum.'

Drone, humming sound; the base note of the bagpipes.

Drones, non-worker bees.

Droop-rumpl't, that droops at the crupper.

Drouk, to drench.

Drouket or *Droukit*, soaked with wet; drenched.

Drouth, drought; thirst.

Drouthie or *Drouthy*, thirsty.

Drucken or *Druken*, drunken.

Drumly, muddy.

Drummock, oatmeal and cold water mixed.

Drunt, pet; sour humour.

Dryin', drying.

Dub, a pool; a puddle.

Duddie, ragged. *Duddies*, ragged clothes.

'To drink their orra duddies.'

Duds, rags; mean clothes.

Dung, worsted; subdued; stricken.

'To see his puir auld mither's pot
Thus dung in staves,'

Dunsh, a heavy push.

Dunt, to throb. *Dunted*, throbbed; beaten.

Dunts, blows.

Durk, a dirk.

Dusht, pushed; attacked.

Dwalling, dwelling.

Dwalt, dwelt.

Dwyne, to decline.

Dyke, a stone fence.

Dyvor, a bankrupt.

'Rot the dyvors in the jails.'

Ear', early.

Earn, the eagle.

'Cliffs, the haunts o' sailin' earns.'

Eastlin, eastern; eastward.

Ee or *E'e*, eye.

E'e-bree, the eyebrow.

Een, eyes. *E'en*, even.
E'en's, even as.

E'en or *E'enin'*, the evening.

E'enow, even now.

Eerie, ghostly; fear-inspiring.

'In mirkest glen, at midnight hour,
I'd rove and ne'er be eerie.'

Eild, old age.

Eke, an addition; also.

Elbuck, elbow.

Eldrich or *Eldritch*, ghostly; frightful.

Ell, a Scots measure—37 inches.

Elshin, a shoemaker's awl.

En', end.

Eneuch or *Eneugh*, enough.

Enfauld, enfold.

Engine, genius.

Enou', enough.

Erse, the Gaelic tongue.

Ether, an adder.

Ether-stane, adder-stone (according to old superstition, a stone formed by adders).

Ettle, aim; intent; to try.

Evermair, evermore.

Eydent, diligent; busy.

'And mind their labours with an eydent hand.'

Fa', fall; lot; try.

'Nae farther can we fa'.'
'Black be your fa'.'
'Gude faith he maunna fa' that.'

Faddomed or *Faddom't*, fathomed.

Fae, foe. *Faes*, foes.

Faem, foam; the sea.

Faiket, excused.

Fain, fond; glad.

Fair fa', good befall; welcome.

'Fair fa' your honest sonsie face.'

Fairin, present from a fair; deserts.

Fairly, evenly; entirely.

Fallow, fellow. *Fallows*, fellows.

Fand, did find; found.

Fareweel, farewell; adieu.

Farl, an oaten cake.

Fash, trouble; care; annoyance.

Fasheous, troublesome.

'Faith they'll maybe fin' them fasheous.'

Fasten-e'en, Fasten's Even; the evening before Lent.

Faucht, fought; a fight.

Fauld, a fold for sheep.

Faun, fallen.

Fause, false.

Fause-house, an empty space in a stack of grain for drying.

Fausant, decent; seemly.

Faut, fault.

Fautor, transgressor.

    'Although he be the fautor.'

Feal, loyal; steadfast.

Fearfu', fearful; frightful.

Fear't, affrighted.

Feat, neat; spruce.

Fecht, to fight; a fight.

Fechtin', fighting.

Feck, the greater bulk.

    'Ye, for my sake, hae gi'en the feck
      Of a' the ten comman's,
        A screed some day.

Fecket, an under waistcoat.

Feckfu', large; ample; handsome.

Feckless, puny; weak; silly.

Feckly, mostly.

Fee, servants' wages.

Feg, a fig.

Fegs, an exclamation—as, Faith !

Feide, feud; enmity.

Fell, keen; biting; nippy.

    'Biting Boreas, fell and doure.'
    'Her weel hain'd kebbuck fell.'

Fell, the cuticle under the skin.

    'See how he peels the skin an' fell.'

Felly, relentless.

Fen or *Fend*, to shift; successful effort.

Ferlie, a wonder; to marvel.

Fetch, to pull by fits; bring.

Fey, strange; fated.

Fidge, to fidget; to wriggle.

Fidgin'-fain, quivering with fondness.

Fient, fiend; a petty oath.

Fient-ma-care, fiend-may-care (devil-may-care).

Fier, sound; healthy.

Fiere, comrade; friend.

    'And here's a hand, my trusty fiere

Fin', to find.

Fish-creel, fish-basket.

Fissle, tingle; bustle.

Fit, foot; footstep.

Fittie-lan', the near horse o the pair in a plough.

    'Thou was a noble fittie-lan'.'

Fizz, to make a hissin noise; fuss.

Flae, flea.

Flaff, to flap.

Flaffin', flapping in the wind

Flaite, did flyte; did scold.

Flang, threw with violence danced wildly.

Flannen, flannel.

Flee, a fly; to fly.

Fleech, to supplicate; t wheedle.

Fleechin', supplicating; wheedling.

'Duncan fleech'd, and Duncan pray d

Fleesh, a fleece.

Fleg, a fright; to scare.

Flether, to scatter; to flatter

Fletherin', scattering; wheedling.

Flewit, a sharp blow.

Fley, to frighten.

Fley'd, frightened.

Flichter or *Flichtering*, t flutter as young nest lings.

Flinders, fragments; broke pieces.

    'Twill mak her puir auld heart, fear,
      In flinders flee.

Fling, to throw; to leap dance.

    'Lowping and flingin' on a crum mock.'

Flingin'-tree, a flail.
'The thresher's weary flingin'-tree.'
Flisk, to fret at the yoke.
Flisket, fretted.
Flisky, skittish.
Flit, to shift; to remove from one place to another.
Flitterin', fluttering.
Flunkie, a liveried servant.
Flyte, to scold.
Flyting, scolding.
Fodgel, dumpy and stout.
'A fine, fat, fodgel wight.'
Foor, fared.
Foord, a ford.
Foorsday, Thursday.
Forbears or *Forebears*, forefathers.
Forby or *Forbye*, besides.
Fore, alive; to the fore.
Forfairn, forlorn; jaded.
Forfoughten, worn out.
Forniawed, worn out.
Forrit, forward.
Fother, fodder.
Fou or *Fu'*, full; drunk.
Foughten, beaten; done out.
Foursome, a set of four.
Foursome reel, a dance by four persons.
Fouth, plenty; enough.
Frae, from.
Fraet, superstition.
Freath, froth.
Fremit, estranged; foreign.
Fremit folk, strangers.
Frien', friend.
Fu', full.
Fud, the scut or tail of a hare.
'Ye maukins, cock your fud fu' braw.'
Fuff, to blow intermittently; puff.
Fuff'd, puffed.
Fumbler, an awkward person.
Fumblin', endeavouring without success.

B.P.

Fur or *Furr*, a furrow.
Furder, further.
Furms, forms; low wooden benches.
Fushion, pith; vigour.
Fushionless, pithless; sapless; without taste.
Fy, an exclamation signifying haste.
'Fy, let us a' to Kirkcudbright.'
Fyfteen, fifteen.
Fyke, to fret; in a fuss.
Fyle, to soil; to dirty.
Fyl't, soiled; dirtied.

Ga', the gall.
Gab, the mouth. *To gab*, to speak fluently.
Gaberlunzie, a beggar.
Gae, to go. *Ga'e*, gave.
Gaed, went.
Gaen or *Gane*, gone.
Gaet or *Gate*, way; manner.
'I gaed a waefu' gate yestreen,'
'And may they never learn the gaets Of other vile, wanrestfu' pets.'
Gaip, to open wide.
Gairs, slashes; coloured insertions.
'My lady's gown has gairs upon't.'
Gang, to go; to walk.
Gangrel, a vagrant.
Gar, to compel; to make.
'Ye gar the lasses lie aspar.'
Gar't, compelled.
Garten, garter.
Gash, wise; sagacious.
Gat, got.
Gate. See *Gaet*.
Gatty, failed in strength; paunchy.
Gaucie or *Gausie*, jolly; large.
Gaud, goad; the ploughstaff.
Gaudsman, the driver at the plough.
Gaun, going.
Gaunt, to yawn.

U

Gawkie, a thoughtless and foolish person.

'Now gawkies, tawpies, gowks, and fools.'

Gaylies, pretty well.

Gear, wealth; goods.

'And gather gear by every wile.'

Geck, to toss the head in scorn.

Ged, a pike.

Ged's-hole, a pool frequented by pike; metaphorically, the grave.

'Wae's me for Johnie Ged's hole now.'

Gentles, gentry.

Gentry, trim and elegant.

Geordie, George. *Yellow Geordie*, a guinea of King George's time.

Get, a child; issue.

Ghaist, ghost.

Gie, to give; *Gies*, gives. *Gied*, gave; *Gien*, given.

Gie's, give us.

Gif, if.

Giftie, diminutive of *gift*.

'O wad some power the giftie gie us.'

Giglets, giggling maidens.

Gillie, diminutive of *gill*.

Gilpey, a young girl.

Gimmer, a two-year-old ewe.

Gin, if; by.

'I'll aulder be gin summer, Sir.'

Gipsey, gipsy; a lively young girl.

Girdle, a round plate of metal for firing cakes on.

'The verra girdle rang.'

Girn, to grin.

Girr, a hoop.

Gizz, the face.

Glaikit, foolish; thoughtless.

Glaizie, smooth and shining.

Glaum, to clutch, *Glaum'd*, clutched.

Gled, a hawk; the kite.

Gleede, a glowing coal.

Gleg, sharp; quick.

Gley, to squint; off the straight.

Gley'd, squint-eyed.

Gleyde, an old horse.

Glib, ready.

Glib-gabbit, with ready tongue.

Glint, to shine briefly. *Glinted*, went brightly past.

Gloamin', gloaming; twilight.

'And darker gloamin' brought the night.'

Glowr, to stare; a stare in wonder.

'I glowr'd as I'd seen a warlock.'

Glowrin', staring with wonder.

Glunch, to frown; to sulk.

Goavan, gazing vacantly.

Gotten, got.

Gowan, the wild or mountain daisy.

Gowany lea, daisied lawn.

Gowd, gold.

Gowden, golden.

Gowdspink, the goldfinch.

Gowff, the game of golf; a dull, heavy stroke.

Gowffin', driving hither and thither.

Gowk, the cuckoo; a foolish person.

Gowl, to howl.

Graff, the grave.

Grain or *Grane*, groan.

Graip, a pronged implement used in farm work.

Graith, harness.

Grannie, grandmother.

Gree, to agree; superiority. *To bear the gree*, to win the victory.

Gree't, agreed.

Greet, to weep.

Greetin', weeping.

rien, to long for; to covet.

'That griens for the loaves and fishes.'

rieve, farm overseer.

rippet, seized hold of.

rissle, gristle.

rit, great. *Grit folk*, great folks.

roanin'-maut, the handsel drink at a child's birth.

Groset, a gooseberry.

ruesome, ill-favoured.

rumphie, a sow.

run', the ground; ground.

runstane, grindstone.

runtle, the snout; the face.

runzie, the mouth or snout.

'She d ghts her grunzie wi' a hushion.'

rushie, thick; of large growth.

Gude or *Guid*, good; the Supreme Being.

Gude e'en, good evening.

Gudefather, father-in-law.

Gudeman, husband; master.

Gude mornin', good morning.

Gudemother, mother-in-law.

Gudes, goods; commodities.

Gude-willie, with good will.

Gude-willie-waucht, a drink with right good will.

'We'll tak a right gude-willie-waucht.'

Gullie or *Gully*, a large knife.

Gulravage, a wild raid; a riot.

Gumlie, muddy.

Gumption, sense; understanding.

Gusty, tasteful; full.

Gutcher, grandfather.

Gut-scraper, fiddler.

Ha', hall.

Ha'-Bible, hall-Bible.

The big ha'-Bible, ance his father's pride.'

Haddie, a haddock.

Haddin', house; home

Hae, have; to accept. *Haen*, had. *Hae't*, have it.

Haet, the least thing. *Fient-haet*, nothing at all.

Haffet, the side of the head.

Hafflin, a good-sized lad.

Hafflins, half-way.

Hag, a scar; an unseemly female.

Haggis, an oatmeal pudding.

Hain, to save; to spare.

Hairst, harvest.

Haith, a petty oath.

Haivers, nonsense.

'Wi' claivers and haivers, Wearing the day awa'.

Hal' or *Hald*, hold; possession.

Hale, whole; healthy; well.

Hallan, partition between the door and the fire-place.

Hallan-shaker, a sturdy beggar.

Hallions, rogues.

Hallowe'en, Hallowmas Eve.

Haly, holy.

Hame, home. *Hamely*, homely; familiar.

Han', hand.

Han'-breed, a hand-breadth.

Han'-waled, carefully selected by hand.

Hangit, hanged.

Hansel, a first gift.

Hansel-throne, a throne newly inherited.

Hap, a wrap; to cover over. *Hap*, hazard. *Ill-hap*, ill-hazard.

Happer, hopper; the hopper of a mill.

Happin', hopping.

Hap-step-an'-loup, hop, skip, and leap.

Harigals, heart, liver, and lungs.

Harkit, hearkened.

Harn, a coarse linen cloth.

'Her cutty sark o' Paisley harn.'

Harns, brains.

Hash, to smash; a big, awkward fellow.

Haud, hold.

Hauf, half.

Haughs, low-lying lands; meadows.

'Let husky wheat the haughs adorn.'

Haurl, to drag roughly.

Haurlin', dragging roughly.

Hauver-meal, half-ground meal.

Haverel or *Haveril*, a half-wit.

Havins, good manners; common sense.

'Put some havins in his breast.'

Hawkie, a cow.

Heapit, heaped.

Hech, an exclamation of wonder.

Hecht, promised.

Heckle, a flax comb; to question.

Hecklebirnie, hell.

Heels-owre-gowdie, heels over body; topsy-turvy.

Heeze, to lift up; to elevate.

Heft, haft; handle.

'The gray hairs yet stack to the heft.'

Heich or *Heigh*, high.

Hein-shin'd, in-shinned.

Hellim, helm.

Hen-broo, hen-broth.

'Kate sits i' the neuk, suppin' hen-broo'

Herrin', herring.

Herry, to rob; to plunder.

Hersel, herself.

Het, hot.

Heugh, a hollow.

Heuk, a book.

Hie, high.

Hilch, to hobble.

Hiney, honey. *Hinny*, sweet.

Hing, to hang.

Hirple, to walk haltingly.

'He hirples twa-fauld as he dow.'

Hirlpin', limping.

Hirsel, a flock of sheep

Hizzie, a lively young woman

Hoast, a cough.

'Colic grips, and barkin' hoast.'

Hodden-gray, coarse gray woollen cloth.

Hoddin', hobbling.

'Here farmers gash in ridin' graith Gaed hoddin by their cotters.'

Hoggie, diminutive of *hog.*

Hog-score, the distance lin in curling.

Hog-shouther, to jostle wit the shoulder.

Hoodie-craw, the hoode crow.

Hool, the husk or outer skin

'Puir Leezie's heart maist lap th hool.'

Hoolie, softly.

Hoord, hoard; to hoard.

Hornie, with horns; th devil.

Hotch, to fidget.

Hotch'd, fidgeted.

'And hotch d and blew wi' might an main.'

Houghmagandie, fornication.

Hov'd, swelled.

'Some ill-brewn drink had hov' her wame.'

Howdie, a midwife.

Howe, a hollow.

Howe-backit, hollow-backed.

Howes, hollows.

Howf, a place of commor resort.

Howkit, digged.

Howlet, an owl.

Hoy, to urge.

Hoy't, urged.

'They hoy't out Will wi' sair advice.'

Hoyte, to amble awkwardly.

Hullions, slovens.

Hunder, a hundred.

Hunkers, with hams on heels.

'Upon his hunkers bended.'

urcheon, a hedgehog.

urdies, the hips; the crupper.

url, to roll over; to drive down.

url't, rolled over; driven down.

ushion, a footless stocking.

yte, mad; crazy.

heir witching, cursed, delicious blinkers,
      Hae put me hyte.'

', in.

cker, an ear of corn.

er'oe, a great-grandchild.

k or Ilka, each; every.

l-deedie, mischievous.

l o't, bad at it.

l-taen, ill-taken.

l-will, bad nature; spite.

l-will'd, bad-natured; spiteful.

l-willie, malicious.

ndentin', indenturing.

ngine, genius; ingenuity.

An a' that kenn'd him round declared
      He had ingin .'

ngle, the fire; the fireside.

ngle-lowe, the flame of the fire.

rede ye, I warn ye; I advise ye.

se, I shall; I will.

sna, is not.

'Ah Nick! ah Nick! it isna fair.'

ther, other.

tsel, itself.

ad or Jaud, a jade.

ads or Jauds, jades.

ag, to prick.

auk, to dally; to trifle.

aukin', trifling.

auner, idle talk.

aup, to bespatter; to splash.

aw, to pour out forcefully; coarse raillery.

Jaw-hole, a deep trench for foul water.

Jillet, a jilt; a giddy girl.

'A jillet b ak his heart at last.'

Jimp, slender.

Jingle, rhyme.

'Hamely, wastlin, jingle.'

Jinglin', jingling.

Jink, to dodge; to frisk.

Jinker, a gamester.

Jinkin', dodging.

Jirkenet, a bodice.

Jirt, to squirt.

Jo, a sweetheart.

'Thou canst love another jo.'

Jocteleg, a large clasp-knife.

Jokin', joking.

Jouk, to duck; to stoop suddenly.

'I jouk beneath misfortune's blow.'

Jow, to swing with sound like a large bell.

Jumpit, jumped.

Jundie, to jostle.

Jurr, a servant lass.

Kae, a daw.

Kail, colewort; broth.

Kail-blade, leaf of the colewort.

Kail-gullie, cabbage-knife.

Kail-runt, stem of the colewort.

Kain, penalty; rent.

Kebars, rafters.

'He ended, and the kebars sheuk.'

Kebbuck, a cheese.

Keckle, to cackle.

Keek, a sly look; to peep.

Keekin'-glass, a looking-glass.

Keekit, peeped.

Keel, red chalk.

Keepit, kept.

Kelpie, a water-demon.

Ken, to know.

Kenna, know not.

Kennin', knowing; in small degree. *A kennin' wrang*, a little wrong.

Kent, a shepherd's staff. *Wi' kent and collie*, with staff and dog.

Kent, knew.

Kep, to catch.

Ket, a fleece.

'Wi' tawtet ket and hairy hips.'

Kiaugh, anxiety.

Kilt, to tuck up; a short skirt.

Kimmer, a girl.

'I'm tauld they're lo'esome kimmers.'

Kin, kindred.

Kin', kind.

Kintlin', cuddling; fondling.

Kintra, country.

'Though he was b.ed to kintra wark.'

Kintra cooser, a travelling stallion.

Kirn, a churn; to churn; a harvest-home.

Kirsen, to christen.

Kist, a chest.

Kitchen, meat or relish eaten with bread.

Kith, kindred.

Kittle, difficult; to tickle.

Kittlin', a kitten; tickling.

Knaggie, with nobs.

Knap, to strike neatly on the top.

Knappin'-hammer, a hammer for breaking stones.

Knowe, a hillock.

Knurl, a churl.

Kye, kine; cows.

Kyle, the central portion of Ayrshire.

Kyte, the belly.

Kythe, reveal; to show.

Laddie, diminutive of *lad*.

Lade, a load.

'I bear alane my lade o' care.'

Laggen, the angle within between the side an bottom of a cask.

Laggen-gird, the end hoop a cask.

Laigh, low.

Lair, learning; lore; mue the grave.

'It kindles wit, it waukens lair.'

'Here Robin lies in his last lair.'

Laird, proprietor (general landowner).

Lairie, muddy; miry.

Laith, loath.

Laithfu', loathful.

Lallan or *Lalland*, lowland.

'Guid braid lallans.'

Lallans, lowlands; lowlan tongue.

Lammas moon, harvest moor

Lammie, diminutive of *lamb* term of endearment to child.

Lampit, limpet.

Lan', land.

Lane, lone.

Lang, long.

Lang syne, long ago.

Lap, leapt; apron.

Lassie, diminutive of *lass*.

Lave, the rest. *The lave*, ti others.

'What's aft mair than a' the lave.'

Lav'rock, the lark.

Lawin', score; reckoning.

'Gudewife, count the lawin.'

Lea, grass land; pasture *Lea'*, leave.

Lea-rig, grass ridge.

Leal, loyal; true.

'Hearts leal, and warm, and kin l.'

Lear, learning; lore.

Leddy, lady.

Lee, to tell a lie; also gras land.

Lee-lang, live-long.

'The lee-lang day.'

eesome, pleasant.

eeze me, a phrase of endearment.
'Leeze me on thee, Robin.'

eister, a fish-spear.

eugh, did laugh.

ibbet, castrated.

ick, to beat ; to lap with the tongue.

ickit, beaten ; lapped with the tongue.

icks, a beating.
'Mony a fallow gat his licks.'

ift, the sky ; a load.

ilt, a tune ; to sing.

immer, a low woman.

impet, limped.

ink, to trip lightly. *Linkin*, tripping along.
'And linket at it in her sark.'

inn, a waterfall ; a cascade.

int, flax. *Lint in the bell*, flax in the flower.

intie, the linnet.

int-white, flaxen-coloured.
'Lassie wi' the lint-white locks.'

ippen, to trust.

ippen'd, trusted.

ippin', full to the brim.

ivin', living.

oan, loaning ; a private road to a farm.

o'ed, loved. *Lo'esome*, lovesome.

oof, the palm of the hand.
'Heaved on high my waukit loof.'

oosome, lovesome.

oot, let.

osh, an exclamation of wonder.

oun, a low fellow.

oup or *Lowp*, leap.

out or *Loot*, to stoop down.

owe, a flame.

owin', flaming.

owin'-drouth, burning desire for drink.

Lown, quiet.

Lowse, to untie.
'An' lowsed his ill-tongu'd, wicked scaul.'

Luckie, dame ; matron.

Lug, the ear.

Lugget, having ears.

Luggie, a wooden dish with handles.

Lum, chimney.
'Till fuff! it started up the lum.'

Lunt, a column of smoke ; to smoke.

Luntin', smoking.

Luppen, leaped.

Luve, love.

Lyart, gray.
'His lyart haffets wearing thin and bare.'

Mae, more.

Maggot's-meat, food for the worms.

Mahoun, Satan.

Mailen or *Mailin*, a farm.

Mailie, Mollie.

Mair, more.

Maist, most ; almost.

Mak, make ; shape.

Mang, among.

Manse, a minister's house.

Manteel, a mantle.

Mark, merk (a Scottish coin), value thirteen shillings and fourpence.
'He gied me thee, o' tocher clear, And fifty mark.'

Mar's year, the year 1715.

Mashlum, mixed corn.

Maskin'-pat, a teapot.

Mauhin, a hare.

Maun, must. *Maunna*, must not.

Maut, malt.

Mavis, the thrush.

Maw, to mow. *Mawin'*, mowing.

Mawn, mown ; a basket.

Maybe, perhaps.

Mear, mare.

Meikle, *Mickle*, or *Muckle*, big; much.

'And twice as meikle's a' that.'

Melder, amount of grain sent to the mill to be ground.

'Ilka melder wi' the miller,
Thou sat as lang as thou had siller.'

Mell, a mallet; to meddle.

Melvie, to soil with meal.

Men', to mend.

Mense, manners; sense; decorum.

Menseless, rude; unmannerly.

Merle, the blackbird.

Messan, a mongrel cur.

Mess John, the parish minister.

Midden, a dunghill.

Midden-creels, dung-baskets.

Midge, a gnat.

Mim, prim.

Mim-mou'd, prim-mouthed; or precise speech.

Minawae, a minuet.

Minnie, mother.

Mirk, dark.

'O mirk, mirk, is this midnight hour.'

Misca', miscall; abuse with the tongue.

Mishanter, mishap; disaster.

Mislear'd, mischievous; unmannerly.

'I wad be kittle to be mislear'd.'

Miss't or *Mist*, missed.

Misteuk, mistook.

Mither, mother.

Mixtie-maxtie, confusedly mixed.

Mizzled, speckled.

Monie or *Mony*, many.

Mools, mould; the grave.

Moop and mell, associate with.

Mou', mouth.

Moudiwart, a mole.

Mousie, diminutive of *mou*

Musie, diminutive of *muse*

Muslin-kail, beefless broth

Mutchkin, an English pint

Mysel, myself.

Mystic-knots, entanglemer made by the bride maids on the bride night-dress, so comp cated as to be ve difficult to untie.

Na or *Nae*, no.

Naebody, nobody.

Naething or *Naithing*, n thing.

Naig, a horse; a nag.

'When I downa yoke a naig,
Then, Lord be thankit, I can beg

Nane, none.

Nappy, strong ale.

Neebors, neighbours.

Negleckit, neglected.

Neist or *Niest*, next.

Neuk, nook.

New-ca'd, newly drive newly calved.

Nick, to indent; to cut int to break.

Nick, a name for the devil.

'Auld Hornie, Satan, Nick, Clootie.'

Nickie-Ben, the devil.

Nicket or *Nickit*, cut int broken off.

Nick-nackets, curiosities.

Niest, next.

Nieve or *Nief*, the first.

Nievefu', a fistful.

Niffer, exchange.

Nit, a nut.

Nocht, nothing.

Noddle, brain.

Norland, northland.

Nowte, cattle.

'To thrum guitars and fecht w nowte.'

)', of.

)! Oh! Och! Ochone! exclamations of distress or longing.

)'erlay, wrap; coverlet.

)'erword, refrain; a phrase often repeated.

)nie or Ony, any.

)rra, odd; extra. [clothes.

)rra duddies, superfluous

)'t, of it.

)ught, aught.

)ughtlins, aught in the least.

)urie, drooping; shivering.

)ursels, ourselves.

)utler, unhoused.

' The deil, or else an outler quey.'

)wer or Owre, over.

)wsen, oxen.

)xter, armpit.

)xter'd, carried or supported under the arm.

)ack, intimate; familiar.

)ack, twelve stones of wool.

'Scores o' lambs, and packs o' woo.'

)aidle, to paddle.

)aidl'd, paddled.

' We twa ha'e paidl'd in the burn.'

)ainch or Paunch, stomach.

)aitrick, a partridge.

)ang, to cram.

' Pangs us fu' o' knowledge.'

)arishen, the parish.

)arritch, porridge.

)at, pot; to put.

)attle, a plough spade.

)aughty, haughty.

)aukie, Pauky, or Pawkie, artful; sly.

)ay't, paid.

)echan, the stomach.

'E'n the ha' folk fill their pechan.'

)echin', panting; blowing.

)enny-fee, small wages.

)enny-weep, small beer.

Pet, a favourite.

Philabeg, a Highland kilt.

Phraise, fair speech.

Phraisin', flattering.

Pibroch, a martial bagpipe air.

Pickle, a small quantity; a grain of corn.

' She gies the herd a pickle nits.'

Pigmy-scraper, an under-sized fiddler.

Pine or Pyne, pain; torture.

Pingle, trouble. [measure.

Pint-stoup, a two-quart

Plack, an old Scots coin, equal to the third part of an English penny.

Plackless, pennyless.

Plaiden, coarse woollen cloth.

Plaidie, diminutive of plaid.

Plew or Pleugh, plough.

Pliskie, a trick.

Plumpit, plumped.

Pocks, wallets; meal bags.

Poind, to distrain; to seize.

Poortith, poverty.

Posie, a garland.

Pouch, pocket.

Pou'd, Pou't, or Pu'd, pulled.

Pouk, to poke; to pluck.

Poupit, pulpit.

Pousie, a hare or cat.

Pout, a chicken.

Pouther, powder.

Pow, the head; the poll.

Pownie, a pony.

Pree or Prie, to taste.

' Rab and Allan came to pree.'

Preen, a pin.

Prief, proof.

Prent, print.

Prigg, to haggle.

Priggin', haggling.

Primsie, precise.

Propone, to propose.

Puddock-stools, toad-stools.

Pund, a pound.

Pyet, a magpie.
Pyke, to pick.
    'Sae merrily's the banes we'll pyke.'
Pyles, grains.
Pystle, epistle.

Quaich, a drinking-cup.
Quaik, quack; the cry of a duck.
Quat, quit; quitted.
Quaukin', quaking.
Quean, a young woman; a lass.
Quey, a young cow.
Quo', quoth.

Rade, rode.
Raep, a rope.
Ragweed, the ragwort.
Raible, to rattle off nonsense.
Rair, to roar. *Rairin'*, roaring.
Raise, rose.
Raize, to madden.
Ramfeezled, fatigued; overpowered.
Ramgunshoch, rugged.
    'Our rumgunshoch, glum, gudeman.'
Rampin', raging in action.
Ram-stam, forward; thoughtless.
Randie or *Randy*, quarrelsome; a shrewish woman.
    'Randie, gangrel bodies.'
Rant, an unskilled song; to rollick.
Rantin', joyous; free.
Rants, merry meetings.
Raploch, home-spun cloth.
Rash, a rush.
    'As feckless as a wither'd rash.'
Rash-buss, a bush of rushes.
Rattan or *Ratton*, a rat.
Raukle, rash; fearless.
    'Auld Scotland has a raucle tongue.'

Raught, reached.
Raw, a row.
Rax, to stretch.
Ream, cream; froth.
Reamin', brim full and frothing.
Reave, to rob; to take by force.
Rebute, rebuff; rebuke.
Reck, heed.
Red or *Rede*, to advise counsel.
    'I red ye weel, tak care o' scaith
     See there's a gully.'
Red-peats, burning turfs.
Red-wat-shod, walking in blood.
Red-wud, stark mad
Reed, smoke; to smoke.
Reekin', smoking.
Reekit, smoked.
Reel, a dance; to spin. [go
Reestit, scorched; refused t
Remead, remedy.
Respeckit, respected.
Rickle, a heap.
Riddle, a sieve; a puzzle.
Rief-randies, sturdy thieves.
Rig, a ridge.
Riggin', roof-tree; the roof.
Rigwoodie, coarse, sapless and touch; the rope c chain that crosses th saddle of a horse's har ness to support th shafts of a cart.
    'Rigwoodie hags, wad spaen a foal'
Rin, run.
Ripp, a handful of ur threshed corn.
Ripplin'-kame, a flax-comb.
Riskit, cracked.
    'Till spritty knowes wad rair't an riskit.'
Rive, to tear; to burst.
Rives, tears.
Rives't, tears it.

Rock or *Roke*, a distaff.

Rockin', a small social gathering, at which the women spin on the rock, or weave a stocking.

Roose, to praise ; to flatter.

Roosty, rusty.

Roun', round.

Roup, sale by auction.

Roupet, hoarse, as with a cold.

Row, to roll ; to wrap.

Row'r, rolled ; roll it.

Rowte, to low ; to bellow.

Rowth, abundance.

Rowthie, having plenty.

Rozet, rosin. [sense.

Rumble-gumption, common

Run-deils, downright devils.

Rung, a cudgel.

' She's just a devil wi' a rung.'

Runkled, wrinkled.

Runt, the stalk of the cabbage or colewort.

Ryke, to reach.

' Let me ryke up to dight that tear.'

Sab, to sob.

' Wi' sighs and sabs she thus began.'

Sabbit, sobbed.

Sae, so.

Saft, soft.

Sair, sore ; to serve.

Sairly, sorely.

Sair't, served.

Sall, shall.

Sang, song ; did sing.

Sark, a shirt.

Sark't, provided with shirts.

Saucy, proud; offish; scornful.

Saugh, the willow.

Saugh-woodies, willow-wands.

Saul, soul.

Saunt, saint.

Saut, salt.

Saut-backets, salt-boxes.

Saw, to sow.

Sax, six. *Saxty*, sixty.

Saxpence, sixpence.

' Hale breeks, saxpence, and a bannock.'

Scaith, hurt ; damage.

Scauld, a scold ; to scold.

Scaur, to scare; a jutting cliff.

Scaur'd, frightened.

Scho, she.

' Guid faith, quoth scho, I doubt ye, sir.'

Scone, a soft, flat cake.

Sconner or *Scunner*, to loathe; to sicken with disgust.

Scraich or *Skraich*, to scream.

Scraichin' or *Skraichin'*, screaming; calling hoarsely.

Screed, to tear ; a rent ; to rattle off.

Scriech, *Scriegh*, or *Skriegh*, to screech.

Scriechin', screeching.

Scrieve, to rant ; to talk or write freely.

Scrievin', gliding gleefully.

Scrimp, scant.

Scrimpit, scanty.

Scroggie or *Scroggy*, thickly grown with stunted shrubs.

Sculdudd'ry, obscenity ; fornication.

See'r, see it.

Sel, self.

Sell't, sold ; sell it.

Sen', send.

Sets, becomes. *Sets her weel*, becomes her well.

Sets aff, goes away.

Settlin', settling.

Shackl'd, shapeless.

' How her new shoon fit her auld shachl'd feet.'

Shaird, a shred.

Shangan, a cleft stick.

' He'll clap a shangan on her tail.'

Shanks, legs. *Shank it*, walk it.

Shanna, shall not.

Shaul, shallow.

Shaver, a barber ; a wag.

Shavie, a trick ; an ill-turn.

Shaw, show ; a wooded dell.

Shearer, a reaper.

Sheep-shank-bane ; ' thinks himsel nae sheep-shank-bane,' thinks himself a person of no small importance.

Sheers or *Shears*, scissors.

Sheugh, a trench ; a wide ditch.

Sheuk, shook.

Shiel, or *Shielin'*, a hut ; a shepherd's cottage ; a shelter.

Shill, shrill.

Shog, a shock ; to shake.

'An' gied the infant warld a shog.'

Shools, shovels.

Shoon, shoes.

Shore, to offer ; to threaten.

Short-syne, a short time ago.

Shouldna, should not.

Shouther, shoulder.

Shure, shore.

Sic, such. *Siccan*, such-like.

Sic-like, such as.

Sicker, secure ; steady.

Sidelins, sidelong ; slanting.

Siller, silver ; money in general.

' Thou sat as lang as thou had siller.'

Simmer, summer.

Sin', since. *Sin'-syne*, since then.

Sindry, asunder.

Skaith, hurt ; damage.

Skeigh, high-mettled ; proud.

Skellum, a worthless fellow.

' She tauld thee weel thou wast a skellum.'

Skelp, a slap ; to run.

Skelpie-limmer, a female scold.

Skelpin', striking ; walking rapidly, or running with sounding steps.

Skelpit, hurried forward.

Skinkin', thin - like soup ; watery.

Skinklin', sparkling ; a small portion.

Skirl, to shriek.

' Skirl up the Bangor.'

Skirl't, shrieked.

Sklent, slant.

Sklented, slanted.

Skouth, range ; scope.

Skriegh, scream.

Skyrin, flaring.

Skyte, to eject forcibly ; a worthless fellow.

Slade, did slide.

Slae, the sloe.

Slap, a breach in a fence ; a gate.

Slaw, slow.

Slee, sly. *Slee'st*, slyest.

Sleekit, sleek ; sly.

Sliddery, slippery.

Sloken, to slake ; to quench thirst.

Slype, a wet furrow.

Slypet, slipped.

Slypet o'er, fell over without noise.

Sma', small.

Smeddum, sense ; mettle.

Smeek, smoke.

' Filled wi' hoast-provoking smeek.'

Smiddy, a smithy.

Smoor'd, smothered.

Smoutie, smutty ; sooty.

Smytrie, a huddled collection.

'A smytrie o' wee duddie weans.'

Snakin', sneaking.

Snapper, to stumble in walking.

Snash, abusive address ; impertinence.

Snaw, snow.

Snaw-broo, melted snow.

Snawie, or *Snawy*, snowy.

Sneck, the latch of a door.

Sned, to crop; to lop off.

Sneeshin'-mill, snuff-box.

Snell, bitter; biting.

Snick, a latch.

Snick-drawin', trick contriving.

Snirt, to snigger.

Snirtle, a sly laugh.

Snool, to cringe; sneak.

Snoove, to go forward creepingly.

Snoov'd or *Snoov't*, sneaked forward.

Snowkit, snuffed and pryed with the nose.

Sodger or *Soger*, a soldier.

Sonsie or *Sonsy*, jolly; ample.

Soom, to swim.

Soor, sour.

Sough or *Sugh*, a light breeze; a heavy sigh.

Souk, to suck.

Souple, supple.

Souter, a shoemaker.

Sowp, a spoonful; a small quantity.

' Wi' sowps o' kail and brats o' claes.'

Sowth, to whistle or hum over a tune.

Sowther, to solder; to make up.

Spae, to divine; to foretell.

Spails, chips; splinters.

Spairge, to bespatter.

Spairin', sparing.

Spak, spake.

Spate, a sudden flood.

Spaul, a limb.

Spavie, the spavin.

' Tho' limpin' wi' the spavie.'

Spavie't, having the spavin.

Spear, to wean.

Speel, the climb.

Speer or *Spier*, to inquire; to ask.

Spence, the parlour.

Spinnin-graith', wheel and rock and lint.

Splatter, splutter.

Spleuchan, a tobacco pouch.

' Deil mak his King's-hood in a spleuchan.'

Splore, a frolic; riot.

Sprachl'd, scrambled.

Sprattle, to scramble; to struggle.

Spreckl'd, speckled.

Spring, a lively tune; a dance.

Sprit, a joint-leaved rush.

Sprittie, dull of sprit roots.

Sprush, spruce.

Spunk, fire; mettle; a spark.

Spunkie, full of spirit; fiery; the will-o'-the-wisp.

Spurtle, a pot-stick for stirring porridge or broth.

Squad, a squadron.

Squatter, to flutter in water.

Squattle, to squat; to crawl.

Squeel, to scream.

Stacher, to stagger.

Stacher'd or *Stacher't*, staggered.

Stack, stuck; a rick of hay or corn.

Staggie, diminutive of *stag*.

Staig, a young horse.

Stan', stand; a stand.

Stane, a stone.

Stang, sting; stuny.

Stank, a pool of standing water.

Stap, step; to stop; stave.

Stark, strong.

Starns, stars.

Starnies, diminutive of *starns*.

Staukin', stalking; walking with dignity.

Staumrel, half-witted.

Staw, a stall; stole; to surfeit.

Stech, to cram.

Stechin', cramming; panting with repletion.

Steek, to shut; a stitch.

Steer, stir; to stir.

Steeve, firm; compacted.

Stell, a still.   [horse.

Sten', to leap; to rear, as a

Stented, erected; set on high.

Stents, dues; assessments.

Step, steep. *Steyest*, steepest.

Stibble, stubble.

Stick-an'-stowe, totally; altogether.

' Folk thought them ruined stick-an'-stowe.'

Stilt, a crutch.

Stimpart, the eighth part of a bushel.

Stirk, a young bullock or heifer.

Stock, a plant of cabbage or colewort.

Stockin', stocking.

Stoited or *Stoiter'd*, staggered; walked stupidly.

Stook, a set of twelve sheaves.

Stot, an ox.

Stound, a sudden pang of the heart.

Stoup or *Stowp*, a measure with a handle for serving liquids.

Stoure, dust in motion; excitement.

' This day the kirk kicks up a stoure.'

Stourie, dusty.

Stowlins, by stealth.

Stown, stolen.

Stoyte, to stagger.

Strade, strode.

Strae, straw.

Strae-death, natural death (death in a straw bed).

Straik, to stroke. *Straikit*, stroked.

Strak, struck.

Strappin', tall and handsome.

Straught, straight.

Stravagin', wandering without aim.

Streek, to stretch. *Streekit*, stretched.

Striddle, to straddle.

Stroan't, spouted forth; pissed.

' An stroan't on stanes an' hillocks' wi' him.'

Stroup, the spout.

Strunt, spirituous liquor of any kind; to swagger.

Studdie, an anvil.

Stumpie, diminutive of *stump*.

Sturt, trouble; vexation.

Styme, a glimmer of light.

' I scarce could wink, or see a styme.'

Sucker, sugar.

Sud or *Shou'd*, should.

Sugh. See *Sough*.

Sumph, a soft, stupid fellow.

Sune, soon.

Suthron, an Englishman.

Swaird, sward; the smooth grass.

Swall'd, swelled.

Swank, tall and lithe.

Swankie, a strapping youth.

Swap, an exchange; to barter.

Swarf, to swoon.

Swatch, a sample.

Swats, a new ale.   [averse.

Sweer, lazy; extremely

Swinge, to lash; to whip.

Swirl, a curl; an eddying blast or pool.

Swith, swift. *Swith awa'*, swiftly away.

Swither, to hesitate; doubt.

Swoor, swore.

Swurd, sword.

Sybow, a young onion.

Syne, then ; since.

' Was made lang syne, Lord knows how lang.'

Tack, lease.

Tackets, shoe-nails.

Tae, toe. *Tae'd*, toed.

' A three-tae'd leister.'

Taen, taken.

Taet or *Teat*, a small quantity.

Tairge, to task ; to cross-question.

' I on the questions tairge them tightly.'

Tak, take. *Tak tent*, take care.

Takin' taking.

Tald or *Tauld*, told.

Tane, the one ; as against *Tither*, the other.

Tangle, sea-weed.

Tangs, tongs.

Tap, top.

Tapetless, without energy ; heedless.

Tapmost, topmost.

' The verra tapmost, tow'ring height O' Miss's bonnet.'

Tappet-hen, a quart measure of whisky.

' The tappet-hen gae bring her ben.'

Tapsalteerie, topsy-turvy.

Targe, a shield.

Tarry-breeks, a sailor.

Tassie, a drinking-cup ; a goblet, generally of silver.

Tauld, or *Tald*, told.

Tawie, tractable ; quiet.

' Hamely, tawie, quiet, and cannie.'

Tawpie, a witless young woman.

Tawted or *Tawtie*, matted together.

Teen, provocation ; vexation.

Teethin' a heckle, putting spikes in a hackle.

Tell'd, told. *Tellin'*, telling.

Temper-pin, the regulating pin of a spinning-wheel.

Ten-hour's-bite, a slight feed in the yoke between regular meals.

Tent, to take heed ; mark.

Tentie, heedful ; cautious.

Tentless, careless.

Teugh, tough.

Teughly, toughly.

Teuk, took.

Thack, thatch.

Thack an' rape, the covering of a house or corn-stack ; used as a simile for comfortable circumstances.

' Thack an' rape secure the toil-won crap.'

Thae, those.

Thairms, small guts ; fiddle-strings.

Thanket or *Thankit*, thanked.

Thankfu', thankful.

Theekit, thatched.

Thegither, together.

Themsels, themselves.

Thick, familiar. *Pack and thick*, confidentially intimate. [bidding.

Thieveless, handless ; for-

Thigger, a beggar.

Thiggin', begging.

Thir, these ; opposed to *Thae*.

Thirl, to thrill ; to bind.

Thirl'd or *Thrilled*, bound.

Thole, to suffer ; to endure.

' How they maun thole a factor's snash.'

Thou'd, thou art.

Thowe, a thaw ; to thaw.

Thowless, slack ; useless.

Thrang, throng ; busy.

Thrapple, the throat.

' See how she fetches at the thrapple.'

Thrave, twenty-four sheaves of corn, in two shocks.

Thraw, to twist; to contend.

Thrawin', twisting; contending.

Thrawn, twisted; stubborn; contentious.

Threap or *Threep*, to argue; to maintain by dint of assertion.

Thresh, to thrash.

Threshin'-tree, a flail.

Thretty, thirty.

Thrissle, thistle.

'Paint Scotland greetin' ow'r her thrissle.'

Throuther or *Through-ither*, through other; pell-mell; confusedly.

Thrum, hum.

Thrums, hums; the unweavable threads at the end of a web.

Thud, a dull, heavy sound; a thump.

Thummart or *Foumart*, a pole-cat.

Thumpit, thumped.

Thysel, thyself.

Till't, to it. *Fa' till't*, begin.

'An', Lord, if ance they pit ye till't.'

Timmer, timber; a tree.

Timmer-prop't, supported by timber.

Tine or *Tyne*, to lose.

Tinkler, a tinker.

Tip or *Toop*, a ram.

Tippence, twopence.

Tirl, to thrill; to strip; to ring.

Tirl'd at the pin, knocked at the door.

Tirlin', uncovering.

Tither, the other.

Tittie, a sister.

Tittlin', whispering and laughing.

Tocher, dowry; marriage portion.

'My tocher's the jewel has charms for him.'

Tod, a fox.

Toddle, to totter; to walk like a child.

To-fa', a building added, leaning to the first.

Toom, empty.

Toop, a ram.

Toun, town; a farm-house.

Tousie or *Towsie*, shaggy; unkempt.

Tout, the blast of a horn or trumpet.

Touzle, to ruffle in romping.

To've, to have.

Tow, a rope; flax.

Towmond, a twelvemonth.

Toy, an old fashion of female head-dress.

Toyte, to totter; to walk like an old man.

'We'll toyte about wi' ane anither.'

Trams, shafts.

Transmugrify'd, metamorphosed.

Trashtrie, small trash.

Trews, trousers. [tricks.

Trickie or *Tricksie*, full of

Trig, spruce; trim.

Trinklin', trickling.

Trinle, the wheel of a barrow.

Trintle, to roll; to trundle.

Tripe, the stomach cooked for eating.

Troggers, hawking merchants.

Troggin', hawked wares.

Troke, to barter; to exchange.

Trow, to believe.

Trowth, troth; a petty oath.

Tryste, an appointment; a cattle fair.

Tug, raw hide; to pull.

'As e'er in tug or tow was drawn.'

ulyie or *Tulzie*, a squabble; a fight.

umbler-wheels, the wheels of a low cart.

wa, two.

wa-three, a few.

wad, it would.

wal, twelve; twelve o'clock.

wal-pint hawkie, a cow that yields twelve pints at a milking.

walt, the twelfth.

wang, twinge.

win, to part with; to give up.

wined, reft; twisted.

wistle, a twist.

yke, a dog.

yne, to lose.

ysday, Tuesday.

ysday'teen, Tuesday in the evening.

lzie, oil.

nchancie, dangerous.

nco, strange; uncouth; very.

'Unco pack an' thick thegither.'

ncos, wonders; news.

nfauld, unfold.

nkend or *Unkenn'd*, unknown.

nsiccar or *Unsicker*, insecure; uncertain.

nskaith'd, unhurt.

po', upon.

pon't, upon it.

squabae, water of life; whisky.

'Wi' usquabae we'll face the devil.'

alentine's dealing, drawing of names by lot on St Valentine's day.

ap'rin', vapouring.

auntie, joyous; proud.

era or *Verra*, very.

Virl, a ring.

Vittle or *Victual*, grain.

Vogie, well-pleased; vain.

'And, wow, but I was vogie.'

Wa', wall.

Wab, web.

Wabster, weaver.

Wad, would; wager; wed.

'I'll wad a groat he gets his fairin'.'

Wadna, would not.

Wadset, a mortgage.

Wae, woe; sad.

Wae worth ! woe befall !

Waefu', woeful.

Waefu'-woodie, the gallows-tree; the hangman's rope.

Waesacks ! alas !

Wae's me ! woe to me ! O the pity.

Wa'-flower, wallflower.

Waft, weft; wool.

Wair or *Ware*, to spend.

Wair't, spend it; spent.

Wair't-on, spent on.

Wale, choice; to choose.

Wal't, chose; chosen.

Walie, ample; jolly; large.

'Clap in his walie nieve a blade.'

Walie ! an exclamation of distress.

'O walie! walie! up yon bank.'

Wallop, to struggle convulsively; to whip.

Wame, the belly.

Wamefu', a bellyful.

Wan, won.

Wanchancie, unlucky.

Wanrestfu', restless.

Wark, work.

Wark-lume, a tool to work with.

Warl' or *Warld*, world.

Warld's-worm, a miser.

Warlock, a wizard.

Warl'y, w rldly.

Warran', warrant.
Warsle or *Warstle*, to wrestle.
Warsled or *Warstled*, wrestled.
Warst, worst.
Wasna, was not.
Wat, wet. *I wat*, I know.
Wat na, wot not.
Wat-shod, wet-shod.
Wattle, a twig.
Wauble, wobble; to reel.
Waught, a copious drink.
Wauken, awake; to awaken.
Waukening, awakening.
Wauket, thickened.
Wauket-loof, a palm thickened by toil.

'I heaved on high my wauket loof.'

Waukin', waking.
Waukrife, wakeful.
Waur, worse; to worst.
Waur't, worsted.
Weanies, diminutive of *weans*.
Weans, children.
Wearie, exhausted.
Wearie-widdle, exhausting contest.
Weasan or *Weasand*, the windpipe.
Wecht, weight.
Wee, little.
Wee things, children.
Weeder-clips, an instrument for destroying weeds.
Weel, well. *Weelfare*, welfare.
Weel-faur'd, well-favoured.
Weel-ken'd, well-known.
Weet, wet; to wet; rain.
We'se, we shall.
Westlin or *Wastlin*, western.
Wether, a sheep two years old.
Wha, who.
Wha e'er, who ever.
Whaizle, to wheeze.
Whalpit, whelped.

Wham, whom.
Whan, when.
Whang, a leathern thong; to flog; a long, thick slice

'Wi' sweet milk cheese in mony a whang'

Whar or *Whare*, where.
Whase, whose.
Wha's, whose; who is.
What reck, what matter.
Whatt, whittled; did whet.
Whaup, the curlew.
Whaur'll, where will.
Wheep, to fly nimbly; to jerk

'O rare! to see your elbuck wheep

Whid, a fib; a lie; to scud.
Whiddin', fibbing; running as a hare.
Whigmaleeries, crotchets silly fancies.
Whingin', complaining; fretting.
Whins, gorse.
Whirlygigums, tawdry ornaments.
Whisht, silence; to be silent
Whisk, to lash; to sweep.
Whisket or *Whiskit*, whisked
Whissle, whistle.
Whitter, a hearty draught.
Whittle, a clasp-knife.
Whunstane, whinstone.
Whup, a whip; to whip.
Whyles, sometimes.
Wi', with.
Wick, a term in curling— strike a stone in a oblique direction.

To guard, or draw, or wick a bore

Widdie, a rope; the gallow
Widdiefu', gallows-worthy.
Widdle, a struggle.
Wiel, a small whirlpool; a eddy.
Wifie, diminutive of *wife*.
Wight, strong.
Wight and wilfu', strong an obstinate.

Wil'-cat, wild-cat.

Willyart, wild.

Willyart-glower, a wild, bewildered stare.

Willy-wicker, a willow sapling.

Wimple, to meander.

Wimpl'd, meandered.

Wimplin', meandering.

'Wh re Doon rins wimplin' clear.'

Win, to gain; to winnow.

Win', wind; the wind.

Win't, did wind; winded.

Winna, will not.

Winnock, a window.

Winnock-bunker, a seat in the window.

Winsome, attractive.

Wintle, a somersault.

Winze, a curse; an oath.

Wi's, with his; with us.

Wiss, wish.

Wi't, with it.

Withouten, without.

Won, to dwell. *Wons*, dwells.

'There's auld Rob Morris that wons in yon glen.'

Wonner, a wonder.

Woo, to court.

Woo', wool.

Wooer-babs, love-knots.

Wordy, worthy.

Worset, worsted.

'Her braw new worset apron.'

Wow! an exclamation of pleasure or surprise.

Wrack, to vex; to destroy; wreck.

Wraith, a ghost.

Wrang, wrong; to injure.

Wud, mad; wild. *Red-wud*, stark-mad.

Wumble, a wimble or gimlet.

Wyle, to decoy; to entice.

Wylie coat, a flannel vest.

Wyling, enticing.

Wyte, blame; reproach; to blame.

Yaff, to bark.

'A yaffin' cur.'

Yard, a garden.

Yaud, an old horse.

Yealings, coevals; born in the same year.

Yell, dry; not giving milk.

'Dawtit, twal-pint hawkie's gaen As yell's the bill.'

Yerd or *Yird*, earth.

Yerk, to lash; to jerk.

Yerket or *Yerkit*, jerked; lashed.

Ye'se, ye shall.

'Ye'se get them a'thegither.'

Yestreen, yesternight.

Yett, gate.

Yeuk, itch. *Yeuks*, itches.

Yeukie, itchy.

Yill, ale.

Yird, earth.

Yokin', yoking; a bout of work; a set-to.

Yon, yonder. *Yon time*, yonder time.

Yont or *Ayont*, beyond.

'Yont the dyke she's heard thee bummin'.

Yoursel, yourself.

Yowe, a ewe.

Yowes, ewes.

Yowie, diminutive of *yowe*.

'An' neist my yowie, sil y thing.

Yule, Christmas.

'Blythe Yule night when we were fou.'

INDEX OF FIRST LINES

INDEX OF FIRST LINES 647